Probings and Re-Probings
Essays in Marxian Reawakening

Edited by
Sankar Ray
Shaibal Gupta

Probings and Re-Probings: Essays in Marxian Reawakening
Edited by Sankar Ray and Shaibal Gupta

First Published 2021

ISBN 978-93-5002-692-2

Published by
AAKAR BOOKS
28 E Pocket IV, Mayur Vihar Phase I
Delhi 110 091 India
aakarbooks@gmail.com

Laser Typeset at
Arpit Printographers, Delhi

Printed at
Sapra Brothers, Noida.

Contents

Preface

Marxism may not be as 'alive' in 2018, his bicentenary, as it was during the two preceding centuries, but one cannot deny that it is as 'relevant' now as it was earlier. This was amply revealed in the International Conference on Karl Marx during June 16-20, 2018 at Patna, organised by the Asian Development Research Institute (ADRI). Indeed, the organisers were simply overwhelmed when more than fifty scholars had sent their substantive papers to the Conference, more than two-thirds of them being from abroad, covering all the contents. The rationale for organising the Conference was not just the historical importance of the event, but the enormous influence that Marxian thoughts still have on the present day social science research. As a social science research institute, it was, therefore, very appropriate for ADRI to organise the Conference. The organisers of the Conference were particularly happy that the Conference was probably the largest among other bicentenary Conferences held across the globe.

In the Conference, quite expectedly, the Marxian issues that the scholars had addressed were as varied as Marx's own writings were, encompassing questions on—economics, politics, society, philosophy and others. Methodologically, these studies have largely followed an inter-disciplinary framework, which has long been a characteristic of Marxian approach to social investigation. We had decided to publish 31 papers of the Conference in two volumes. The first volume, 'Karl Marx's Life, Ideas and Influences: A Critical Examination on the Bicentenary', was published by Palgrave in 2019, incorporating 16 papers. This volume is the second one, incorporating the remaining 15 papers.

It will be difficult to classify the papers in this volume thematically, but it is satisfying to note that three of these papers related to India—one on economics by Archana Aggarwal (modes of surplus extraction), the second by Helene Fleury and Damien Ehrhardt on culture (Maithil village) and the third by Shannon Brincat on philosophy (ancient Lokayat tradition). India is also covered in two other papers—one by Craig Brandist tracing the origins of Marxist oriental studies, and the second by Eugenio Lo Sardo re-examining the writings of Marx on Opium Wars, that revealed the character of colonial exploitation in China and India.

The concept of class divisions plays a major role in Marxian analysis of social dynamics of a capitalist society. But parallel to class division, there are other divisions that are too obvious and they have widely attracted the attention of social scientists, both Marxian and others. One of them is the gender division of the society and the other racial. Two of the papers in this volume (Chirashree Das Gupta and Edoardo Schinco) analyse the gender issue in a Marxian framework for a more comprehensive understanding of the phenomenon. Similarly, again utilising a Marxian framework, Kipton Jensen examines the history of Black Marxism in America to help us understand the strategy of African Americans to flight the forces of racism.

Although the functioning of the capitalist system has undergone much change since the days of Marx, certain basic traits of the system still remain unaltered. The fact of exploitation of hired labour is certainly one of them. In his paper, C. Saratchand analyses this phenomenon, although in a restricted context. One can also include in this category the paper by Riccardo Bellofiore presenting a Macro Monetary Theory of capitalist production. The analysis presented here covers the monetary dimensions of capitalism under the present circumstances, when monetary instruments and institutions have made huge proliferation, both nationally and internationally, to sustain the system. This phenomenon was absent during the early phase of capitalism.

The writings of Marx, as we all know, cover not only economics, but many other dimensions of the society and the state. The present volume has three papers on these dimensions—one on nature of elite (Giulietto Chiesa), the second on Marx's critical theory (Julio Boltvinik) and the third on alienation (K Sunitha V). Together, these authors draw our attention to the role of societal power structures in the present day world.

Although the Marxian literature provides valuable insights on the functioning of the capitalist society, the paper by Jean Joseph Boillot in this volume argues that, along with the gains, the Marxian tradition has also caused some losses to human wisdom. This is primarily because of the orthodoxy of many Marxian scholars or political leaders. In the paper, the author substantiates this important observation, citing several historical events. Finally, this volume also includes a paper by Roberto Massari, describing how Che Guevara had tried to understand the Marxian theories, parallel to his heroic political activism. Interestingly, although Che was a great devourer of books, he had no pretention about his theoretical knowledge about Marxism.

I have reasons to hope that this volume will not only enlighten its readers about some major trends in Marxian studies across the world, but it will also help them identify social issues that demand immediate academic attention, not just from Marxian perspective, but from other perspectives as well. I am very thankful to the editors of this volume—Sankar Ray and Shaibal Gupta for compiling this volume, which must have required substantial professional ability. Thanks are also due for Neeraj Kumar who had provided valuable assistance to the editors. Finally, I express my deep gratitude to Lord Meghnad Desai and Professor Gopa Sabharwal, without whose cooperation the Conference would not have achieved its desired goal.

Prabhat P Ghosh
Director, ADRI

Note

A total of 9 papers out of the 15 in this collection are based on dedicated memorial lectures delivered at the conference. They are as follows:

1. The Shapurji Saklatvala Memorial Lecture on 'Ancient Indian Dialectics and Marx' was delivered by Shannon Brincat.
2. The Gyorgy Markus Memorial Lecture on 'Marx's Theory of Prehistory: In Memory of Gyorgy Markus. My Great Master Whom I Never Met' was delivered by Julio Boltvinik.
3. The Friedrich Engels Memorial Lecture on 'The Origins of Marxist Oriental Studies in the USSR and Its Stalinist Distortion' was delivered by Craig Brandist.
4. The D.D. Kosambi Memorial Lecture on 'A Short History of Black Marxism in the USA' was delivered by Kipton E Jensen.
5. The Maurice Dobb Memorial Lecture on 'The Untimely Marx: Marx's Critique of Political Economy and the Political Dimension of Critical Economics' was delivered by Riccardo Bellofiore.
6. The Pablo Neruda Memorial Lecture on 'Guevara and Marx: Critical Remake of an Old Film' was delivered by Roberto Massari.
7. The Antonio Gramsci Memorial Lecture on 'From Hegemony to Full Control: Which Kind of Elite, If Any, is Necessary for the Masters of the Universe? Reading Antonio Gramsci about the Role of Intelligentsia, Yesterday and Tomorrow' was delivered by Giulietto Chiesa.
8. The Nikolay Bukharin Memorial Lecture on 'Karl Marx and the Opium War' was delivered by Eugenio Lo Sardo.
9. The P.C. Joshi Memorial Lecture on 'Marx or Utopia and Ideology Against Wisdom' was delivered by Jean-Joseph Boillot.

Introduction

This publication on Marx is based on papers presented at the International Conference entitled *Karl Marx—Life, Ideas, Influence: A Critical Examination on the Bicentenary*, organized during June 16-20, 2018 in Patna, under the aegis of the Asian Development Research Institute (ADRI). Incidentally, this is the second volume based on the conference papers. The first volume, entitled *Karl Marx's Life, Ideas, and Influences: A Critical Examination on the Bicentenary*, published by Palgrave Macmillan, has 16 essays in total and is edited by the Marcello Musto, Babak Amini and Shaibal Gupta. The present volume contains a set of 15 additional papers.

This Bicentennial Conference on Marx was a follow-up to a conference on Marx, in a small sub-divisional town of Begusarai in Bihar (India) in 1968 to celebrate his 150th birth anniversary. The canvas of the Begusarai Conference was limited to the theme entitled 'Marx and India'. In contrast, the canvas of the Patna Conference was much wider, both geographically as well as thematically. The Patna Conference was dedicated to the memory of Dr. Pijushendu Gupta and Professor Radhakrishna Chowdhury, the duo who had organized the Begusarai Conference. In the Patna Conference, there were 38 dedicated lectures in memory of distinguished philosophers, economists, academics and political figures who had either influenced Marx or were influenced by him. The scholars from all the continents had taken note of this conference and shared it among their own circles. Such were the reverberations of the Patna Conference that renowned scholars of Marx, like Dr. Alessandra Mezzadri from SOAS London, have noted its significance and the versatility of the first volume which has now been widely accessed by researchers all over the world. This year, 2020, marks the bi-centenary of Friedrich Engels, 150th birth anniversary of both V.I. Lenin and David Borisovich Riazanov, the latter arguably the greatest Marxist scholar of the twentieth century and the founder and director of the Institute of Marx and Engels in Lenin's last years.

We are indeed in an era of Marxian renaissance. For the global working class, it is time to recognize that it alone holds the possibility of a civilized alternative to capitalism, an inherently exploitative and iniquitous system. The neo-liberal finance capital, the driver of post-USSR globalization, was violently shaken due to the 'sub-prime mortgage crisis' that erupted in 2008, and kept devastating the US economy for at least three years. It pushed the US economy towards a near-unmanageable recession and had a contagion effect on the global capitalist order. This led Frédéric Lordon, a distinguished Marxist to write an essay in October 2008 in *Le Monde* diplomatique, captioned 'The Day Wall Street Became Socialist'. He termed such circumstances as a 'financial gust', generating 'a multiplication of comments on the moralization of capitalism', slapping an imperative for 'regulation to punish the culprits'. Lordon continued to write: "Some go much further. Wall Street as we have known it will cease to exist. So, Karl 'Bernanke' and Vladimir Ilich 'Paulson' are not out of the woods. The red star cap fits them like suspenders to a pig, but at least they understood that they had to keep it screwed on the head all the time necessary, unlike the mad, mad liberals who call 'laissez-faire-les-insolites' and the moral of the purge." Henry Paulson was then the chief of Goldman Sachs that completely collapsed and Ben Bernanke, the US Fed chief. The rest is history.

With all the major bourses of the world in tailspin in 2008, even monetary economists, including those from the Chicago School of Monetary Economics, built by the Nobel laureate

Milton Friedman, looked up to Marx's *Capital*. Bookstores witnessed queues for the three volumes of *Das Capital* as never before. They had to pay for unflinching faith in Keynesian, neo-Keynesian, and neo-classical Keynesian economics.

Twelve years after the sub-prime crisis, now we are faced with what Lordon coined as 'Coronakratch'. Economic pain is now excruciating the stock market in the US. The social distancing has forced the closure of just about any business where human beings congregate. The restaurant, live-entertainment, tourist, and airline industries are being crushed. Public and private mass-transit systems—many already unprofitable—are facing budgetary crises. This scenario is everywhere the world over. The economic ramifications of the coronavirus are so visible on the healthcare system. But it is only the beginning. Lockdowns are authoritarianism in disguise.

Marx, as Anitra Nelson observed succinctly, was a "nineteenth-century political intellectual", unconstrained by the disciplinary rigour or specialization insisted on by the late twentieth-century academia. Marx's writings can be studied as sociology, philosophy, politics, economics, history, and even as literature, though if studied from simply one perspective, his work loses much of its richness and original message. An interdisciplinary approach is especially pertinent to Marx's theory of money, which is definitely not just an economic theory. Marx was a scholar and a revolutionary."

The papers in this volume cover issues that are varied and debatable. A comprehension of these papers would be facilitated if their basic premises are noted before they are read. To start with, Shannon Brincat in his Shapurji Saklatvala Memorial Lecture, titled 'Ancient Indian Dialectics and Marx', delivered at the conference, traces the origin of dialectical reasoning in India—the cosmogonic speculations in the Rig-Veda, Brihadaranyaka Upanishad, Mahabharata and Ramayana. "The first forays into dialectics in India shared a common social problem with other Axial civilizations: extreme social disparities under hierarchical divisions, and a period of profound technological, productive, and social growth," he stated.

Following the era of the Vedas (1500-800 BCE), the so-called Classical or Brahminic period (800-200 BCE), Karl Jasper's Axial Age dialectical thought emerged in traditional practices and beliefs, alongside the interpretation of the Vedas. The Hindu, Buddhist, Jain and other schools of thought, the heterodox and the orthodox Darśanas, individual mystics and Renouncers followed, but all locked in deep disputes over metaphysics. It was an inevitable consequence of religious and social order, still in vogue in Indian social life. The trajectory of growth across a range of civilizations, alongside a number of ontological assumptions, is related to the concept of dialectics: (i) the world, and everything in it, undergoes constant change (the doctrine of flux); (ii) everything in the cosmos is internally related (however close or distant that relation may be), reflecting the idea of interconnection or interdependency, otherwise known as the philosophy of internal relations) and (iii) these processes of the internal relations between all things are the forces for the change that one observes and experiences as humans in the phenomenal world. He finds a fascinating impact of this constancy of flux, desiring to better understand our world through interdependency, internal relations, and change. This indeed guides 'humanity towards a more emancipatory future'.

The author narrates the brave front of the "Lokāyata or later Cārvāka school in the fragments of the Bārhaspatya Sūtras, namely, perception, inferential doubt, and empiricism within a materialistic conception of the cosmos, rejecting the Vedas, doctrines of Karma/Samsara, and the notion of the afterlife." He noted the persecution by the Brahminic orthodoxy, but regrets 'sadly we have lost much of their knowledge'. The element of doubt or scepticism in dialectical thought remained a key defence against the imposition or over-reach of metaphysical dogma in sync with Marx's dialectical method, the very foundation of emancipatory politics today. Things changed with the advent of the 'Nyaya' school of thought, with 'four kinds of dialectical relations, the most unique of which is the svarupa relation, viśesanatā (the relation between object and sense-organ)'.

The György Márkus Memorial Lecture on Marx's Theory of Prehistory by Julio Boltvinik is about Marx's philosophical anthropology (defined by Lukacs as 'ontology of the social being'), and his Paris Manuscripts of 1844, as systematized and developed by Márkus of the Budapest School of Studies in Marxism and Anthropology. Anthropology is strewn in *Paris Manuscripts* (*Economic and Philosophical Manuscripts of 1844*), *German Ideology, Grundrisse* and *Capital*. For Marx, "the Human Essence is to be found in work, sociality, and consciousness, and in universality which embraces these three moments and expresses itself in each of them." Human beings in Márkus is a self-created community, a historical product through an incessant process of change. Marx's anthropological ontology defines the human being as a social being, comprising sociality, activity, historicity, genericity and the like. Márkus concentrates on human essence, evolved naturally and historically, developing new powers and needs through changing strategies of socially organized work.

In *Capital*, Marx reproduces the Franklinian definition of man: a 'tool-making animal', alongside alienation of 'human essence', taken away from the proletariat. Márkus quotes Marx: "...the society of this estranged man is the caricature of a true community, of his true generic existence... a consequence of the division of labour and the separation and opposition between mental and physical labour... the true essence" of man. This essence lies precisely in the presence of this self-activity, whereby he creates and forms his own subjectivity. The individual becomes a human individual precisely because of active engagement, since he appropriates some of the objectified results and achievements of previous human progress. Ideologies creep in with "distorted-alienated expressions of the separation and alienation of thought from praxis", manifest in the scientific and technology that excludes the internal need for man, imposed by an external need. "The working instruments created by the STR go beyond the limits of mechanical machines and assume functions that convert them, in principle, into autonomous production complexes". The reversal happens when man ceases to produce the things that the same things can produce and devote himself to a creative activity or human flourishing, "once the material forms of human activity give it the character of an active manifestation of itself, the external necessity, determined by the need for subsistence, yields its place to the internal need of man; in that moment, human activity becomes a human need, which exists for itself and enriches man; then the abstract contradictions between work and pleasure, between work and free time, disappear: human activity is merged with life". Human prehistory, according to Marx, then comes to an end and 'History of mankind begins'.

The paper 'The Origins of Marxist Oriental Studies in the USSR and Its Stalinist Distortion' by Craig Brandist endorses Michael Kemper's inference that post-colonialists, specifically Foucauldian theorists, attempt to discredit Marxism as an extreme form of 'European Enlightenment thinking', consigning 'Marxism to the dustbin of Eurocentrism for forging a historical myth of post-colonialism's own radical origin.' This is in the way of understanding Hegel's writing on India. Brandist relates the post-colonial intent to instances of Eurocentrism and its 'arrogant and arrogating narrative' among some Marxists. Brandist is backed by Robert Young's perceptive study *White Mythologies: Writing History and the West* (1990). Young's strong disagreement with Althusser is noted by Brandist who asserts that Marx's early writings are insufficiently understood. He points to their hyphenation from 'Hegelian prejudices about the orient', despite revival of the same in the recent works of some Marxists. The author indicts the Stalin era for crushing of opposition currents that "dramatically affected oriental studies. Centralization of the Soviet state in order to compete militarily with hostile powers also required the subordination of anti-colonial struggles to the foreign policy interests of the USSR." He states with profound agony: "Some of the most sophisticated, talented and innovative thinkers in the field were fired, imprisoned or even killed, while their places were often taken by opportunists and sycophants who sought to shape the field into a dogmatic sphere narrowly subservient to the requirements and doctrines of the state. Statutory authority trumped scientific authority in all questions, including which positions could legitimately be regarded as Marxist". Brandist imbibes strength from the pioneering work of Aleksei Petrovich Barannikov (1890-1952). He states 'the caste dynamics in the formation of Indian national languages and literatures' would not have generated fresh interest in academia, endorsed by some other scholars.

Brandist refers to the Goan Buddhist Dharmanand Kosambi, father of Damodar Kosambi, one of the founders of Marxist studies in Indian history. The former had come in touch with Fyodor Shcherbatskoy (aka Theodor Stcherbatskoy), Leningrad-based Buddhologist, in Bombay in 1910, and later came closer to him while teaching Pali at the short-lived Institute of Buddhist Culture for a number of months. Dharmanand Kosambi felt an urge to study Buddhism as an atheistic, rationalist philosophy countering Brahminism. Unlike the Bihari polymath Rahul Sankrityayan, who too was converted to Buddhism, he kept himself at bay from dogmatic perspectives of Indian Communists loyal to Stalinism.

"The black man was stolen from his native land, from his wife and child, brought to these shores and made a slave. He was chained, whipped and robbed by his 'white superior', while the son of his 'superior' raped the black child before his eyes," writes Kipton E. Jensen in his paper 'A Short History of Black Marxism in the USA'. The paper provides for a broad debate on the segregation into Black Marxism. The American Left "relegated the struggle of Blacks to a subsidiary position in the revolutionary movement". Nikhil Pal Singh raps Marxist tradition for failure to sympathize with the struggle against racism in the history of capitalism, while Abigail Bakan's version of Marxism "circumvented, dismissed for its apparent tendency to emphasize class relations and economic materiality to the exclusion of other forms of oppression and other ways of understanding domination", Jensen cites. Marxian alienation and oppression as 'central to the reproduction of capitalist exploitation' is basic to go into the theme. Keeanga-Yamahtta Taylor sticks to the primacy of class angle, arguing that, 'gross inequality' is needed by capitalism for "various political, social, and ideological tools to divide the majority". The author remembers Eugene Debs who read *Das Kapital* in an Illinois jail during the Pullman Strike in 1895 and had contested for the US President election five times. He is also famous for his classic work, *The Negro in Class Struggle* (1903). Jensen draws 'instructive parallels between Marx and Debs'.

The author maps 200 years of the 'historical epicycle of Black Marxism' as 'a singular signifier' for the universal struggle for freedom and equality in America, collinearly with Angela Davis, once a leading functionary of the Communist Party of USA. She "would have us construe slavery as the most extreme form of un-freedom, the reality rather than the metaphor, slave ownership rather than the 'slavery of wage labour'." Given the concrete reality of 'the most brutal forms of unfreedom, enslavement', she posits Black Marxism in American historiography as "collective consciousness of an oppressed people (that) entails an understanding of the conditions of oppression and the possibility of abolishing these conditions, the most extreme form of human alienation," through reduction of persons 'to the status of property'.

Jensen imbibes the Damodar Kosambi model of chronological order of successive developments in the means and relations of production to scan the five periods of slavery—1818, 1868, 1918, 1968, and 2018. The Atlantic slavery is "the cornerstone of capitalist exploitation, appropriation, and dispossession over centuries". Approximately 12.5 million enslaved Africans were transported to the Americas between 1500 and 1866; 10.7 million survived the dreaded 'Middle Passage'.

Hélène Fleury and Damien Ehrhardt in their paper 'From Early Marx to Véquaud's Countercultural Indophilia: Similar

Aesthetics Founded on Romanticism and Communitarian Utopia' substantiates a theoretical synergy between Marx's aesthetic mindset and Yves Véquaud's counter culture. Although Marx did not theorize aesthetics of his own, yet aesthetic reflex is embossed in his 'life-path, from poetry to philosophy'. Véquaud's essays on Mithila paintings are seminal.

Following a hippie trail, during a two-year stay in Nepal, India and Ceylon, beginning in 1969, Véquaud first saw the Mithila paintings that inspired him to make several travels to Mithila and meet many rural painters. This led him to discover 'a canonical form of the counter-culture': the back-to-the-land-movement in communitarian utopias within the Maithil village. Icons in his frame of utopian counter-society were prophetic figures of legend, between holiness and genius. Their success involves both the personalization of means as well as the depersonalization of the ends of the success, namely the creation of objects crystallizing values recognized beyond the author (Véquaud). It was traditionally reserved for heroes and saints. This literary fantasy bears witness to a picturesque vision of India within an orientalizing episteme. The Maithil Republic, praised by him, was of Arts, through a pastoral myth and art religion, prevalent during the first Romanticism. The revolutionary spirit no longer resided in the proletariat, but in some 'new working class', the young intelligentsia and the social or gender fringe groups. He made a neo-tantric interpretation of Mithila paintings too in line with the hippie craze for oriental esotericism.

Véquaud studied in depth Marx's early writings and Freud's psychoanalysis. Scanning existentialism, feminism, and anti-colonialism, he wrote 'a radical critique of alienation felt by individuals in everyday life, recreation and family, but also a fulfilment of human's essence to be most in conformity with nature'. This critical approach is a step towards 'a transformation in cultural realms' 'through oppositional subcultures preceding social and political changes. Alternative lifestyles aim at redistributing leadership'. Fleury and Ehrhardt are of the view that the 'Marxian vision of art differs greatly from socialist realism and even from the neo- (if not post-) Marxist philosophy of critical theorists like Adorno and the Frankfurt School.

Kumari Sunitha V. in her paper, 'Sartre and Alienation: A Marxian Perspective' posits Jean Paul Sartre's ideation of alienation in the French philosopher's basic frame of existentialism and the latter's postulates. Sartre "addresses the fundamental problems of human existence: death, nothingness, freedom, bad-faith, anxiety, political commitment, the meaning of existence itself." He remains an 'existentialist in his Marxist phase and during his final overtly anarchist phase'. The paper sequentially summarizes Sartre's Being and Nothingness, segregates existence from essence (despite a gap in his definition of existence), that of freedom from necessity and separation of subject from object that form the crux of Nothingness in Existentialist philosophy. 'Man is the being through whom nothingness comes to the world'.

For Sartre, the origin of nothingness makes a man a non-being. Destruction, a form of change in consciousness is, for Sartre, a purely human act, since for destruction to exist there must be 'first a relation of man to being—that is, a transcendence, and within the limits of this relation, it is necessary that man apprehends one being as destructible'. The act of questioning or interrogation is performed by dissociation of man from the causal series of being or the causal order of the world. This is affected by nihilating withdrawal, Sunitha infers. For Sartre, freedom is inseparable from man, there being no difference between the being of man and his being free which the author thinks 'an exaggerated view of human freedom'. One finds a combinatorial commutation in the Existentialist guru's words "there is no determinism; we are free, we are condemned to be free".

She interprets the Marxian concept of alienation as something where "everything seems to happen as if men experienced their alienation and their reification first in their own work, where in actuality each one lives first as a child, in his parents' work", while he thinks 'people continue to live this alienation, products of their parents' design; they are never fully able to overcome this early distortion of character'. That is Sartre's problematic in this content, she stresses. To Marx, under capitalism, alienation of labour's product is only expressed by the alienation in the activity of labour itself; but Sartre's position is distinctively different. He stated, "I don't believe that the relations production is the primary one... There are neighbourhoods of workers who have settled in the cities... What unites them more profoundly beyond the mode of production is that they are human beings." There lies Sartre's inconsistency. He ignores the exploitative content in human alienation. Framed in a perspective of conflict, Sartre's descriptions of human relations are a perverse form of human alienation, completely different from Marxian alienation whose essence is 'wage slavery'.

Riccardo Bellofiore's paper 'The Untimely Marx: Marx's Critique of Political Economy and the Political Dimension of Critical Economics' is an illuminating discourse of 'Capital: A Critique of Political Economy—A Methodological Elaboration'. 'Critique, contrary to criticism, recognizes the inner truth of political economy; it does not merely criticize its shortcomings.' Pointing at the dichotomy into classical and vulgar (vulgar economists' focus on circulation, without referring circulation back to production), he emphasizes the hiatus between fetish-character and fetishism, the role of dialectics, and the difference between reading, interpreting and reconstructing. He also discusses "multiple meanings of abstract labour and socialization, the role of money as a commodity for the labour theory of value, the 'method of comparison' in grounding valorization (the emergence of gross profits) as the constitution of capital from class struggle in production, the real subsumption of labour to capital." Being unfinished, the magnum opus needs a critical appraisal.

Marx's original approach was towards "the logic of capital in two distinct and successive moments. The first step was the inquiry about capital in general (all that it is common to capitals); the second step was the inquiry about the many capitals (competition among capitals). The second step should have been dealt with only after he had completed the first. To understand why, let us ask: what is 'competition' for Marx? Competition has two meanings for Marx, and these two meanings are not well understood by interpreters, or are conflated," Bellofiore states convincingly.

Marx highlighted the 'macro-social (class and monetary) foundation of the capitalist process as the pumping out of new value from the working class (and thus of the extraction of surplus value) by total capital'. Starting off with money and the commodity, he moved to capital, single capitalist as average representative of total capital labour market and relations between labour and capital - working class, Bellofiore asserts, being "tied to capital as a whole by a relation of slavery: the free and equal bargaining of the individual worker was just a necessary 'objective illusion'."

During Marx's bicentenary, Bellofiore drew a sort of balance sheet and thought it untimely due to 'the fall of the Berlin Wall and the collapse of the USSR' to talk about a crisis of Marxism. Keeping in mind his practical materialism, the author is of the view that Marx is an instance where "the failure(s) of his project of 'liberation' and 'exit' from the capital relation puts in question his oeuvre", although Marxism is not in a crisis at all.

Roberto Massari's 'Guevara and Marx: Critical Remake of an Old Film' is a long epistemological journey into an almost unknown theoretical area. He chanced upon the original copy of Che's Bolivian diary at the Banco Central de Bolivia basement in La Paz in 1996 when the Bolivian government had given him and his associates free access to the A-73 safe-deposit box, of which five pages contained a list of 109 book titles (15 of which marked with a red cross), divided by months (November 1966 - September 1967), giving an idea of his academic yearning. They came across the original copy in Spanish of Pombo's diary, believed to have disappeared after its translation into English and the red loose-leaf notebook with the diary pages from November 7 to December 31, 1966, as also the German leatherette agenda with the diary pages from January 1 to October 7, 1967. The list of books reflects Guevara's quest—from Marx to Mao, Engels to Liu Shaoqi,Lenin to Trotsky and Stalin to Milovan Djilas, as also Benedict Croce, C. Wright Mills, etc. Che had no pretension and he had admitted, "he had twice tried to deepen his understanding of the philosophy of 'maestro Hegel', always ending up defeated but with the conviction of having to start philosophical studies from scratch". Massari notes, he was a Marxist, interested in Marxology, and 'a great devourer of books throughout his life'.

Absence of serious Marxist material in Cuba, Che felt, made room for "the Soviet bricks that have the disadvantage of not letting you think, because the party has done it for you and you have to digest". The erstwhile USSR was then helping Cuba financially. Guevara criticized "seguidismo ideológico" (ideological tailism/khvostism) towards Soviet and French authors, when the CP of France (PCF) was under the ideological supervision of Roger Garaudy. He proposed that works by Marx, Engels, Kautsky, Hilferding, Luxemburg, Lenin, Stalin and many contemporary Marxists who are not totally scholastic be published.

He read widely, from Franz Mehring's biography of Marx to Jewish Italian Marxist Rodolfo Mondolfo, who emigrated to Argentina in 1939, alongside texts of the 'Young Marx' era, and Engels' Anti-Duhring. He had learnt from leprologist Doctor Hugo Pesce ('who will provoke, perhaps unknowingly, a major change in my attitude towards life and society'), Trotskyist friend Armando Hart (whom he addressed as 'tu amigo Trotsky' or your friend Trotsky) and notably his first wife and mother of Hildita who was 'Professor' of Marxism to Che. She had a degree in economics and an anti-orthodox Marxist training with roots in Apra (or more genuinely Latin American) and not Sovietic (Stalinist and dogmatic). Guevarian Marxism, as Michael Löwy wrote, was revolutionary humanism in contrast to rigidly anti-humanist positions of Althusser. He was more inclined to Lenin than Marx. However, the names of Marx, Lenin or other famous Marxists are totally absent in his famous *Bolivian Diary*, but Trotsky is the exception.

The controversial—if not disputatious—relationship between Marxists (including Marxian scholars who neither support official Marxist parties, nor agree to be branded as Marxists) and feminists is an engaging theme.

Edoardo Schinco's paper 'Historical Process and Gender Essentialism from a Dialectical Point of View: A Contribution to a Marxian Feminist Theory', presents a kaleidoscope of controversies around liberal equality, implying an equal treatment for all, irrespective of sex or gender and not formal equality of opportunity deriving from individuals' negative rights. Reframing of the concept of equality is due to feminists and also categorization of 'sexual difference' to reverse the discriminatory use of sex towards a broader concept of justice and negation of conservatives who adhere to the hangover of women's submission to men, on the plea of biological differences. 'The Origin of the Family, Private Property and the State' by Engels was a distinctive break in this context. In the *Paris Manuscripts of 1844*, Marx pointed out 'how the eternal economic laws described by liberal thinkers were rather contingent laws, dependent on capitalism itself.'

Marx, Schinco stresses, was not aware of his gradual convergence with Hegel's point of view, specifically Left Hegelians' interpretation of Hegelian thought sans theorization of a totalitarian philosophical system that ended up in oppressive universality. "Hegel attempted to bridge the gap between transcendence and immanence by assuming universality...". The author endorses the third wave of feminism of Michel Foucault's that inspired Western feminism in defining the concept of sexuality and his anti-universalist philosophical perspective alongside Judith Butler's philosophical framework. Foucault reduces 'every transcendence to an absolute immanence, instead. One of the most common risks of this position is the implicit relativism'.

Foucault's thought helped deepening of the critical analysis of universalism as a form of hidden cultural hegemony in contemporary feminism 'a sort of Trojan horse against subaltern cultures'. Schinco also praises Italian feminist Carla Lonzi's *The Manifesto of the Feminine Revolt* (1970) or *Let's Spit on Hegel* (1974) for demolishing male culture and fundamental principles of patriarchy. Capitalism inherited oppression of women rather than produced it alongside the rise of private property to engender an imbalance between the sexes as each man's need for power over each woman. The paper tangentially touches upon Post-Structuralism, Feminism and transgender people whose gender identity from the sex assigned at birth is recognized very lately, despite their existence before the last century. Schinco suggests "dialectic essentialism" for understanding the essence as a historically dynamic universality in tackling discriminations into latest feminist and trans issues.

Chirashree Das Gupta's paper, 'Revolution, Emancipation and Social Reproduction', is based on the Marxist-Feminist conceptualization of social transformation. She critically surveys the methods involved in the institutional reorganization of reproduction in societies aiming at revolutionary transformations, having summed up the three attempted transformations—the Russian, Chinese and Cuban Revolutions. She supposes 'the growth of productive forces as the focus of extensive transformation, rather than egalitarian institutionalization of social reproduction, undermine the material dialectics of revolutionary emancipation'. Controversies about the content of socialism in the twentieth century notwithstanding, the paper considers them as 'all-pervasive' as 'the reorganization of social reproduction way beyond the tenets of welfarism had been the greatest promise of revolutionary emancipation from patriarchy and social oppression', namely, from the tyranny of family, private property and the state; and the conscious political attempt of collectivism rather than individualism forming the basis of new 'individualities'. "The sociological genealogy of the attempts at 'Marxist' theorizing in the judgment(s) of socialist attempts at social transformation has implications of the level of abstraction as to whether it helps one understand the processes of social transformation towards the creation of an emancipatory society breaking free of alienation." The hyphenation from the class basis of production relations, Das Gupta asserts, went along transformation of the domain of state-society relationships under the nation-state aberration during the Stalin era, new standards in food, healthcare, housing, education and clothing and providing women visibility and better remuneration as workers notwithstanding. She refers to ujamaa after independence in Tanzania, where women joined the paid labour force in agriculture through the process of villagization, although 70 per cent were in private hands. "The abstract conceptualization of conflict, contest and the dialectics of transformation limited to the sphere of production" were conflictual with Marx's and earlier Marxist understanding of the institutional unit(s) of organization of society.

Archana Aggarwal's paper 'Manufacturing Profits: Modes of Surplus Extraction at the Lower End of Global Value Chains (GVCs)' is an empirical study on the low value adding enterprises which are one of the facets of globalized production and a new form of international division of labour. Such enterprises proliferated in Delhi and adjoining areas in the post-reform (1991) years, including parts of Uttar Pradesh (general manufacturing), Haryana (automobile, electronics, and textiles) and Rajasthan (marble, leather, and textiles). Basically, there are two chains—producer-driven (automobiles) and buyer-driven (apparel and consumer electronics). The high rates of profits are generated through cheap labour, aside from ensuring competitiveness. These GVCs have made India a global "hub for the automobile supply chain, as well as 'manufacturer' of readymade garments and also consumer electronic goods for global 'buyers'." The paper scans the mechanisms employed by firms located in the automobile, apparel and consumer electronics and how they extract surplus and profits, primarily based on interviews with workers employed in some of these firms, a high percentage of them being contractual labour. She looks through the Marxian lens to understand the modes of surplus extraction. "An overwhelming use of non-regular workers, long hours of work, overtime, reduced breaks, wages lower than the value of labour power, increasing the productivity of labour without accompanying wage increases in the same proportion and intensification of work are common across all sectors and industries in the area under study."

Giulietto Chiesa's paper, 'From Hegemony to Full Control—Which Kind of Elite, If Any, Is Necessary for The Masters of The Universe? Reading Antonio Gramsci about the Role of Intelligentsia, Yesterday and Tomorrow', looks into the potential of the Marxian method as a useful tool for the construction of a new theory to confront the current complexity of capitalism with features profoundly different from its early phases, when the monstrosity inseparable from wanton destruction of the earth's limited resources was not there and nor was there the 'inhuman technological acceleration', both financial and global. Marx, he thinks, "could not foresee the effects that capitalist production, by revolutionizing itself, could have produced, both on the evolution of the species and on the relationship between the organic and inorganic world". The capitalism underwent a technological revolution, throwing off its original features with 'money map of abstract corporate finance, designed by the 'banking system' that compels the 'state' to condescend and surrender, with corruption sans checks, served by an 'army of its exegetes (the economists), its soldiers (mainstream media) and its policemen (the secret services)'. The transformation and accumulation are based on 'production of money by means of money' or 'producing money from nothing', burying the cycle 'commodity-money-commodity'. The explicit crisis of liberal democracy is nakedly reflected in Europe with the institutions of liberal democracy losing control over the dynamics of money. All this strengthens 'the abstract corporate finance, in an obscure and unpredictable way', demolishing the Western collective structurally. The task, he strongly believes, is return to the trajectory of revolution which is to overturn the 'money map' that enslaves "the whole of mankind and forces mankind and nature into a deadly zero-sum game. We need a conscious movement of peoples, of human masses, able to understand the collective necessity of a struggle for survival". For Gramsci or Marx, it was not possible to imagine that one day someone could accumulate huge amounts of data (metadata), not to speak of predicting from such data "reactions and preferences of millions or billions of individuals; or to anticipate their desires, their fears, their elementary urges—statistically, through digital algorithms."

Eugenio Lo Sardo's essay 'Karl Marx and the Opium War' revives the debate about Marx's writings on the opium wars, particularly the Second Opium War (1856-1860), waged by Britain and France. For historians studying the colonial era, the two opium wars over questions of trade, diplomacy, national dignity and, last but not the least, drug trafficking, drowned the 'Middle Kingdom' into the 'Century of Humiliation,' forcing the weak Chinese governments to cede territory and sign unequal treaties. Now the conflict is termed as deeply counterintuitive. Although Marx scripted 'a perfect description of the opium trade', which tied Indians and Chinese to a mortal knot, these essays are pickings from numerous articles, published in the *New York Tribune*. They were, Marx himself admitted, essentially journalistic, and they needed extensive follow-up. But that did not happen. The author recalls relevant quotes from Marx on how the colonial rulers compelled Indian ryots 'to engage in the poppy culture', enticing them with 'money advances'. He adds, "The Government runs everything" and quotes Marx. "It keeps the wholesale manufacture of the deleterious drug a close monopoly in its hands; watches by a whole army of official spies its growth, its delivery at appointed places, its inspissation and preparation for the taste of the Chinese consumers, its formation into packages especially adapted to the conveniency of smuggling, and finally its conveyance to Calcutta." All this was to generate fabulous profits. 'Every chest costed about 250 rupees and was sold at the Calcutta auction at a price ranging from 1,210 to 1,600 rupees', from there passed on officially to 'the speculators thence to pass into the hands' of the smugglers who land it in China'.

The author elucidates the British motive of opium trade, referring to *Das Kapital*: England "sends silver to India, and buys opium ...all of which goes to China to lay down funds to purchase the silk". China, Eugenio Lo Sardo notes, disinterested in 'English merchandises, it was a market closed to them. The Chinese had always produced all they wanted. They were in credit, a huge credit towards the more industrialized countries!'

Reference to the French historian Fernand Braudel, author of *La Méditerranée* and *Ecrits sur l'histoire,* is important for academics in further understanding of Opium Wars to fathom into Braudel's reflections on the intellectual framework of his historical studies to penetrate beneath the surface of political events as also cycles of production, wages and prices, grids of communication and trade, etc.

For Jean-Joseph Boillot, the Marxist system has in-built 'theoretical weaknesses' in its 'quick evolution into ideology', and its orthodoxy (implying applied Marxism of the twentieth century) has turned it into a religion, further into an 'utopian project', instead of 'rational thought and political project' that Marx envisioned. He thinks a 'dispassionate critique of Marxist thought and its utopia is overdue in quest of 'more humane economies, more just societies and better harmony among humans and with nature'. His paper, 'Marx or Utopia and Ideology Against Wisdom', trichotomizes Marx into the philosophical Marx, the political Marx and finally the economist Marx. He endorses four theses, following Erik Olin Wright's 'Envisioning Real Utopias'. They are: (a) long-term unsustainability of capitalism under the effect of its own internal contradictions and law of falling rate of profit, (b) anti-capitalist class struggle together with global proletarianization of the entire world population and polarization into two blocks of a wealthy elite and others, leading to 'communist revolutions' as Lenin visualized in some parts of the world, despite failures in countries like India, 'the most exploited colony', (c) collapse of capitalism through its overthrow by the oppressed classes including the proletariat and its communist vanguard party, where capitalism dominates largely within the framework of the parliamentary system, and (d) transition into the 'socialist system'.

The essay is very briefly a descriptive rather than academic survey of alternatives covering the Mao and post-Mao periods of China, Nehruvian period of India (inclined to Soviet macro-economic planning) and the drift to very short-term meanderings during the premiership of Indira Gandhi, recalling the prognostics of 'totalitarian drifts' (Orwell). Marxism, like all 'isms,' has 'costs probably greater than their benefits', he infers.

C. Saratchand's paper, 'Exploitation and Oppression under Bourgeoisdom', examines the relationship between exploitation and oppression, focusing on the role of caste, gender, race, communalism, etc. in the frame of monopolization (leaning on centralization and concentration of capital) and proliferation of the bourgeoisie. By proliferation, he means a process of participation of 'new entrants make it into the ranks of the bourgeoisie'. He thinks gender, race, caste and communalism cause unequal rates of exploitation, and there exists 'a whole host of social practices that reproduce the social differences between the two or more types of workers'. He identifies 'interiorization' of race (or any other type of social oppression) in the class struggle.

For him, Stalin's theory of heterogeneity amongst the proletariat into three strata, pitting 'pure-blooded' proletarians against the other two, is very relevant in understanding the class struggle. In contrast, he puts Marx into an interrogation box. "Some writings of Marx may be construed to imply that there is a tendency towards the creation of a homogeneous proletariat", he claims, citing that the rate of surplus value was equal in each branch of production in Marx.

However, his claim that the term 'bourgeoisdom' was introduced in Vol. I of *Capital* (f.n 22) is not factual.The word in the original text is 'Bürgertum'. Marx wrote in *Das Kapital*: "In ihrer mystifizierten Form ward die Dialektik deutsche Mode, weil sie das Bestehende zu verklären schien. In ihrer rationellen Gestalt ist sie dem Bürgertum und seinen doktrinären Wortführern ein Ärgernis und ein Greuel, weil sie in dem positiven Verständnis des Bestehenden zugleich auch das Verständnis seiner Negation, seines notwendigen Untergangs einschließt, jede gewordne Form im Flusse der Bewegung, also auch nach ihrer vergänglichen Seite auffaßt, sich durch nichts imponieren läßt, ihrem Wesen nach kritisch und revolutionär ist." (*Das Kapital,* Band I, Hamburg 1872, Nachwort zur zweiten Auflage'). The English translation is: "In its mystified form the dialectic became German fashion because it seemed to transfigure the existing. In its rational form, it is a nuisance and an abomination to the bourgeoisie and its doctrinaire spokesmen, because it includes in its comprehension and affirmative recognition of the existing state of things, at the same time also, the recognition of the negation of that state, of its inevitable breaking up; because it regards every historically developed social form as in fluid movement, and therefore takes into account its transient nature not less than its momentary existence; because it lets nothing impose upon it, and is in its essence critical and revolutionary.' *Capital,* Volume I Hamburg 1872, Afterword to the second edition.Thus, Marx's 'Bürgertum' should not be termed 'Bourgeoisdom'.

Sankar Ray
Shaibal Gupta

1

Ancient Indian Dialectics and Marx

Shannon Brincat

Introduction

India is the birthplace of dialectical thinking in our world—or it is the first written record of such a form of philosophical and critical thinking. My research has been concerned with tracing how dialectical thinking developed in the Axial Age, across a range of civilisations. In this paper, I highlight some of the key aspects of dialectics in Ancient Indian thought—elements that I believe need to be reclaimed in contemporary critical theory to revitalise dialectical thinking today. There are a number of ontological assumptions that inform my conception of dialectics: (i) that the world, and everything in it, undergoes constant change (the doctrine of flux); (ii) that everything in the cosmos is internally related (however closely or distant that relation may be) (which is the idea of interconnection or interdependency, otherwise known as the philosophy of internal relations), and; (iii) that these processes of the internal relations between all things are the forces for the change that we observe and experience as humans in the phenomenal world. Humankind has been fascinated with this constancy of flux, desiring to better understand this existential given of our word between interdependency, internal relations, and change. Yet this has also been equally concerned with a knowledge interest: to help direct ourselves, to guide humanity toward a more emancipatory future. And my firm belief is that the best way to understand our world—

and perhaps even guide this process of change toward desired ends—is through dialectical analysis. It is not only the best approach for grasping transformation and change, it is the *only* one that takes this ontology as the basis of its method. This is why dialectics was so fundamental to Marx's thought, and why I think it must remain so for any self-professed critical theory of society today.

We can examine dialectics in any number of ways. Firstly, we could focus on the way it has been defined or how it has been conceived by individual thinkers. This this would mean particular forms of dialectics would then stand in for the whole (i.e. the Hegelian system). Whilst there is much to say about how such towering figures advanced dialectical thinking in some of the most important and profound ways, they do not cover all of its aspects nor are they without their significant limitations (Hegelian objective idealism, for example). Secondly, we could look at how a particular school of dialectical thought deploys this form of analysis (i.e. Dialectical Materialism, or Daoist Dialectics, and so on). But this would only broaden the circle by degree—certain forms necessarily excluded. The third option, and what I have undertaken in my research, is to define dialectics by its constitutive elements: its logical components (from non-contradiction to context, from vantage point to syllogism and many others); its methods (such as dialogue, and open-ended, truth seeking inquiry); and its ontology (internal relations and flux). It is from these expansively defined constitutive elements that we can then examine how dialectics has been composed and added to, expanded and contracted, in human thought—whether of individual dialectics or dialectical schools—over time. Using this constitutive method allows us to do at least four things: to historically trace how dialectics has emerged to what it is today; to compare the various forms of dialectical thinking as against other dialectical forms, schools, and individual thinkers; to evaluate different dialectical forms by what they emphasise and what they leave out in their dialectical analysis; and to a purposive reconstruction—one that is more inclusionary of the many different strands of dialectics and which can retrieve those aspects otherwise lost or down-played. Taken together, this can help lead us toward a more robust method of dialectics for thinking through today's problems.

We can identify dialectical thinking thousands of years before it was understood by Hegel and mastered by Marx, by tracing its origins outside of the Western philosophical canon, and instead locating its emergence from the period that Karl Jaspers named the Axial Age (so from around 800 BCE to around 300 or 200 BCE). This historical narrative identifies a number of civilisations that begin to pivot (hence the name)—as if on an axis—away from long accepted myths and localised knowledge towards thoughts of *transcendence*. Transcendence, here, is not in the Kantian sense but rather a shift toward second-order thinking, largely beginning with movements in thought to speculation about the cosmos and our relation to it, rather than acceptance of myth or deity. It is in this moment of the so-called 'Great Transformation' that dialectical thinking emerges, and in ways that reveal it to be seemingly global (though not universal) in its formation. That is, dialectics emerges across a variety of cultures whose contact was minimal though by no means independent of each other.[1] And from here we can observe the remarkable shared characteristics across the Vedic, Buddhist, Daoist, Greek, Jewish, Persian, and on into Islamic and Scholastic dialectical systems. This begins within the Axial period, as Jaspers wrote:

"What is new about this age...is that man becomes conscious of Being as a whole, of himself and his limitations. He experiences the terror of the world and his own powerlessness. He asks radical questions. Face to face with the void he strives for liberation and redemption. By consciously recognising his limits he sets himself the highest goals."[2]

By approaching this era via the historical record provided in philosophical texts, we can begin to move beyond the usual tropes that dismiss these dialectical systems under gross misunderstandings: that Indian dialectics remains magical (or lost to the domination of the Brahmins); that Budhist dialectics remains mystical (concerned with release of the soul and not release on earth); or that Daoism remains strictly authoritarian (via its veneration of monarchy rather than balance). There is ample evidence of such readings, to be sure. But they do not cover everything, nor does their presence taint everything else so that these systems must be dismissed in their totality. Rather, it is more productive for us to reconstruct these dialectical systems in order to find what we can use of them today: to retrieve from them old or lost ways of thought that can help us to analyse and understand social life today…

So What is Dialectics?

Dialectics means many things, to many different people. But consistent across most of its forms are three elements: an ontology of flux and relations, methods of dialogue and logic, and a purpose (or knowledge-interest) in the possibility of consciously directing change. Dialectics is not a theory and does not do anything: instead, I think it is best conceived as a way of thinking—an 'approach' to thought itself—that helps one to bring into view the relations between things and the possibilities for change within this expansive context of interactions. This is its unique feature and the reasons for its utility for research and critical thought.

The ontology of flux is relatively uncontroversial as nearly everyone would agree that change is constantly taking place in some form—'one can never step into same river twice' as the old saying of Heraclitus reminds us. The unique aspect of dialectics here is that the emphasis on flux forces analysis to include how things happen as part of what a thing or phenomena is. It is not a simple cause/effect model other surfaced notion of causation but a historical and relational notion of change. It replaces the idea of a thing or phenomena as separate and static, with "process"—process contains the things history and its possible futures as the thing in-itself. Hence Marx saw the historical relation of capitalism as the conditions of emergence for communism. The key aspect of dialectics is that it places reality as flux at the forefront of its analysis.

The methods of dialogue are also relatively straight forward. For example, some of the first forms of dialectical thinking in Ancient India adopted a question/answer method between various ascetics, the so-called *vāda-vitandā* approach. In the Western canon this method is best known through Plato's dialogues that involve the method of Elenchus (how two or more people engage in a debate over a specific problem until they reach a point of contradiction and attempt to work through it to resolution or exhaustion). Sometimes these dialogical forms become so sophisticated that they develop into fully articulated or formalised systems of logic: and we can observe these in Ancient India through Nyaya logic, and also in the Gelugpa Budhist tradition (that continues today in Tibet), or even the closed logic of the Christian Scholastics. It was this openness to critique that typified the Axial period in the Upper Ganges where the many different orthodox and heterodox schools competed and integrated many ideas and concepts throughout this formative period.

Yet if there is one key part of dialectics that I would emphasise—and one that has also been consistently affirmed by Professor Bertell Ollman, the leading figure in Marxist-dialectics as well—it is the philosophy of internal relations. This could be otherwise labelled the study of the 'relations inside the whole' because 'internal' may wrongly imply we are looking at the individual make-up of a particular thing/object, when we are in fact concerned with the whole in which it relates.The philosophy of internal relations treats the relations in which anything stands as essential parts of what that thing is: the parts of the whole are not separated from each other but are inherently related. Changing one part of one thing, changes all the other individual units and the whole as well. As such, the assumed identity of one thing, abstracted and separated from all others, is not really the thing in-itself but is mere appearance: one-sided, and ultimately false. And this is really the revolutionary aspect of dialectical thinking because it overturns the commonsensical and superficial view that makes things/objects appear static and independent of one another, leading to a distorted and incomplete picture because these relations are abstracted away. Instead, dialectics looks at how a certain thing or phenomena has become what it is, and, the broad set of relations (its interactive context) in which it is located. The philosophy of internal relations goes to the history of the thing and its possible futures in relation to all other things. So whereas non-dialectical thinkers look for external causal agents to explain change, dialectical thinkers attribute the main responsibility for all change to the inner contradictions of the system in which it occurs and which form the possible tendencies—the horizon—of future change. But these are tendencies only: dialectics is not a teleology leading to prediction or some determined end.

Now, in West this philosophical tradition of internal relations stretches from Parminides, through to Spinozza and Hegel, to Marx and Dietzgen. But it has earlier and non-Western counterparts that formed in ancient India. For example, Buddhism's notion of (Pratītyasamutpāda) 'interdependent origination' that draws attention to the realisation that every *thing* and every *event* is the result of previous *things* and *events*. Here, no *thing* or *event* is born of itself—a thing is both 'that which *is* put together' and 'that which *puts* together'. We can think of later examples, outside of India, such Daoism's Ten Thousand Things (sometimes translated as 'myriad creatures'). This phrase expresses the multiplicity of things in the phenomenal world (all things under 'sky and earth'), not only in their status as objects (with internal yin/yang forces) but in their relations with one another that produces the cosmic constancy of change. A passage from the *Zhuangzi* states: "So we say: That is derived from This, and This is also dependent upon That."

It is this relationalism that, in turn, leads to the dialectical notion of change symbolised as a spiral. So perhaps best known is Engels account that, following Marx, says that dialectics reveals that everything is made of the mutual penetration of polar opposites (or contradiction), and the negation of this relation leads to gradual change. He calls this the 'spiral form of development'—Or what Katie Brown calls the 'cycles of elevating proportion'. Change progresses in a spiral-movement (i.e. it is not circular or necessarily progressive).[3] Nothing is lost in this process; new things arise in their interconnection with others, and preserved in the arms of the spiral. This spiral image does not make an implicit judgement on whether change is progressive or regressive, it is what is possible within given relations themselves.

Dialectical thinking is not particular or unique to any civilisation but emerged across a range of civilisations during the Axial Age, albeit in ways that differ in terms of emphasis according to the social problems that this form of critical thinking was directed (i.e. some who emphasise change/flux, others on dialogue, and logic, others on relations). What appears common to them all is the use of dialectics in terms of exploring metaphysical questions. When myth and accepted custom were questioned, it was dialectics—the method of doubt—that was germane to open discussion on questions that could not be proven or demonstrated.

The shift—the axis—in human consciousness that took place in India, and elsewhere, involved three changes:

1. The movement from the mythos/mundane to the transcendental or metaphysical;
2. The beginnings of a recognition of historical unity (or what Jaspers calls 'solidarity');
3. And the realisation of 'historical self-comprehension', the idea that humans could direct their own history

In this milieu, thinking was greatly advanced by taking a dialectical approach: thinking became its own object; critical thought was used to attempt to convince or persuade others (and hence the importance of rational argumentation and dialogue); the exploration of contradictions and opposites that remained related to one another rather than considered as binary or exclusive; and perhaps most importantly, the questioning of all previously accepted ideas, customs, and traditions. In this revolutionary period, according to Jaspers, thinkers began to ask "radical questions":

> All this took place in reflection. Consciousness became once more conscious of itself, thinking became its own object. Spiritual conflicts arose, accompanied by attempts to convince others through the communication of thoughts, reasons and experiences. The most contradictory possibilities were essayed... opposites which nonetheless remained related to one another, created unrest and movement to the very brink of spiritual chaos.... As a result of this process, hitherto unconsciously accepted ideas, customs and conditions were subjected to examination, questioned and liquidated. Everything was swept into the vortex.[4]

There were sociological and material conditions that provided the context for this shift and which where shared across all of these civilisation regions: the formation of small city-states with independent (or sovereign) existence; reciprocal intercourse of trade; massive improvements in agriculture; and widespread urbanisation. The question of the degree of inter-civilisational cross-fertilisation of ideas between these civilisations, and especially dialectics as a method of thought, can only be speculated on.

Jaspers gives an unfortunate religious and Eurocentric interpretation to this process—how he "orders" history—which we can readily dismiss. Rather, the most important question when ordering this history is looking for the "profound common element" to these Axial Age civilisations which, I argue, lies in how each of these societies began to think dialectically. Regardless of the degree of the interrelation between these civilisational groups (something that only future historical work will be able to uncover) all of these civilisations developed sophisticated dialectical systems because of an urgent imperative or knowledge interest to: think through oppositions/contradictions as inherently related. Rather than conceptualising beginning/end, dark/light and so on as binary oppositions and separate, thinkers began to see them as correlatives, that is, mutually implicated in the other. This breakthrough allowed these societies to engage with new transcendental and metaphysical questions in an open form, that of rational dialogue between opposed ideas rather than through force or authority—and this was especially true in Ancient India through the orthodox dharsanas, the heterodox schools, and the ascetics and Renouncers...). In the absence of old accepted traditions of authority (like myths or tribal kings), and in societies in which no class or sect dominated, each had to settle their metaphysical conceptions through critical thinking. In these conditions dialectics became a key tool and weapon one wielded by a new intellectual elite: the ascetics in India, wandering thinkers in China, philosophers of Greece, prophets of Israel and so on.

Axial Age civilisations began to think dialectically because they were confronted with similar social conditions such as the massive transformation from agrarian into urban centers, and faced similar metaphysical questions under the loss of old sources of legitimacy or authority or tradition, such as the post-Vedic system in Ancient India. We have vast amounts of evidence in the philosophical texts that have survived to us that reveal how dialectics was a unifying thought process across the Axial Age civilisations. This literature documents how the various movements and schools, or sometimes even individual thinkers, began to think dialectically. And underlying all these intellectual movements was a shared goal of "mutual comprehension." That is, even though they were each "concerned about the same problems" they were *not* bound by the same truth, which therefore required a methodology to be able to assent to contending "propositions."

Ancient Indian Dialectics

The first forays into dialectics in India shared a common social problem with other Axial civilisation: extreme social disparities under hierarchical divisions, and, a period of profound technological, productive, and social growth. After the composition of the Vedas (between 1500-800 BCE), India in its so-called Classical or Brahmanic period (between 800-

200 BCE)—a timeline that fits within Jasper's Axial Age—was a land of profound change. It was a time when traditional practices, beliefs, and interpretation of the Vedas were reassessed... Out of this milieu would come many schools of thought—Hindu, Budhist, Jainist and other schools, the heterodox and the orthodox Darśanas, individual mystics and Renouncers—all locked in deep disputes over metaphysics that was of fundamental consequence for religious and social order as a whole. Indeed, these remain at the core of Indian social-life today.

The East Ganges basin, east of modern-day Patna, was the focus of this Axial revolution. The Brahmana of the Hundred Paths (Śatapatha *Brāhmana*) offers a reason for this site: that the Gadank river had never been "burnt over" by Agni (Vaisvanara), the messenger and fire god in Vedic thought. It meant the Orthodox Brahmins of the Western Doab (those from the so-called 'land of the holy stages') had not penetrated beyond this point.[5] In this place between a western orthodoxy and an emerging heterogeneous, urban society in the east provided the site for intense social and intellectual disputes that would propel Indian's Axial Age. What was unique was not just the overall material development that I have already highlighted (such as urbanisation, improvements in agriculture, and small kingdoms) but the new intellectuals and the awareness of change that led radical innovative thinking. So from the worldview of Vedic ritualism gave way to philosophical speculations on the relation between immanence and transcendence.

The texts to which dialectical thinking would be first applied in Ancient India are some of the earliest examples of written philosophy: the *Rigveda* and on into the *Ramayana* and *Mahabharata*. The *Rigveda* contains passages that trace cosmogonic speculation, with its hymns on deities (especially in Books 1-10) that examine the origins of the universe and god,[6] and its later interpretation offer early attempts to think through the contradictions that arise when the mind speculates on the nature of cosmic origins. As is well known, there were numerous cosmogonies and no single or standard cosmogony within Ancient India, or indeed contemporary Indian thought. This hotbed of contested ideas of cosmological origins provided highly fertile soil for the development of dialectical thinking into the nature of the phenomenal and metaphysical. Arguably, it is the *Nāsadīya Sūkta* (0:129-6), one of the cosmogonic hymns, that expresses most clearly the type of speculation that would propel dialectics forward. This hymn it attempts to think through the seeming opposition of being/non-being at the point of creation, that is, to think beyond the impasse between the divine or autogeneration of the cosmic idea. But it breaks off at the point of answering this: positing that this may never be knowable. Even more important that in its open skepticism, is how the texts raises ideas of other worlds, dawns, and times—speculations that provided the grounds for thinking through to the transcendent during the Axial Age.

In turn the *Bhagavad Gita*, juxtaposed the polarities of good and evil, creation and destruction, in both a metaphysical and spiritual sense and for their profundity in thinking through relations of opposites.[7] More specifically, it is the delusion of the binary opposition between good/bad that is said to be one of the principle sources of error.[8] One of the first to instances of 'both-and' thinking operative in the *Bhagavad Gita* in the dialogue between Arjuna and Krishna. Arjuna is stuck within thinking in 'either/or' categories not yet realizing that Krishna's categories are not 'either/or' but 'both-and'. The latter is a dialectical way of thinking in which "opposites do not exclude each other but complement each other."[9] This 'both/and' thinking was taken up in the Axial Age, exemplified in the *Isha Upanishad*'s account of Brahma as *both* nirguna Brahman (without qualities) *and* saguna Brahma (with qualities). Yet, even today, many remain stuck in their interpretation of the *Bhagavad Gita* at the point of formal contradiction. As shown by Dorter, these apparent contradictions disappear when they are seen as arguments that are related dialectically rather than analytically. Rather than being solved by conceptual distinction or terminological clarification, it requires a change of perspective or context. For example, Krishna's statement that Brahman [as the ultimate metaphysical reality] is 'neither existent [sat] nor non-existent [asat]' (13.12) is meaningful only at the point where thought pushes through the paradox of thinking existence/being within a sensory or phenomenal frame: "If we understand existence in terms of presence in space and time, and non-existence as absence from space and time, the source of space and time itself can neither be said to exist or not exist."[10] The text compels thought to move dialectically, to push through to a mutual understanding of contradiction rather than opposition.

So how was dialectics first defined in these debates from Ancient India, and, how does this term translate across time to us today? Matilal provides a range of answers to this question. For him, the most relevant Sanskrit term seems to be *vāda* (or *vāda-vivāda*), defined as a bifurcating or divisive debate,[11] and for this reason Matilal refers to dialectic as the Ancient Indian 'art of philosophical disputation'.[12] He sets the scene in post-Upanishad India (we can assume the period between 800-300 BCE) in which philosophy was, as he describes it, "brisk, critical and controversial." As he writes: "No subject was considered too sacred for criticism and refutation." Here the Vedic cosmogony—the theory of the universe, both the mundane and the transcendent, were radically disputed amongst a plethora of schools and individuals. As such, one of the unique features of Ancient Indian dialectics was its spirit of knowledge-seeking. A passage from the Questions of Milinda (*Milinda-pañho*) captures this cooperative intention behind dialectics eloquently: "When the scholars debate with one another" [it says] "... there is summing up and unravelling, there is also defeat, and yet the scholars do not get angry at it."[13] Consequently, *vāda* and *vāda-vitandā* were upheld as most productive because each involved "honest seekers after truth" within a formal context of "honest and fair debate aimed at the refutation only of the opponent's thesis."[14]

Dialectical thinking also held great practical utility. An exemplar was use of dialectics in the law courts in Indian society at the time. Solomon shows how legal disputes involved dialectics both in the procedures of intellectual debates, and, syllogistic statements of arguments.[15] The *Manusmriti*, a legal text on dharma that engages questions of law, rights, and conduct, provides that in cases where "doubts arises" regarding the interpretations of the dharmas, an assembly of ten persons was required to deliberate the matter. This assembly expressly includes a dialectician (alongside Vedic scholars, a logician, and laypeople from different groups i.e. a student, household member, and retiree).[16] Such a rigorous process, and the specific inclusion of a dialectician, demonstrates the level of respect for dialectical thinkers during the Axial period and their capacities for exploring matters in doubt.

The other key aspect of dialectics was that it provided a means for critical, dissenting positions to be expressed in a medium accessible to others, whether orthodox or heterodox. For example, one of the most significant challenges to orthodoxy during this time emanated from the Lokāyata or later Cārvāka school found in the fragments of the *Bārhaspatya Sūtras*. This school insisted on perception, inferential doubt, and empiricism within a materialistic conception of the cosmos. This school rejected the Vedas, doctrines of Karma/ Samsara, and the notion of the afterlife. They were persecuted by Brahmin and sadly we have lost much of their knowledge. For them, insisting on sense-perception was a defence against the deception and exploitation that could come about through adherence to the Vedas. Importantly, their adherents were usually labelled negativists (*nastikah*)[17] because through logical argumentation they would negate Brahma, the practice of sacrifice, and the authority of the Vedas. As a famous story goes, when the Brahmins defended animal sacrifices by claiming the sacrificed go to heaven, Cārvāka members asked why the Brahmans did not then kill their aged parents to speed them on their way to heaven also? The element of doubt or scepticism deployed with dialectical thought remained a key defence against the imposition or over-reach of metaphysical dogma.

Turning to the importance of relationism within Ancient Indian thought, the *Vaiśenika Sutra* held that both the phenomenal and the 'supra-sensual' worlds exist objectively but that the latter could only be considered from a dualist position, the former from a materialist one. This cosmology contributed to a profound shift in thinking. The Vaiśenika theory of matter rendered the phenomenal world as consisting of countless, eternal atoms (*paramanu*)—when these atoms interacted generated the cause of all dynamism and movement in the world. This inherence is the source of motion, cause, and change in the phenomenal world—giving Vaiśenika a much wider, relational account of *prakriti* and the patterns of change they could observe in the natural world. Knowledge could obtain a complete understanding of the world of experience, thereby rendering liberation (or Moksha) in material rather than only spiritual terms.[18] In many respects, Nyāya develops this atomistic ontology of Vaiśenika but also made important contributions to epistemology and logic using dialectics. Nyāya recognised illusion and other forms of error in thought were not absolute barriers to liberation but were either flawed, incomplete, or absent cognition—they could be overcome by 'right reasoning' that followed an appropriate Pramanas (epistemology). Soul could be liberated or released (moksha or samsara) through such correct knowledge. In order to ensure accurate knowledge, Nyāya systematised thought to include no less than sixteen principles—though I will focus only on its unique syllogism of five parts, for which Nyāya is most commonly associated with dialectical logic.

This syllogistic method was not deployed for exploring things either known (that could be demonstrated) or unknown (that would require demonstration) but for those in dispute or doubt. This is crucial because it was intended as the "science of inference for the sake of others," that is, areas of doubt or where thought was in contestation and it focused on the intersubjective nature of persuasion and the possible inferences that interlocutor and audience may make. Two components warrant special attention. The first was the denial of any affirmative-negative dichotomy. Regarding dichotomies, the Naiyayikas argued that the absence of something should be regarded as another type of an (irreducible) attribute or quality (akhanda) rather than a form of non-identity. For example, 'this pot is blue' can be known by perception, whereas to know a negation, i.e. 'this pot is not blue' requires inference. Nyāya logic implies that our perceptual apparatus—and I would add memory of comparisons and forms of authority to establish and confirm such knowledge—are sufficient to give both affirmation and denial as assertions, especially in obvious cases. So, for example, regarding the contradictory statement 'It is a blue pot' and 'The pot is not blue' would seem logically inconsistent—they cannot be both true at the same time ('A' and 'not A'). It may be inferred that 'The pot is not blue' because of the positive fact that it is some colour other than blue. However, for Nyāya logicians, in such a move the negative has not been eliminated from the facts but merely "smuggled back into them in the (dis)guise of otherness or difference." That is, they do not readily infer that the non-blue pot must be a colour other than blue, not because this is not a valid inference but because it is not concerned with this level of either/or negation. The fundamental importance of this position is that it pushes thought to oppositional correlatives rather than either/or determinations. For example, when we refer to light/dark, it is their relation that is necessarily implied as conjunction and opposition: without the other, neither would have quality. This would then hold true for all oppositions in which their qualitative dimension is a gradation to be measured by 'more' or 'less' that exhausts itself in the nuances of their detailed qualitative difference. Nuance is a relational quality, *not* a separation of either/or. Arguably, much of the limitations of the contemporary 'politics of identity' could be overcome by engaging with this type of dialectical thinking.

The second component relates to the four kinds of dialectical relations that Nyāya identifies, especially its most unique one, the *svarupa* relation, viśesanatā (the relation between object and sense-organ, but also ontologically over and above the object of awareness). The relation of svarupa/viśesanatā refers to something related to something by a relation to something else, a process of relation that could seemingly be endless.[19] This is best seen as a clear articulation of the philosophy of internal relations—things are not merely tied by secondary relations, these relations must be seen as part of the things in themselves. Nyāya thus postulated a "peculiar" kind of relation, a svarupa relation, which is not to be taken as different from its relata but somehow intrinsic to the thing it-self. For Nyāya, there is no *a priori* necessity for the relation to be taken as different in all cases from its relata. What this thinking pushes toward is an account of a peculiar relation of a thing related to an other that must be seen as *part* of the thing in-itself—a key theme later echoed and modified by Hegel, Marx and Dietzgen. That is, whereas some would separate these aspects as endless forms of relations, each separate in their identity, and separate in the causal function, *svarupa* refers to an existential quality 'of/between' that is a constitutive attribute of its being.

A final example comes from the concept of *Anekāntavāda*—the many sidedness of reality—a concept unique to the Jainist School. In this line of thinking, substances undergo endless change but what we humans perceive are merely single facets of this process. Judgment is therefore conditional: it is true only in the context where the object it refers to remains the same. What is of importance is that Jainist thought detected a powerful limitation to identitarian logic (well before Adorno or other negative dialecticians) in that judgement must remain humble, even sceptical, of its ability to know the object. The complexity of reality cannot be expressed in a single way because it has a multiplicity of aspects—and hence Jainism erected a way of analysis to understand these various dimensions of truth. To gain knowledge/experience from only one naya (individual character) is, for a Jainist, to become like one of the seven blind men who, each feeling separate parts of an elephant, conclude the single part they hold represents the elephant's true form. To ensure we account for all these many sides, the method of the seven-fold predications, Syādvāda,[20] was deployed that when taken together form a system of logic necessary and sufficient to exhaust the possibilities of *all* knowledge claims. So Syād'—loosely translated as 'from some viewpoint' or 'may be'—is affixed to every statement to demonstrate its conditional or partial aspect and the logician must go through all of them to show that they have taken in all perspectives.

Conclusion

Having outlined just a few of the many ways that dialectics was developed and used in Ancient India, it is important to reflect on the knowledge interest that gave such an impetus to dialectics. Dialectics was the tool and weapon used to bolster any side of the disputed metaphysical claims regarding the cosmogony of the post-Vedic world within Axial Age India. Consequently, in many ways the dialectical forms of thought that emerged in Ancient India were essentially parasitic on the Vedic cosmology of which it was made to interrogate. Orthodox ascetics and darśanas rarely ventured outside of this transcendent realm or even asked questions of the mundane. Aside from the Cārvāka, many of its proponents were relatively concerned with using dialectics to explore the material world. In many ways, this led to an ambiguous and paradoxical outcome: dialectics was bound to a set of metaphysical concerns that gave both its motivation to strive into unknowns and yet stunted its wider development and application. Dialectics performed an invaluable service for metaphysical debates but the manner in which it was pressed into service solely for these needs meant the subordination of its wider critical functions and potential.

Ancient India dialectics was thus caught in contradiction. On the one hand, the shared basis of the Vedic cosmogonic speculation meant that all sects, ascetics, and philosophers—whether orthodox or heterodox—shared the view of flux: that "The only permanence is the permanent transience."[21] On the other hand, there was the forced separation of all things in the dharmic role, later formalised in varna, and social hierarchy. The Brahmin could officiate liturgy and ritual, and the lower castes could hope that it had some cosmic effect, but that was the extent of the practical relation between the mundane and the transcendent. Nondualism retained two worlds in everyday lived experience. Moreover, the Brahmin no longer needed the gods for they had made them compliant to their will through knowledge of ritual in the mundane. They were *the* gods in practice now. In its place, evidence adduced from intuition (*jnana*) or revelatory experience of the Brahmins, denigrated the experience/knowledge of the human condition in *prakti*. As Ancient Indian thought became bound in on itself, there would be no more Axial breakthroughs.

The limited application of dialectics in Ancient India leads to a fundamental external critique: its failure to grasp fully internal relations. Premised on the Vedic notion of inherence that was caught between nondualism *and* the practical separation of the mundane from the transcendent (and domination of the former by the latter), meant a full articulation of relations was not made, at least within the orthodoxy. In this cosmology, we were all Ātman-Brahma and yet separate from it. Here, it tended to forget that the construction of the worlds, its multiplicity and transience from Vedic cosmology, was ordered by human mind. The whole was revealed only in certain parts, and most of which the Brahmin had re-established the understanding of the two worlds and varna in ways that actually fragmented the whole. So, whereas the philosophy of internal relations admits a practice of abstraction that allows for an even greater variety of second-order relations,[22] it was precisely this aspect that was shut down at the close of India's Axial Age. To riff on Marx and Engels' famous opening of the *Manifesto*, we could say:

> Between the Brahmin and Cārvāka; philosopher and sophist;

Mutakallim and Falasifa; in a word, dialectician and non-dialectical thinker, have stood in constant opposition to one another, carried on an uninterrupted, now hidden, now open fight, a fight that each time ended, either in a revolutionary reconstitution of thinking or in the relative closing of thought...

NOTES

1. The extent to which these civilisation interacted and shared knowledge-systems is a matter of speculation. Yet given what we know of trade and travel routes of this period, it is highly likely there was both cross-pollination of dialectical thought and also auto-generation of dialectical systems particular to each locale.
2. Karl Jaspers, *The Origin and Goal of History*.
3. See F. Engels, "The Dialectic of Nature," in *Karl Marx, Frederick Engels: Collected Works: Frederick Engels:* Vol 25, Intl Publishers, 1987.
4. K. Jaspers, *The Origin and Goal of History*, 2.
5. See H. Kulke, "The historical background of India's axial age," in *The Origins and Diversity of Axial Age Civilisations*, (Ed. S.N. Eisenstadt), NY: SUNY, 1986: Chapter 16.
6. L. Renou (ed.), *Hinduism*, NY: Washington Square Press, 1963: 7.
7. S.S. Joarder, "Pondering Dialectical Nature in Indian Thoughts," *Philosophy and Progress: Vols. LI-LII*, January-June, July-December, 2012.
8. Note: Krishna embraces dualism when he praises nonviolence but not its complement, violence. This appears as one of the very few times duality is retained but it is only retained because both are characterised by attachment and difference, whereas in the latter pair only violence is attached and nonviolence unattached. As explained by Dorter, precisely because Arjuna does not want to fight, his fighting would not be an act of violence, i.e. attached. To act from dharma rather than desire exempts the action from being violent. See K. Dorter, "A Dialectical Reading of the Bhagavadgita," *Asian Philosophy*, 2012, 22(4): 320.
9. R. C. Zaehner, *The Bhagavad-gita with a Commentary on the Original Sources*, New York: Oxford University Press, 1973: 200.
10. Dorter, "A Dialectical Reading of the Bhagavadgita," 308.
11. I thank Jonardon Ganeri for a discussion on this point.
12. All quotes taken from Bimal Krishna Matilal, *Logic, language and Reality*, Delhi: Motilal Banarsidass, 1985: 1-22.

13. Milinda-pañho, 2.6. For details account of these various forms of Indian logic, see Jonardon Ganeri, "Indian Logic," 1-94, available at: https://philpapers.org/archive/GANIL.pdf
14. Matilal, *Logic, Language and Reality*, 16-17, 19.
15. E.E. Solomon, Indian Dialectics, 1976-1978, 93 cited in J. Bronkhorst, *Buddhism in the Shadow of Brahmanism*, London: Brill, 2011.
16. See Matilal in Biderman, Shlomo and Scharfstein, Ben-Ami (eds.), *Rationality in Question*, Leiden: E. J. Brill, 1989: 203.
17. E. Frauwallner, *History of Indian Philosophy, Vol. II*, Delhi: Motilal Banarsidass, 1997: 215.
18. On this see O. Leaman, *Key Concepts in Eastern Philosophy*, London: Routledge, 1999: 269.
19. "When we talk of x as being related to y by the relation r, we have first to relate x to y by r, and then relate r (which is also a property) to x by, say, r', and r to y by, say, r", another relation. This again may require that x should be related to r' by a further relation r'." See Bimal Krishna Matilal and Daniel H. H. Ingalls, *The Navya-Nyāya Doctrine of Negation: The Semantics and Ontology of Negative Statements in Navya-Nyāya Philosophy*, Cambridge: Harvard University Press, 1968: 40.
20. The Syādvāda are: (1) May be, it is; (2) may be, it is not; (3) may be, it is and it is not; (4) may be, it is indescribable; (5) may be, it is and yet is indescribable; (6) may be, it is not and it is also indescribable; (7) may be, it is and it is not and it is also indescribable. See Sancheti Asoo Lal, *First Steps to Jainism (Part Two)*, Jodhpur: Sumcheti Trust, 2001: 91.
21. See E. Shils, "Some Observations on the Place of Intellectuals in Max Weber's Sociology, with Special Reference to Hinduism," in *The Origins and Diversity of Axial Age Civilizations* (S.N. Eisenstadt ed.), NY: SUNY, 1986: 433.
22. Bertell Ollman, *Dance of the Dialectic*, Chicago: University of Illinois Press, 2003: 73.

2

Marx's Theory of Prehistory

In Memory of György Márkus. My Great Master Whom I Never Met

Julio Boltvinik

1. Overview

Departing from the premise that the best homage to Karl Marx in his bicentenary is the development of his thought. This lecture is an attempt to put together two aspects of his thought, which have remained isolated from each other, and try to show that together they constitute Marx's Theory of Human Prehistory.

The *first aspect* is Marx's philosophical anthropology (MPhA) or 'ontology of the social being', as Lukács called it, present in his 1844 *Economic and Philosophical Manuscripts* (EPhM) (but not only there), which has been masterfully systematised and developed by György Márkus (1934-2016) in *Marxism and Anthropology* (M&A) 1971/1978), with a passage in *Grundrisse* (pp. 704-06, Penguin Books, 1973) which might be identified by a central idea it puts forward: that the *objective limit of capitalism* (OLC) is reached as science and technology (S&T) are applied to production.[1] Thus, while MPhA explains the *genesis* of man, *anthropogenesis*, or the *Beginning of Human Prehistory*, the passage referred from the *Grundrisse* signals *the End of Human Prehistory* according to the meaning given to prehistory by Marx. Seen together they constitute *Marx's theory of human prehistory*. The following two quotations show that for Marx humanity remains in prehistory as long as it has not overcome scarcity and antagonistic social forms.

> The bourgeois relations of production are the last antagonistic form of the social process of production... at the same time the productive forces developing in the womb of bourgeois society ***create the material conditions for the solution of that antagonism.*** **This social formation brings, therefore, the prehistory of human society to a close** (Prologue to *Contribution to the Critique of Political Economy*, 1859; referred as Preface to *A Critique of Political Economy* in David McLellan, *Karl Marx, Selected Writings*, Oxford University Press, p. 426).

> In a more advanced phase of communist society, when the enslaving subjugation of individuals to the division of labour... have disappeared; when labour is no longer just a means of keeping alive but has itself become a vital need; when the all-round development of individuals has also increased their productive powers and ***all the springs of collective wealth flow more abundantly***—**only then can society wholly cross the narrow horizon of burgeois right and inscribe on its banner: from each according to his capacities, to each according to his needs!** (*Critique of the Gotha Programme*, 1875, in *Karl Marx, Political Writings*, Vol. 3, Verso 2010, p. 347)

In *M&A* Márkus says that Marx "distinguishes man from animal by his specific life activity, which constitutes his most proper essence. Man's life activity is *work*. Work is first of all an activity which *is aimed not directly but only through mediations at the fulfilment of needs...*" Márkus adds that "Man himself creates his increasingly complicated means [of labour] in the form of separate, independent objects. And in *Capital* Marx reproduces the Franklinian definition of **man as *a tool-making animal*"** (M&A, p. 6). This, together with other traits (sociality, consciousness, universality and freedom) and the most essential fact that man makes himself, makes his own history, constitutes the human essence in the Marx-Márkus (MM) perspective.

Going to *Grundrisse* and the *End of Human Prehistory*, the objective limits of capitalism (OLC) are met by the application of S&T to production, whereby the

> ...creation of real wealth comes to depend less on labour time (LT) and the amount of labour employed than on the power of the agencies set in motion... [there appears a] monstrous disproportion between LT applied, and its product... *No longer does the worker insert a modified natural thing as middle link between the object and himself; rather, he inserts the process of nature, transformed into an industrial process, as a means between himself and inorganic nature, mastering it...* The *theft of alien labour time, on which the present wealth is based,* appears as a miserable foundation in face of this new one... *Production based on exchange value breaks down, and the direct, material production process is stripped of the form of penury and antithesis.* (pp. 704-06)

Radovan Richta et al. (1969) and André Gorz (1999) have further developed the contents of this passage. I review Marx's and these authors' ideas and try to move forward, particularly on what should be done to delink the end of capitalism from apocalypses, following Gorz and other authors.

2. MPhA and Anthropogenesis: The Beginning of Human Prehistory

According to Marx-Márkus's (MM) conception, "the Human Essence (HE) is to be found in *work, sociality,* and *consciousness,* and in *universality* which embraces these three moments and expresses itself in each of them" (M&A, p. 36). Although *man shares with other species its characteristic as natural active being,* the difference between man and animal lies in their different life activities: while animal activity is directed exclusively to seize and consume the objects of its needs directly, *human work is an activity directed to need satisfaction not directly but through mediations.* (p. 4) *This has many consequences to which I will refer, with some detail, infra.* Let's state now only that these mediations broaden continually the range of things which might serve as objects of work, thus converting man into a ***natural universal being,*** *potentially capable of transforming in object of his/her needs and activity all natural phenomena* (p. 6), and that the more he/she broadens the objects of her/his activity, the more he/she develops her/his human capacities and human *needs* (pp. 9-10).[2]

In work (but not only in it) the conditions for ***man as a social being*** *are also given, which means that man cannot lead a human life except in his/her relation to other human beings and as a consequence of this relation*. In fact, work is always social in a double sense: 1. it is group work or else men produce for each other; and 2. the activity of the producer is always a historical-social activity in the sense that the means of work employed and the capacity to use them rely always in the appropriation and application of productive forces and forms of activity created by previous generations (pp. 16-25). **Man is constituted thus as a *social universal being*.**

The universality of the human essence expresses itself in the three traits described above: in dealing with work we can describe man as a ***natural-universal being;*** in discussing man's social characteristics, man can be qualified as a ***socio-universal*** and ***historical-universal*** being; lastly when broaching man's conscience, we characterised man as a ***universally conscious being.***

Márkus adds an additional trait of the human essence: ***man as a free being***. Before broaching this feature let's go back to work, which is central for this lecture and try to give a more detailed account. Márkus starts by saying that Marx's point of departure is the conviction that "man is a part of nature", a material, alive, sensuous, natural being, which can only subsist by his constant exchange or metabolism with nature; man attains this exchange through his own life-activity: *he is an active natural being*. "Man is a *finite, limited* entity, a dependent-conditioned and suffering entity, which is to say that the objects of his drives exist outside him, as independent objects from him; yet these are the objects of his need, indispensable, essential for his performance and the confirmation of the forces of his own being. These objects constitute, so to say, his *inorganic body.*" (p. 3).

In a general sense this can be said of all other animals

as well. "But man is not only a natural being; he is a *human* natural being". (Marx, EPhM, 162; A&M, p. 4). It is necessary, therefore, to characterise man as *specifically human*, as a *species being* (or even better as a *generic* being, a being of the genus; in German *Gattungswessen*), which implies the opposition between man and animal. (A&M, p. 4).

"The cause and at the same time the essence of this difference between man and animal has to be sought in the respective life activities of man and animal". "Both animal and man can satisfy their needs only through their own activity. But animal activity is confined exclusively to seizing and consuming the given natural objects of their need: *it directly coincides with the process of active need-fulfilment.* Therefore, it is a *limited* life activity". It can only transform into objects of its activity and of its life those objects whose physical, chemical, etc. properties satisfy its genetically fixed needs. (A&M, p. 4).

First and foremost, what distinguishes man from animals is his specific life activity, which constitutes his most proper essence. Man's life activity is *work. "Work is first of all an activity which is aimed not directly but only through mediations at the fulfilment of needs."* (p. 5) *But work is also a conscious free activity.* The object of work only becomes suitable for human use because work transforms it. Mediation is present: "1. As the mediating activity, the *living labour* itself which precedes and makes possible, the human use (the consumption) of the object. 2. As the *instrument of labour* which man interposes between him and the potential object of his needs and which serves as the conductor and transformer of his activity". (p. 6) "While the animal's instruments of labour, i.e. its *organs* evolve and change only in the uncontrolled millennial process of biological evolution, man himself creates his increasingly complicated means in the form of separate, independent objects. And in *Capital* Marx reproduces the Franklinian definition of man (in English) as *a tool-making animal.*" (Márkus, p. 6). Márkus points out the following consequences of this human specific activity:

1. As human activity is not aimed without mediations to the

satisfaction of needs, "but in the useful transformation of the material form of natural substances, it constantly increases *the range of environmental things and materials which can act as objects of that activity.* On the one hand work makes things suitable for human consumption and so affects the widening of the scope of consumable objects. On the other hand, objects which cannot be individually consumed even in transformed form, may find a useful application as means of the productive activity itself... *Consumption and use become different categories* (which does not happen among animals)." Already in his material life, in his activities of subsistence the human being *appropriates* nature in a growing degree; his "inorganic body" shows a historical tendency to growth, his interrelations with nature become more and more complex and many-sided, less rigidly determined by biological constraints. (p. 6)

2. This reproduction [i.e. of human individuals in the historical process of production, Márkus] although it appears as appropriation of the objects by the subjects in one respect, appears in another respect also as formation, *subjugation of the objects to a subjective purpose*; their transformation into results and repositories of subjective activity (Márkus quotes *Grundrisse* p. 489]. Work, production, means not only the appropriation of nature as object by man as subject, but also the *objectification* (Vergegenständlichung) of the subjective agent and his activity... In general, historical development replaces natural environment by *a socio-cultural milieu* which is the result of the productive activity of earlier and present generations and the elements of which embody human capacities, represent the objectifications of the "essential powers of man (menschliche Wesenkrafte)" (p. 7). As a consequence of the fact that man lives in a hyper-humanised world in which human capacities and needs developed in the past are found as fairy godmothers, in their objectified form, at the cot's headboard, in which the results of all previous social development are at his disposition in material form, *it is possible for man to start his development not in the "beginnings of the first principle", but in the point that previous generations have bequest. Work, the objectivation of human nature, constitutes the possibility of history as such.* (Translated from the Spanish edition of M&A, p. 22; in the English edition, p. 8, this brilliant statement becomes dull). Note that not only are human capacities objectified in

labour products, but also human needs. Work, however, changes not only the object at which it is directed, but also the labouring subject itself: *it transforms not only the external nature but transforms man himself:* ...the producers change, too... they bring out new qualities in themselves, develop new powers and ideas, new modes of intercourse, new needs and new language (*Grundrisse*, Penguin Books, 1973, p. 445).

3. The historical creation of new human objects...implies not only that man extends his activity over new realms of nature, but also... that *man appropriates new human essential potentialities, new properties and new human capacities*. Generally, we may say that *man forms and develops his own production capacities by objectifying them*... (p. 9 English; combined with translation from the Spanish edition, pp. 23-24). The subjective appropriation of some means of production implies the formation of an integral activity which puts the means and the object in the necessary relation for obtaining the outcome desired by the subject. Capacities thus appear as transpositions of specific objective natural connections into the sphere of the subject's activity... Man is capable, then, of transforming into laws, into principles of his own activity, a broader and broader range of natural connections and regularities. (pp. 9-10 English; p. 24, Spanish).

4. Each singular act of human activity presupposes the pre-existence of a *need*... but in the historical process as a whole that relation is inverted. The needs that effectively determine production are not the original needs in their natural harshness, but the needs originated in production itself.[3] '...needs are produced .... just as are products and the different kinds of work skills. The greater the extent to which historic needs—needs created by production itself—social needs which are themselves the offfsprings of social production and intercourse, are posited as *necessary, the higher the level to which real wealth has become developed. Regarded materially, wealth consists simply in the manifold variety of needs.*' (*Grundrisse*, p. 527; I have made the quote to coincide with the source, eliminating the errors it contained). It is the object produced by man which origins the human collective need of it. (Again I combined the English (p. 10) and the Spanish (p. 27) editions).

Now I turn to man as a free being, the additional trait that

Márkus includes in the concept of human essence. (This is discussed in the last two pages of M&A: 57-59). "Man is a generic being not only in that he practically and theoretically makes his own genus (Gattung)... his object, but also in that he treats himself... as a *universal* and therefore *free being*" (*Economic and Philosophical Manuscripts*, EPhM, p. 293, quoted by Márkus[4]). Marx rejects, according to Márkus, the idealist interpretation of freedom as independence from the real world, as exemption from external influences and determinations; and sustains that the concept of freedom has for Marx a double, intimately linked, abstract-negative, and concrete-positive meaning. *In the negative sense freedom is freedom from something;* it means man's capacity to *liberate* himself through his real activity from those concrete conditions, relations, characteristics which have turned historically into limitations, chains, upon the manifestation of his socially formed personality. The possibility of this liberation in general is already implied in the fact of human self-consciousness. Man can make the social and —in some sense and within limits— even the biological determination of his life the object of his activity, i.e. something that he can consciously influence and change. An animal is immediately one with its life activity, it is not distinct from it, it *is* that activity. Man makes his life activity itself into an object of his will and consciousness. He has conscious life activity [...] ***Conscious life-activity directly distinguishes man from animal life activity. Only thereby is he a generic being...*** Only because of that is his activity free activity (p. 328, Penguin edition of the EPhM, but I keep Márkus's use of "generic being" instead of "species-being").

This negatively understood freedom, says Márkus, this constant release and liberation from limitations, is at the same time, in its historical tendency, also something *positive*: *power which man procures for himself.* It means the development of man's control and domination over the forces of nature, external nature as well as man's own nature; it means the widening of the scope of human possibilities, *it is the formation and cultivation of human creativity, of the essential powers of man, beyond any limitation, as an end in itself.* (M&A, p. 58)

> But the historical development of man towards the creation and increase of this freedom on the scale of whole society *has not,* up to this point, *coincided with the formation of free individuals.* The man of the alienated capitalist society, a man who is, in general, liberated from the *personal dependencies* and constraints characteristic of earlier ages, is an 'abstract' and that also means a *fortuitous', accidental individual* —that is, he is a man whose life and activity, hence the manifestations of his individuality, though free in a legal sense, are in fact determined by conditions and social circumstances that act objectively and independently of him, conditions which have a 'chance' quality for him. *Hence, he is a man for whom his life does not constitute the expression of his personality, does not mean the realization of his individual potential, the actualization of his freedom.* Liquidating private property and the naturally given [*spontaneous* in the Spanish edition] division of labour, transcending alienation, communism first creates the conditions for a truly free human development and individual life... *The freedom of the individual, made possible through the elimination of the antagonism between human essence and existence,* social and individual development, objectification and self-realization… means that each individual will be able to choose himself consciously within the (historically circumscribed) range of the objective possibilities offered to him by the whole of social development and to realize them in his life harmoniously, *depending on his decision, on his needs, capacities and interests.* (M&A, pp. 58-59)

Márkus develops, in an extensive way, in the third and last chapter of M&A, how human essence (HE) manifests itself in history. He starts by denying that HE is the ensemble of those fundamental traits which remain untouched by the historical development of mankind, which are inseparable from man as such and are characteristic of every human individual in any form of social life. This interpretation, says Márkus (p. 36), cannot be reconciled with Marx's texts: As a result of alienation it is precisely 'human essence' which is alienated and *taken away* from the proletariat (in the sense that it cannot realise it in its own life)". Márkus says that we come to the same conclusion if we examine the specific (and above analysed) *content* of Marx's notion of human essence. The universality of man, which figures in Marx as a particular tendency of the overall historical *development*, can hardly be understood at all as a constant feature or condition of individual men (p. 37).

Work, sociality and consciousness *can* indeed be conceived as necessary and permanent traits of every human individual, but when conceived in this way their meaning loses those philosophical characteristics which Marx took to be their substance. Work, from being free self-activity in which man forms, develops and appropriates his own capacities, becomes under the circumstances of alienation a forced and externally imposed activity resulting in the increasing one-sidedness and deformation of its subject. Thus, this activity is not 'work' in the anthropological-philosophical meaning of this term but merely abstract labour (p. 38). This difference is clearly shown in the fact that Marx in the *German Ideology* [Márkus ignores the fact that Engels is co-author of this text] repeatedly considers the "abolition [*Aufhebung*] of [abstract] labour" to be one of the most fundamental preconditions of a communist society (M&A, p. 38). The case is similar with man's sociality. Naturally the individual is always a 'social being' but in capitalism the dependence of the individual on the social whole does not mean collective existence. Márkus (p.38) quotes Marx: "The *society* of this estranged man is the caricature of a *true community*, of his true generic existence" ("Excerpts from James Mill's Elements of Political Economy" in *Karl Marx. Early Writings* Penguin, op. cit., pp. 264-65). Finally, "the situation is again analogous in the case of consciousness", which is "an attribute belonging to every human individual, to every normal member of the species *Homo sapiens*", but as a consequence of the division of labour and the separation and opposition between mental and physical labour:

> The empirical, everyday consciousness of individuals has become increasingly divorced from the generic development of social consciousness and self-consciousness, from the progress

> made in the social spheres of intellectual production, i.e. in sciences and arts; it has become fetishistic, a prisoner of socially conditioned appearances distorting reality... Corresponding to this... ideologies have evolved, distorted-alienated expressions of the separation and alienation of thought from praxis. (M&A, pp. 38-39)

On the basis of the above, continues Márkus, the interpretation of 'human essence' as an "ensemble of fundamental and invariant traits found in every human being would seem to be unacceptable" (p. 39). Márkus (overcoming some difficulties) arrives at an original and profound vision of the Marxian concept of the Human Essence and of Human History:

> The point here... is not simply that there are certain abstract traits which remain invariant through the historical transformation and change of the 'nature' of concrete, real men, but above all, that this never-ceasing formation of 'human nature' is itself a *unified process* which can be comprehended and characterised in its unity... *Marx meant... by 'human essence' primarily those characteristics of the real historical existence of mankind which make it possible to comprehend history as a continuous and unified process that has a development tendency. The universality of man... and his freedom mark the general direction of the historical progress of humanity, while the characterisation of man as a conscious social being engaged in material productive self-activity refers to those necessary traits, those dimensions of this total developmental process on the basis of which the above historical tendency unfolds...* (pp. 39-40)

Additionally, Márkus adds in an endnote:

> This conception of history assumes and presupposes the acceptance of a definite *perspective* (i.e. the *affirmation* of determinate, presently existing *social needs* that point in the direction of this perspective, the *affirmation of the* ***radical needs*** of the proletariat) *and the choice of values emerging from, and determined by, this perspective*. The concept of 'human essence' locates, articulates and explicates precisely these values and at the same time it indicates the basic conditions of their realization through an analysis of the real '*condition humaine*' that is history... The Marxian concept of 'human essence' necessarily presupposes

> and encloses the moment of *practical choice,* that of decision in the social conflicts of the present and between presently given social possibilities; it contains within its very theoretical content the moment of *praxis,* namely of a *revolutionary* praxis radically transforming the existing state of affairs. (Note 12 to Chapter 3, p. 76)

Agnes Heller, in her book (1972) gives further force to the association of the perspective derived from the conception of the Human Essence and values. She says:

> We sustain that in Marx's *Oeuvre* two axiological axioms are present from which all values and all value judgements that he sustains are derived. These axioms are centred on the ontological primary category (not derivable empirically from any other thing): **human wealth,** which is the multilateral unfolding of the essential forces (powers) of the *Human Species*. The *First Marxian Axiological Axiom* says: 'Anything that contributes, or promotes, the enrichment of the species essential forces *is a value*'. The *Second Axiological Axiom* states: 'The supreme value is the circumstance in which *individuals can appropriate the species wealth*'. In fact, *Marx derives all values from these two axiological axioms*. (I had no access to the English edition of this book by Heller, so I am translating from the Spanish version *Hipótesis para una Teoría Marxista de los Valores*, Grijalbo, Barcelona, 1974, pp. 27-28)

Márkus states that *according to Marx,* "It is just the fact that man has a *history* (in the strict sense of the term) that constitutes the real specificity of human existence, and therefore to abstract man from this historicity would mean to disregard his most essential trait." (p. 40). "History is the process of human 'self-creation', a continuous process whereby man forms and transforms himself through *his own* activity, through *his own* work, in the direction of an increasing freedom and universality". And Márkus adds brilliantly:

> And the principal characteristic, the 'true essence' of man lies precisely in the presence of this *self-activity whereby he creates and forms his own subjectivity*. The individual becomes and is a *human* individual precisely because he actively engages and participates in this process, and this is possible only because

> he has appropriated some of the objectified results and achievements of previous human progress... Thus the real unity of the human species itself cannot be truly comprehended apart from this historical process, but only in and through it. This unity is actually nothing else but the inner *unity and continuity of the process of human history*. So if we mean by 'philosophical anthropology' some extra or suprahistorical (or even simply ahistorical) characterisation of human traits, then Marx *has no* anthropology, and he would deny the usefulness of such an anthropology for the understanding of man's *essence*. If, on the other hand, we would understand by anthropology an answer given to the question about 'human essence', an attempted resolution of the question 'what is essentially man?', then there is a Marxian 'anthropology', only it is not *an abstraction from history but rather an abstraction of history itself*. [The Spanish translation: *it is not an abstraction of history but rather the abstract of history*, makes clear that Márkus meant that it does not exclude history but *is* the generalisation of history]. That is, Marx's conception is diametrally opposed to all those trends of thought which sharply divide and counterpose anthropology and sociology, which set the study of man's 'essence' in opposition to the socio-historical study of man. For Marx the 'human essence' lies precisely in the 'essence' or inner unity of the total social development of humanity. (pp. 40-41).

Márkus adds a central idea: "The bearer or subject of the 'human essence' for Marx is not the single individual but *human society* apprehended in the continuity of its historical change and development". (p. 41)

History, continues Márkus:

> Can be apprehended as a *unified process* only from the point of view of *society*...from this perspective it appears not only as *technological progress* but also as *anthropological progress*, as the continuous broadening and deepening of the range of the capacities (abilities in the English translation), needs, forms of intercourse and knowledge evolved by the whole of society. From the point of view of the *social whole*, history unfolds itself as the process of man's progressive universalisation and liberation. But this process has not meant, up to now, in history, the emergence

> of increasingly universal and free *individuals.* From the point of view of individuals there is no unified and unequivocal criterion with the help of which we could comprehend history as evolution ('development' in the English translation)... From the individual point of view we cannot characterise the historical process with *a single, definite direction, —due to its contradictory tendencies.* That is, regards individuals, there is no single criterion which would make it possible to describe unambiguously succeeding historical eras as 'more advanced' or 'superior'. Can the men of today's civilisation, who clearly have both more extensive and more variegated needs and broader possibilities of their satisfaction, be valued more highly ('set over' in the English translation) the individuals of previous historical epochs for whom the circle of these possibilities was undoubtedly much more limited, but who were able, *en masse* (albeit within definite limits) to fulfil their need for creative and meaningful work —which, as a general phenomenon, is impossible in our days amidst capitalist social relations?... The universalisation of the human genus does not necessarily mean the historical formation of increasingly universal and many-sided individuals. This total historical tendency can be realized through the diversification and extension of relations and intercourse between 'one-dimensional', limited, narrow particular or, as Marx would say, 'abstract' individuals as well. (pp. 42-43)

Márkus states that at this point *Marx's 'anthropology' is closely related to his theory of alienation*. I cannot deal with Márkus' full discussion here, but only quote a few phrases that pinpoint his very insightful text on alienation.

> The social power, i.e. the multiplied productive force, which arises through the cooperation (*Zusammenwirken*) of different individuals, as it is determined within the division of labour, appears to these individuals, *since their cooperation is not voluntary but naturally given,* not as their own united power but as an alien force existing outside of them, of the origin and goal of which they are ignorant, which they thus cannot control... This is alienation... (p. 43)
>
> The concept of alienation serves to characterize not merely the economic sphere but the totality of social life...So in the

> political sphere it refers to the state as 'alienated public power' and 'illusory community', becoming independent from the real (and privatized) life of individuals; as regard to human relations in general... to the reification of the intercourse and commerce between individuals and to their ensuing atomization that follows the dissolution of 'naturally given' communities; in the sphere of intellectual production to the fetishization of everyday consciousness and to the appearance of ideologies which translate the separation of mental from physical labour into the sway of ideas over matter and material life (p. 44).
>
> Under conditions of alienation, *the discrepancy between individual and social development*... necessarily ensues... *Alienation is nothing but this discrepancy,* whereby the historical progress of mankind is separated from the development of single individuals, whereby the self-formative and creative aspects of human activity appear only in the larger context of the social whole, but are not present on the effects of the individual activity upon the concerned individual himself. Alienation, therefore, is nothing but ***the separation and opposition of human essence and man's existence*** in the sense Marx has applied these terms. And transcending alienation means the elimination of this disaccord and conflict between human essence and existence—that is, the creation of the historical development which ends the inverse and antagonistic relationship between the wealth and many-sidedness of social life and the impotence, paltriness and one-dimensionality of the lives of individuals. The end of alienation thus means the creation of such social conditions under *which it will become possible to judge the general level of societal development, of human progress, by the developmental level of single individuals, when the universality and freedom of human genus will be directly expressed in the free and many-sided lives of men.* (pp. 45-46; italics in last phrase, added)

Only with the historical-practical transcendence of alienation, points out Márkus, can the human essence become a concrete determination 'for itself', characterising the living individuals and their real communities. And it is for this reason that communism wins Marx's moral affirmation as a society which makes possible the *simultaneous* and interrelated free development of the human genus *and* of the individual men, and therefore the 'adequate' realisation of the HE (p. 48). And Márkus concludes:

> And this is what differentiates mankind's *'prehistory'*, that is, that history which is not yet 'the *actual* (wirkliche) history of man as an already posited (vorausgesetztes) subject but only man's act of creation (Erseugungsakt), the *history of his origin'* (EPhM, p. 317), from his future 'actual', real history. For the concept of 'prehistory', which traverses Marx's whole life work, is not to be understood as a simple metaphor. The process of human genesis is, according to Marx, not completed with the formation of *Homo sapiens* as a biological species... Indeed, this is only the starting point and foundation from which man's *socio-historical genesis,* the genesis of man as a 'generic being' departs and begins. *This social genesis is the process of 'prehistory'*, which at the end, gives rise to the human species as *mankind,* as a real and conscious unity of globally interacting and interconnected individuals, on the one hand, and to the concrete, many-sided and multidimensional human individuality which truly *represents* the historically achieved stage of development of the 'genus', on the other... Alienation in this context is *not merely a negative precondition* for the unfolding of human essence (as the earthly 'vale of tears' is to salvation), but —in a contradictory form— also its *positive* formative period... Only through the era of alienation... are the purely 'naturally given', local and restricted communities dissolved, and only thereby does an increasingly broader sphere of human intercourse unfold, one which at the end virtually embraces mankind as a whole (world market)... Finally... only through the processes of alienation can that positive wealth of objectified human needs [not wants, as the English translation writes] and capacities emerge which constitutes the fundamental *objective* precondition of human emancipation. (pp. 48-49).

Figure 1 is a graphic representation of MPhA as elaborated by Márkus

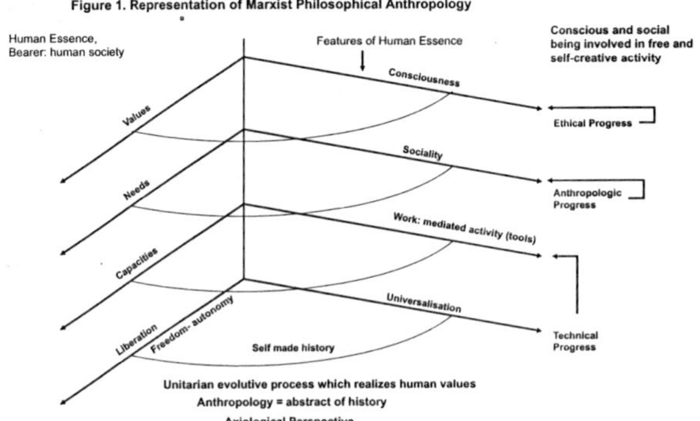

Figure 1. Representation of Marxist Philosophical Anthropology

3. The Role of Tool Making in Human Genesis According to Palaeo-Anthropology

If we can speak about human freedom but not on salmon's freedom, it is because the life of salmons is controlled by instincts while ours is not. This is a central aspect of the rupture and its result is *biological liberty of human beings*. I explore now the role of tool making (or the mediated nature of human work) in human genesis. I begin with Stringer and Andrews (2005),[5] which emphasise the non-directed character, with many casual elements, of the process which generated the birth of the human being and the rare fact that we are the only species of the gender *Homo*, which was not the case in various moments of the past. Before proceeding further, I want to introduce an idea which Marx expresses in *Capital* and which is not, as explicitly as one would desire, broached by Márkus: that human work is distinguished from animal activity by the fact that the form of the product is prefigured in the mind of man before it is actually produced. Richard Leakey (2001)[6] analyses the experimental work done by Nicholas Toth, which proves that in the fabrication of the first stone tools (by *Homo habilis*, 2.5 million years ago, called Olduvaian as they were first found in Olduvai Gorge), which were small very sharp stone chips used to cut skin, meat, wood and other soft materials, their producers did not have the specific forms of the tool in their mind. Toth argues that, nevertheless, to produce them they required a superior brain capacity to that of present day apes. Leakey describes the position of other authors which sustain that present-day apes do have the required manipulative skills, and the spatial concepts, to manufacture these tools, which Leakey refutes by noting the failure of the experiments which have tried to teach them to manufacture them. On the contrary there is consensus that the Achulean tools, which were first produced 1.4 million years ago (by *Homo erectus*) required their producers to have a mental template of what they wanted to produce, in other words, that they intentionally imprinted a specific form into the material. There is also consensus that this task required advanced cognitive capacities. Leakey points out that the development of Olduvaian or Achulean tools allowed the human being to incorporate (through hunting or scavenging) meat into their diet, widening its survival and reproductive possibilities. Leakey and Toth date 1.4 million years ago, the first conclusive evidence of work "in a form which belongs exclusively to human beings" (Achulean tools) to express it with Marx's words. On these bases, I posit four initial stages in the use and development of tools by the human being (and its ancestors): eventual use of tools (apes); systematic use of natural tools (bipedal apes); semi-conscious manufacture of tools (*Homo habilis*); and conscious manufacture of tools (*Homo erectus*). This is associated with the growth of the human brain through natural selection. If in a given population (which has a given distribution of brain sizes) the persons with the largest brains are more successful in producing tools, their survival and reproductive probabilities will be larger, which will produce the growth of the average brain.

Leakey interprets a text by Darwin from the *Descent of Man* as positing the simultaneity of three aspects of the human evolution: the erected posture, the size of the brain and the making of tools. The quotation by Leakey (2001, op. cit. p. 5) is as follows:

> If it be an advantage to man to stand firmly on his feet and to have his hands and arms free, of which, from his pre-eminent success in the battle of life, there can be no doubt, then I can see no reason why it should not have been advantageous to the progenitors of man to have become more and more erect or bipedal. They would thus have been better able to defend themselves with stones or clubs, to attack their prey, or otherwise to obtain food... But the hands and arms could hardly have become perfect enough to have manufactured weapons, or to have hurled stones and spears with a true aim, as long as they were habitually used for locomotion and for supporting the whole weight of the body, or, as before remarked, so long as they were especially fitted for climbing trees.[7]

But as can be seen, the alleged Darwinian package is not contained in the quotation, which rather sustains the thesis that bipedal walking *is a necessary (but not sufficient) condition to use and produce tools or weapons*. The big temporal gap in the appearance of bipedal walking and the first manufactured stone tools (5 million years) would invalidate Darwin's package according to Leakey. My hypothesis is that during such a long period our ancestors used natural tools and weapons and produced tools and weapons made of soft materials, which leave no archaeological tracks. Bipedal walking is thus a precondition for the other two aspects of human evolution.

In the writings of Aura Ponce de León[8] I have found an excellent (but not named as such) definition of work as mediated activity: In "Cognitive Archaeology" she points out that tool making is evidence of a cognitive level beyond that of other species and that "the transformation of the world in a conscious and systematic way and with a *purpose oriented eventually to other time and place, beyond the present activity,* is a conduct that is far from being widely shared by other species although some signs of it have been identified in other superior apes." (p. 90). The phrase in italics is an excellent definition of mediated work, showing that some paleo-anthropologists concur with Marx's definition of mediated work. I have also found in her writings (*Homo* Genus) a reason as to why tool making cannot be an instinctive activity: as she argues that transformation of the world, and tool making as part of it, *are intentional activities*. This she contrasts with bipedal walking and the growth of the brain which are biological processes.

If it is not still clear that among paleo-anthropologists there is also present the notion of a rupture that gave birth to human beings, the following quotation from Phillip V. Tobias should dissipate any doubt:

> Dobzhansky, in his posthumous Raymond Dart Lecture (1977) recognised two great steps forward in the development of life. The *First Transcendence* was the Origin of Life itself, the *Second Transcendence*, the coming of Man with his futuristic survival kit. *Homo habilis*, the meek hominid, announced the Second Transcendence to the world, and neither hominids nor the world *could be the same again*. Thenceforth, man's behaviour, adjustments, survival, came to be determined more and more by what he could do with his hands under his watchful eyes and the control of his planning, foreseeing, anticipating and agile brain. (1979, pp. 85-92)

The issues rose by Darwin, Leakey, Ponce de León and Dobshanzky reinforce the central ideas of Marxian philosophical anthropology (MPhA). The Tobias citation shows that for paleo-anthropologists there was a great rupture provoked by the manufacture of stone tools (especially the Achulean tools), concurring with MM perception that the mediated character of human work distinguishes *Homo* from all other species.

In trying to identify further what the sciences of evolution are sustaining with respect to the human mind, in particular trying to elucidate *if they are in a condition of identifying the how and when life became conscious of itself*, which is as Fromm identifies the Great Rupture, I look at work by Arsuaga Ferrreras and Martínez Mendizábal[9], who give an account and oppose those views (e.g. Chomsky's) which reject that cognitive human capacities developed gradually by natural selection as was argued by Darwin. They analyse both the growth of

the brain and the anatomy of our speaking apparatus. They conclude that the necessary development of the brain for speech had to precede the adaptation of the peculiar speaking human system; that human speech is as old as two million years and that its development followed a gradual process of natural selection. Ponce de León in "Cognitive Archaeology" discusses the findings by Wynn on the intelligence of those which manufactured Achulean stone tools (especially hand axes). Wynn concludes that they had already developed advanced cognitive capacities. Nevertheless, Ponce de León tells us that the study of consciousness in our ancestors is still something to be done.

The overall conclusion I derived from my brief incursion into paleo-anthropological literature is that of reinforcing MM convictions on the central role of tool making in human essence.

4. Objective Limit of Capitalism (OLC). Marx's Vision of the End of Prehistory and Current Evidence.

4.1 The passage of the Grundrisse (pp. 704-06, Penguin edition)

I adopted the expression OLC from what Jorge Veraza pointed out reacting to a presentation of mine regarding the passage object of this section. In it, after exposing the central change that big industry implies for production by applying science and technology (S&T) to it, Marx concludes, to which the expression OLC fits well, that:

> The *surplus labour of the mass* has ceased to be the condition for the development of social wealth, *just as the non-labour of the few*, for the development of the general powers of the human intellect. With that, production based on exchange value breaks down, and the direct, material production process is stripped of the form of penury and antagonism.

Although the notion of an objective limit must also be extended to the objective natural limits of the planet, here I refer only to the meaning it has in the *Grundrisse*.

It is a remarkable text that raises the OLC in terms of the

social relations of production, and *casts serious doubts about the current validity of the law of value*. A century later Radovan Richta *et al.* in *Civilization at the Crossroads* (op. cit.) and 130 years later André Gorz in *Reclaiming work. Beyond the wage-based society*, retook some of Marx's arguments. Next, I enumerate in a synthetic way the contents of the *Grundisses's* passage:

1) Capitalism (production of value) is *governed by the assumption* that the amount of labour time (LT) is the decisive factor in the production of *wealth*.
2) But with big industry the creation of wealth becomes less dependent on LT than on the power of the agencies set in motion, power that depends only on the advance of S & T and its application to production.
3) A quantitative disproportion between LT and product is generated, as well as a qualitative imbalance between abstract labour and the power of the production process it superintends.
4) Labour appears next to the production process (as watchman and regulator) instead of being included within it and being its chief actor.
5) Instead of the tool interposed between man and the object, an industrial process is now interposed.
6) The great foundation-stone ceases to be the direct human labour that is replaced by the development of the social individual who appropriates the general productive force (understanding and mastery of nature).
7) The *theft of alien LT*, surplus value, on which the present wealth is based, appears as a miserable foundation in face of this new one.
8) As soon as labour in the direct form has ceased to be the great well-spring of wealth, LT ceases to be its measure and exchange value must cease to be the measure of use value.
9) The *surplus labour of the mass ceases to be* the condition of

the development of social wealth, just as *the non-labour of the few,* for the development of the human intellect.

10) Production based on exchange value breaks down and the production process is stripped of the form of penury and antagonism.
11) Necessary LT is minimised.
12) The liberated time and the means created for all correspond to the artistic and scientific development of individualities.
13) Capital is the living contradiction: while reducing LT to a minimum, it considers it as the only measure and source of wealth.
14) It calls to life the powers of science and nature so that the creation of wealth is independent of LT but wants to measure with it the gigantic social forces created.
15) Nevertheless, it wants to confine these powers so that the value created remains value.
16) The productive forces and social relations that, for capital, with its limited foundation, are mere means to produce value, are the material conditions to blow this foundation sky-high.
17) Machines are organs of the human brain created by the human hand: objectified power of knowledge; the development of fixed capital reveals the degree to which the *general intellect, which is now the central productive force, controls the conditions of the social process.*

This passage from the *Grundrisse* can be read as Marx's assertion that the development of science and its application to production, lay the foundations so that the exploitation of human labour is no longer required; that the material bases of a post-capitalist society are given; that *capitalism is coming very close to its objective limit, and that human prehistory is coming to an end.* The objective limit of capitalism takes the form of *the necessary delinking between work and income and thus, of the end of wage-based society.*

4.2 The Scientific-Technological Revolution (STR): Towards Total Automation

Capitalism, in its relentless pursuit for profits, constantly revolutionises production techniques. It has generated three industrial revolutions: the 1st Industrial Revolution of the 18th century centred on coal and the steam engine and its multiple applications in factories and in rail and maritime transport; the second industrial revolution of the 20th century was based on the internal combustion engine, oil, electricity and the telephone. In both, machinery replaced a significant proportion of direct human labour. In many branches of industry, workers increasingly became supervisors of automatic machinery. But this machinery was based exclusively on mechanical principles, which have limits. Marx in 1857-58 only knew the first revolution and, nevertheless, given his genius, appreciated its deep meaning.

The Scientific and Technical Revolution (STR), initiated towards the end of the Second World War, introduced cybernetics, information technology, computers, artificial intelligence and robotics. It unleashed a spiral of technological development that may be called the Third Industrial Revolution, which covers all productive activities, including services. With the STR the mechanical machinery is replaced by what Richta et al. (op. cit., 1968) called *autonomous production complexes*. The stability of capitalism is very easily shaken by the decrease in wages/employment, because falling effective demand leads the economy into crisis, since production cannot be sold. The displacement of agricultural and industrial employment by mechanical machinery was replaced by the growth of employment in the tertiary sector (commerce and services). But now this sector is also being automated.

The evidence, not very obvious for those who do not want to see, shows that there are not enough new labour-intensive, commodified and lucrative activities to create enough new wage jobs to compensate for those lost due to

automation, and that this gap is becoming larger every year. Although this transformation can take decades to produce all its consequences, it has been silently contributing to economic crises, stagnation, unemployment, underemployment and to the generalisation of precarious employment (the precariat as Guy Standing aptly calls it), to poverty and hunger. But the full consequences may come before the time when a high percentage of the population of working age has been displaced by automation. As Martin Ford (2009) has stated:

> As automation begins to eliminate jobs in an increasingly wide range of industries and occupations, its impacts are clearly not going to be kept a secret [...] As a growing percentage of the population is exposed to evidence of ongoing losses, many people will begin to experience a greatly heightened level of stress and worry ... they will cut back on consumption, perhaps quite dramatically, and will try to save more in anticipation of a very uncertain future [...] if this would occur in a critical mass of the consumers [...] we could be clearly pushed in a very dark scenario [...]a dramatic downward economic spiral would almost certainly be precipitated. (pp. 109-10)

As a result of the unstoppable advance of automation, capitalism will fall into ever more severe crises until it becomes completely non-viable. This is what Marx predicted in the passage of the *Grundrisse.* A little more than a century later, a group of scientists led by Robert Oppenheimer, argued that cyber-technologies were forcing a change in the relationship between income and work and urged the US President and Congress "to consider guaranteeing all citizens, as a matter of law, an adequate income." Their text, published on the first page of the *New York Times* (March, 1963), says:

> The continuance of the income-through-jobs link as the only major mechanism for distributing effective demand—for granting the right to consume—*now acts as the main brake on the almost unlimited capacity of a cybernated productive system.*

Compare the final phrase (in italics) with Marx's Prologue to the *Contribution to the Critique of Political Economy* (1859) (especially the phrase in italics):

> At a certain stage of development, the material productive forces of society come in conflict with the existing relations of production [...] *From forms of development of the productive forces these relations turn into their fetters.*

Jeremy Rifkin predicted in 1995, a new era in which services will be increasingly automated. Not only routine personal services but also more complex services are being taken over by intelligent machines. The retail trade is also being automated. In a later book (2014) Rifkin says:

> Big-data, advanced analytics, algorithms, Artificial Intelligence (AI) and robotics are replacing human labor across the manufacturing industries, service industries and knowledge and entertainment sectors, leading to the very real prospect of liberating hundreds of millions of people from work in the market economy in the first half of the 21st century (p. 121)... Today near workerless factories run by computer programs, are increasingly the norm, both in highly industrialized countries and developing nations (p.123) ... [Many] blame the loss of blue collar jobs on the relocation of manufacturing to cheap labor markets such as China. The fact is that something more consequential has taken place. Between 1995 and 2002, 22 million manufacturing jobs were eliminated in the global economy while global production increased by more than 30 percent... Even China shed 16 million factory workers while increasing its productivity... Manufacturers that have long relied on cheap labor in their Chinese production facilities are bringing production back home with advanced robotics that are cheaper and more efficient.... (p. 124)

Martin Ford shows his concern at the economists' rejection of the idea that technology displaces human work, dismiss those who worry about technological unemployment as neo-Luddites and have coined the term *neo-Luddite fallacy*. Ford correctly perceives that off-shoring is a prelude to automation: "many jobs that are currently being relocated will be, in the future, fully automated [...] Off-shoring is the small wave that distracts you, automation is the big one further out that you don't see coming."

In a more radical vein, André Gorz, says:

> We must dare to prepare ourselves for the Exodus from 'work-based society': it no longer exists and will not return. We must be bold enough to choose the Exodus. There is nothing to be gained from the symptomatic treatments of the 'crisis', because there is no crisis: a new system has been installed that tends to massively abolish work. (1999, p. 1)

As can be seen there is a diagnostic coincidence, in the main points, among the authors cited, but Gorz argues that "it is not this abolition of work which we should object to, but its claiming to perpetuate that same work, the norms, dignity and availability of which it is abolishing, as an obligation, as a norm, and as the irreplaceable foundation of the rights and dignity of all" (Ibid.). Gorz discusses the nature of the work that is being eliminated:

> What Rifkin calls the 'end of work' is the end of what everyone has become accustomed to call 'work'. It is not work in the anthropological or philosophical sense of the term. It is not the labour of the parturient woman, nor the work of the sculptor or the poet... It is, unambiguously, the specific 'work' peculiar to industrial capitalism, the work we refer to when we say 'she does not work' of a woman who devotes her time to raising her own children, but 'she works' for one who occupies even a small part of her time to bringing up other people's children..." (op. cit., p. 2)

From the preceding analysis, I conclude that the development of productive forces compatible with capitalism is coming to an end. This leads to the OLC. Industrial expansion to capture the very cheap and docile labour of the global south appears as temporary steps before the complete automation of production is attained.

Rifkin predicted in 2003 that the 21st century would face the end of mass work. "This is the anthropological point where we are, *we have a technological revolution that can create a renaissance or a great social upheaval,* we can make a leap forward for the generation of their children or we can have years, decades and generations of instability and restlessness." The renaissance option (*the beginning of human history*) can be related to the following ideas by Richta et al. (op. cit., pp. 35-36 of the Spanish edition: Artiach, Madrid, 1968; my translation to English), with which this lecture ends:

> The working instruments created by the STR go beyond the limits of mechanical machines and assume functions that convert them, in principle, into *autonomous production complexes* [...] **the subjective aspect of production, invariable for centuries, is modified: the functions of direct production carried out by the simple labour force progressively disappear**; technology increasingly supplants man in the direct functions of execution, maintenance, manipulation and, finally, regulation ...*It radically modifies the place occupied by man. It ensures the triumph of the automatic principle in the broadest sense of the term.*
>
> Complex automation is liberating man from his direct participation in the production process, from his role of simple 'gear' in the machine system and offers him, in return, the role of promoter, creator and director of the technical production system.
>
> We can expect that the process of the STR will absorb traditional simple industrial work, *which does not constitute an internal need for man, but is imposed by an external need. On the other hand, once man ceases to produce the things that the same things can produce, the possibility opens up before him to devote himself to a creative activity that mobilises all his forces, that tends to the research of new ways, to the expansion of his capacities. [I would add: to human flourishing].*
>
> The general diffusion of this type of human activity will mark in fact the overcoming of labour [*let's add, the beginning of human history*]. Indeed, once the material forms of human activity give it the character of an active manifestation of itself, *the external necessity, determined by the need for subsistence, yields its place to the internal need of man; in that moment, human activity becomes a human need, which exists for itself and enriches man; then the abstract contradictions between work and pleasure, between work and free time, disappear: human activity is merged with life".*

Human prehistory, according to Marx, comes to an end. History of mankind begins.

NOTES

1. György Márkus, *Marxism and Anthropology. The Concept of the 'Human Essence' in the Philosophy of Marx,* Van Gorcum Publishers, Assen, The Netherlands, 1978. There is a second edition in English with an introduction by Axel Honneth and Hans Joas: Modem-Verlag, Australia, 1988, which takes the text of the book from the 1978 edition. Although I mainly worked with the excellent Spanish translation by Manuel Sacristán, *Marxismo y 'antropología'*, Grijalbo, Barcelona, 1973 and México, 1985, I have based the wording and quotations in this lecture mainly on the 1978 English edition
2. Unfortunately, the English translation of M&A translates *Bedürfnisse* as *wants* instead of *needs* which is the correct translation and also the usual one. A note from the translators (including Márkus himself) arguing why they opted for this translation, turns upside down the usual use of the terms wants and needs in English and makes many paragraphs of the English translation unusable. I have followed the Spanish translation in these (and some other) cases. This big mistake might explain why M&A is so little known by English-speaking scholars.
3. Here I have adopted the usual (and correct) translation of *Bedürfnisse* as *needs*, and not as *wants* as the translators of the English edition have done.
4. Márkus quotes a difficult to get English edition of the EPhM. In the Penguin edition (in Karl Marx, *Early Writings*) this sentence is on page 327. Márkus has changed the usual (and incorrect) translation of Gattung to English as species-being, by the more precise "genus".
5. Chris Stringer and Peter Andrews, *The Complete World of Human Evolution*, Thames and Hudson, London, 2005, 240 pp.
6. Richard Leakey, *The History of Humankind. Unearthing our Family Tree*, Phoenix, London, 2001.
7. The first part of the paragraph is from page 72 of the Penguin Books edition (2004) and the second part (starting from 'But the hands..') is from page 71, showing that Leakey is not very careful in handling his sources.
8. "Arqueología cognitiva: atisbos de la mente homínida" (Cognitive archaeology: signs of the hominid mind), *Ludus Vitalis*, Vol. X, No. 18, México, 2002, pp. 89-109; and "Género *Homo*: ¿modificar o conservar el ambiente?" (*Homo* genus: modify or conserve the environment?), in Jorge Martínez Contreras (editor), *Senderos de*

la conservación y de la restauración ecológica. Evaluación crítica y ética, Centro de Estudios Filosóficos, Políticos y Sociales Vicente Lombardo Toledano, México, 2005. In what follows these works will be quoted as "Cognitive Archaeology" and "*Homo* gender".

9. "El origen de la mente" (The origin of the mind), *Investigación y ciencia,* No. 302, November 2001, Barcelona.

REFERENCES

Darwin, Charles, *The Descent of Man*, Penguin Classic, 2004.

Ferrreras Arsuaga and Martínez Mendizábal, "El origen de la mente" (The origin of the mind), *Investigación y ciencia,* No. 302, November 2001, Barcelona.

Ford, Martin, *The Lights in the Tunnel. Automation, Accelerating Technology and the Economy of the Future,* Acculant Publishing, San Bernardino, CA, 2009.

Gorz, André, *Reclaiming Work. Beyond the Wage-Based Society,* Polity Press, 1999.

Heller, Agnes, *Toward a Marxist Theory of Value* (Southern Illinois University, 1972).

Leakey, Richard, *The History of Humankind. Unearthing our Family Tree,* Phoenix, London, 2001.

Márkus György, *Marxism and Anthropology. The Concept of the 'Human Essence' in the Philosophy of Marx,* Van Gorcum Publishers, Assen, The Netherlands, 1978. There is a second edition in English with an introduction by Axel Honneth & Hans Joas: Modem-Verlag, Australia, 1988, which reproduces the text of the 1978 edition. [Although I mainly worked with the excellent Spanish translation by Manuel Sacristán, *Marxismo y 'antropología',* Grijalbo, Barcelona, 1973 and México, 1985, I have based the wording and quotations in this lecture mainly on the 1978 English edition, but I have frequently combined both translations. In some cases this has been necessary to avoid the mistakes incurred in the English translation; in other cases the Spanish translation seemed better].

Marx, Karl, *Economic and Philosophical Manuscripts* (*1844*), in Marx, Karl, *Early Writings,* Penguin Classics, 1992, pp. 279-400.

—— "Excerpts from James Mill's Elements of Political Economy" in *Karl Marx, Early Writings* Penguin Classics, 1992, pp. 259-278.

—— Prologue to *Contribution to the Critique of Political Economy,* 1859, referred as Preface to *A Critique of Political Economy* in David Mc Lellan, *Karl Marx, Selected Writings,* Oxford University Press, pp. 424-428.

—— *Grundrisse. Introduction to the Critique of Political Economy*, Penguin Books, 1973.

—— *Critique of the Gotha Programme*, 1875, in *Karl Marx, Political Writings*, Vol. 3, Verso 2010, pp. 339-359.

—— *Capital. Vol. I*, Penguin Classics, 1990.

Ponce de León, Aura, "Arqueología cognitiva: atisbos de la mente homínida" (Cognitive archaeology: signs of the hominid mind), *Ludus Vitalis*, Vol. X, No. 18, México, 2002, pp. 89-109.

—— "Género *Homo*: modificar o conservar el ambiente?" (*Homo* genus: modify or conserve the environment?), in Jorge Martínez Contreras (editor), *Senderos de la conservación y de la restauración ecológica. Evaluación crítica y ética*, Centro de Estudios Filosóficos, Políticos y Sociales Vicente Lombardo Toledano, México, 2005.

Richta, Radovan et al. (*Civilisation at the Crossroads*, original Czech edition, 1968; in English, 1969, International Arts and Sciences Press, reissued 2018 by Routledge; Spanish Edition, *La civilización en la encrucijada*, Artiach, Madrid, 1968.

Rifkin Jeremy, *The End of Work*, G.P. Putnam's Sons, NY, 1995.

—— *The Zero Marginal Cost Society*, Palgrave Macmillan, New York, 2014.

—— "Tiempo libre para disfrutarlo o hacer filas de desempleados", in Luis J. Alvarez, *Un mundo sin trabajo*, Editorial Dríada, México, 2003.

Stringer, Chris and Peter Andrews, *The Complete World of Human Evolution*, Thames and Hudson, London, 2005, p. 240.

Tobias, Phillip V., "Men, Minds and Hands: Cultural Awakening Over Two Million Years of Humanity", *South African Archaeological Bulletin*, Vol. 34, 1979, pp. 85-92.

3

The Origins of Marxist Oriental Studies in the USSR and its Stalinist Distortion

Craig Brandist

While Marxists may find much to object to in the work of the French sociologist and historian Michel Foucault, there is no denying his historical work shone an important and revealing light on hitherto neglected aspects of repression and domination. Cultural historians also made some important contributions by employing his ideas, especially in combination with those of Edward Said, to reveal previously unacknowledged dimensions of colonial rule. Since such approaches dominated postcolonial studies in the 1980s, however, they have tended to become rather mechanical applications of an unquestioned repertoire of conceptions. Theoretical or phenomenal novelties are few and far between as this or that cultural phenomenon is treated as a problem to be 'solved' by applying a preconceived set of ideas. The limitations of this procedure have become even clearer to those not content to remain within the bounds of this preconceived framework. The enclosure of postcolonialism within the paradigm of '*power/knowledge*', involving denial of any historical truth irreducible to the present-day interests of the historian and those he or she serves, has seriously compromised its claims to veracity. Moreover, the inflated and under-theorised sphere of 'discourse' that Foucault employed throughout his work, and which was passed on to his followers with little critical reflection, has proven deeply problematic. As Christopher Norris (2015, 204) argues, the conflation of the linguistic employment of the term to mean any body of language larger than the sentence with the 'hugely extended range of meaning that it [discourse – CB] can signify things like "body of knowledge," "*Weltanschauung*," "ideology," "professional code," "cultural way of life," "habit of thought," "scientific belief system," "dominant structure of assumptions,"' and the like, often obscures more than it reveals. French structuralism with its focus on binary oppositions and Althusser's conflation of such structures with inescapable forms of ideology here meets Nietzsche's 'will to power', which is allegedly everywhere and inescapable.

Invocations of a closed, orientalist discourse that dates back to the Enlightenment and beyond, structured around a series of binary oppositions: the rational, democratic and progressive West versus a mystical or religious, despotic and stagnant East, have now become as repetitious and unproductive as the clichés of official Soviet condemnations of Western imperialism. This can be explained by both the sociology of academic practices and, as we shall see, by the fact that there is a genetic relationship between the two. In much postcolonial theory the Manichaean visions of the Cold War struggle over the decolonising world, each side of which articulated closed systems of values and conceptions, has now morphed into a dichotomy of East and West. Characterisations of the former often secrete, if not openly present, a romantic image of an organically whole, pre-colonial culture that became fractured by the incursion of a colonial rationality. All individual utterances among those operating within the Western episteme ultimately succumb to institutionalised discursive forms.

Many important factors have been obscured by this monologic caricature. One is the highly contested dialogues between the radical, atheistic currents within the Enlightenment, beginning with Spinoza's philosophy, and those moderate *philosophes* determined to reconcile the advance of science with religious prejudices and the established social order on which Jonathan Israel (2006) has written in detail. In reality, the rise of colonialism acted on this field in complex ways (2006, 590–614). Another is the fact that the narratives developed by Indo-European philology, that formed the basis of what Edward Said called 'orientalism', and that 'endowed orientalism with its most important technical characteristics' (1995 [1978], 131), was nothing like a unified discourse of European Enlightenment. Rather, it emerged from a meeting of distinct sections of two complex and already class-divided societies. Indo-European philology emerged from unequal collaboration between European philologists and Brahman pandits who were bidding for cultural authority (Karttunen 2015, 59-63; Mani 2015, 191-201). The poststructuralist theory of language relegated considerations of these complex historical processes that were refracted through discursive interaction to, at best, matters of secondary importance.

Said's eclectic 1978 book *Orientalism* certainly contributed to the elision of these crucial dimensions, and he encouraged a number of misconceptions about Marxism and the Orient. However, later, more 'hardline' Foucauldians, with little of Foucault's own sophistication, forgot, or more likely simply ignored, Said's own reservations and caveats about Foucault. They also overlooked Said's debt to Marxist thinkers. We will return to the latter issue in due course, but, significantly, Said regarded Foucault's attitude to power as 'flawed', with the central problem deriving 'from his insufficiently developed attention to the problem of historical change' (Said 1983, 222). Contra Foucault, Said insisted that 'individual writers' do leave a 'determining imprint' on an 'otherwise anonymous body of texts constituting a discursive formation like Orientalism'. For Said (1995 [1978], 23) it was the 'dynamic exchange between individual authors and the large political concerns shaped by the... great empires' that need to be foregrounded rather than a closed circle of discourse. Finally, Foucault's identification of a discourse with a rationality of domination was a matter of considerable concern for Said. As he expressed it in 1983, there is 'a sensible difference between... *Logos* and words: we must not let Foucault get away with confusing them with each other, nor with letting us forget that history does not get made without work, intention, resistance, effort, or conflict, and that none of these things is silently absorbable into micronetworks of power' (1983, 245).[1]

Hegel and India

As postcolonial theory developed, a typical target of attack was Hegel's disparaging, and undoubtedly prejudiced, comments about Indian thought. The idea of a unitary discourse of 'Orientalism' is superficially convincing here, but the matter is not so simple. As Rathore and Mohapatra have shown, some of Hegel's most notorious interventions were primarily directed against his own German contemporaries, the Romantics who he held over-enthusiastically to have exaggerated the wisdom found in the *Gita* (2017, 24). When posturing against his rivals Hegel 'rode roughshod over the subtle distinctions which, during cooler and more contemplative moments, he himself took great pains to tease out, articulate and explore' (2017, 80). Indeed, Hegel regarded Indian thought significant enough for him constantly to engage with it throughout his career and to write some 80,000 words on the topic. While redolent with caricatures characteristic of the age of imperialism, 'insofar as he touches on central farcical and corrosive tenets of Brahminism', Hegel's critique shares much with 'a long history of other pre-eminent Indian critics of the origins, perpetuation, and persistence of caste in India, from Buddha, Kabir, Ravidas, Tukaram, Guru Narnak—all either scarcely known or unknown to Hegel—to his contemporary Jyotirao Phule, to recent pioneers such as Periyar, Iyothee Thass, and B.R. Ambedkar' (2017, 32).

Whatever Hegel's orientalist failings they pale before those of Nietzsche and Heidegger, the European philosophers central for poststructuralist critics of Eurocentrism. Both were proponents of the 'Greek romance of philosophy' that promoted an image of classical Greece 'as the pure origin of modern Europe, writing out of this genealogy the influence of Pharaonic and Hellenistic Egypt on Greek culture, and of the Islamic world on mediaeval Christendom' (Callinicos 1995, 180-181). Nietzsche did, of course, have some respect for Indian thought when it came to pursuing a new order of rank between classes: the *Laws of Manu* became the model for his 'new aristocracy' or 'new ruling caste' in Europe, but this is often passed over in silence (Figueria 2015 [2002], 55-56).

The Postcolonial Critique of Marxism

Failure adequately to understand Hegel's writing about India is significant because it prepared the ground for postcolonalist attempts to discredit Marxism as 'an extreme form of European Enlightenment thinking' (Kemper 2006, 6). Foucauldian postcolonial theorists needed to consign Marxism to the dustbin of Eurocentrism in order to forge a historical myth of postcolonialism's own radical origin. For all its emphasis on emancipation, argued Robert Young in his widely received book of 1990, *White Mythologies: Writing History and the West*, Marxism is 'implicated in the link between the structures of knowledge and the forms of oppression… that has become known as Eurocentrism' because its 'unifying… arrogant and arrogating narrative' always involves the 'creation, subjection and final appropriation of Europe's "others"' (2004 [1990], 33; Callinicos 1995, 180). While Young managed to land some justified blows on Althusser, his approach was marked by significant overgeneralisations. While one can certainly find instances of Eurocentrism in the work of some Marxists, postcolonial critics have often failed to acknowledge the many Marxist works that not only developed a critique of the imbrication of much Western scholarship about the orient with imperialism, but also criticised specific Marxist works that were marred by the same assumptions. One example of the latter was Bryan S. Turner's book *Marx and the End of Orientalism* (1978), published the very same year as Said's *Orientalism*, with which Young engaged, fleetingly, only in the introduction to the second edition of his book. Turner, Young argued, was urging the '"de-colonisation" of the European

Marxist tradition' (2004 [1990], 2), whereas, in actual fact, Turner (1978, 7–8) noted only that Marx's early work was still insufficiently separated from Hegelian prejudices about the orient, and that these reappeared in certain works by contemporary Marxists. On this issue, as many others, noted Turner, 'there is no such thing as a homogeneous tradition of Marxist analysis' (1978, 8). To his credit, Young has more recently adopted a rather more nuanced perspective on the role of Marxism in the development of the postcolonial critique, but his earlier comment stands as symptomatic of the time when poststructuralist assumptions about unified, if unstable, discourses were dominant.

When looking at perspectives on the development of Oriental Studies in the USSR the same monologic approach is still very much in evidence (though far from universal). In a recent work on the problems of the historiography of the Orient, veteran Russian Orientologist Leonid Alaev (2018, 45-46) argues that Marx was a fundamentally Eurocentric thinker who regarded the pattern of economic development he discerned in western Europe as universal and 'laid aside the problem of the specific evolution of various societies'. Rather than correcting this bias, Alaev continues, later Marxists were concerned 'exclusively with the establishment of a single line of development to be ascribed to all peoples'. Historian of Soviet Islam, Michael Kemper makes effectively the same claim when he argues that 'the classical Marxist conception' of the development of all societies is the 'concept of five universal socio-economic stages' (primitive society, slave-holding society, feudalism, capitalism and socialism), what in Stalin's time came to be referred to as the '*piatichlenka*' (2009, 35). Marxism allegedly sought to locate all societies on a pre-established scheme of stadial development, and this was the basis of a unitary 'discourse of Soviet orientalism' that from the outset of the Russian Revolution functioned 'to turn the Orient into an instrument of Soviet Russia' (Kemper 2010, 449). Marxists writing about the 'East' in the USSR, he argues, developed a 'discourse' that 'was itself pure "Orientalism" (in the sense of Edward Said)', they 'unquestionably put their knowledge at the disposal of the state, which used it for ruling and thoroughly transforming... contemporary Muslim societies' (Kemper 2009, 46).

The elements of truth in these statements are combined with a series of conflations and overgeneralisations. In the 1930s there really was a concerted effort to homogenise Soviet perspectives on the East and to use the knowledge generated as a resource for the imperial domination of the Soviet 'East' and the subordination of the independence movements across the colonial world to the foreign policy of Moscow. Part of this was indeed the development of a unilinear model of social development, which was presented in Marxist terminology. However, as we will see, simply to extrapolate this model, let alone a putative Orientalist 'discourse', back into the debates of the 1920s, and then to extrapolate from this to the writings of Marx himself, is highly problematic.[2]

In terms of practical application, there is a fundamental difference between the Bolsheviks' attempt to win leadership in a revolutionary struggle against a common adversary and treating an ally simply as an instrument. As I have argued elsewhere at length (Brandist 2015) the many debates about the strategy of hegemony before and after the Revolution focused specifically on this distinction, and it is no coincidence that these came to an abrupt end when Stalin declared that socialism had been achieved in the USSR. It is significant that even historians who are hostile to the entire Bolshevik project are generally compelled to acknowledge that policies towards the 'peoples of the East' in the 1920s was quite different to what prevailed from the end of that decade. To square this particular circle even sophisticated historians tend to revert to a form of conspiracy theory. A concrete recent example is the well-researched and documented book on *Buddhism in the USSR from 1917 to 1946*, by the Russian historian Fedor Sinitsyn (2013). The author duly notes the tolerant approach taken by the Soviet government towards Buddhists in the first half of the 1920s, but then declares such tolerance was a 'deception' [*obman*], for Buddhism, along with other religions was 'not only an ideological opponent but an existential enemy' (2013, 58). The *a-priori* requirement to uphold a narrative of continuity between the Bolsheviks plans in the early 1920s and the assault on Buddhist monasteries at the end of the decade, in the face of considerable evidence of discontinuity, leads to a trope of masks and plots. Yet while the study is valuable for its rich store of factual information, evidence that subterfuge was actually taking place in the early 1920s is absent. Rather, pronouncements of the Party leadership made both in public and behind closed doors at this time are quite different to those at the end of the decade. The years 1925-28 represent a transitional period when bureaucratic forces ceased to observe the earlier policy towards the religious institutions of the oppressed peoples of the Russian Empire, including Buddhists, which had foregrounded constructive engagement. The possibility that the ruling party could have changed in fundamental ways between 1917 and 1930 does not receive any serious consideration. Yet what if, as Said suggested, continuity of terminology and of rhetoric (words) obscures a sharp discontinuity of rationality (*logos*)?

Marxism, Positivism and the 'Peoples of the East'

The important changes in Marx's own ideas during his long career, and his increasingly critical approach to the conceptualisations and generalisations of the positivist historians on which he relied for much of his information, have been the focus of a number of scholars recently (see, for instance, Habib 2006; Anderson 2010; Achcar 2013). In these accounts, Marx's mature engagements with non-Western societies appear more as exploratory attempts to discern the so-called 'laws of motion' of specific historical formations than attempts to locate societies on a pre-established timeline.

Recent scholarship on Marx convincingly shows that he never aspired to the construction of a unified discourse of 'Marxism' and indeed repeatedly rejected attempts by those who sought to create one. Indeed, many of Marx's most influential texts were left incomplete and unpublished at his death, being finalised by editors. The Marx-Engels Institute in Moscow played a particularly important role in this creation of apparently canonical texts. Indeed, Marx's incomplete and fragmentary texts only began to be published without editorial interventions in the still far from complete second *Marx Engels Gesamtausgabe* (*MEGA*) that began to appear in 1975. As Michael Heinrich (2015), who is writing the first intellectual biography of Marx since these texts appeared notes, even Marx's most influential published texts were only parts of 'fundamental theoretical projects' that remained unfinished, such as the first book of the *Contribution to the Critique of Political Economy* (1859) or the first volume of *Capital* (1867/1872). Such projects remained unfinished because Marx was a thinker who was constantly learning and developing his theoretical conceptions, and he increasingly studied non-Western societies, which complicated and ultimately compromised his plans.

Trotsky's historical writings on the particularities of Russian historical development, in which he outlined the principle of combined and uneven development, marked a further step in this direction (see Banaji 2010; Anievas and Nisancioglu 2015). Naturally such developments were not given due consideration by those writing within the officially sponsored and regulated sphere of 'Soviet Marxism'.

So where did the idea of a unified Marxist discourse on the orient come from? It has some roots in the somewhat mechanical evolutionism of some Second International Marxism, such as Plekhanov's insistence, in his arguments with the Russian populists, that Russia would have to pass through the stage of capitalist production before socialism could even be put on the agenda. This approach owed more to the evolutionary narratives of contemporary positivism, which dominated Russian thought in late imperial Russia and beyond, than to the mutually constituting dialectic pioneered by Marx (see especially Steila 1991). The work of leading positivist thinkers like Auguste Comte, John Stuart Mill, E.B.

Tylor and Herbert Spencer appeared in Russian translation often within a year of their original publication, and were widely received. A unilinear pattern was further affirmed by the proponents of so-called 'legal Marxism', for whom the arrival of capitalism and of bourgeois democracy were viewed as synonymous. Interestingly a variant of this idea has reappeared in certain strands of subaltern studies to show that India has never fully achieved the status of a capitalist state. Not only did all this contradict Marx's late engagements with Russian revolutionaries, which remained unpublished till the late 1920s, but it was decisively rejected by Lenin, Trotsky and others who led the October Revolution of 1917. It was decisively revived and canonised in the Stalinist period when the positivist search for universal laws of social development, with mentally-conceived stages (in Comte's case theological, metaphysical and positive stages) was confused with the so-called 'laws' of the dialectic presented in Engels's (unfinished) *Dialectics of Nature*, compiled, edited and published by the Marx-Engels Institute in 1927.

If Plekhanov laid the groundwork for the Stalinist model of social development, it was imperial Russia's late specialists on the 'East' that laid the foundations of Stalinist oriental studies. A particularly clear case is the great historian of Central Asia Vasilii Bartol'd (1869-1930), who welcomed the positivist search for universal laws of social development but argued that 'sociology' remained grounded one-sidedly on facts gathered by historians relating to European societies. A truly universal sociology had, he maintained, to look beyond Europe, which constitutes only a small minority of the societies, which enter into 'world-historical intercourse' (Bartol'd 1977 [1911], 207). In the absence of a wider base of evidence, a speculative philosophy of history had arisen, propagating an unscientific notion of 'progress' and a series of stereotypes (Bartol'd 1977 [1911], 220–22). While 'progress' became an established characteristic of the West, 'stagnation' became a perceived characteristic of the 'East' among educated Europeans (Bartol'd 1966 [1903], 303). While most European writers about Eastern societies viewed their development as a 'self-contained process' defined by racial origin, Bartol'd praised recent German historians, such as the Assyriologist Hugo Winckler, for showing that 'the history of the ancient East, just as much as that of Europe, was determined by the influence of one nation on another and the distribution of the culture of one or several advanced nations over an ever wider geographical region' (Bartol'd 1977 [1911], 233–34). On the basis of such research, Bartol'd pursued what he considered a more scientific 'law of "evolution", i.e. the gradual and consequential change in all the conditions of life of human societies' (Bartol'd 1977 [1911], 222). The direction of evolution was clear: 'the gradual convergence of an ever greater number of separate societies' (Bartol'd 1977 [1911], 208).

While sharply critical of British and French oriental studies for their ideological biases, manifested in the binary oppositions that were later identified as 'orientalist', Bartol'd's work promoted Russia's own Eurasian and territorially coterminous imperial project. He argued scholars must highlight and celebrate the cultural achievements of the peoples of the East and in doing so contribute towards their 'peaceful convergence... with Russia': 'the peoples of the East will believe in the superiority of our culture all the more when they are convinced we know them better than they know themselves' (Bartol'd 1963 [1900], 610). As Vera Tolz (2011) has shown, late imperial 'Orientologists' like Bartol'd, Indologist Sergei Ol'denburg (1863-1934) and archaeologist and philologist of the Caucasus region Nikolai Marr (1865-1934) sought to strengthen the Empire by promoting a hybrid identity among the various peoples of Russia. Simultaneously the subject peoples should be encouraged to take pride in their local cultures and in the imperial civic space they shared. These figures would play an important role in the formation of Soviet oriental studies and in the practical work of building the USSR.[3] While the Imperial authorities had no time for their proposed multicultural nationality policy, this was precisely the project of '*korenizatsiia*' (indigenisation or nativisation) that emerged from the Twelfth Party Congress in 1923.

By the time of the sixteenth Party Congress in the summer of 1930, the positivist 'convergence of an ever greater number of separate societies', and the multicultural form of Empire that Bartol'd, Marr and other 'orientologists' had espoused, was Party policy. Stalin now argued that national cultures would, and indeed should, merge into a unity 'in both form and content' under socialism. The peoples of the USSR were now allegedly converging because of the USSR's movement towards 'socialism in one country'. However, until there was a final victory of socialism on a global scale this convergence would remain limited to a unity of ideological 'content' coexisting with a 'flowering' of various 'forms' of national culture (Stalin [1930] 1954, 380). While Bartol'd died within weeks of Stalin's speech, Marr and his followers deliberately invoked it to win official support for their own espousal of the convergence and merger of all languages.

Early Soviet Oriental Studies

In the 1920s though, the positivist approaches of the pre-Revolutionary period were but one strand of nascent Soviet oriental studies, which remained a complex field subject to competing intellectual and political forces till the end of the decade. Young Soviet Marxists were coming into the field, seeking to overthrow existing paradigms and guide political intervention in the colonial world, but hampered by a paucity of expertise in oriental languages and cultures. As in many areas they relied on the older generation of specialists for factual information, while attempting a critique of their principles of generalisation and conceptualisation. At the same time, a generation of radical intellectuals from the colonial world, seeking support from the Revolutionary regime, found themselves in dialogue with Bolshevik leaders in the Communist International and participating in its newly formed educational institutions such as the University of the Communist University of the Toilers of the East (KUTV).

Indian, Chinese and Arab Communists played particularly important roles (see, *inter alia*, Persits 1973; Datta Gupta 2006; Kosach 2001; 2009). From this interaction a vigorous debate about how to bring Marxism to bear on non-Western societies ensued, with a wide range of approaches coming into view. With the formation of the All-Russian Scientific Association of Oriental Studies (*Vserossiiskaia nauchnaia assotsiatsiia vostokovedeniia*, VNAV) formed within the Commissariat of Nationalities (*Narkomnats*) in December 1921. The definition of the 'East' now shifted to mean all areas of the world adversely affected by imperialism. As the director of the Eastern section of the Comintern, Georgii Safarov (1891–1942) noted in his 1922 book *Problemy Vostoka* (Problems of the East), Marxists needed to respond to the 'question of the East' as posed by the realities of imperialism and the state of the class struggle. In present conditions this meant the 'ways and means through which the backward countries of the East would be incorporated into the global capitalist economic system', and it 'elevated this question to the status of a matter of principle'. The task was to help the labouring masses of the East shorten their path from pre-capitalist means of production to communism and so avoid the suffering inflicted by capitalist development (Safarov 1922, 25–26). The goal was to achieve something approximating a *smychka* (alliance or union) between the proletariat of industrialised countries and the labouring masses of the colonial world against the common enemy: international capitalism.

VNAV published a significant journal, *Novyi Vostok*, throughout the 1920s and gave rise to some significant and varied scholarship, such as Gurko-Kriazhin's work on Turkey, Sultan-Zade's work on Persia or Safarov's work on Turkestan and (later) on China. A range of works developed new perspectives on the origin and development of Islam, aimed at informing policy both within the USSR and relations with the colonial world. The problem was these works understandably prioritised the enlightenment of the popular masses about the East, in order to combat religious and other prejudices, above elaborating an alternative to the established and refined ideologies of the pre-Revolutionary intelligentsia. Indeed, persistent Russian chauvinist ideas among many Party members, about which Lenin voiced concern on more than one occasion, meant that the prioritisation of popular-scientific works about the 'peoples of the East' was a priority even within the Party itself (for a good overview of the problem see Harris 1990, 101-15). As Gramsci noted in his Prison reflections on the NEP-era USSR, Marxists thus formed intellectual alliances with 'extraneous tendencies' (Gramsci 1971, 392) such as philosophical materialism and positivism. Marxism thus 'combined into a form of culture which was slightly higher than the popular average (which was very low) but was absolutely inadequate to combat the ideologies of the educated classes' (Gramsci 1971, 392–393).

At the same time, however, students of established Orientalists from the pre-Revolutionary era assimilated aspects of Marxism that gave their work a new character. These works were generally less immediately subjected to immediate political pressures since they concerned matters of history and culture more than politics in the narrow sense. Nikolai Konrad's studies of Japanese history, language and literature (1927, 1935) was one clear example of a certain Marxist *perestroika* that took place among what Gramsci called 'traditional intellectuals'. More directly connected with political questions was the work of a new generation of linguists involved in the codification and standardisation of the languages of the peoples of the Soviet East. Linguists like Evgenii Polivanov and Nikolai Iakovlev made crucial contributions not only to the study of individual languages, but also in the development of sociological linguistics. The promotion of the languages and cultures of the peoples of the former colonies of the Russian Empire also facilitated the rise to prominence of a number of scholars from the former colonies of the Russian Empire, such as the Buryat scholar Tsyben Zhamtsarano (1880-1942) and the Armenian historian Iosif Orbeli (1887-1961).[4] This accompanied splits among

Muslim and Buddhist intellectuals, with the emergence of significant movements of 'renovationists' (*obnovlentsy*), and of 'national communists', seeking to make common cause between formerly oppressed religious communities and the Soviet government.

VNAV illustrated some of the potential paths open to incipient Marxist oriental studies, and the shift of traditional intellectuals working within state institutions towards Marxism showed the rising prestige of Marxist ideas among specialists. The shift towards subordination of Oriental Studies to political expediency was illustrated by the Scientific-Research Association for work on the Socio-Economic Problems of the Soviet and Foreign East formed at KUTV in 1927. As a Party institute linked directly to the Comintern, the Association and its journal *Revoliutsionnyi Vostok* (The Revolutionary East) provided *post-hoc* justifications for the zigzags of the Comintern policy from the defeat of the Shanghai uprising till the Great Purge of 1937. When Party institutes effectively annexed state institutes in 1929 and the administration required that research supported the drive for forced industrialisation and the collectivisation of agriculture, the environment within which oriental studies operated changed fundamentally. Just as, in the field of literature and literary studies, where belligerent advocates of proletarian culture were encouraged and supported in harassing and denouncing fellow travellers and representatives of the avant-garde, so in oriental studies the same phenomenon took place. Indeed, the same people were sometimes involved, such as Il'ia Vardin (pseudonym on the Georgian critic Illarion Vissarionovich Mgeladze, 1890-1941), who had attacked fellow-travellers on the grounds that 'he who cannot look through Communist Eyes is not able artistically to reflect the objective truth' (Tamazishvili 2008, 80) and now moved on to attacking non-Party specialists in Oriental studies on the same basis. By 1930 this had degenerated to accusing such figures, and VNAV in general, of concealed Menshevism and allying with 'social-fascism' (Tamazishvili 2008, 121).

In 1930 VNAV lost its autonomy and was incorporated into the Communist Academy, which pursued a narrow struggle 'on the oriental studies front' (Safarov 1931).

The crushing of opposition currents dramatically affected oriental studies. Centralisation of the Soviet state in order to compete militarily with hostile powers also required the subordination of anti-colonial struggles to the foreign policy interests of the USSR. Perspectives that failed to support these policies were denounced, while those that supported them were officially promoted. Soviet specialists in oriental studies consequently became some of the most persecuted groups of intellectuals in the USSR. Some of the most sophisticated, talented and innovative thinkers in the field were fired, imprisoned or even killed, while their places were often taken by opportunists and sycophants who sought to shape the field into a dogmatic sphere narrowly subservient to the requirements and doctrines of the state. Statutory authority trumped scientific authority in all questions, including which positions could legitimately be regarded as Marxist. Only areas relatively distant from immediate political concerns retained the possibility of more diverse and critical engagements. Here one might mention the work of Aleksei Petrovich Barannikov (1890-1952), whose discussion of the caste dynamics in the formation of Indian national languages and literatures are worthy of renewed attention (Barannikov 1937; 1941; 1948).

Indian Dialogues

Despite the tragic fate of incipient Marxist oriental studies in the 1930s, and the subordination of Communist Parties to the pronouncements of Moscow, the USSR remained surprisingly open to fellow-traveller intellectuals from Asia.[5] Particularly interesting in this regard are the visits to the USSR by Indian fellow-traveller intellectuals involved in the anti-caste movement in this period.

While the importance of caste divisions within the Labouring masses of contemporary India had been considered by the Comintern in the early 1920s (Roy, Datta Gupta and

Vasudevan 1999, Vol. 1, 116-25), the most influential Indian member of the Comintern, M.N. Roy, did not systematically discuss the question of caste till his expulsion from the Comintern at the end of that decade. While in prison in the 1930s, Roy began to reconsider Indian politics and history from a perspective that sought to cleanse Marxism of its Stalinist accretions (Roy 2016 [1932]). The Brahmanical social order and the precedent of Buddhism as an egalitarian, anti-caste and atheistic movement were now considered systematically in his writings. In the Party itself such complexities and specificities were largely neglected. Caste was considered to be a feudal survival that was destined to disappear with the development of capitalism and so did not need to be considered systematically in the development of policy. After a period in which renovationist currents in Soviet Buddhism were welcomed and engaged in a constructive fashion, from 1929 the government regarded all such currents extremely negatively. Indeed, renovationists were (like many reformist currents during the 'third period') often regarded as more dangerous than conservative Buddhists who were openly hostile to Soviet power (Sinitsyn 2013, 69). The subsequent repressions deprived intellectuals seeking to unite Buddhism and Marxism within the anti-caste movement of a credible, corresponding movement within the USSR itself and encouraged hostility from within the Indian Communist Party. While this did not, preclude productive engagements that led to theoretical advances, parties loyal to Moscow undermined attempts successfully to adapt political practice to Indian conditions.

One of the earliest visitors to the USSR in this category was the Goan Buddhist Dharmanand Kosambi who, with the support of Indian Comintern activist Virendranath Chattopadhyaya and future Prime Minister Jawaharlal Nehru, travelled to Leningrad to attend an international conference on Buddhist culture in 1929 (Roy, Datta Gupta and Vasudevan 1999, Vol. 1, 339-40), after which he stayed on teaching Pali at the short-lived Institute of Buddhist Culture for a number of months. He visited Leningrad for a second time in 1932. Apart from his interest in Marxism and the changes in the USSR, Kosambi was attracted to the work of Leningrad Buddhologists led by Fedor Shcherbatskoy (aka Theodor Stcherbatsky), who he had met in Bombay as early as 1910 (Vigasin 2008, 246). Shcherbatskoy was especially interesting for Indian radicals because of his treatment of Buddhism primarily as an atheistic, rationalist philosophy that had evolved in opposition to Brahmanism and had achieved a level of sophistication rivalling that of European philosophy. Kosambi's overall experience in the USSR was, however, ambivalent, for his admiration of economic achievements, the development of education and gender equality coexisted with less comfortable observations of the repressions involved with collectivisation and of religious communities, including Buddhism. Reflections on the USSR and the need for the Buddhist commitment to non-violence to be combined with Marxism in India are important parts of Kosambi's written work (Kosambi 2010 [1935]). His subsequent influence on perhaps the most important anti-caste campaigner of the independence movement, B.R. Ambedkar, who was sympathetic to Marxism but having considerable problems dealing with the dogmatic perspectives of Indian Communists loyal to Stalinism (Teltumbde 2017), is a matter for further research. Dharmanand's influence on his son Damodar, the founder of Marxist history in India, must have been significant indeed. The critical distance Damodar maintained from Soviet unilinear narratives that runs throughout his Marxist histories of ancient India owes much to this.

Another illustrative case is the Bihari polymath Rahul Sankrtityayan who, like Kosambi, converted to Buddhism, which he understood as 'atheist humanism... social egalitarianism, and a system of reason... compatible with the modern world' (Ober 2013, 141). Also like Kosambi, Sankrityayan had spent some years as a wandering Buddhist monk, but had visited Tibet several times where he collected important Sanskrit manuscripts, xylographs and pictorial art (Gerke 1998). While in Tibet in 1929, Sankrityayan was told about the emergence of renovationists among Soviet Buddhists, who claimed Marxism and Buddhism were compatible (Ober 2016, 300).[6] After a number of attempts, he travelled to Leningrad to work with Shcherbatskoy in the winter of 1937-38, amid Stalin's Great Terror, which claimed most members of the Leningrad school of Buddhology apart from Stcherbatsky himself. Unlike Kosambi, however, Sankrityayan's closeness to Stalin's Russia was enhanced by his time in Russia, during which time he married one of Shcherbatskoy's students and they had a son (Vasil'kov 1998). He became increasingly critical of Buddhism in the absence of a historical-materialist perspective on history, and joined the Indian Communist Party on his return to India in October 1939. In 1945 he returned to Leningrad to teach in the Department of Indian Philology at Leningrad University at Leningrad University, returning to India after independence in 1947, only to be expelled from the Indian Party in January 1948. Sankrityayan's prodigious literary output is impressive both in the number and variety of his publications, but we see an early attempt to consider the development of Indian religions and their relations to the specific forms of social organisation in some of his Tibetological works and philosophical reflections such as his essay on Buddhist dialectics (Sankrityayan 1970). Such work made possible later Marxist excursions into the study of Indian philosophy and religions such as Debiprasad Chattopadhyaya's landmark study of *Lokāyata* (1959). It is no coincidence that Chattopadhyaya then proceeded to edit and publish the work of Shcherbatskoy in English translation.

Finally, Tamil leader of the Self-Respect movement, Periyar E.V. Ramaswami visited Moscow in December 1931 till March 1932, where he became an honorary member of the League of the Militant Godless. The practice of the Russian atheist movement was important for Periyar since he held that Hinduism had been the main obstacle to revolutionary change in India, but he retained considerable sympathy for Buddhism. On Periyar's return to India socialism became a central part of his outlook, leading to the development of the so-called Erode programme in which the founder of the Communist Party in Tamil Nadu Malayapuram Singaravelu Chettiar (1860-1946) played a leading role (Murugesan and Subramanyam 1975, 67-84). Singaravelu, it is worth noting, had been President of the largest Buddhist revivalist organisation in Madras, the Maha Bodhi Society, and had worked closely with the key anti-caste campaigner and Buddhist revivalist Iyothee Thass.[7] Thass's critique of Brahmanism, like that of Jotirao Phule before him, had much in common with the semantic palaeontology being developed by Marx and his followers in the USSR in the 1920s and 1930s (Brandist 2018), and Singaravelu's attempts to 'indiginise' Marxism in India in the 1930s owed much to these earlier movements, and to the convergence of the anti-caste movement and the revival of Buddhism in India (see Geetha and Rajadurai 1998; Vaitheespara and Venkatasubramanian 2015).

These cases amply illustrate the potential that existed for Indian Marxists to engage in a productive dialogue with indigenous forms of Indian socialism that emerged in the anti-caste movement and took forms that drew upon renovationist Buddhism. Stalinism ultimately obstructed any sustained and organised engagement, ultimately driving a wedge between the communist and anti-caste movements the effects of which persist today. This was symptomatic of the alienation from the USSR that would be felt by many intellectuals from the decolonising world as the Communist Parties were subordinated to Moscow's foreign policy agenda. This was only to increase in the context of the Cold War.

The Cold War and After

The bipolar world order that emerged with the beginning of the Cold War consolidated institutionally the polemical face of a unitary Soviet oriental studies. Soviet orientalism (*sovetskoe vostokovedenie*) was defined in contrast to its other, 'bourgeois orientalism' (*burzhuaznoe vostokovedenie*). An ideological struggle between 'bourgeois' and 'Soviet' orientalisms began to appear in Soviet publications as the necessary corollary of the struggle for the allegiance of decolonising nations.

In 1949 the journal *Voprosy istorii* (Questions of History) published a leading text '*Neotlozhnye zadachi sovetskikh istorikov-vostokovedov*' ('Urgent Tasks of Soviet Historian-Orientalists', Anon 1949) setting out the terms of the ideological struggle within oriental studies. Here we learn that 'bourgeois oriental studies serve imperialism in an extraordinarily vigorous manner and strive "to prove" the historical inevitability and even the "necessity" of the rule of the Western colonial powers over the multi-million masses, who are lagging behind in their progress and, therefore, "incapable" of independently deciding the fate of the East themselves' (Anon 1949, 5). Such scholars produce 'false, pseudo-historical "theories" and "conceptions"', which may 'differ in details and on particular points but they bear a testimony to a complete unity on the principal and fundamental question' (Anon 1949, 5). This involved the propagation of a particular type of exoticism about 'the special type of "Eastern soul"', relishing 'unimportant details of the religious cults or repeat entertaining palace-anecdotes about dynastic histories' (Anon 1949, 6). Soviet orientalist-historians were encouraged 'to facilitate with the help of their own studies the exposure of the false theories of the bourgeoisie' (Anon 1949, 6).

This sentiment, with the rhetoric somewhat softened, reappeared in the 1951 edition of the *Great Soviet Encyclopaedia* and the delineation of a Soviet orientalism distinct from that of the West gained importance particularly as a result of the April 1955 Bandung Conference which eventually led, in 1961, to the formation of the Non-Aligned Movement. Perspectives on the tasks of Soviet as opposed to bourgeois orientalism were further developed at the First All-Union Conference of Orientalists in Tashkent in June 1957, at which continuities between pre- and post-Revolutionary Russian Oriental studies were stressed (Gafurov 1957, 13–14), beginning with the publication of the *Complete Works* of Bartol'd (Bustanov 2014, 65–70). These perspectives were subsequently conveyed to many intellectuals from the various national liberation movements who were educated at such institutions as the Patrice Lumumba People's Friendship University in Moscow, founded in 1960, the same year that the USSR hosted the 25th International Congress of Orientalists. Here senior Politburo member Anastas Mikoian gave a speech declaring that henceforth 'the peoples of the Orient themselves create their own history, their culture, their economy; in this way the peoples of the orient have been promoted from being objects (matter) of history to the rank of creators'. This speech, and a number of other Soviet sources, were quoted in the Egyptian Marxist Anouar Abdel-Malek's 1963 article 'Orientalism in Crisis' (1963, 122), where the author also contrasted the persistence of 'Europeocentrism' in the West with the 'truly colossal effort in the field of modern orientalism' in the USSR since the Bandung Conference (1963, 127). Abdel-Malek's article was one of the most important sources for Said's ideas about orientalism (Tolz 2006; Said 1995 [1978]), and it would be no exaggeration to say that *Orientalism*, which was almost entirely a critique of the tropes of British and French Oriental Studies that had been inherited by mainstream US intellectuals, was to a considerable extent a recapitulation of 'bourgeois orientalism'.[8]

The idea of competing bourgeois and Soviet orientalisms was, however, no more than a crude and highly selective summary, an opportunistically deployed formula derived from long and intense debates about the relationship between knowledge about the colonial world and the policies of the various colonial powers in the revolutionary period. Sometimes this was tacitly acknowledged in post-Stalin Soviet scholarship, as in the 1963 survey article 'The Study of the History of India in the USSR 1917–1934' where then young orientologist, Leonid Alaev (1963: 167), notes 'Soviet scholars came to the correct evaluation of imperial policy in India as the result of a long struggle of opinions'. The 'evaluation' ultimately regarded as 'correct' was not settled on because a position proved internally persuasive by virtue of factual accuracy or rigour, but according to its correspondence to Stalin's policies and those of his successors.

The influence of the USSR over intellectuals in the decolonising world depended on the resources at its disposal, its effectiveness in countering US imperialism and the extent to which the Soviet model of state-led development actually worked. All these factors declined sharply from the end of the 1970s, punctuated by the disastrous policy adopted, under Soviet pressure, by the Tudeh Party in the Iranian Revolution of 1979, the ill-fated Soviet invasion of Afghanistan the same year and the unravelling of the statist model under pressure of the internationalisation of capital. Just as the USSR's political influence waned, however, structuralist and poststructuralist thinkers who were alienated by the practice of the French Communist Party were seeking to justify their withdrawal from collective politics in the wake of the events of Paris in 1968. They began treating Marxism as a unitary discourse of power/knowledge. They also worked to give Said's eclectic work on Orientalism a more unified theoretical edifice, and in doing so drew, in some cases unwittingly, upon the Stalinist model of 'bourgeois orientalism' as a model for orientalist discourse. Separated from its putative opponent, this discourse now included Marxism as a subset, or even an exemplary instance.

The problem is that any systematic consideration of the history of Marxist thought about non-Western societies was rendered irrelevant, and it has taken a number of decades for the question to return to the agenda. This is, however an issue worthy of considerable attention for reasons both scholarly and political.

NOTES

1. For a general discussion of Said's critical remarks about Foucault and the difference between Said's project and that of postcolonial studies see Brennan (2006, 91-125).
2. In the case of Alaev, one wonders the extent to which this amounts to a self-criticism of his many 'Marxist' works of the

late Soviet period. Caricature of Marxism in its entirety may serve to detract attention from the author's own adherence to the Stalinist schema of historical development.

3. For an example of how the agenda of these thinkers was adapted to the requirements of Soviet oriental studies in the 1930s see Ol'denburg (1931).
4. See Iuzbashian 1986; Tolz 2015.
5. For valuable overviews of Soviet cultural relations on an international scale see Clark (2011) and David-Fox (2011).
6. The page reference given in the dissertation appears to be in error.
7. Thass (referred to as Pandit Ayodhidas) and Singaravelu were also acquainted with Kosambi, on which see Kosambi (2010 [1912-24], 130-147).
8. This, I think, provides the most coherent answer to Alaev's (2018, 35-36) question as to why Said's book 'did not frighten' Russian orientalists.

REFERENCES

Abdel-Malek, Anouar, 1963. 'Orientalism in Crisis', *Diogenes,* 11: 103–40.

Achcar, Gilbert. 2013. 'Marx, Engels and Orientalism: On Marx's Epistemological Evolution'. In *Marx, Orientalism, Cosmopolitanism.* London: Saqi Books, pp. 68–102.

Alaev, L.B., 1963. 'Izuchenie istorii Indii v SSSR 1917–1934'. *Narody Azii i Afriki,* 2: 160–172.

Alaev, L.B., 2018. *Problematika istorii Vostoka.* Moscow: URSS.

Anderson, Kevin, 2010. *Marx at the Margins. On Nationalism, Ethnicity and Non-Western Societies,* Chicago and London: Chicago University Press.

Anon, 1949. 'Neotlozhnye zadachi sovetskikh istorikov-vostokovedov', *Voprosy istorii* 4: 3-8.

Anievas, A. and Nisancioglu, K. 2015. *How the West Came to Rule: The Geopolitical Origins of Capitalism.* London: Pluto Press.

Banaji, J. 2010. *Theory as History: Essays on Modes of Production and Exploitation.* Leiden: Brill.

Barannikov, Aleksei Petrovich, 1937. 'Prem Sagar i ego avtor'. In Lallu Dzhi Lal, *Prem Sagar.* Translated and Edited by A.P. Barannikov. Moscow and Leningrad: Akademiia Nauk SSSR. pp. 5–91.

——— 1941. O nekotorykh polozheniiakh v oblasti indologii'. *Sovetskoe vostokovedenie,* 11: 169–86.

——— 1948. 'Tulsi Das i ego Ramaiana'. In Tulsi Das, *Ranaiana ili*

Ramacharitamanasa. Translated and edited by A.P. Barannikov. Moscow and Leningrad: Akademiia nauk SSSR. pp. 9–106.

Bartol'd, Vasilii Vladimirovich 1963 [1900], 'Rech' pered zashchitoi dissertatsii', in *Sobranie sochinenii,* Vol. 1, Moscow: Vostochnaia literatura.

——— 1966 [1922] 'Mussul'manskii mir', in *Sobranie sochinenii,* Vol. 6, Moscow: Nauka.

——— 1977 [1911], 'Istoriia izucheniia vostoka v Evrope i Rossii', in *Sobranie sochinenii,* Vol. 9, Moscow: Nauka.

Brandist, Craig. 2015. *The Dimensions of Hegemony: Language, Culture and Politics in Revolutionary Russia*. Leiden: Brill.

Brandist, Craig. 2018. 'Nikolai Marr's Critique of Indo-European Philology and the Subaltern Critique of Brahman Nationalism in Colonial India'. *Interventions: International Journal of Postcolonial Studies*. https://doi.org/10.1080/1369801X.2017.1421043

Brennan, Timothy, 2006. *Wars of Position: The Cultural Politics of Left and Right,* New York: Columbia University Press.

Bustanov, Alfrid K., 2014, *Soviet Orientalism and the Creation of Central Asian Nations*. London: Routledge.

Callinicos, Alex, 1995. *Theories and Narratives: Reflections on the Philosophy of History*. Oxford: Polity.

Chattopadhyaya, Debiprasad, 1959. *Lokayata: A Study in Ancient Indian Materialism*. New Delhi: People's Publishing House.

Clark, Katerina, 2011. *Moscow, the Fourth Rome: Stalinism, Cosmopolitanism, and the Evolution of Soviet Culture, 1931-1941*. Cambridge MA: Harvard University Press.

Datta Gupta, S. 2006. *Comintern and the Destiny of Communism in India 1919-1943: Dialectics of Real and a Possible History*. Kolkata: Bakharahat Seribaan.

David-Fox, Michael, 2011. *Showcasing the Great Experiment: Cultural Diplomacy and Western Visitors to the Soviet Union, 1921-1941*. Oxford & New York: Oxford University Press.

Figueira, Dorothy, 2015 [2002]. *Aryans, Jews, Brahmins: Theorizing Authority Through Myths of Identity*. New Delhi: Navayana.

Gafurov, B.G. 1957. 'Aktual'nye zadachi sovetskogo vostokovedeniia', *Vestnik Akademii Nauk SSSR,* 9: 13–24.

Geetha, V. and S.V. Rajadurai, 1998. *Towards a Non-Brahmin Millennium: From Iyothee Thass to Periyar*. Calcutta: Samya.

Gerke, Barbara, 1998. "Tibetskie otkrytiia Rakhula Sankrit'iaiany." *Arivarta,* 2: 127-43.

Gramsci, A. 1971. *Selections From the Prison Notebooks*. London: Lawrence and Wishart.

Habib, Irfan, 2006. 'Marx's Perception of India'. In Iqbal Husain (ed.) *Karl Marx on India*. New Delhi: Tulika Books, pp. xxix–liv.

Harris, Nigel, 1990. *National Liberation*. Reno: University of Nevada Press.

Heinrich, Michael, 2015. "Je ne suis pas marxiste". *Neues Deutschland*, January 24, 2015. English translation here: https://libcom.org/library/%E2%80%9Eje-ne-suis-pas-marxiste%E2%80%9C (accessed 10 May 2018).

Israel, Jonathan, 2006. *Enlightenment Contested: Philosophy, Modernity, and the Emancipation of Man 1670–1752*, Oxford: Oxford University Press.

Iuzbashian, K.N. 1986. *Akademik Iosif Abgarovich Orbeli 1887-1961*. Moscow: Nauka.

Karttunen, Klaus, 2015. 'The Beginnings of Indology and Modern Historiography in India'. In Klaus Karttunen (ed.) *History of Indological Studies*. New Delhi: Motilal Banarsidass, pp. 53-78.

Kemper, Michael. 2006. *Studying Islam in the Soviet Union*, Amsterdam: Vossiuspers Uva.

Kemper, M. 2009. The Soviet Discourse on the Origin and Class Character of Islam, 1923–1933. *Die Welt des Islams* 49: 1–48.

Kemper, M. 2010. Red Orientalism: Mikhail Pavlovich and Marxist Oriental Studies in Early Soviet Russia. *Die Welt des Islams* 50(3–4): 435–476

Konrad, Nikolai, 1927. *Iaponskaia literatura v obraztsakh i ocherkakh*. Leningrad: IZhVIa.

Konrad, Nikolai, 1935. *Vostok: Literatura Kitaia i Iaponii*. Moscow: Academia.

Kosach, Grigorii G. 2001. *Krasnyi flag nad Blizhnim Vostokom? Kompartii Egipta, Palestiny, Sirii i Livana v 20-30-e gody*. Moscow: RGGU.

Kosach, Grigorii, G. 2009. *Kommunisty Blizhnego Vostoka v SSSR. 1920-1930-e gody*. Moscow: RGGU.

Kosambi 2010 [1912-24]. 'A Narrative (Nivedan)'. In *Dharmanand Kosambi: The Essential Writings*, 53-219. Ranikhet: Permanent Black.

Kosambi, Dharmanand. 2010 [1935], "Civilization and Non-Violence." In *Dharmanand Kosambi: The Essential Writings*, 327–57. Ranikhet: Permanent Black

Mani, Braj Ranjan 2015. *Debrahmanising History: Dominance and Resistance in Indian Society*. New Delhi: Manohar.

Murugesan, K. and C.S. Subramanyam. 1975. *Singaravelu- First Communist in South India*. New Delhi: People's Publishing House.

Norris, Christopher, 2015. *Deconstruction After All: Reflections and*

Conversations. Brighton: Sussex Academic Press. Ebook.

Ober, Douglas. 2013. " 'Like Embers Hidden in Ashes, or Jewels Encrusted in Stone': Rāhul Sānkrtyāyan, Dharmānand Kosambī and Buddhist Activity in Late British India." *Contemporary Buddhism*, Vol. 14/1: 134-148.

Ober, Douglas. 2016. *Reinventing Buddhism: Conversations and Encounters in Modern India, 1839–1956*. PhD dissertation. Vancouver: University of British Columbia.

Ol'denburg, S.F. 1931. *Zapad i Vostok v sovetskikh usloviiakh*. Moscow: Gosizdat.

Persits, M.A. 1973. *Revolutionaries of India in Soviet Russia*. Moscow: Progress Publishers.

Rathore, Aakash Singh and Rimina Mohapatra, 2017, *Hegel's India: A Reinterpretation*, Oxford: Oxford University Press.

Roy, M.N. 2016 [1932]. 'Materialism in Indian Philosophy'. In *M N Roy Reader: Essential Writings*. 3 Vols. Edited by Bhaskar Sur and R.M. Pal. New Delhi: Aakar Books. Vol. 1. pp. 19–44.

Roy, Purabi, Sobhanal Datta Gupta and Hari Vasundevan (eds) 1999. *Indo-Russian Relations 1917-1947: Select Documents from the Archives of the Russian Federation*, 2 vols. Calcutta: Asiatic Society.

Safarov, G.I. 1922. *Problemy Vostoka*. Petrograd: Gosizdat.

Safarov, G.I. 1931. 'Polozhenie na vostokovedcheskom fronte'. *Biulleten zaochnoi konsul'tatsii v Institute Krasnoi Professury* 2: 40–58.

Said, Edward Wadie 1995 [1978], *Orientalism: Western Conceptions of the Orient*, Harmondsworth: Penguin.

——— 1983. *The World, the Text and the Critic*. Cambridge Mass.: Harvard University Press.

Sānkrityāyan, Rāhul. 1970. "Buddhist Dialectics." In *Buddhism: The Marxist Approach*. New Delhi: Peoples Publishing House: 1–8.

Sinitsyn, F.L. 2013. *Krasnaia buria: Sovetskoe gosudarstvo i buddizon v 1917-1946gg*. St. Petersburg: Izd. A. Teren'tva.

Stalin, J.V. 1954 [1930]. 'Political Report of the Central Committee to the Sixteenth Congress of the C.P.S.U.(b.)'. In *Works*, Vol. 12, Moscow: Foreign Languages Publishing House, pp. 242–285.

Stcherbatsky, T. 1932. "The Doctrine of the Buddha." *Bulletin of the School of Oriental and African Studies*, 6: 867–896.

Steila, Daniela, 1991. *Genesis and Development of Plekhanov's Theory of Knowledge: A Marxist Between Anthropological Materialism and Physiology*. Dordrecht: Kluwer.

Tamazishvili, A.O. 2008. Vladimir Aleksandrovich Gurko-Kriazhin: Sud'ba boitsa "Vostokovednogo fronta". In *Neizvestnye stranitsy otechestvennogo vostokovedeniia*, 3, ed. V.V. Naumkin, et al., 32–136. Moscow: Vostochnaia literatura.

Teltumbde, Anand. 2017. 'Introduction: Bridging the Unholy Rift'. In B.R. Ambedkar, *India and Communism*. New Delhi: Leftword Books.

Tolz, Vera, 2006. 'European, National and (Anti-)Imperial: The Formation of Academic Oriental Studies in Late Tsarist and Early Soviet Russia', in Michael David-Fox et al. (eds.), *Orientalism and Empire in Russia*, Bloomington: Slavica.

Tolz, Vera, 2011. *Russia's Own Orient: The Politics of Identity and Oriental Studies in the Late Imperial and Early Soviet Periods*. Oxford: Oxford University Press.

Tolz, Vera, 2015 'Reconciling Ethnic Nationalism and Imperial Cosmopolitanism: The Lifeworlds of Tsyben Zhamtsarano (1880-1942)', *Asiatische Studien*, 69(3):723-746.

Turner, Bryan S. 1978. *Marx and the End of Orientalism*. London: Allen & Unwin.

Vaitheespara, Ravi, and Rajesh Venkatasubramanian. 2015. 'Beyond the Politics of Identity: The Left and the Politics of Caste and Identity in Tamil Nadu, 1920–63', *South Asia: Journal of South Asian Studies*, 38:4, 543-557.

Vasil'kov, Ia. V. 1998. "Rakhula Sankrit'iaiana i Rossiia." *Ariavarta*, 2: 115–126.

Vigasin, A.A. 2008. *Izuchenie Indii v Rossii (Ocherki i materialy)*. Moscow: Stepanenko.

Young, Robert, 2004 [1990]. *White Mythologies: Writing History and the West*. Second edition. London: Routledge.

4

A Short History of Black Marxism in the USA

Kipton E. Jensen

> "To learn about the present in light of the past also means to learn about the past in light of the present. The function of history is to promote a profounder understanding of both past and present through the interrelation between them" (E.H. Carr, as quoted in Kosambi, 1962: 62).

Recognition of difference and conflictual social relationships constitutes the methodological starting point of anti-oppression theorists. These range from critical race and postcolonial scholars to traditional and heterodox Marxists alike (Dhamoon 2010; Rein 2007; Bannerji 1995). Exploitation is one of the paradigmatic 'conflictual social relations,' to be sure, but so too are alienation and oppression. As Abigail Bakan puts it: "Alienation and oppression are central to the reproduction of capitalist exploitation" (2014: 103). The capitalist system in particular and competitive culture in general depends upon separation if not conflict between individuals. The focus of this essay is on freedom qua non-alienation. It shows how racialised differences in the USA have been used to suppress freedom.

Nikhil Pal Singh suggests that while there are important exceptions, "thinkers in the Marxist tradition have largely failed to give sustained and sympathetic attention to this issue [viz. the role of racism in the history of capitalism]" (2017: 79). This frustration with how the American Left has "relegated the struggle of Blacks to a subsidiary position in the revolutionary movement" (Haywood, 1978: 234) reaches back at least as far as Hubert Harrison, who A. Philip Randolph called the "father of Harlem radicalism." In recent years, at least in the USA, writes Abigail Bakan, "Marxism is often acknowledged but circumvented, dismissed for its apparent tendency to emphasise class relations and economic materiality to the exclusion of other forms of oppression and other ways of understanding domination" (2014: 99). And while some declare an inherent incompatibility of a Marxist perspective with consistent anti-racism (Robinson, 2000), or that Marxism should be rejected as Eurocentric and the victim of Orientalism (Said, 2003; Anderson, 2010), Bakan believes—citing many Marxists who are also race and gender theorists[1]—that the divide is by no means definitive.

Keenga-Yamahtta Taylor, for one, perhaps as an exemplar, sees racism through the lens of class and class with an eye fixed on race. "Because of the gross inequality it produces," writes Taylor, "capitalism requires various political, social, and ideological tools to divide the majority—racism is one among many oppressions intended to serve this purpose" (2016: 205-06). Malcolm X put his finger on the problem, in 1964, at the founding rally of the OAAU, when he quipped: "You can't have capitalism without racism" (Heron, ed. [1964] 1990; also, Taylor, 197). Scholars like Zerilli and Laclau argue that "there is no trans-historical group that can stand in for the universal" and that "an appropriate signifier must be determined in each period by political contestation" (2008: 45; also in Dawson, 173 ff.). There are nevertheless compelling reasons for focusing on the history of slavery and the ideology of racism as a critical reflection of the brutal dialectics of class struggle in the USA. The historiographical epicycle of Black Marxism in the USA, over the past 200 years, is a singular signifier for the universal struggle for freedom and equality in America as a whole.

Angela Davis would have us construe slavery as the most extreme form of un-freedom, the reality rather than the metaphor, slave ownership rather than the "slavery of wage labor." (The analogy or simile is instructive, but the ways that slavery is dis-analogous to wage-labour is also meaningful.) Although one could limit the term "Black Marxism" to Marxists who are Black, I wish to use Black Marxism in the broader sense of a hermeneutical turn in American historiography. Following Dawson and Badiou, I want to "regain a politically constituted definition of 'black'" (Dawson, 2013: 177) that is "less the demand of a social faction or community to be integrated into the existing order than something which touches on a transformation of the order as a whole" (Badiou, 2001: 109). Charles Mills is surely right to suggest that "in understanding the workings of a system of oppression, a perspective from the bottom up is more likely to be accurate than one from the top down" (1997: 109). Better yet is Angela Davis's observation in "Lectures on Liberation" that "[t]he collective consciousness of an oppressed people entails an understanding of the conditions of oppression and the possibility of abolishing these conditions" (Davis, 2010[1969]: 49). In this essay I focus on five periods—viz. 1818, 1868, 1918, 1968, and 2018—as illustrative of what might be called the "Kosambi-model" of "presenting, in chronological order of successive developments in the means and relations of production" (1951: 23)," a historiographical model in which "to learn about the present in light of the past also means to learn about the past in light of the present" (ibid.).

1. The State of the Union in 1818: Slavery and 'the Rosy Dawn of Capitalism'?

> Atlantic slavery was the cornerstone of capitalist exploitation, appropriation, and dispossession over centuries. It also bequeathed an enduring devaluation of black life (Singh, 2017: 96).
>
> *Freedom* and *slavery* constitute an antagonism. There is no need for me to speak either of the good or of the bad aspects of freedom. As for slavery, there is no need for me to speak of its bad aspects. The only thing requiring explanation is the good side of slavery. I do not mean indirect slavery, the slavery of

the proletariat; I mean direct slavery, the slavery of the Blacks in Surinam, in Brazil, in the southern regions of North America. Direct slavery is just as much the pivot of bourgeois industry as machinery, credit, etc. Without slavery you have not cotton; without cotton you have not modern industry. It is slavery that has given the colonies their value; it is the colonies that have created world trade, and it is world trade that is the pre-condition of large-scale industry, thus slavery is an economic category of the greatest importance (Marx, *The Poverty of Philosophy: A Reply to M. Proudhon's Philosophy of Poverty*, New York, International Publishers, 1847: 94-5).

In der wirklichen Geschichte spielen bekanntlich Eroberung, Unterjochung, Raubmord, kurz: Gewalt, die grosse Rolle (Marx, 1867, "Die Sogenannte Urspruenglichen Akkumulation").

When Marx was born in Triers, in 1818, slavery was the law of the land in America. Approximately 12.5 million enslaved Africans were transported to the Americas between 1500 and 1866; 10.7 million survived the dreaded Middle Passage (Gates, 2015). Alongside the horrors of chattel slavery, which was well-established in the US by 1818, and often justified along similar ideological lines, the exponential accumulation of capital included or entailed the slaughter and dispossession of native Americans. For some, these atrocities comprise two sides of "a wooden nickel."[2] Keenga-Yamahtta Taylor defines capitalism quite curtly as "an economic system based on the exploitation of the many by the few" (2016: 205). In *Black Marxism*, Cedric Robinson defines 'racial capitalism' as "the development, organisation, and expansion of capitalist society pursued essentially racial directions, so too did social ideology. As a material force, then, it could be expected that racialism would inevitably permeate the social structures emergent from capitalism." Marx saw quite clearly that capitalism came into the world "dripping from head to toe in blood" and also that "the turning of Africa into a commercial warren for the hunting of black skins signalled the rosy dawn of the era of capitalist production." Manning Marable claims that "the ordeal of slavery was responsible for accelerating the economic and political power of Europe and North America over the rest of the mostly non-white world" (2000: 7).

In 1818, 200 years ago, America was still quite young. Fifty years earlier, the US was itself a British colony. Frederick Douglass took some small amount of consolation in the fact that America was so young, in 1852, since youth inspires the hope if not the promise of maturation and mutual recognition in the trenches if not also reconciliation and redemption at the mountaintop. In his "Oration at the Corinthian Hall," Frederick Douglass adumbrated and admonished the glaring inconsistencies inherent in singing peons to freedom and prosperity on Independence Day in the USA:

> The existence of slavery in this country brands your republicanism as a sham, your humanity as a base pretense, and your Christianity as a lie. It destroys your moral power abroad; it corrupts you politicians at home. It saps the foundation of religion; it makes your name a hissing, and a byword to a mocking earth (July 5, 1852).

James Monroe was the fifth President of the United States. And while it is true that Monroe once declared that slavery was "one of the evils still remaining, incident to our colonial system," it is also true that Monroe owned as many as 250 slaves—and he never freed any of them. (Monroe inherited his first slave when he turned 16 years of age.) As President, Monroe formed the American Colonisation Society (ACS), which advocated for the repatriation of slaves to Africa: indeed, the capitol of Liberia, Monrovia, is named after Monroe. This was not the first—nor the last—contradiction or pernicious paradox that characterises the history of the USA. In her luminous "Lectures on Liberation," Angela Davis states that "[o]ne of the most acute paradoxes present in the history of Western society is that while on a philosophical plane freedom has been delineated in the most lofty and sublime fashion, concrete reality has always been permeated with the most brutal forms of unfreedom, enslavement" (2010[1969]: 45).

The first five presidents of the USA owned slaves. Aptheker describes the solidarity exhibited amongst the slaveholders and planter-class in the first half of the 19th century as "the most closely knit and most important single economic unit in the nation, their millions of bondsmen and millions of acres of land comprising an investment of billions of dollars. This economic might had its counterpart in political power, given its possessor's dominance within the nation and predominance within the South" (1965: 19). Two hundred years ago, back in 1818, racial domination was an explicit if not unabashed and brutal element in the plantocratic management of capitalist society. We sometimes think that, for Marx, wage labour emerged from the dissolution of slavery or serfdom, and was the pre-condition of bourgeois society. But slavery also existed within bourgeois society. It is in this sense that Singh amends Marx's axiomatic statement: Capital ceases to be capital without the ongoing differentiation of free labour *and slavery,* waged labor *and unpaid labor* as its general creative basis (2017: 88). Beyond the hyper-exploitation inherent to racial differentiation, we would do well to discuss alienation. *The Narrative of Frederick Douglass* describes slavery as something worse than merely the exploitation of Black labour: for Douglass, slavery represented a totalizing claim on the lives of Black people. "The most extreme form of human alienation," writes Angela Davis, "is the reduction [of persons] to the status of property" (2010: 53). The consequences of slavery are still with us today. Indeed, Manning Marable goes so far as to say that "[s]ince the demise of slavery, and the emergence of modern capitalism, the process of Black underdevelopment has expanded and deepened" (2000: 7).[3]

2. The State of the Union in 1868: Postbellum Southern Reconstruction

> "The dominant ideology of society was that of the plantocracy, a dictator of labour and land with no democratic pretensions" (Robinson, 153).
>
> "Either poverty must use democracy to destroy the power of

property, or property in fear of poverty will destroy democracy" (Thomas Rainboro, quoted in Robinson, 188).

The starting point of the development that gave rise to the wage labourer as well as to the capitalist, was the servitude of the labourer. The advance consisted in a change of form of this servitude, in the transformation of feudal exploitation into capitalist exploitation." (Marx, 1868, "The Secret of Primitive Accumulation").

In 1868, 150 years ago, five years subsequent to the Emancipation Proclamation,[4] the year that the XIV Amendment was passed, in the wake of the civil war, the year Du Bois was born, the year that Marx published the first volume of *Capital: A Critique of Political Economy* in London, twenty years after the publication of the *Communist Manifesto,* the "free labor of the enslaved" was abolished de jure but African Americans were still not free.[5] For the emancipated slave, thought Marx, "the capitalist relationship appears to be an improvement in one's position on the social scale," and it was, but Marx also believed that wage-labor constituted enslavement of a different sort. In 1855, Douglass observed that "by encouraging enmity of the poor labouring white man against the blacks," slaveholders and overlords of a similar type, "succeed in making the white man almost as much a slave as the black man himself." De facto slavery did not disappear in 1868. Similar to what Marx called the "unending circle of capitalism," the racial-capitalist political economy characteristic of the antebellum period was preserved and reproduced in various ways in postbellum America.

In their "Address of the International Working Men's Association," written in November 1864, just one year before Lincoln was assassinated, Marx wrote:

> . . . the working classes of Europe understood at once, even before the fanatic partisanship of the upper classes for the Confederate gentry had given its dismal warning, that the slaveholders' rebellion was to sound the tocsin for a general holy crusade of property against labor, and that for the men of labour, with their hopes for the future, even their past conquests were at stake in that tremendous conflict on the other side of the Atlantic.[6]

German culture in general and Marxism or at least Hegelianism was so prominent as to be virtually dominant in the USA in the 19th century. The St. Louis Hegelians viewed the civil war as a concrete expression of the dialectical antitheses that constituted the world historical process. The Ohio Hegelians, mostly Marxists, included August Willich. He fought alongside Marx in the Rhineland campaigns before emigrating to the United States. There he was "one of four Marxists to rise to the rank of general in the Union Army" (Goetzmann, 1973: 45) who construed the civil war as a conflagration between the workers of the world and the capitalist overlords. Through Ambassador Adams, Lincoln noted:

> Nations do not exist for themselves alone, but to promote the welfare and happiness of mankind by benevolent intercourse and example. It is in this relation that the United States regard their cause in the present conflict with slavery, maintaining insurgence as the cause of human nature, and they derive new encouragements to persevere from the testimony of the workingmen of Europe that the national attitude is favored with their enlightened approval and earnest sympathies.

Though Lincoln and Marx would have disagreed on other fronts, they did seem to agree that labor rather than capital was the source of value and that exploitation was abominable.[7] Some will argue, from Du Bois to Dawson, that Lincoln had no intention of emancipating the slaves and that the decision was purely strategic; Black Marxists of various sorts, both old and new, would insist that we look more closely at how the civil war was actually won, i.e. in terms of quasi-deterministic materialism, than an ideological myth concerning a quickened Christian conscience in the form of the Emancipation Proclamation. Some scholars would encourage us to focus most explicitly on "the General Strike," which Du Bois viewed as a world historical event that inaugurated "the most extraordinary experiments of Marxism that the world, before the Russian Revolution, had seen" (1935: 58). In *Black Reconstruction* (1935), Du Bois describes the role of the conscientious historian in this way:

> What we have got to know, so far as possible, are the things that actually happened in the world. . . . the historian has no right, posing as a scientist, to conceal or distort facts; and until we distinguish between these two functions of the chronicler of human action, we are going to render it easy for a muddled world out of sheer ignorance to make the same mistake ten times over (722; quoted in Robinson, 228).

What actually happened, thought Du Bois, was something far more instructive when it comes to analysing the psycho-social dynamics of revolutionary class or race consciousness. Robinson puts it this way:

> [W]hat Du Bois termed a 'General Strike' was the total impact on the secessionist South of a series of actions circumstantially related to each other: some 200,000 Black workers, most of them slaves, had become part of the Union's military forces. These, and an even larger number of Blacks, had withdrawn their productive labour and paramilitary services from the Confederacy; transferring a substantial portion of them to the Union. In addition, tens of thousands of slaves and poor whites had emigrated from the South. The former were escaping slavery, the latter their poverty and the demands and ravages of war in which they had no vested interest. The result was to critically weaken the secessionists. The ordering of these diverse actions was then a consequence of the social order to which they were reactions. The contradictions within southern society rather than a revolutionary vanguard knit these phenomena into a historical force. After the war, a different ordering would be required to integrate these phenomena into a political movement. This could be accomplished if only the ruling ideologies of the society were transcended. This was not done (230).

Du Bois certainly respected Marx's insight into economic relations, plus his observations about the alienation inherent in capitalist modes of production, but he also thought that Marx was a product of his own place and time. Though appreciative of Marx, who Du Bois must have understood quite well, given his studies in Berlin, Du Bois said he never felt obliged "to dogmatise with Marx or Lenin" (*Crisis*, July 1921; reprinted in MOON as "The Negro and Radical Thought"). In "Karl Marx and the Negro," written in 1933, in *Crisis*, Du Bois wrote:

> It was a great loss to American Negroes that the great mind of Marx and his extraordinary insight into industrial conditions could not have been brought to bear at first hand upon the history of the American Negro between 1876 and the World War. Whatever he said and did concerning the uplift of the working class must, therefore, be modified so far as Negroes are concerned by the fact that he had not studied first hand their peculiar race problem here in America.

What really constituted the 'historical forces' during the period in question, thought Du Bois, was animated by the ideologies of race and individualism rather than a conscious contradiction between the modes of production and the relations of production. In America, at least, thought Du Bois, racism constituted a historical force that, as Robinson puts it, "precluded the emergence of a strong labour movement" (229). What really happened, according to Du Bois, what obstructed class consciousness and solidarity, suggests Robinson, was racial capitalism. During the same period in American history, in the midst of the Reconstruction years, 1867-1877, extra-legal measures were taken to subjugate Black labour to white wage-labourers in the South.[8]

Robinson claims in *Black Marxism* that Du Bois offers a critique of Marxism as adapted to the geo-political situation in America, some of those criticisms are theoretical and others constitute a discrepancy apropos matters of fact, e.g. the role of slavery to the emergence of capitalism, "the revolutionary force of slave and peasant labourers" as distinct from a "reactionary industrial working class," and the importance of American Reconstruction to the development of capitalism as a world system. Robinson encourages us to reconsider not only how "Lenin and Trotsky understood the peasantry differently from Marx and Engels" but also to compare "the descriptions found in Marx and Engels of peasant life with those of Du Bois concerning the slaves and poor whites" (235; for Du Bois's discussion, see BR, 121-122). The comparison is indeed instructive. "Beneath its appearance as a 'feudal agrarianism' lay the real relation of slavery to the emergence of modern capitalism," writes Robinson, and that slavery "was not a historical aberration, it was not a mistake in the otherwise bourgeois democratic age—it was, and its imprints continued to be, systemic (200).

Robinson believes that Du Bois's account of the General Strike constitutes a constructive critique of Marxism. Indeed, by 1918, Du Bois himself criticised the American Socialist Party's ideologues for praising the successes of the Russian peasantry while ignoring the achievements of American Blacks. The economic foundation for class antagonism was challenged during this period by proposals to radically alter land tenure, which, again Robinson, "the white ruling class averted by getting poor whites to scapegoat and chastise the black workers." As Du Bois put it: "The masters feared their former slaves . . . they lied . . . they forestalled the danger of a united Southern labour movement by appealing to the fear and the hate of white labour" (BR: 633). Poor whites were pitted against still poorer Black workers. Du Bois also understood the degree to which even poor whites were compensated with "a public and psychological wage."[9] Again Robinson:

> The ideology of racism in combination with self-interest functioned to pit immigrant and poor white workers against the Black worker and the slave. And after the Civil War, the same social consciousness divided the working classes—immigrant and white—from ex-slave.

Du Bois saw it coming when he recognised how "the plight of the white working class throughout the world today is directly traceable to slavery in America, on which modern commerce and industry were founded, and which persisted to threaten free labour until it was partially overthrown in 1863" (30; 203). After Reconstruction, by 1880, with an undercapitalised South, writes Robinson, "northern capitalists constructed their own form of slavery (in Mexico, the Philippines, Haiti, the Caribbean, and the Pacific Islands (231).

3. The State of the Union in 1918

> 1. The black man was stolen from his native land, from his wife and child, brought to these shores and made a slave. He was chained and whipped and robbed by his "white superior," while the son of his "superior" raped the black child before his eyes. For centuries he was kept in ignorance and debased and debauched by the white man's law. . . The African is here and to stay. How came he to our shores? Ask your grandfathers, Mr. Anonymous, and if they will tell the truth you will or should blush for the crimes (Debs, 1903).
>
> 2. Politically, the Negro is the touchstone of the modern democratic idea (Hubert Harrison, 1911)
>
> 3. Ten thousand times has the labour movement tumbled, fallen and bruised itself, and risen again; been seized by the throat, choked and clubbed into insensibility; enjoined by courts, assaulted by thugs, charged by the militia, shot down by regulars, traduced by the press, frowned upon by public opinion, deceived by politicians, threatened by priests, repudiated by renegades, preyed upon by grafters, infested by spies, deserted by cowards, betrayed by traitors, bled by leeches, and sold out by leaders, but notwithstanding all this, and all these, it is today the most vital and potential power this planet has ever known, and its historic mission of emancipating the workers of the world from the thralldom of the ages is as certain of ultimate realisation as is the setting of the sun [Debs, "An Ideal Labor Press," *The Metal Worker* (May 1904)].

One approach to discussing racial capitalism during this period consists in contrasting Du Bois and Debs. This is what David Roediger does, or attempts to do, in his *Class, Race, and Marxism* (2017); the tack was taken first by him back in 2006 in an article titled "Retreat from Race and Class."[10] Du Bois claimed—in the "Address to the Nations of the World" (1900) and the *Souls of Black Folk* (1903)—that the great issue of the 20th century was "the color line"; and yet, the leading voice of Socialists if not Marxists of the period, Eugene Debs, who was jailed twice and who ran for President from behind bars in

1920, claimed that—and this is the innuendo in question—the socialist movement in America as distinct from the CPUSA, which was founded in 1919, could and probably should offer "nothing special" to African Americans. Debs added that "the class struggle is colorless." Eugene Debs was considered to be the voice of the blue denim masses in America in 1918, but he was also deeply concerned about the egregious hyper-exploitation of African Americans. Debs did acknowledge "that the white heel is still on the black neck is simply proof that the world is not yet civilised. The history of the Negro in the United States is a history of crime without parallel."[11]

When it comes to understanding the American Left in 1919, perhaps the best representative thinker for our purposes is Hubert Harrison (1883-1927), described by Perry as "the most class conscious of race radicals and the most race conscious of the class radicals." Not altogether unlike Du Bois in 1918, Harrison argued that supporting African Americans was "the crucial test of socialism's sincerity" (1921 in Dawson, 30; Perry, 180). Robinson would have us focus on Lenin as the person who best understood the strategic value of recruiting African Americans into the Party, at the 4th INTCOM, in 1922, in a missive titled the "Negro Question," as defending the principle of self-determination, which Lenin supported, but Debs did write his first essay on the topic: "The Negro in Class Struggle," in 1903, and subsequently in his reply to "Mr. Anonymous,"[12] who quipped that "it would jeopardise the best interests of the socialist party if you insist on political equality for the Negro" (November 25, 1904), viz. "The Negro and His Nemesis" (1904), published in *International Social Review*. Some would contend that Debs wasn't really a Marxist at all. Consider V.F. Calverson's assessment, in 1933, of Debs's loyalty to Marx, viz. that "his Marxism, if it could be called such, was more instinctive than intellectual."[13]

Not altogether unlike Marx, Debs's critique of capitalism began with a sober recognition that "[t]hose who produce should have, but we know that those who produce the most—that is, those who work hardest, and at the most difficult and most menial tasks, have the least" (1927: 5). Debs seems to have intellectually understood the role of racial ideologies in America and elsewhere in arresting or otherwise retarding the evolutionary or teleological development towards class consciousness and revolutionary solidarity. Debs believed both early and late that it was "only through an organised struggle in the labour and socialist movement ... that the Negro would win equality." This idea still appeals to a wide array of critical race and class theorists. Perhaps the alleged "instinctive" dimension of Debs's Marxism is captured in his oft cited claim that "while there is a lower class, I am in it, and while there is a criminal element I am of it, and while there is a soul in prison, I am not free." Debs often insisted that "for myself, I want no advantage over my fellow man, and if he is weaker than I am, all the more is it my duty to help him."[14] Similar to Debs's 1918 commemoration lecture 'Honoring Marx,' 100 years ago, I'm keen to focus more on the manner of man he was than the particular theories he espoused. Debs conceded that "no pen or tongue could possibly do Marx justice," but he came pretty close in his own description of Marx as a "triumphant awakener of the long-asleep and the revolutionary leader of the long-enslaved masses" ([1918] 2007: 473; also in Brommel, 1978: 208).[15]

Debs first read *Das Kapital* in an Illinois jail, where he was imprisoned in 1895 for his role in the Pullman Strike. Instructive parallels can be drawn between Marx and Debs, to be sure, but it is also true that—as Thoreau put it in "Walking" (1851)—the Mississippi was "a Rhine stream of a different kind." By 1918, Harrison was taking his message of Black Marxism, as it were, to the South; by 1918, Harrison had left the Socialist Party, fallen out with Du Bois, and was in the process of founding the Liberty League, which provided a platform for Garvey and the UNIA. In the 1920s, the dominant voice on the left was the CPUSA; at about the same time, Stalin became more prominent than Marx within the Party. According to Robinson: "Stalin, himself a member of a Russian national minority, had been the authority through which the COMINTERN and the American Communist Party had come to recognise Blacks as an oppressed nation" (227). By the late 1920s, the CPUSA had a "black belt thesis" (i.e. the self-determination concession); CPUSA gained additional credibility for their role in the Scottsboro Boys Case in 1931. Dawson writes the fire stirred by the American Left, at its peak, somewhere between 1918 and 1932, was quickly and unceremoniously extinguished or otherwise contained for most of the 20th century, especially following the First World War. For African Americans on the Left and within the Black radical tradition, the ideological trajectory runs from Marx in American Socialism into the 1920s to Lenin or Stalin within the CPUSA in the 1930s until the 1950s, when America began fighting proxy wars against communism, and Mao at the peak of the Black Power movement, e.g. the Black Panthers (see "Ten Point Program"), by 1968 in the USA.

Very few Americans were familiar with the "Champaran Satyagraha," in 1918, in Patna. Nor were they aware of one of the emerging leaders of that movement, a young lawyer recently returned from South Africa, Mahatma Gandhi. But they were keenly interested in the *Satyagraha* as well as *Ahimsa* by the time Howard Thurman and his wife, Sue Bailey, visited Gandhi in his ashram in 1936. At the first meeting of the Southern Negro Leaders Conference, later called the Southern Christian Leadership Conference (SCLC), in 1957, Bayard Rustin asked Martin King, "Do you remember what Gandhi told Howard Thurman in India, many years ago?" He then recited Gandhi's seemingly prophetic words that "it may be through the Negroes that the unadulterated message of non-violence will be delivered to the world.'" By the time he met Gandhi, Thurman distinguished quite clearly and concisely the religion of Jesus from the injustices that are historically inseparable from the institution of Christianity. Thurman suggested in 1948, the year of Gandhi's death, in *Jesus and the Disinherited,* that the teachings of Jesus had a special significance for "those with their backs against the wall." Martin Luther King claimed that the revolutionary consciousness achieved in America during the early civil rights movement combined the political stratagems of Gandhi with the "love-ethic of Jesus" or the compassion of the Buddha. Thurman was sympathetic to Gandhi's doctrine of non-violence prior to their meeting in India and it was easy to draw analogies between the plight of the colonized masses in India or in South Africa and the historiographical narrative of super-exploitation of Blacks in America, especially in the South. Martin Luther King, who visited India in 1959, famously referred to Gandhi as "the guiding light of our technique of non-violent social change" (*Papers* 5: 231). King argued that the Gandhian philosophy was "the only morally and practically sound method open to oppressed people in their struggle for freedom" (*Papers* 4: 478).

4. The State of the Union in 1968

> In his 1968 manifesto, *Where Do We Go from Here: Chaos or Community?* and especially in the final chapter titled "World House," King admonished and implored us to "shift from a 'thing' oriented society to a 'person' oriented society." (King, 184).
>
> "The oppressed people of this earth make up a majority, not a minority" (Malcolm X, D: 173; Haywood, 1978: 629).
>
> In his 1968 poem, "On Justice," in his *Scottsboro Limited,* Langston Hughes wrote:
>
> "That Justice is a blind goddess
> Is a thing to which we blacks are wise:
> Her bandage hides two festering sores
> That once perhaps were eyes."

By 1968, the year that Martin Luther King was assassinated as part of a sanitation workers' strike in Memphis, African Americans were still not free. Many if not most African Americans were, as King put it in 1966, "trapped in an air-tight cage of poverty." By 1968, Thurman and King were reconsidering yet consistently devoted to the methods of non-violent yet active resistance against social and economic injustice, whether racism or poverty and militarism. The closest we came to a truly revolutionary position was the "Poor People's Campaign" in 1968. King was advocating the basic living wage 50 years ago. In the past fifty years, since the PPC of 1968, things have not really improved for most African Americans. Marable Manning wrote: "The citadel of world capitalism, the United States, has never liked to admit that millions of its citizens are poor" ([1983] 2000: 53). Divergence between labour productivity and worker compensation between 1948 and 1973, labour productivity rose by 96.7% and hourly compensation rose by 91.3%; comparatively, between 1973 and 2013, productivity rose by 74.4% and hourly compensation rose only by 9.2%. In 1928, the top 1% collected 19.6% of all income; in 1973, the top 1% collected 7.7% of all income; and in 2013, the top 1% collected 19.3% of all income. Political economists must also acknowledge disproportionate underemployment and low-wage jobs for African Americans, still: "The problem is not only unemployment, it is under or sub-employment . . . people who work in full-time jobs for part-time wages" (King, 03/1968; Pitts, 2015: 29).

In one of his final speeches before returning to Memphis, celebrating 100 years since the birth of W.E.B. Du Bois, in Atlanta, in a speech titled "Honoring Du Bois," in 1968, Martin Luther King said: "We must finally admit that Du Bois was brilliant and that he was a communist."[16] (But was he, really, and if so, to what extent or with what provisos?) Du Bois died in Ghana in 1963, on the very day that King delivered his "I Have a Dream" [originally, "Normalcy Never Again"] on the steps of the Lincoln Memorial in Washington DC. This coincidence of times and places merits further consideration: the underlying conditions from 1868, 1918, and 1968 remain the same or at the very least betray family resemblances when it comes to what King called the ugly triplets: racism, poverty/materialism, and imperialism/militarism.

It has become fashionable to discuss the "radical" King. Though it is sometimes suggested that King abandoned his commitment to active yet non-violent resistance, which is not true, it is true that King was increasingly committed to addressing structural inequalities rather than relying on moral persuasion to combat what he called the ugly triplets of racism, materialism (or, elsewhere, poverty), and militarism (or, alternatively, imperialism). King was increasingly convinced that the goals of labour and the goals of African Americans were one and the same. In his seminal "All Labour Has Dignity," in 1956, and in a passage that King amends when it comes to honoring Du Bois in 1968, King concluded saying:

> ... Dr. Du Bois' greatest virtue was his committed empathy with all the oppressed and his divine dissatisfaction with all forms of injustice. Today we are still challenged to be dissatisfied. Let us be dissatisfied until every man can have food and material necessities for his body, culture and education for his mind, freedom and until rat-infested, vermin-filled slums will be a thing of a dark past and every family will have a decent, sanitary house in which to live. Let us be dissatisfied until the empty stomachs of Mississippi are filled and the idle industries of Appalachia are revitalized. Let us be dissatisfied until brotherhood is no longer a meaningless word at the end of a prayer but the first order of business on every legislative agenda. Let us be dissatisfied until our brother of the Third World—Asia, Africa, and Latin America-will no longer be the victim of imperialist exploitation but will be lifted from the long night of poverty, illiteracy, and disease. Let us be dissatisfied until this pending cosmic elegy will be transformed into a creative psalm of peace and 'justice will roll down like waters from a mighty stream.'

King was maligned by the establishment, both the government and corporate elites, as a communist sympathiser, initially because of his work with unions, but later because of his criticisms of the Vietnam War. Who else but a communist could advocate for equal rights for African Americans? Officially, King sought a third way, what he considered to be a synthesis of capitalism and communism, in the form of 'democratic socialism.' In private, as early as 1952, King was quite adamant about his opposition to an economic system that "takes necessities from the masses to give luxuries to the classes" (1962, see Honey, 2018: 31).[17] Increasingly, King described his loyalty to the religion of Jesus in ways that echoed with Howard Thurman's view, which the latter associated with Eugene Debs's claim—though Thurman rarely acknowledged the author of the quote, for political reasons, in the midst of McCarthyism and the Red Scare—that "[w]herever there is a man in jail, I am not free.

"During the black power era there were no dominant national leftist organisations like the Socialist Party before the First World War or the Communist Party after the 1920s," writes Michael Dawson. It is interesting to note that Black radicals and nationalists of this period spoke less of Marx and Lenin or Stalin than they did about Mao Zedong's "On Contradiction" or "On Practice" (Dawson, 122; also see Harold Cruse, "Revolutionary Nationalism and the Afro-American," *Studies on the Left*, 1962: 72 ff.). Angela Davis offered a Marxist analysis to the notion of freedom as non-alienation, as opposed to the pseudo-concept of freedom as capacity to exploit other people, in her 1969 "Lectures on Liberation," but she also appreciated Mao's conviction that knowledge came from the people: "The collective consciousness of an oppressed people entails an understanding of the conditions of oppression and the possibility of abolishing these conditions" (Davis, 2010[1969]: 49). In "Black Like Mao: Red China and Black Revolution," Robin Kelley and Betsy Each write that "Black radicals came to see China as the beacon of Third World revolution and Mao Zedong thought as the guidepost" (1999: 8).

5. The State of the Union in 2018: Where Do We Go from Here, Again?

> . . . the rapaciousness of transnational corporation and the superrich grows without limit (Dawson, *Blacks In and Out of the Left*, 178).

> As long as white men can be taught to believe that the presence of black men threatens their means of existence, so long will their attitude be one of enmity. So long as the fallacy of economic

> fear survives, so long will the economic competition create race prejudice (Hubert Harrison).

> Capitalism makes an accumulation of misery a necessary condition, corresponding to the accumulation of wealth. Accumulation of wealth at one pole is, therefore, at the same time accumulation of misery, the torment of labour, slavery, ignorance, brutalization and the moral degradation at the opposite pole, i.e., on the side of the class that produces its own product as capital (Marx [1867]1976: 799).

Taylor suggests that while Marx is often dismissed for ignoring issues of race, he most certainly did acknowledge that "capitalism used racism to justify plunder, conquest, slavery" and that it would also "use racism to divide and rule—to pit one section of the working class against and, in doing so, blunt the class consciousness of all" (206). State-sanctioned violence, what Marx called the "bloody legislation against the expropriated," is perhaps the exception rather than the rule when it comes to the management of capitalist society in 2018; but race remains, writes Bruce Baum, "one of the most important axes of social power and inequality in the contemporary world" (2006: 118). Marx claims that mature capitalism occurs when "the silent compulsion of economic relations set the seal on the domination of the capitalist over the worker." Surplus if not slave-labour is what built America's economic prowess. Though it was in the colonies that the approach was applied with impunity, Marx thought that "European capitalism's emergence was rooted in the pilfering, rape, and destruction of natives, colonial subjects, and Black slaves" (ibid.). Following Taylor:

> capitalism creates a false scarcity: the perception that need outstrips resources. When billions are spent on war, police-brutality settlements, and publicly subsidized sports stadiums, there never seems to be a shortage of money. But when it comes to schools, housing, food, and other basic necessities, politicians always complain about deficits and the need to curb spending and cut budgets (212).

Just because the plutocrats and oligarchs, whether plantocrats in the South and manufacturing magnates in the North, could no longer legally expropriate and exploit Black bodies as they had in earlier phases of American history didn't mean that they wouldn't find other means of oppressing and disenfranchising the vast majority of the Black (and also white) workers of the world. Michelle Alexander has made this point repeatedly in her *The New Jim Crow* (2010). See also see Manning Marable's chapter on "Black Prisoners and Punishment in a Racist/ Capitalist State" in *How Capitalism Underdeveloped America*, pp. 105 ff.). Taylor sees what Marx, Douglass, Du Bois, Debs and King all saw—with perfect clarity—was that the "slavery and the intense racism that flowed from it not only resulted in the oppression of slaves but also threatened the stability of the white working class by creating a downward pressure on wages in general. It was impossible to compete with free labour of the enslaved" (Taylor, 2016: 208). As if to add insult to injury, writes Dawson: "Yet those on the bottom are told both that the state is too poor to help them and that we live in society ordered by free markets where institutions and citizens succeed or not on their own merits" (182).[18]

Tentative Conclusion

> Criticism has plucked the imaginary flowers on the chain not in order that man shall continue to bear that chain without fantasy or consolation, but so that he shall throw off the chain and pluck the living flower (Marx, Proudhon Essay).
>
> We must analyse the historical foundations of underdevelopment, and articulate a theory of social transformation which will overturn capitalism, patriarchy, and white supremacy (Marable, 2000: 10).
>
> It should be beautiful, and powerful, but it should also work. It should have something in it that enlightens; something in it that opens the door and points the way (Toni Morrison, "Rootedness," 1982).

In 1936, Thurman met Gandhi to discuss the relative merits of applying the methods of active yet non-violent resistance (as practised in the salt campaign) to the civil and human rights movement in the USA. Thurman was often heard reciting the wonderful words of Eugene Debs, usually without mentioning Debs by name, since Debs was considered to be, in the midst of the Red Scare in the USA, a subversive citizen and a communist sympathiser:[19]

> Your Honor, years ago I recognized my kinship with all living beings, and I made up my mind that I was not one bit better than the meanest on earth. I said then, and I say now, that while there is a lower class, I am in it, and while there is a criminal element I am of it, and while there is a soul in prison, I am not free.

How much have things changed, in the US, in India, across the world, since the birth of Marx two hundred years ago or even since 1968, 50 years ago, in terms of racial discrimination and poverty?[20] As a critical race theorist, but also a Marxist of a certain sort, Charles Mills challenges us to recognise that race is "central to the making of the modern world" and that, echoing Marx's fine dictum, the 11th of the Theses on Feuerbach, viz.*"es kömmt drauf an, die Welt [nicht nur zu interpretieren, sondern auch sie] zu verändern,"* we must "seek to understand structures of social oppression for the emancipatory purpose of transforming them" (2003: 199).

I want to conclude with a paragraph or two devoted to D.D. Kosambi's application of Marxism to historiography in India. Kosambi defined history as "the presentation, in chronological order of successive developments in the means and relations of production" (1951: 23). In his *Exasperating Essays: Exercises in the Dialectical Method* (1957), Kosambi defined historiography somewhat differently. Kosambi would ask us to carefully consider the plight of the most exploited and the least free in 2018, in the US, in India, in Africa, but he would also have us recognise the material and ideological forces that conspire to perpetuate systems of domination, whether in terms of caste, race, gender, or sexual orientation. Analogies have been drawn in the past between, e.g. the Dalit population in India and the plight of Black people in America. In 1946, Ambedkar drew the analogy in a letter he wrote to W.E.B. Du Bois.[21] In 1959, when visiting a school in Trivandrum, Martin Luther King was introduced by the principal as a "fellow untouchable from the United States." Although initially "shocked and peeved," as Razdan reports, King later recalled that as he began to think "about the fact that 20 millions of my brothers and sisters were still smothering in an airtight cage of poverty in an affluent society. And as I thought about this, I finally said to myself, yes, I am an untouchable and every Negro in the United States is an untouchable."[22]

Frederick Douglass admonished the Black intelligentsia, back in 1852, that they should "have to do with the past only as we can make it useful to the present and to the future." This essay seeks to understand the past—e.g. in 1818, 1868, 1918, and 1968—because it is still relevant in 2018. Kosambi occasionally cited E.H. Carr to clarify what he took to be the political function of history: "To learn about the present in light of the past also means to learn about the past in light of the present. The function of history is to promote a profounder understanding of both past and present through the interrelation between them" (1962: 62). In closing let us also recall Du Bois's wise dictum that concealing the facts and distorting what actually happened "render it easy for a muddled world out of sheer ignorance to make the same mistake ten times over" (722; quoted in Robinson, 228).

NOTES

1. Bakan here cites Robin Blackburn (1997, 2011), Angela Davis (1983), W.E.B. Du Bois (1969), C.L.R. James (1989), August Nimtz (2003), Walter Rodney (1972), Eric Williams (1944); we might also add Keenga-Yamahtta Taylor (2016). Bakan also discusses various anti-racist theorists who acknowledge the importance of certain elements of Marxism (e.g. Carole Boyce Davies, Ania Loomba, Charles Mills, Sherene Razack, Nikhil Pal Singh, and Ella Shohat) as well as those who, like David Roediger, "attempt to develop analytic tools to bridge the theoretical gap" (2014: 100 ff.)
2. Fitzhugh writes—in *Sociology for the South*—that "[d]espite the

mawkish sensibility of the age, practical men are . . . pursuing the same course; they slay the Indians hip and thigh, as in the days of Moses and Joshua, and enslave the negroes" (286-7; in Roediger, 107); Roediger adds: "Enslaving Africans was on this view the nurturant flipside of the white managerial genius that killed off the Indians" (ibid.).

3. Marable elaborates: "Underdevelopment is not the absence of development; it is the inevitable product of an oppressed population's integration into the world market economy and political system. Once 'freed,' Black Americans were not compensated for their 246 years of free labour to this country's slave oligarchy. . . . Sharecropping and convict leasing were followed by industrial labour at low wages. . . . The constant expropriation of surplus value created by Black labour is the heart and soul of underdevelopment" (2000: 7).
4. In 1865, the Confederacy surrendered unconditionally. The Emancipation Proclamation in 1863, combined with the 13th Amendment, theoretically destroyed the "peculiar institution" of slavery in the US. Taylor has been helpful in demonstrating the many ways, proximate and remote, that Blacks are still not free. (Since the very moment that Slaves were *de jure* liberated from slavery, the capitalist machine has morphed into less egregious or overt but equally egregious forms—wage labour rather than chattel slavery—of exploiting the vulnerable and disinherited to such an outrageous degree that it constitutes *de facto* slavery.)
5. "In reference to you, coloured people, let me [viz. Abraham Lincoln in Richmond, VA, days after the unconditional surrender of the Confederacy] say God has made you free. Although you have been deprived of your God-given rights by your so-called Masters, you are now free as I am, and if those that claim to be your superiors do not know that you are free, take the sword and bayonet and teach them that you are for God created all men free giving to each the same rights of life, liberty, and the pursuit of happiness" (quoted in Taylor, 2016: 192).
6. See https://www.marxists.org/archive/marx/iwma/documents/1864/lincoln-letter.htm
7. In his first message to Congress in December 1861, Lincoln criticised the "effort to place capital on an equal footing with, if not above, labor in the structure of government." Instead, he insisted, "labour is prior to and independent of capital. Capital is only the fruit of labour . . . . Labour is the superior of capital

and deserves much the higher consideration" (https://www.jacobinmag.com/2012/08/lincoln-and-marx).

8. Jim Crow laws were implemented in 1878. Ida B. Wells documents—in *Southern Horrors* (1892)—the role of lynching as a systemic means of keeping African Americans de facto enslaved, alienated, oppressed, and exploited. Also see Preston King, CRISSP, "Ida Wells and Nonviolent Resistance in the South."
9. Singh writes: "The association of whiteness with wages through the monopolisation of fields of employment has been widely discussed. Less fully examined has been how the elevation of whiteness to the threshold of nationality actively links freedom with the management of public authority, specific mechanisms of violence, and an operational notion of (racial) nemesis" (2017: 94-95).
10. David Roediger first published this useful thesis in the *Monthly Review*, 58 (July-August 2006), 40-51; he republishes and amends the earlier article as the first chapter of his recent *Class, Race, and Marxism* (2017).
11. Eugene Debs, "The Negro in the Class Struggle," *International Socialist Review*, 4 (November 1903), marxist.org; also see David Roediger, *Class, Race, and Marxism* (Verso, 2017), pp. 33 ff.
12. Mr. Anonymous, who identified himself as "a staunch member of the Socialist Party, allegedly from Elgin, Illinois, advised Debs to peruse Thomas Dixon's "The Leopard's Spots." As an aside, Debs wrote a speech in which he praised John Brown, who was hanged in 1859, for his leading role in the Harper's Ferry Massacre, as "history's greatest hero."
13. In *Democracy's Prisoner*, Ernest Freeberg reminds us that "Debs was born in the Midwest, and his fight against capitalism was inspired as much by Tom Paine, Walt Whitman, Wendell Phillips as it was Karl Marx" (1999: 18). Debs's fight against capitalism was widely publicised: "Of course, Socialism is violently denounced by the capitalist press and by all the brood of subsidised contributors to magazine literature, but this only confirms the view that the advance of Socialism is very properly recognized by the capitalist class as the one cloud upon the horizon which portends an end to the system in which they have waxed fat, insolent and despotic through the exploitation of their countless wage-working slaves" (Debs, 1900, *Internationalist Socialist Review*). For more on Thomas Paine and early American socialism, see Sean Monahan's "Reading

Paine from the Left" (2015, Jacobin).

14. "The Negro and His Nemesis" in the *International Socialist Review* (January 1904).
15. For Debs on Marx, see "Karl Marx: An Appreciation" (1918) and "Marx and the Young People" (1918).
16. In 1968, in a speech titled "Honoring Du Bois," King wrote: "Some people would like to ignore the fact that he was a Communist in his later years. It is worth noting that Abraham Lincoln warmly welcomed the support of Karl Marx during the Civil War and corresponded with him freely. In contemporary life the English-speaking world has no difficulty with the fact that Sean O'Casey was a literary giant of the twentieth century and a Communist or that Pablo Neruda is generally considered the greatest living poet though he also served in the Chilean Senate as a Communist. It is time to cease muting the fact that Dr. Du Bois was a genius and chose to be a Communist. Our irrational, obsessive anti-communism has led us into too many quagmires to be retained as if it were a mode of scientific thinking."
17. As early as 1951, King made so bold as to declare: "I am convinced that capitalism has seen its best days in America, and not only in America, but in the entire world. It is a well-known fact that no social institution can survive when it has outlived its usefulness. This, capitalism has done. It has failed to meet the needs of the masses."
18. Michael Dawson proposes a wide array of recommendations for restraining what he calls "the voracious maw of capitalism," including the case for reparations and something along the lines of the 'truth and reconciliation' process in South Africa, which is more about agency and recognition than about extracting revenge in terms of monetary compensation, as well as an "unlearning attachment to regimes of injustice" (pp. 182 ff.). Ta-Nehisi Coates wrote an interesting article on reparations for the *Atlantic* in 2014.
19. "Now my friends, I am opposed to the system of society in which we live today, not because I lack the natural equipment to do for myself, but because I am not satisfied to make myself comfortable knowing that there are thousands of my fellow men who suffer for the barest necessities of life. We were taught under the old ethic that man's business on this earth was to look out for himself. That was the ethic of the jungle; the ethic of the wild beast. Take care of yourself, no matter what may become

of your fellow man. Thousands of years ago the question was asked: "Am I my brother's keeper?" That question has never yet been answered in a way that is satisfactory to civilized society. Yes, I am my brother's keeper. I am under a moral obligation to him that is inspired, not by any maudlin sentimentality, but by the higher duty I owe to myself. What would you think of me if I were capable of seating myself at a table and gorging myself with food and saw about me the children of my fellow beings starving to death?" (Debs, 1918).

20. "While the overall poverty rate for all Americans is about at the same level today, at 12.7%, as it was in 1968, "deep poverty," defined as having income below half the federal poverty level, has risen from 3.7% in 1975 (earliest available) to 5.8% in 2016. And because our population has added more than 122 million people since 1968, this means that 15 million more people are poor today than they were 50 years ago."
21. http://credo.library.umass.edu/view/pageturn/mums312-b109-i132/#page/1/mode/1up
22. https://kinginstitute.stanford.edu/encyclopedia/india-trip

BIBLIOGRAPHY

Alexander, Michelle. 2010. *The New Jim Crow: Mass Incarceration in the Age of Colorblindness.* New York: New Press.

Anderson, Kevin. 2010. "Marx at the Margins: On Nationalism, Ethnicity, and Non-Western Societies," *Global Discourse,* 2:2, 174-182.

Aptheker, Herbert, and David Walker. 1965. *One Continual Cry: David Walker's Appeal to the Colored Citizens of the World, 1829-1830, Its Setting & Its Meaning.* Aims Historical Series No. 1. New York: Published for A.I.M.S. by Humanities Press.

Bakan, Abigail B., and Enakshi Dua, eds. 2014. *Theorizing Anti-Racism: Linkages in Marxism and Critical Race Theories.* Toronto: University of Toronto Press.

Bannerji, Himani. 1995. *Thinking Through: Essays on Feminism, Marxism and Anti-Racism.* Toronto, Ont.: Women's Press.

Baum, Bruce. 2006. *The Rise and Fall of the Caucasian Race: A Political History of Racial Identity.* New York: NYU Press.

Badiou, Alain. 2013. *Ethics: An Essay on the Understanding of Evil.* London: Verso.

Blackburn, Robin. 2011. *The American Crucible: Slavery, Emancipation and Human Rights.* London: Verso.

Brommel, Bernard J. 1978. *Eugene V. Debs: Spokesman for Labor and*

Socialism. Chicago: Charles H. Kerr.

Carr, Edward Hallett. 1962. *What is History? The George Macaulay Trevelyan Lectures Delivered in the University of Cambridge January-March 1961*. First American ed. The George Macaulay Trevelyan Lectures, 1961. New York: Alfred A. Knopf.

Coates, Ta-Nehisi. 2014. "The Case for Reparations." *The Atlantic Monthly* 71–54 :(5) 313.

Cruse, Harold. 1962. *Revolutionary Nationalism and the Afro-American*. Indianapolis, Ind.: Bobbs-Merrill.

Dawson, Michael C. 2013. *Blacks in and Out of the Left*. The W.E.B. Du Bois Lectures. Cambridge, Mass.: Harvard University Press.

Davis, Angela. [1969] 2010. "Lectures on Liberation," reprinted as the "Introduction" to Douglass, Frederick. 2010. *Narrative of the Life of Frederick Douglass, an American Slave, Written by Himself: A New Critical Edition*. Open Media Series. San Francisco: City Lights Books.

Debs, Eugene V. [1903], 1918, 1948. *Writings and Speeches of Eugene V. Debs*. New York: Hermitage Press.

Dhamoon, Rita Kaur. 2010. "Democracy in Crisis: Violence, Alterity, Community." In *Democracy, Accountability and Disruption*. Manchester: Manchester University Press.

Dixie, Quinton Hosford, and Peter R. Eisenstadt. 2011. *Visions of a Better World: Howard Thurman's Pilgrimage to India and the Origins of African American Nonviolence*. Boston: Beacon Press.

Douglass, Frederick, and National Black Caucus of Librarians. Chicago Chapter. [1852] 1976. *The Meaning of July Fourth to the Slave: Oration Delivered in Corinthian Hall, July 5, 1852*. Chicago: Chicago Chapter, National Black Caucus of Librarians.

Du Bois, W.E.B. [1903] 2007. *Black Reconstruction in America: An Essay Toward a History of the Part Which Black Folk Played in the Attempt to Reconstruct Democracy in America, 1860-1880*. The Oxford W.E.B. Du Bois. New York: Oxford University Press.

Freeberg, Ernest. 2008. *Democracy's Prisoner: Eugene V. Debs, the Great War, and the Right to Dissent*. Cambridge, Mass.: Harvard University Press.

Fitzhugh, George. 1854. *Sociology for the South: Or, the Failure of Free Society*. Richmond, Va.: A. Morris.

Gates, Henry Louis. [2014] 2015. "How Many Slaves Landed in the US?" in *The Root*, see https://www.theroot.com/how-many-slaves-landed-in-the-us-1790873989.

Goetzmann, William H. 1973. *The American Hegelians: An Intellectual Episode in the History of Western America*. Edited by Dickson Pratt. New York: Knopf.

Haywood, Harry. 1978. *Black Bolshevik: Autobiography of an Afro-American Communist*. Chicago, Illinois: Liberator Press.

Honey, Michael K. 2018. *Going Down Jericho Road: The Memphis Strike, Martin Luther King's Last Campaign*. New York: W.W. Norton.

Hughes, Langston, and Arnold Rampersad. 2001. *The Collected Works of Langston Hughes*. Edited by Arnold Rampersad, Dolan Hubbard, Leslie Catherine Sanders, Donna Sullivan Harper, Christopher C. De Santis, Dianne Johnson, Steven C. Tracy, Joseph McLaren, and Dellita Martin-Ogunsola. Columbia: University of Missouri Press.

James, C.L.R. 1989. *The Black Jacobins: Toussaint L'ouverture and the San Domingo Revolution.*, 2nd ed., rev. New York: Vintage Books.

Kaldor, Mary, and Polly Vizard. 2011. *Arguing About the World: The Work and Legacy of Meghnad Desai*. London: Bloomsbury Academic.

Kelley, Robin D.G., and Betsy Esch. 1999. "Black Like Mao: Red China and Black Revolution." *Souls* 1(4): 6–41.

King, Martin Luther, Clayborne Carson, Peter Holloran, Ralph E. Luker, Penny A. Russell, and Ralph Luker. 1992. *The Papers of Martin Luther King, Jr*. Berkeley: University of California Press.

______. 2010. *Where Do We Go from Here Chaos or Community?* The King Legacy. Boston: Beacon Press.

King, Preston T., and Walter E. Fluker. 2005. *Black Leaders and Ideologies in the South: Resistance and Nonviolence*. London: Routledge.

Kosambi, D.D. 1966. *Ancient India: A History of Its Culture and Civilization*. [American ed.]. New York: Pantheon Books.

______. 1977. *Exasperating Essays: Exercises in the Dialectical Method*. Calcutta: India Book Exchange.

______. 1962. *Myth and Reality: Studies in the Formation of Indian Culture*. Bombay: Popular Prakashan.

Laclau, Ernesto. 2008. "Is Radical Atheism a Good Name for Deconstruction?" *Diacritics* 38 (1/2).

Marable, Manning. 2000. *How Capitalism Underdeveloped Black America: Problems in Race, Political Economy, and Society*. South End Press Classics, V. 4. Cambridge, Mass.: South End Press.

Marx, Karl, and H. Quelch. 2005 [1847]. *The Poverty of Philosophy: Being a Translation of the Misère De La Philosophie (a Reply to "La Philosophie De La Misère" of M. Proudhon)* Elibron Classics Replica ed. United States: Elibron Classics.

Mills, Charles W. 2003. *From Class to Race: Essays in White Marxism and Black Radicalism*. New Critical Theory. Lanham, Md.: Rowman & Littlefield.

______. 1997. *The Racial Contract*. Ithaca: Cornell University Press.

Monahan, Sean. 2015. "Reading Paine from the Left." *Jacobin Magazine*. https://www.jacobinmag.mcom/2015/03/thomas-paine-american-revolution-common-sense

Morrison, Toni. 1982. "Rootedness" in Evans, Mari. 1984. *Black Women Writers (1950-1980): A Critical Evaluation*. 1st ed. Garden City, N.Y.: Anchor Press/Doubleday.

Nimtz, August H. 2003. *Marx, Tocqueville, and Race in America: The "Absolute Democracy" or "Defiled Republic"*. Lanham, Md.: Lexington Books.

Perry, Jeffrey Babcock. 2009. *Hubert Harrison: The Voice of Harlem Radicalism, 1883–1918*. New York: Columbia University Press.

Pitts, Steven. 2015. "Low-Wage Work in the Black Community in the Age of Inequality." In *#BlackWorkersMatter*. Neighborhood Funders Group.

Rein, Sandra. 2007. "Reading Dunayevskaya: Engaging the Emergence of Marxist Humanism, 1930-1955", Ph.D. Dissertation. Department of Political Science, University of Alberta.

Robinson, Cedric J. 2000. *Black Marxism: The Making of the Black Radical Tradition*. Chapel Hill, N.C.: University of North Carolina Press.

Rodney, Walter. 1972. *How Europe Underdeveloped Africa*. London: Bogle-L'Ouverture Publications.

Roediger, David R. 2017. *Class, Race, and Marxism*. London. Verso Press.

Roediger, David R., and Elizabeth D. Esch. 2014. *The Production of Difference: Race and the Management of Labor in U.S. History*. New York: Oxford University Press.

Said, Edward W. 2003. *Orientalism*. Penguin Classics. London: Penguin.

Singh, Nikhil Pal. 2017. *Race and America's Long War*. Berkeley: University of California Press.

Taylor, Keeanga-Yamahtta. 2016. *From #BlackLivesMatter to Black Liberation*. Chicago, Illinois: Haymarket Books.

Thoreau, Henry David, and Richard Dillman. 2001. *The Major Essays of Henry David Thoreau*. Albany, N.Y.: Whitston Publishers.

Thurman, Howard. [1948] 1996. *Jesus and the Disinherited*. Boston: Beacon Press.

Wells-Barnett, Ida B., and Jacqueline Jones Royster. 1997. *Southern Horrors and Other Writings: The Anti-Lynching Campaign of Ida B. Wells, 1892-1900*. The Bedford Series in History and Culture. Boston, MA: Bedford Books.

Williams, Eric Eustace. 1994. *Capitalism & Slavery*. Chapel Hill:

University of North Carolina Press.

X, Malcolm, and George Breitman. 1990. *Malcolm X Speaks: Selected Speeches and Statements*. Grove Weidenfeld Evergreen ed. New York: Grove Weidenfeld.

Zerilli, Linda G. 2008. "Toward a Feminist Theory of Judgment." *Signs: Journal of Women in Culture and Society* 34:295–317.

5

From Early Marx to Véquaud's Countercultural Indophilia

Similar Aesthetics Founded on Romanticism and Communitarian Utopia

Hélène Fleury
Damien Ehrhardt

Véquaud was a French writer, a contributor to the *Nouvelle Revue Française* (NRF), a translator, a film director, and a curator, today mostly known for his essays on Mithila paintings.[1] In this paper, we aim to show the indirect impact of Marx's ideas on Véquaud as a player of the countercultural Indophilia. We hypothesise that, in the case of Véquaud, the traces of Marx go beyond the ideological references of the counterculture. We will try to assert this hypothesis in particular with the similarity of vision between both authors concerning the so-called "communitarian Indian village" as a counter-model challenging capitalist society, but stemming from a persistent Western orientalist imaginary and primitivist schema. This essay deals with, first, an overview of the different stages of Marx's aesthetics, presented here with only a little though to other Marxist theorists, and second, a discussion of different aspects of Véquaud's writings connected to Marx's ideas and counterculture.

1. Marx's Aesthetics: An Overview

1.1. *Marx as a Romantic Poet (1835-37)*

Karl Marx's first foray into writing goes back to the years 1835-37.[2] As a poet, he was marked in particular by E.T.A. Hoffmann's and Fichte's romanticism and his own academic studies about ancient literature and German classical aesthetics. The young Marx wrote poems inspired by the love for his fiancée, Jenny von Westphalen,[3] but his poetry treats also romanticist themes as the primacy of feeling and human emotions, the situation of artists separated from "normal" life, the struggle against philistines, or the opposition to an abstract and dehumanised world. In the poem "An die Sterne", the coldness of the shining stars may appear far from heart-warmth, mildness and soul. In his diatribes against physicians (among others "An die Mediziner"), he criticises their approach consisting of understanding human beings merely through the study of anatomy and physiology. Life cannot be reduced to the abstraction of science. For Marx many physicians are philistine because they "exaggerate their own importance, while ignoring the needs of others."[4] The poem "Der Spielmann" (The Minstrel) expresses the artist's isolation and his diabolical dimension: described as a dealer in black magic, he lives in the dark-side of the soul.[5]

1.2. *Marx as Early Philosopher: Organic Unity in the Material and Social Worlds (1837-41)*

In 1837, Marx left his vocation of a poet to become a philosopher. He combines poetry and prose, art and knowledge, fields that he considered to have been separated for a too long time.[6] Therefore, it is not surprising that he read Hegel, who aims to reunify everything under the metaphysics of the Absolute. But Marx was against the abstraction of Hegel's philosophy that he wished to escape.

The then widespread notion of organic unity plays a crucial role in Marx's oeuvre. In his dissertation on late Greek philosophy[7], the atom is regarded as the material basis of the world, but it symbolises also individual self-consciousness. Within a complex body, the atoms cannot be seen isolated from one another. As a higher unit, this complex body bears witness to the diversity of the world and its societies. In this perspective, Marx disapproved the abstract principles of the French Constitution of 1793 that may lead to a "world of uniform and independent atom-citizens"[8], far from the living forces of society as an essential entity for human beings.

1.3. *Marx's 'Not Written Aesthetics': The Artist Creates Freely Organic Forms in an Organic Society (1841-42)*

After a life-path leading him from poetry to philosophy, Marx would have been well placed to write on aesthetics, which is what he did. With Bruno Bauer he worked in 1841-42 on a critique of Hegel's vision of art and religion. But the two works written within this continuity in 1842 on Christian art are not extant[9] as well as his later contribution in 1857 on aesthetics for the *New American Cyclopaedia*.[10] So, if a "systematic Marxist aesthetics does not exist",[11] it is understandable that the Marxian aesthetics can be described as "a not written" one.[12] However, art is evoked here and there in Marx's oeuvre, and his approach to art is often integrated into more general considerations. The notebooks of 1842 give a few ideas about the supposed content of his not extant works on Christian art. Those notebooks introduce the idea of fetishism applied to religion: the latter worships the materiality of things. In contrast, art seeks to create organic forms through the intermediary of imagination. For Marx, this is how to explain the dryness of religious art.[13] The origin of the organic conception of art lies in a free society which has to be organic too. Therefore, in 1842, Marx advocates for the autonomy of literature in his defence of press freedom against Prussian censorship.[14] For him, the fight against censorship is a precondition for resistance.

Marx distinguished two worlds governed by the same organic principles, coexisting freely one in relation which each other: the real and the artistic ones. Isn't there a similarity with the early romanticist *zwei-Welten Modell*?[15] In that "two-worlds" model, both universes are not parallel, but interconnected: the negation of the real world provides access to the artistic one, which in turn retroacts onto the real one. The main difference between the early romanticist vision and the Marxian one is the fact that the latter did not oppose a poetic world, seen in positive terms, to a trivial one, judged negatively. Marx is more and more attached to the reality perceived through our senses and give less and less importance to idealism.

1.4. *The First Political Economical Works: Alienation as an Emerging Concept (1844-45)*

In 1844-45, Marx wrote his first political economical works: the *Parisian Manuscripts* and the *Holy Family* (the latter together with Engels). The *Parisian Manuscripts* developed the notion of "alienated" and "estranged" work (*entäußerte, entfremdete Arbeit*), which is constituted by: 1. *The estrangement of things:* as working is not belonging to the worker's intrinsic nature, the production exercises power over him as an alien object; 2. *Self-estrangement:* the relation of the worker to his activity considered as not belonging to him, as an activity turned against him; 3. *Man's species-being:* the worker as a being alien to him, to his own body, his external nature and human aspect; 4. The *estrangement of man from man* as a consequence of the estrangement from his production, his life activity and his species-being. Marx deplores that narrow-minded relationships leading to equally narrow-minded senses are left, after the human being had improved his mastery of the five senses during a large part of the history of mankind. To put an end to that situation, different forms of communism are determined whose highest expression implicates the abolition of private property as human self-estrangement. In the *Parisian Manuscripts,* Marx emphasises a Feuerbachian critique of Hegel: The negation of the negation is conceived as a contradiction in itself, and not as a restoration of religion and theology.[16] Indeed, German idealism has been seeking a new prophet for new times, supposed to found a new religion as mankind's last and greatest work. This critique of Hegelian speculative theory is developed further in *The Holy Family or Critique of Critical Critique,* written in opposition to the group of Young Hegelian around Bruno Bauer. Contrary to their mysticism, Marx and Engels stress "the natural and human connection between the world system and world events" and the "real connection between man and nature".[17]

1.5 *From the* German Ideology: *Towards a Re-Aesthetised Communist Society (1845-)*

Althusser regarded the *German Ideology: The Theses on Feuerbach* as an "epistemological break" (*coupure épistémologique*) between the "ideological" period of the Early Works and the "scientific" period after 1845.[18] Furthermore, the *German Ideology* has been canonised in the 1920s-30s as the founding text of the materialist conception of history. Surely, the periodisation and canonisation can be easily deconstructed. Nevertheless, from 1845, Marx and Engels would criticise the aesthetic visions of the Young Hegelians—including Feuerbach—and show the interdependence between, on one hand, the art and the creative spirit of the artist, on the other hand, the history of economic and political life in society. They develop less an aesthetics than an analysis and critique of capitalism as a social system. For both authors, art and creativity are called upon to play a major role in the perspective of a new re-aesthetised communist society in a time of disalienation.

In the ideal society, everybody is engaged in various day-to-day activities, including the arts. There is no more division of labour, even between artists and non-artists: "In a communist society there are no painters but only people who engage in painting among other activities".[19] As long as this utopia cannot be achieved, the economic structure of society may not be isolated from artistic production: hence the need for a mediation between base and superstructure. Marx posed this problem in 1859 in the preface to *A Contribution to the Critique of Political Economy*:

> In the social production of their life, humans enter into definite, indispensable relations that are independent of their will, relations of production which correspond to a definite stage of development of their material productive forces. The sum of these relations of production constitutes the economic structure of society, the real base, on which rises a legal and political superstructure and to which correspond definite forms of social consciousness. The mode of production of material life conditions the social, political and intellectual life process in general. It is not the consciousness of humans that determines their being, but on the contrary, their social being that determines their consciousness.[20]

As shown by Terry Eagleton, "each element of a society's superstructure—art, law, politics, religion—has its own tempo of development, its own internal evolution, which is not reducible to a mere expression of the class struggle or the state of the economy".[21] For Marx, the ancient Greeks were able to produce high art "not *in spite of* but *because of* the undeveloped state of their society".[22] Because of the capitalistic division of labour, the harmony or 'measure' *(Maβ)* between human beings and Nature is broken. That harmony was possible in ancient Greece, not yet affected by the bourgeois consumer society.

Marx and Engels also gave examples of pre-capitalist societies, among others the guilds' organisations in the Middle Ages, and the village community in India. In European medieval towns, individual guilds are unaffected by a higher division of labour. Every workman had to master a whole round of tasks and be able to make all that was to be made with his tools. He was absorbed in his work and capable of rising to a "narrow artistic sense" (*bornierter Kunstsinn*).[23] Marx wrote extensively on India, in particular in his articles for the *New York Daily Tribune* in the years 1853-58. He examines the basic mechanics of pre-colonial India, criticises the British rule and its consequences—he shows in particular how British actions had been undertaken with the aim of benefiting British capitalists, and analyses the course of India's development.

But the most significant for our purpose is Marx's vision, influenced by Hegel, of the presumed "idyllic" Indian village community as a pre-capitalist immutable form of organisation. In the *Capital*, he stresses the prevalence of "possession in common of the land" and the mode of production able to sustain a "natural economy" through the union of handicrafts and agriculture. Only the surplus becomes a commodity when it circulates outside the village.[24]

Marx and Engels were looking for societies which are distant in time (Antiquity, Middle Ages) and space (India and other Asian countries), with a pre-capitalist mode of production. But for them, these essentialised visions are neither the reflection of a Golden Age nostalgia nor the dream of an elsewhere. They consider, in different steps, the way to break away capitalism, pursuing the ideal vision of communist society.

2. Véquaud's Aesthetics and its Similarities with Marx's Ideas

2.1. *Véquaud, an Agent of the Counterculture*

Véquaud was not politically committed, but his anti-institutional temperament matched the mood of the counterculture. In a letter to his friend Arland, then the director of the journal *NRF* and a recognised and influential writer in France, Véquaud wonders: "Do you know that I am a hippie? Some French people, have referred to me as such: 'Yes, the French hippie with a beard!' But what is a hippie?"[25]

Some groups were called hippies as early as 1964 in San Francisco. Living on the margins of the dominant way of life, they refuse work as it is imposed, practice non-violence, free love and spontaneous creation. They dream of being "on the road" rather than "on the job". They built a counter-culture, a concept formed in 1969 by Theodor Roszak.[26] This notion encompasses their anti-establishment dimension, be it political, social or "existential", counter to the "bourgeois" ideals. Some of them, in the wake of their literary precursors of the Beat

Generation, among them Ginsberg or Burroughs, pursue a quest for holistic experience.[27] During the 1960s, groups like hippies or *Kommune 1* saw cultural and art freedom as the key to political liberation, and infused cultural space with political meaning.[28] For many of them, challenging cultural norms was a means to confront social and economic inequities.

*2.2. **Counterculture and "Heterodox" Marxisms***

Counterculture had been fed by the neo-Marxism developed by the Frankfurt School in the intellectual and artistic world since the 1920s. During the 1960s, the language of protest drew its ideological references not mainly from the "orthodox" Marxist-Leninist tradition, but essentially from "heterodox" Marxisms: Frankfurt School, critical thought, New Left, (neo)-anarchism, (politically committed) surrealism, Council communism, and situationism.[29]

At that time, Marx's early writings as well as psychoanalysis, existentialism, feminism, and anti-colonialism contribute to develop a radical critique of alienation felt by individuals in everyday life, recreation and family, but also a fulfilment of human's essence to be most in conformity with nature. Marcuse and Lefebvre are bound by the daily revolution, thought respectively as counter-culture and revolutionary festival. "Alienation", as the word of the moment or *mot-moment*,[30] embodied the prevailing Freudo-Marxism in the 1960s. With this critical thought, a transformation in cultural realms is expected through oppositional subcultures,[31] preceding social and political changes. Alternative lifestyles aim at redistributing leadership.

These critical perspectives had never been central for theoretical debates among institutionalised Marxism. Within this context, the critique of exploitation is re-centred on the one of alienation in the capitalist world, which appeals to the liberation of anyone's creativity.[32] So, everybody becomes an artist to a higher stage, that is to say producer-consumer of a "total cultural creation".[33] Generalised creativity can be understood as the "essential weapon of the revolutionary movement".[34] The utopia of generalised creativity follows Marx's critique of the social division of labour and its hierarchies of legitimacy.

2.3. *Véquaud's Indian Enchantment Through the Prism of the Counterculture*

For a brief moment in 1968, a "third way" seemed to have been a possibility, a new orientation beyond the Cold War and its Western and Eastern blocs, transcending capitalism and communism, encompassing the non-Western world.[35] The theoretical writings about the critical thought in the 1960s imply a worldwide re-mapping: the "epicentre of the global politics"[36] was located in South East Asia, Africa and Latin America, rather than in the Western world, situated on the periphery. The pair South/North tends to replace that of East/West. In the course of this re-mapping, India personifies a specific counter dimension.

The revolutionary spirit no longer resided in the proletariat, but in some "new working class",[37] the young intelligentsia and the social or gender fringe groups. This spirit was spreading among non-Western peoples and at the margins of Western society. Within this context, the desire to remove oneself from society—Timothy Leary's "turning on, tuning in, and dropping out"[38]—appears to spread predominantly in Western countercultural movements, when the battle for representation and inclusion may be less crucially at stake. Nevertheless, the 1960s' Indophilia as a fully-fledged component of counterculture sounded to be relegated to the fringes; it may be ascribable to intrinsic aspects, probably presumed to conflict with neo-Marxist positions as the search for spiritual awakening, the quest of holistic experience involving "extraordinary" perceptions, previously evoked.[39] Véquaud also developed a neo-tantric interpretation of Mithila paintings, in line with the hippie craze for oriental esotericism. His *Flower Power* tantric version of Mithila paintings, extols the body and hedonism, presumed to allow to approach an essential gendered unity expressing

Living Life.[40] As underlined by Hugh Urban, neo-tantrism arose in Western popular culture and the hippie movement in the form of a cult of ecstasy, presumed to involve higher consciousness and tantrism.[41]

2.4. *Véquaud's Early Writings: Traces of Counter-Cultural Romantic Revolt*

From his first writings, Véquaud followed on the heels of anti-bourgeois Romanticism and critical thought:

- *The extolling of emotions and body*: The hippie movement called into question the self-control required to maintain one's rank or place, such as the body *hexis*. Emotions are liberated from the social constraints of daily-life lived as alienation. Here, the body signifies the rejection of dominant norms and upper-class reserve.[42] For example, in *Le voyage en écriture*, a forced hairdressing session is felt as a traumatic, symbolic amputation.[43] An anti-conformist body *hexis* based on natural body postures is extolled. Later, his travel books on India are characterised by a "creative bubbling"[44] stemming from a cult of pleasure and a hedonistic way of life. Exalted emotions, linked to experiences of transgression, and the questioning of social points of reference leads to a feeling that anything is possible. The feeling of festive (party) liberation and freedom are associated with a spiritual register. In 1974, the initiation given by the Dalai Lama was described as "one of the most extraordinary parties which you could see in life".[45] These literary fantasies entail colourful sensorial descriptions, allowing to open the "field of the possibilities" (*champ des possibles*).[46] The prevalence of affects matches with romantic hippie values, in opposition with cold and abstract knowledge, identified as stemming from colonisation as an antidote to romance and imagination.
- *The critique of the values of the bourgeoisie*: Véquaud refused the social finiteness and the bourgeois mandate of remunerated work and family. In *Le Voyage en écriture*,

life is represented as a train from which we must jump in order to escape from despondency,[47] reminding Timothy Leary. Véquaud questioned also the function of education, which socialised children to accept hierarchy, in particular in a provocative article entitled: "The parents don't love their children, the proof is that they put them in school".[48] This rejection of educational connections leads him to give up teaching and to invest in the writing that he considered as a vocation, after being awarded in 1967 by the Félix Fénéon literary price. Thus, Véquaud experienced a broke and happy hippie bohemia.

- *The praise of bohemia*: If Véquaud was able to accumulate cultural and artistic capital, his economic one remained very fragile. But he defied the petty bourgeois way of life, from which he originated, to seize the liberality of manners, presumed associated with the aristocracy and the upper-class, while experiencing precariousness. So, Véquaud's semi-autobiographical writings revived a myth of bohemia, inseparable from a vocational art definition, whose singularity regime reinforces the figure of the marginal genius. He evolved in a Bourdieusian "economic world turned upside down",[49] depending on different modalities:
    - *Regarding the means for subsistence*: He managed situations which he presumed to be temporary, without too much concern for saving money;
    - *Concerning the autonomy of the field of artistic creation*, the narrator of his novels aspire to a freedom auspicious to creation. In *Le Voyage en écriture*, he scoffs at a dreary routine and enjoins to drop out: "Open your head, wash well your memory, (...) this story is not yours. Go through, go through".[50]
    - Finally, as for posterity postponed, *Yves Véquaud strove for glory and not for gain*, contrary to the bourgeois artist who expects success, in particular a financial one, and immediate notoriety.

Marx and Véquaud wished at first to make writing their vocation. Both appropriated common themes of early Romanticism which are also those of counterculture: the exaltation of emotions, the critique of philistines or bourgeoisie, the praise of bohemia or the cursed artist at the margins of the society. The common denominator between both authors can be found in the notion of romanticism in the broader meaning of the sense forged by Löwy and Sayre.[51] They define romanticism not only as a literary trend but more widely as an anti-establishment *Weltanschauung* against rationalization and commodification of human relationships. This opposition to the capitalist modernity aspires to re-enchant the world, beyond egotistical calculation, machinery of rationalism and utilitarian approach to the environment. Thus emerges a religious philosophy of nature, praising in particular the return to a notion of organic unity.

2.5. *Véquaud's Communitarian Maithil Village Utopia*

Started in 1969, his hippy trail took him to India, Nepal and Ceylon (just before the creation of Sri Lanka). He discovered Mithila paintings in New Delhi and went to Mithila several times to meet village painters. Véquaud expressed a canonical form of the counter-culture: the back-to-the-land-movement in communitarian utopias within the Maithil village. His fantasy model shares the suspension of dominant norms like *phalansterie,* monachisms or communes, involving widened households, collective care of children, and egalitarian rotation of domestic tasks. Gender, patriarchy, and family are redefined. He notes that men often do nothing else than keeping their lastborns on the knees.[52] In the West, "one can count on the fingers of one hand the women painters who shine through their art. Here, (...) two hundred, three hundred women make marvels".[53] According to him, in India, "the example is not rare of societies where women are freer and more powerful than in ours".[54] These projective presumptions, putting forward a phantasmagorical experience of gender resocialisation, are reiterated in his writings. Here Mithila paintings contribute to "undoing gender",[55] emphasising the impact of the feminist cause. This village utopia serves his quest of alternative prophecies.

It renews an epitomised unchanging tradition opposed to mass and technocratic society. The rise of the "information age" is accompanied by nostalgia for older ways of making things. As the romantic critics of the Victorian age praised Indian craftsmanship, Véquaud attributes the perfection of Maithil art to a timeless village. Folk art is misunderstood as homogeneous, stable and rural. He champions a return to a pre-industrial, holistic community. He urges people to leave towns as Madhubani to find hamlets where the Maithil civilisation stays alive. From his standpoint, the preserved culture of Mithila embodies the culture of India. His utopia expresses a romantic nostalgia for the *Heimat* embodied in an elsewhere, through which arise the *Sehnsucht* of a lost Eden. He attempts to re-enchant the world. Which he does by heroizing the women painters.

Yves Véquaud emphasises in his writings a revealing interpretation of the icons of his utopian counter-society. The Maithil women painters are presented as prophetic figures of legend, between holiness and genius. From his standpoint, "to paint better than her neighbour is to be devout, as it were to become a priestess". The artistic success of painters involves both the personalisation of means as well as the depersonalisation of the ends of the success, namely the creation of objects crystallising values recognised beyond the author. It was traditionally reserved for heroes and saints. This literary fantasy bears witness to a picturesque vision of India within an orientalising episteme. Véquaud praises a sort of Maithil Republic of Arts, through a pastoral myth and art religion, prevalent during the first Romanticism. His narratives reflect a male Western style for representing the painters. They bore less relation to Maithil painters than to a crisis (in Western) self-representation.

There are many similarities between Marx's and Véquaud's visions of the Indian village: the idyllic and timeless character, the pre-industrial or pre-capitalist holistic community based on the union of arts/handicrafts and agriculture. If counterculture tends to free individuals from collectivity, the holistic model of the Indian village marks a return to Marx's notion of organic unity. Besides, Indophilia prevails at Marx's and Véquaud's time. Marx was living during Raymond Schwab's "Oriental Renaissance". Reading the first published translations of Sanskrit, artists and intellectuals thought then to discover an echo of humanity's origins, nearest of an harmonious nature and the divine. The Indophilia of the 1960s underlines a similar cultural movement of romantic contestation, associated to a second "oriental renaissance", as underlined by Raphaël Rousseleau.[56] At last, these two visions of the Indian community matches with Löwy's and Sayre's category of "revolutionary and/or utopian romanticism". The difference between both is that Véquaud's literary fantasy reveals more the nostalgia of an enchanted elsewhere, while Marx renewed pre-capitalist models—as the Indian village—in order to lay the groundwork for the communist society of the future.

For the young Marx and Véquaud, freedom and especially artistic freedom is crucial. In this sense, socialist realism may be considered as the negation of the aesthetics of the Early Marx. On the other hand, countercultural orientalism as represented by Véquaud can be seen on a more obvious way as heterodox Marxisms as the negation of socialist realism. So we are tempted to say that Véquaud's vision is the "negation of the negation" of the ideas of the Early Marx. One more reason to explain the similarity of both, following respectively a *Zeitgeist* characterised by romanticism and Indophilia.

NOTES

1. Among others: Yves Véquaud, *L'art du Mithila* (Paris: Les Presses de la Connaissance, 1976); *Die Kunst von Mithila*, trans. Cornelia Pechota and Hilde Weber (Genève: Weber, 1977); *The Art of Mithila. Ceremonial Paintings from an Ancient Kingdom*, trans. George Robinson (London: Thames and Hudson, 1977);

The Women Painters of Mithila (New York: Thames and Hudson, 1977). Even though they are controversial, the writings mark a *Flower Power* turn, emphasising a *kairos* in the international reception of Mithila paintings. But the posterity of these few works, which neglects the remainder of his work, is simplistic. Véquaud published novels, stories, and essays such as *Le monsieur imaginaire* (Paris: Éditions du Seuil, 1961), *Le petit livre avalé* (Paris: Gallimard, 1966), *Le voyage en écriture* (Paris: Gallimard, 1966), *Monarque* (Paris: Gallimard, 1967), or the exhibition catalogue *Mithila: Les femmes, leurs peintures et la faveur des dieux* (Paris: musée des arts décoratifs, and Gap: Musée départemental de Gap, 1977). He edited Victor Hugo's *La Légende des siècles* (Paris: la Différence, 1989) and translated poems of Federico Garcia Lorca, in *La désillusion du monde: choix de poèmes* (Paris: la Différence, 1989). To this might be added the movie *Mithila*, a "docu-fiction" directed by Ludovic Segarra, Georges Luneau, and Yves Véquaud (1974, Çapital Films, production. Broadcasting: LS Productions, ORTF. Paris, Bry-sur-Marne: INA).

2. Frank Biewer, "Karl Marx (1818-1883) und Friedrich Engels (1820-1895)," in *Klassiker der Soziologie der Künste: Prominente und bedeutende Ansätze*, ed. Christian Steuerwald (Wiesbaden: Springer Fachmedien, 2017), 25-27.
3. Biewer, 25.
4. William M. Johnston, "Karl Marx's Verse of 1836-1837 as a Foreshadowing of His Early Philosophy," *Journal of the History of Ideas* 28, No. 2 (April- June 1967), 264.
5. Johnston, 267.
6. Letter to his father, November 10, 1837, Karl Marx, and Friedrich Engels, *Werke* (Berlin: Dietz Verlag, 1968), 40: 3-10.
7. Karl Marx, "Differenz der demokritischen und epikureischen Naturphilosophie nebst einem Anhange", PhD diss., Universität Jena, 1841. In Marx/Engels, *Werke* (Berlin: Dietz Verlag, 1968), 40: 257-373.
8. Mikhail Lifshitz. *The Philosophy of Art of Karl Marx*, trans. Ralph B. Winn (London: Pluto Press, 1976), 24.
9. "Über christliche Kunst" and "Über Religion und Kunst mit besonderer Beziehung auf christliche Kunst", cf. Frank Biewer, "Karl Marx (1818-1883) und Friedrich Engels (1820-1895)." In *Klassiker der Soziologie der Künste: Prominente und bedeutende Ansätze*, ed. Christian Steuerwald (Wiesbaden: Springer Fachmedien, 2017), 21-22.

10. Margaret A. Rose, *Marx's Lost Aesthetic. Karl Marx and the Visual Arts* (Cambridge: Cambridge University Press, 1984), 83.
11. Anil Bhatti, "Some Reflections on Marxism and an Aesthetic of Resistance. An Essay," *Interpreting the World to Change it. Essays for Parbhat Patnaik*, ed. Chandrasekhar and Jayati Ghosh (New Delhi: Tulika Books, 2017), 238.
12. Hans P. Thurn, *Kritik der marxistischen Kunsttheorie* (Stuttgart: Ferdinand Enke Verlag, 1976), 17. See also the title of the first part of Biewer, 21: "Eine nicht geschriebene Ästhetik".
13. Lifshitz, 32-39.
14. "Debatten über Preßfreiheit und Publikation der Landständischen Verhandlungen," in Karl Marx, and Friedrich Engels, *Werke* (Berlin: Dietz Verlag, 1976), 1: 28-77.
15. Hans Heinrich Eggebrecht, *Musik im Abendland: Prozesse und Stationen vom Mittelalter bis zur Gegenwart* (München: Piper, 1996), 595.
16. Karl Marx, and Friedrich Engels, *Werke* (Berlin: Dietz Verlag, 1968), 40: 465-588.
17. Friedrich Engels, and Karl Marx, *Die heilige Familie, oder Kritik der kritischen Kritik: Gegen Bruno Bauer & Consorten* (Frankfurt/M.: Literarische Anstalt [J. Rütten], 1848), 266: "Die kritische Kritik, welche der ‚romantischen Kunst' das ‚Dogma der Einheit' zum Vorwurf macht, setzt, um ein ‚wahrhaft einiges Ganze', um eine ‚wirkliche Einheit' zu erhalten, an die Stelle des natürlichen und menschlichen Zusammenhangs zwischen Weltzustand und Weltbegebenheit, einen phantastischen Zusammenhang, ein mystisches Subjekt-Objekt, wie Hegel an die Stelle des wirklichen Zusammenhangs von Mensch und Natur ein absolutes Subjekt-Objekt, das die ganze Natur und die ganze Menschheit auf einmal ist, den absoluten Geist setzt".
18. Louis Althusser, *Pour Marx* (Paris: Éditions La Découverte, 1965).
19. Karl Marx, and Friedrich Engels, *Werke* (Berlin: Dietz Verlag, 1978), 3: 379: "Bei einer kommunistischen Organisation der Gesellschaft fällt jedenfalls fort die Subsumtion des Künstlers unter die lokale und nationale Borniertheit, die rein aus der Teilung der Arbeit hervorgeht, und die Subsumtion des Individuums unter diese bestimmte Kunst, so daß es ausschließlich Maler, Bildhauer usw. ist und schon der Name die Borniertheit seiner geschäftlichen Entwicklung und seine Abhängigkeit von der Teilung der Arbeit hinlänglich ausdrückt. In einer kommunistischen Gesellschaft gibt es keine Maler, sondern höchstens Menschen, die unter

Anderm auch malen".

20. Ibid., 13: 8-9: „In der gesellschaftlichen Produktion ihres Lebens gehen die Menschen bestimmte, notwendige, von ihrem Willen unabhängige Verhältnisse ein, Produktionsverhältnisse, die einer bestimmten Entwicklungsstufe ihrer materiellen Produktivkräfte entsprechen. Die Gesamtheit dieser Produktionsverhältnisse bildet die ökonomische Struktur der Gesellschaft, die reale Basis, worauf sich ein juristischer und politischer Überbau erhebt, und welcher bestimmte gesellschaftliche Bewußtseinsformen entsprechen. Die Produktionsweise des materiellen Lebens bedingt den sozialen, politischen und geistigen Lebensprozeß überhaupt. Es ist nicht das Bewußtsein der Menschen, das ihr Sein, sondern umgekehrt ihr gesellschaftliches Sein, das ihr Bewußtsein bestimmt".
21. Terry Eagleton, *Marxism and Literary Criticism* (London: Methuen & Co., 1976), 13.
22. Eagleton, 11.
23. *Die deutsche Ideologie*, in Karl Marx, and Friedrich Engels, *Werke* (Berlin: Dietz Verlag, 1978), 3:52.
24. Ibid., 23:378.
25. Véquaud's letter to Arland, March 9, 1971: "Savez-vous que je suis hippie ? Des Français qui ne savaient pas mon nom m'ont désigné ainsi : 'Mais si, le hippie français avec la barbe!' Qu'est-ce qu'un hippie ?".
26. Theodore Roszak, *The Making of a Counter Culture: Reflections on the Technocratic Society and its Youthful Opposition* (Garden City: Doubleday & Co, 1969).
27. Raphaël Rousseleau, "Introduction: les années 60 comme seconde renaissance orientale?", international conference *Counter-Culture in Indian Arts: Neo Tantric Painting, Literature, Music & Dance in the 1960s-80s* [coordinators: Tiziana Leucci and Raphaël Rousseleau], Paris, Musée du Quai Branly, May 28, 2015.
28. Samantha Christiansen, and Zachary A. Scarlett, *The Third World in the Global 1960s* (New York and Oxford: Berghahn Books, 2013), 1.
29. Michel Trebitsch, "Voyages autour de la Révolution—Les circulations de la pensée critique—de 1956 à 1968" in *Les années 68: Le temps de la contestation*, ed. Geneviève Dreyfus-Armand, Robert Frank, Marie-Françoise Lévy, Michelle Zancarini-Fournel, with the collaboration of Maryvonne Le Puloch (Paris: Editions Complexe, 2008), 69-89.

30. Pierre Nora, *Les idées en France*, quoted by Michel Trebitsch, "Voyages autour de la Révolution: Les circulations de la pensée critique de 1956 à 1968," in *Les années 68: Le temps de la contestation*, ed. Geneviève Dreyfus-Armand et al. (Paris: Editions Complexe, 2008), 86.
31. Carole Fink, Philip Gassert, and Detlef Junker, *1968: The World Transformed* (Washington: German Historical Institute and Cambridge University Press, 1998), 25.
32. The situationist Raoul Vaneigem claimed in 1967 that "creativity is the best-shared thing in the world" ("La créativité est la chose du monde la mieux partagée"), cf. Raoul Vaneigem, *Traité de savoir-vivre à l'usage des jeunes générations* (Paris: Gallimard, 1992), 253.
33. Tom McDonough, *Guy Debord and the Situationist International: Texts and Documents* (Cambridge MA: The MIT Press, 2002), 299.
34. This is the case, within the 1968's context in France, for some anti-establishment collectives as in particular the 22 March movement and numerous Action Committees. "La contre-révolution est une science qui s'apprend", *Tribune of March 22*, June 5, 1968, reproduced in Alain Schnapp, and Pierre Vidal-Naquet, *Journal de la Commune étudiante* (Paris: Seuil, 1968), 511-512.
35. Carole Fink, Philip Gassert, and Detlef Junker, *1968: The World Transformed* (Washington: German Historical Institute and Cambridge University Press, 1998), 27.
36. Henning Marmulla, "Rethinking the Writer's Role: Enzensberger and Cuba—or a Story of Self-Censorship", in *A Revolution of Perception? Consequences and Echoes of 1968*, ed. Ingrid Gilcher-Holtey, (New York/Oxford: Berghahn, 2014), 17.
37. Carole Fink, Philip Gassert, and Detlef Junker, *1968: The World Transformed* (Washington: German Historical Institute and Cambridge University Press, 1998), 24.
38. Timothy Leary quoted by Samantha Christiansen, and Zachary A. Scarlett, *The Third World in the Global 1960s* (New York and Oxford: Berghahn Books, 2013), 9, and Timothy Leary, *Turn On, Tune In, Drop Out* (Oakland: Ronin Publishing Inc., 1965).
39. For instance, as soon as 1958, the Situationist International condemned in radical terms the Beat movement and its literary precursors of the Flower Power Indophilia by asserting: "l'odeur d'œufs pourris que répand l'idée de Dieu enveloppe les crétins mystiques de la beat generation", in "Le Bruit et la Fureur", *Internationale Situationniste*, no 1 (June 1958), 4, quoted by Anna Trespeuch-Berthelot, "L'interface situationniste et ses

paradoxes," in *Les "années 68": circulations révolutionnaires*, ed. Ludivine Bantigny, Boris Gobille, and Eugénia Palieraki. Rennes: Presses Universitaires de Rennes, 2017, 161-182.

40. Yves Véquaud, *L'art du Mithila* (Paris: Les Presses de la Connaissance, 1976), 16.
41. Hugh Urban, "The Power of the Impure: Transgression, Violence and Secrecy in Bengali Sakta Tantra and Modern Western Magic", *Numen* No. 50 (2003), 223.
42. Julie Pagis, *Mai 68, un pavé dans leur histoire: Événements et socialisation politique* (Paris: Presses de Sciences Po, 2014), 108.
43. Yves Véquaud, *Le voyage en écriture* (Paris: Gallimard, 1966), 67-68: "Les ciseaux cliquettent. Leur nickel glacé donne la chair de poule. (...) Mais aussitôt vous sentez les mâchoires qui broutent, les incisives qui rasent, remontant le long de votre peau, mouton, mouton aux dents serrées qui vous épile.(...)Vous baissez la tête car les glaces sont agressives et vous lancent à la face votre haut en forme d'œuf (...)".
44. Pagis, 109.
45. Yves Véquaud, "Lettre de Bodh Gaya: Quand le Dalaï Lama donne une initiation," *Le Monde*, May 12-13, 1974, 12: "l'une des fêtes les plus extraordinaires qui se puissent voir dans la vie".
46. Pagis, 110.
47. Yves Véquaud, *Le voyage en écriture* (Paris: Gallimard, 1966), 15-16: "Rien n'est définitif encore. On pourrait se sauver. (…). On hésite. (…) C'est trop tard. On remonte déjà (…). Il y a un moment précis, où le train (…) hésite avant de gravir la pente (…). Peut-être avez-vous été sensible à ce temps mort? (…). La prochaine fois, il me sauvera. Je sauterai".
48. Yves Véquaud, "Les parents n'aiment pas leurs enfants, la preuve en est qu'ils les mettent à l'école", *Le Monde* (February 1980).
49. Pierre Bourdieu, *Les Règles de l'art—Genèse et Structure du champ littéraire* (Paris: Éditions du Seuil, 1992); Nathalie Heinich, *Être artiste: les transformations du statut des peintres et des sculpteurs* (Paris: Klincksieck, 1996).
50. Véquaud, *Le voyage en écriture*, 159-60: "Ouvrez votre tête, lavez bien votre mémoire, (…) laissez-la s'apaiser au grand vent. (…). Cette histoire n'est pas la vôtre. (…). Passez, passez".
51. Michaël Löwy, and Robert Sayre, *Révolte et mélancolie: Le romantisme à contre-courant de la modernité* (Paris: Payot, 1992).
52. Yves Véquaud, "The Women-Artists of Mithila," *Atlas*, No. 85 (July 1973), 88: "les hommes ne font souvent rien, si ce n'est

garder leurs derniers-nés sur les genoux."

53. Ibid., 85: "En Occident, on peut compter sur les doigts d'une main les femmes peintres qui brillèrent par leur art. Ici, dans les deux hameaux où nous avons vécu, deux cents, trois cents femmes exécutent des merveilles."
54. Ibid., 75: "L'exemple n'est pas rare en Inde de ces sociétés où les femmes sont plus libres et plus puissantes que dans les nôtres."
55. Judith Butler, *Undoing Gender* (New York and London: Routledge, 2004).
56. Raphaël Rousseleau, "Introduction: les années 60 comme seconde renaissance orientale?", international conference *Counter-Culture in Indian Arts: Neo Tantric Painting, Literature, Music & Dance in the 1960s-80s* [coordinators: Tiziana Leucci and Raphaël Rousseleau]. Paris, Musée du Quai Branly, May 28, 2015.

BIBLIOGRAPHY

Althusser, Louis. *Pour Marx*. Paris: Éditions La Découverte, 1965.

Biewer, Frank. "Karl Marx (1818-1883) und Friedrich Engels (1820-1895)." In *Klassiker der Soziologie der Künste: Prominente und bedeutende Ansätze*, edited by Christian Steuerwald. Wiesbaden: Springer Fachmedien, 2017, 21-44.

Bourdieu, Pierre. *Les Règles de l'art—Genèse et Structure du champ littéraire*. Paris: Éditions du Seuil, 1992.

Butler, Judith. *Undoing Gender*. New York and London: Routledge, 2004.

Christiansen, Samantha, and Zachary A. Scarlett. *The Third World in the Global 1960s*. New York and Oxford: Berghahn Books, 2013.

Eagleton, Terry. *Marxism and Literary Criticism*. London: Methuen & Co., 1976.

Eggebrecht, Hans Heinrich. *Musik im Abendland: Prozesse und Stationen vom Mittelalter bis zur Gegenwart*. München: Piper, 1996.

Fink, Carole, Philip Gassert, and Detlef Junker. *1968: The World Transformed*. Washington: German Historical Institute and Cambridge University Press, 1998.

Garcia Lorca, Federico. *La désillusion du monde: choix de poèmes*. Translated by Yves Véquaud. Paris: la Différence, 1989.

Heinich, Nathalie. *Être artiste: les transformations du statut des peintres et des sculpteurs*. Paris: Klincksieck, 1996.

Hugo, Victor. *La Légende des siècles: poèmes choisis et présentés par Yves Véquaud*. Paris: la Différence, 1989.

Leary, Timothy. *Turn On, Tune In, Drop Out*. Oakland: Ronin Publishing

Inc., 1965.

Lifshitz, Mikhail. *The Philosophy of Art of Karl Marx*. Translated by Ralph B. Winn. London: Pluto Press, 1976.

Löwy, Michaël, and Robert Sayre. *Révolte et mélancolie: Le romantisme à contre-courant de la modernité*. Paris: Payot, 1992.

Marmulla, Henning. "Rethinking the Writer's Role: Enzensberger and Cuba—or a Story of Self-Censorship." In *A Revolution of Perception? Consequences and Echoes of 1968*, edited by Ingrid Gilcher-Holtey. New York and Oxford: Berghahn, 2014.

Marx, Karl, and Friedrich Engels. *Werke*. Berlin: Dietz Verlag, 1961 [Vol. 13], 1962 [Vol. 23], 1968 [Vol. 40], 1978 [Vol. 3].

McDonough, Tom, *Guy Debord and the Situationist International: Texts and Documents*. Cambridge MA: The MIT Press, 2002.

Pagis, Julie. *Mai 68, un pavé dans leur histoire: Événements et socialisation politique*. Paris: Presses de Sciences Po, 2014.

Roszak, Theodore. *The Making of a Counter Culture: Reflections on the Technocratic Society and its Youthful Opposition*, Garden City: Doubleday & Co., 1969.

Rousseleau, Raphaël. "Introduction: les années 60 comme seconde renaissance orientale?", international conference *Counter-Culture in Indian Arts: Neo Tantric Painting, Literature, Music & Dance in the 1960s-80s* [Coordinators: Tiziana Leucci and Raphaël Rousseleau]. Paris, Musée du Quai Branly, May 28, 2015.

Schnapp, Alain, and Pierre Vidal-Naquet. *Journal de la Commune étudiante*. Paris: Seuil, 1968.

Thurn, Hans P. *Kritik der marxistischen Kunsttheorie*. Stuttgart: Ferdinand Enke Verlag, 1976.

Trebitsch, Michel. "Voyages autour de la Révolution: Les circulations de la pensée critique de 1956 à 1968." In *Les années 68: Le temps de la contestation*, edited by Geneviève Dreyfus-Armand, Robert Frank, Marie-Françoise Lévy, and Michelle Zancarini-Fournel, with the collaboration of Maryvonne Le Puloch. Paris: Editions Complexe, 2008, 69-89.

Trespeuch-Berthelot, Anna. "L'interface situationniste et ses paradoxes." In *Les "années 1968": circulations révolutionnaires*, edited by Bantigny Ludivine, Boris Gobille, and Eugénia Palieraki. Rennes: Presses Universitaires de Rennes, 2017, 161-182.

Urban, Hugh. "The Power of the Impure: Transgression, Violence and Secrecy in Bengali Sakta Tantra and Modern Western Magic", *Numen* No. 50 (2003), 269-308.

Vaneigem, Raoul. *Traité de savoir-vivre à l'usage des jeunes générations*.

Paris: Gallimard, 1992.

Véquaud, Yves. *L'art du Mithila* [with photographs by Edouard Boubat]. Paris: Les Presses de la Connaissance, 1976. *Die Kunst von Mithila.* Translated by Cornelia Pechota, and Hilde Weber. Genève: Weber, 1977. *The Art of Mithila. Ceremonial Paintings from an Ancient Kingdom.* Translated by George Robinson [Preface by Ajit Mookerjee]. London: Thames and Hudson, 1977. *The Women Painters of Mithila.* [Preface by Ajit Mookerjee]. New York: Thames and Hudson, 1977.

——. *Le monsieur imaginaire.* Paris: Éditions du Seuil, 1961.

——. *Le petit livre avalé.* Paris: Gallimard, 1966.

——. "Lettre de Bodh Gaya: Quand le Dalaï Lama donne une initiation," *Le Monde,* May 12-13, 1974, 12.

——. *Le voyage en écriture.* Paris: Gallimard, 1966.

——. *Mithila: Les femmes, leurs peintures et la faveur des dieux* [exhibition catalogue]. Paris: musée des arts décoratifs, Gap: Musée départemental de Gap, 1977.

------. *Monarque.* Paris: Gallimard, 1967.

------. "The Women-Artists of Mithila," *Atlas,* No. 85 (July 1973), 70-92.

Filmography

Mithila, codirected and coproduced by Ludovic Segarra, Georges Luneau, and Yves Véquaud, assistant director: Surya Dev, 1974. Duration: 53 min 17s. Capital Films, production. Broadcasting: LS Productions, ORTF. Paris, Bry-sur-Marne: INA.

6

Sartre and Alienation
A Marxian Perspective

Kumari Sunitha V.

Jean Paul Sartre (1905-1980) is one with Parmenides and Plato in his contention that the chief problem of philosophy is the problem of 'Being'. It is mainly due to his plays, stories and novels that existentialism becomes a popular literary movement after the Second World War. Following Husserl and Heidegger, he adopts the phenomenological method and takes existentialism to its limits. He is the only existentialist who later on sees the limits of the movement he is leading and tries to term with Marxism in his later writing, though unsuccessfully. Sartre claims to have uncovered the reading of Marxism, yet he takes a diametrically opposed position with respect to the notion of alienation. He is always an existentialist, who addresses the fundamental problems of human existence: death, nothingness, freedom, bad-faith, anxiety, political commitment, the meaning of existence itself. He remains an existentialist in his Marxist phase and during his final overtly anarchist phase.

Sartre considers Man as a person in the world. He wants to understand Man in his total situation, though he does not think that Man could be interpreted completely in terms of material relations. There is, according to Sartre, a conflict between Man and the world and we cannot ignore it. We try to point out that Sartre's basic idea is Being-in-the-world, though sometimes he is more emphatic on the reality of human alienation, while at other times he tries to bring to focus the greater concern for the world. His philosophical investigations display a series of dialectical relations between man and the world. His philosophy has been a quest to situate man in the world, but he has not been quite successful as his dialectics is more of a dialectics of consciousness than of dialectic proper between Man and the world.

In *Being and Nothingness,* Sartre begins with an appreciation of the phenomenological method, which, according to him has achieved significant results in philosophical investigation. He writes, "Modern thought has realized considerable progress reducing the existent to the series of appearances which manifest. Its aim was to overcome a certain number of dualism which embarrassed philosophy and to replace them by the monism of the phenomena".[1] He not only separates existence from essence but also does not give any proper definition of existence. In his phenomenological ontology there is 'nothing' concealed behind the appearances, which embody full reality. Sartre, in his philosophy, separates freedom from necessity, subject from object and particular from universal. He says, "We can equally well reject the dualism of appearance and essence. The appearance does not hide the essence but reveals it".[2] After rejecting dualisms like potential and actual, appearance and being etc., he himself retains another main dualism, that of mind and body, which, he says, are "radically separated regions of being".[3] Whatever is positive and objective is being-in-itself.[4] And whatever is subjective and negative is called being-for-itself.[5] Sartre further says that man is a union of being-in-itself and being-for-itself, or subject and object. The concrete, he remarks, "is man within the world in that specific union of man with the world which Heidegger, for example, calls, Being-in-the-world".[6]

Sartre characterises man as a being constituted by non-being. The action of questioning (interrogation), absence (negative judgments) and destruction, as elements of the being of man, show that man's being is fundamentally the origin of nothingness. Destruction implies that a thing loses its present state. But that change can have meaning only before a witnessing consciousness. Destruction for Sartre is purely a human act because "in order for destruction to exist there must be first a relation of man to being—that is, a transcendence, and within the limits of this relation, it is necessary that man apprehends one being as destructible".[7] The act of questioning or interrogation is performed by dissociation of man from the causal series of being or the causal order of the world.[8] This is affected by 'nihiliating withdrawal'. In interrogation, we ask a question and this pre-supposes ignorance. It is a non-being. The answer to the question may be either affirmative or negative. If the answer is negative it is clear that we appear before some non-being. Sartre, thus, comes to the conclusion that "Man is the being through whom nothingness comes to the world...."[9] Whenever one raises a question, he argues, one puts oneself at a distance from the object questioned and from oneself. The answer, even the affirmation which involves negation, he calls the non-being of limitation. The 'non-being of knowing,' the possibility of 'non-being of being in the transcendent being' and 'the non-being of limitation'– this triple non-being'[10] characterises every question and the being of the one who questions. His identification of man with consciousness (immanence) and with 'nothingness' as a reality of this immanence is stated as follows: "Evidently it is necessary to find the foundation of all negation in a nihiliation which is exercised in the very heart of immanence; in desolate immanence, in the pure subjectivity of the instantaneous cogito we must discover the original act by which man is to himself his own 'nothingness'".[11] Thus, man, defined in terms of nothingness and pure subjectivity, is first detached from whatever is determinate, objective and real being. And when the basic determinations of man's objective social existence are nihilated, the subject or consciousness also becomes nothing because Sartre thinks that consciousness is consciousness of something which it is not, and the "consciousness as it is shown in the discussion on the "meaning of question, 'is a being', the nature which is to be conscious of the nothingness of its being". Or it arises "in the World as a No."[12]

What is it about man that occasions this nothingness? According to Sartre the answer is freedom. Freedom is discussed in relation to the will, in relation to facticity and finally in relation to responsibility. The will can never be the condition for freedom; it is simply the psychological manifestation of it. The will pre-supposes the foundation of an original freedom in order to be able to constitute as will. Man is free. Freedom in relation to facticity gives rise to a situation. The situation is impossible to clearly distinguish the contribution of freedom and the determinants of brute circumstance. This accounts for the paradox of freedom. There is freedom only in situation and there is situation only through freedom. Sartre delineates five structures of situation in which freedom and facticity interpenetrate each other: my place, my past, my environment, my fellowmen (the other), and my death.

In so far as freedom always interpenetrates facticity, man becomes wholly responsible for himself. To Sartre, freedom is inseparable from man. There is no difference between being of man and his being free. Sartre usually has an exaggerated view of human freedom; no doubt because of the claims in the existentialism and humanism lecture and later in *Being and Nothingness,* that "there is no determinism; we are free, we are condemned to be free".[13] Condemned because he himself is thrown into the world. Free because he is responsible for his own actions or what he does. "I am responsible for everything, in fact, except for my very responsibility, for I am not the foundation of my being."[14] His abandonment of freedom is an expression of facticity. Thus Sartre argues that since man has no determination, he is completely free and responsible for his own actions.

In Sartre's literary work, *Iron in the Soul,* Mathieu Delarue, the previously inefficient schoolteacher, acts meaningfully and decisively for the first time in his life. "Mathieu was in a hurry. He kept his eye on his man; he had plenty of time. The German army is vulnerable. He fired. The man gave a funny little jerk and fell on his stomach, throwing his arms forward like somebody learning to swim."[15] In the narrative, Mathieu's shooting of the German infantryman is a freely chosen and deliberate act for which he alone is responsible. It is a deeply significant act—metaphysically, personally and politically. Metaphysically, it is the determination of life. Personally, it is Mathieu's recognition of his freedom; "for years he had tried, in vain, to act,"[16] Sartre reminds us. Politically, it is the commitment to resist the forces of right-wing totalitarianism. "Just time enough to fire at the smart officer, at all the Beauty of the Earth, at the Street, at the Flowers, at the Gardens, at everything he had loved. Beauty dived downwards like obscene bind. But Mathieu went on firing. He fired. He was cleansed. He was all-powerful. He was free."[17]

To be man is to be conscious and to be conscious is to be nothingness and nothingness is freedom. This is what Sartre means when he says that in man existence precedes essence. The abandoned and lonely human being has a negative relation to the being-in-itself (that is, objective being), to others as well as to itself. The world is an organised instrumental complex, 'caused'[18] by man in order to realise his ends and it is always 'surpassed,'[19] because consciousness cannot be identical with a certain object, it cannot simply be. One's body is also one of the 'obstacles' which he nihiliates and surpasses so far as he is not an object. Sartre writes, "...to have a body is to be the foundation of one's own nothingness and not to be the foundation of one's being: I am my body to the extent that I am; I am not my body to the extent that I am not what I am. It is by my nihiliation that I escape it. But I do not thereby make an object of it, for what I am is what I perpetually escape. The body is necessary again as the obstacle is to be surpassed in order to be in the world; that is, the obstacle which I am to myself. In this sense it is not different from the absolute order of the world, this order which I cause to arrive in being by surpassing it toward a being to come, toward being-beyond-being. We can clearly grasp the unity of these two necessities: being-for-itself is to surpass the world and to cause there to be a world by surpassing it...."[20]

Bad-Faith (Self-Alienation)

According to Sartre Nothingness, freedom and anxiety provide the conditions, which make possible the movement of bad-faith. To him bad-faith is a form of self-deception (alienation), which in making use of freedom denies it. In lying, one hides the truth from others. But in bad-faith, one hides the truth from oneself. Bad-faith does not come from outside. In fact, a freedom founded on nothing cannot help negating itself. Sartre describes men in bad-faith to substantiate this very assumption that a freedom may be and is negated by itself without any external coercion or manipulation. "But consciousness affects itself with bad-faith."[21]

This state of man's existence arises on the basis of the unity of facticity (of limited objective presence) and transcendence.[22] Man as a facticity is what he is; he is in itself, just as any other object. But he is at the same time a transcendence, one who negates his present condition and transcends it towards what is not. So transcendence or man's free being projects itself as a thing of its own and thus nihiliates freedom. In fact, Sartre conceives man as a being, which is what it is not and which is not what it is. To put it concretely, man is a consciousness than he is a thing and not consciousness and not a thing. Because consciousness is a perpetual negation, it negates itself to be an object and negates its objectivity (facticity) to be what is not (transcendence)[23] This dualism of man's being becomes an ontological basis for bad-faith (self alienation). Let us analyse the Sartrean concept of bad-faith with his examples. First of all, we could take his example of a woman who consents to go out with an amorous suitor. She must decide but she seeks to postpone the decision. It is at this time that the bad-faith comes into play. She leaves her hand in his, but does not notice that she is doing so. She becomes 'a thing,' all intellect divorces her soul from her body and transforms her body into an object or thing into the mode of 'being in itself'. Her hand becomes a 'thing'; neither consenting nor resisting, she loses her subjectivity, her freedom and her responsibility for decision. She exists in bad-faith.[24] From this example, Sartre states that the bad-faith or alienation comes to play through decision or choice. His conception of bad-faith is one of the better-known ideas of his philosophy, but it is too often misunderstood as either a purely ethical notion or as a specific problem which he employs as a foil against Freud. The woman is deceiving herself concerning the intentions of her companion, but Sartre does not want to say that she is simply deceiving herself about him. She is deceiving herself about her own desires and intentions as well as about her own sexual nature. The woman lies to herself, she knows that she is being treated as a sexual object but will not allow herself to realise this. She knows the truth, on the one hand, but refuses to disclose it to herself on the other. Given the thesis of translucency of consciousness, which has been defended in *The Transcendence of the Ego* and *Being and Nothingness,* the nature of hiding is mysterious, to say the least. Where in consciousness is thus truth to hide if there is no content of consciousness? Furthermore, who is doing the hiding and from whom? Sartre tells us that bad-faith is a pre-reflective phenomenon. (As evidenced that a person in bad-faith need not and usually does not know that he is in bad-faith.) Thus there is no self to 'possess the truth' and no self to hide the truth.

Conversely, Sartre has cited the bad-faith of the woman who denies her sexuality. He distinguishes two kinds of people in bad faith. One kind, he calls, 'cowards'. They hide from their freedom in a facade of solemnity or with deterministic excuses. Those who deny not only their freedom but that of others, Sartre calls, swine. In *Nausea,* for example, Roquentin concludes his tour of the portraits of the bourgeois officials in the city museum with the comment, "You bastards". They felt that they had the natural or God-given right to exist and to occupy their social location of wealth and privilege and suppress the freedom of others. In fact, it may be plausibly argued that there is not a single character in his works that escapes bad-faith. Garcin of *No Exit* has been accused of bad-faith for his refusal to face his own cowardice; Mathieu and Boris of *The Age of Reason* reject their freedom in spite of their continuous insistence that they are free men; nearly all of Sartre's women (Inez and Estelle of *No Exit*, Electra of the *Flies*, Marcelle of *The Age of Reason*, Lizzie in *The Respectful Prostitute*, Jessica of *Dirty Hands*) are in bad-faith by virtue of their sexuality.

Let us see how Sartre exemplifies bad-faith with a waiter in the café, "...his movement is quick and forward, a little too precise, a little too rapid. He comes toward the patrons with a step a little too quick. He bends forward a little too eagerly; his voice, his eyes express an interest a little too solicitous for the order of the customer. Finally there he returns, trying to imitate in his walk the inflexible stiffness of some kind of automaton while carrying his tray with the recklessness of a tightrope-walker by putting it in a perpetually unstable, broken equilibrium, which he perpetually re-establishes by a light movement of the arm and hand. All his behaviour seems to us a game. He applies himself to chaining his movements as if they were mechanisms, the one regulating the other; his gestures and even his voice seem to be mechanisms; he gives himself the quickness and pitiless rapidity of things."[25] If the waiter adopts such a regulated behaviour pattern, is it simply a matter of internal negation of consciousness, or are there external norms of that society, which condition him to be an automaton? Of course, Sartre does not deny the fact of social conditioning,[26] but even then asserts that the man in question is playing at being a waiter. As if there is an abstract image of a waiter posited beyond the being of the waiter in question and he is simply trying to represent it. He says, "But if I represent myself as him, I am not he; I am separated from him as the object from the subject, separated by nothing, but this nothing separates me from him, I cannot be he I can only play at being him, that is imagine to myself that I am he.... What I attempt to realise is being-in-itself of the café-waiter, as if it were not just in my power to confer *their* values and *their* urgency upon my duties and the rights of my position, as if it were not my free choice to get up at each morning at five o' clock or to remain in bed, even though it meant getting fired."[27] Thus every state of bad-faith (self-alienation) slavery becomes a free choice of one who is subject to this state. This is how in Sartre's existentialist system being-for-itself becomes being-in-itself, "subject becomes object and nothing becomes everything".[28]

Being -for-Others: Look as Alienation

The distinction between man and world though mutually exclusive, is not collectively exhaustive. There is a third manner of being called being-for-others. One's relationship with Others (society) is manifested through 'look'.[29] The other looking at me as well as me looking at the other apprehend each other as an object and a subject. Subject is freedom but when the other looks or is looked at the freedom is suddenly objectified, subject becomes an object. Sartre invites us to imagine one listening through a door and looking through a keyhole, suddenly one sees a footstep behind; one will be under the gaze of the other. One feels shame. Shame, however, is shame before another. "I am ashamed of myself as I appear to the other," because the Other puts me in the position of an 'object"[30] His own body is not an object for him. It is object from the perspective of another, and another's body is an object from his perspective. In this situation it is not a psychological option for him to sincerely doubt that other people exist or have minds. Under the attempts of being-for-others, Sartre attempts a refutation of solipsism, offers a phenomenology of the body and a rather pessimistic ontology of human relations. Sartre's refutation is based on human relations. Paradigmatically, shame. Being-for-others is, therefore, a kind of bad-faith. In fact, what is realised by the presence of the other is that I am an object possessing a 'definite nature' beyond me and determined by another. This is what Sartre calls an 'original fall'. It is a solidification and alienation of my own possibilities. The other as a look is only that–my transcendence transcended. Of course I am still my possibilities in the mode of non-thetic consciousness of these possibilities. But at the same time, the look alienates them from me.[31] It is Sartre's view that there is no human encounter where one party does not psychologically dominate the other: one is master and one is slave.

Consciously or not, the phenomenology of human relations that Sartre offers essentially operates within the parameters of Hegel's master and slave dialectic in the 1807 *Phenomenology of the Spirit*.[32] There self-conscious beings are depicted as mutually constituting through a struggle for recognition—a power struggle where one party may bestow or withhold psychological identity from another, a complex dialectic where the freedom of one is sought in the control of the other.

Sartre concludes his understanding of human relations as follows: "As a temporal spatial object in the world, as an essential structure of a temporal spatial situation in the world, I offer myself to the other's appraisal. This also apprehend by the pure exercise of the cogito. To be looked at is to apprehend one-self as the unknown object of unknowable appraisals—in particular, of value judgments. But at the same time that in shame or pride I recognize the justice of these appraisals, I do not cease to take them for what they are—a free surpassing of the given toward possibilities. A judgment is the transcendental act of a free being. Thus being-seen constitutes me as a defenseless being for a freedom, which is not my freedom. It is in this sense that we can consider ourselves as 'slaves' in so far as we appear to the other. But this slavery is not historical result—capable of being surmounted—of a life in the abstract form of consciousness. I am a slave to the degree that my being is dependent at the centre of a freedom which is not mine and which is the very condition of my being. In so far as I am the object of values, which come to qualify me without my being able to act upon these qualifications or even to know it I am enslaved. By the same token in so far as I am the instrument of possibilities, which are not my possibilities, whose pure presence beyond my being I cannot even glimpse, and which deny my transcendence in order to constitute me as a means to ends of which I am ignorant—I am in danger.

This danger is not an accident, but the permanent structure of being-for-others."[33]

Conflict as Perverse Form of Human Alienation

Sartre says that his descriptions of human relations have to be understood within the perspective of conflict. Conflict is ultimately a conflict over freedom. The relation between men thus projected is one of 'possession,'[34] possession of freedom itself by the other and the meaning of such a relationship is conflict.[35] In trying to define one's own essence through the exercise of free choice, he or she tries to repress the freedom of the other. Simultaneously the other is doing the same. It follows that the perverse form of bad-faith called 'being a swine' is at the root of human relations.

Why, we might object, should not conflict be overcome in love? Why should not two human beings, who perhaps care more for each other than they do for themselves, feel secure in each other's freedom and not threaten one another's psychological security? Sartre's reply is that love is conflict. Even love is desire to possess the freedom of the beloved and it also involves the 'alienation of lover'.[36] Referring to love, Sartre says, "The lover's freedom, in his very efforts to make himself beloved as an object by the other, is alienated by slipping into the body-for-others. Here, in fact, we encounter the true ideal of lover's enterprise: alienated freedom."[37] Hence, hatred is co-existent 'fundamental attitude' of being-for-others.[38] Sartre says that in both these attitudes, love and hate, we fail because neither of us can possess nor be possessed absolutely so far as everybody is a consciousness or transcendence. Man, therefore, has fallen in the circle of love and hate to "be indefinitely tossed from one to other of the two fundamental attitudes".[39] Sartre here thinks that the object of love is an in-itself and that if it becomes a subject the relation is lost. In love the object of love is both the object and the subject at the same time. Love is not just a passive relation, but an active-passive relation in which two persons are involved.

Sartre speaks of the dialectics in human relationships in

which human beings are always in conflict with one another. This is not something based on the experience of history. What Sartre says goes against the findings of psychologists that animals, including human beings, have both a self-preservative and gregarious instinct. It is not possible to explain the gregarious instinct on the basis of the self-preservative instinct. For there are many cases where man works for a social ideal while sacrificing his own gain. But we cannot deny that there are ideals of friendship and unity in which human beings recognise themselves as individuals. If all men are free, in the Sartrean sense, and each of them has a need, it is quite possible that they can freely choose an ideal that would promote social harmony. Conflicts between individuals may exist, but that is not the whole story.

It is impossible to conceive a communal relationship from this utterly negative, individualistic standpoint. According to Sartre, the consciousness of 'we' is derived from the fact that at a time more than two subjects may be objectified by a Third and in relation to the Third the former two see themselves as 'We objects,'[40] who are transformed into an object for the latter. Sartre very easily fits class-consciousness into this scheme by saying that it is defined by another class. "The oppressed class can, in fact, affirm as a We-subject at the latter's expense...."[41] In the same breath he describes the 'crowd' whose "monstrous materiality and profound reality (although only experienced) are fascinating for each of its members, each one demands to be submerged in the crowd-instrument by the look of the leader".[42] And what about the 'we'-consciousness of humanity as a whole? Sartre says that it is an empty concept, a pure indication of a possible extension of the ordinary usage of the 'us'. Each time we use the 'us' in this sense (to designate suffering humanity, sinful humanity, to determine an objectively historical meaning by considering man as an object, that is developing its potentialities) we limit ourselves to indicate a certain concrete experience to be gone in the presence of the absolute Third; that is, of God. Thus the limiting concept of humanity (as the totality of the 'us' object) and limiting-concept of God imply one another.[43]

Sartre concludes his description of collective consciousness with its supposed two modes of 'us-object' and 'we-subject' with the assertion that whereas the consciousness of the 'us-object' is a proof of his thesis of alienating and alienated relations of the second kind, the consciousness of 'we-subject' or free inter-subjectivity is a secondary and purely subjective experience *Erlibnis*.[44] And thus negating every possibility of free human (social) relationship, he transforms the 'for-itself' which is supposed to arise as a nihiliation of the being-in-itself (object) and as a freedom, into its direct opposite, into in-itself. He says, "We learned first that the for-itself was the nihiliation and the radical negation of the in-itself, at present we establish that it is also by the sole fact of meeting with the other and without any contradiction totally in itself, present in the midst of in-itself."[45] Though he calls this being-in itself of for-itself an outer aspect of the latter it seems that whatever freedom there is it is surrounded by bondage from all sides. It is more evident in his concept of the fundamental project of human existence.

In the context of inter-personal relations, we have seen that Sartre defines man's basic attitude towards others as that of possession, which is reflected in love as well as hatred, and which is the basis of perpetual conflict amongst men. Now in the context of man's fundamental project, he discovers another desire, the desire to be. He writes, "Fundamentally man is the desire to be, and the existence of this desire is not to be established by an empirical induction, it is the result of an a priori description of the for-itself, since desire is a lack and since for-itself is the being which is to itself its own lack of being."[46] The desire of the for-itself is to be in-itself, to be a positive being, just like an objective reality. But, Sartre says that neither subject nor object is an entity, which has its own foundation. Consciousness, therefore, desires to be in-itself, which has its own foundation. The for-itself desires to be in-itself-for-itself or object-subject with its own foundation. This entity, Sartre says, is God. "Thus the best way to conceive of the fundamental project of human reality is to say that man is the being whose project is to be God."[47] The fundamental desire to be, in fact, is ultimately produced by the desire to have. Sartre says that action is a 'transitional category' and what counts is "desire to be or desire to have".[48] To have the object is to be the object and the basic meaning of having object is 'appropriation of the world'.[49] This way Sartre leads to totality as being-for-itself-in-itself and again to God, which he regards as the fundamental choice of one's freedom realised in all being and having. The entity as this God is, the fundamental project of man to be God falls to pieces. Man is subject and wants to be substantive an objective subject which he cannot be because he is a being which is not. Therefore Sartre says, "... the idea of God is contradictory and we lose ourselves in vain. Man is a useless passion."[50]

Approach to Marxism

Sartre, of course, has seen the limits of the existentialist philosophy and gravitated towards Marxism in his later works. But even after accepting the Marxist interpretation of history as valid, he retains existentialist premises either in pure or veiled forms. But we can see how he views man and his estrangement, especially in his later major philosophical work, *The Critique of Dialectical Reason.*

Jean Paul Sartre provides a useful summation of the controversy surrounding proposals to integrate existentialism with Marxism. It was a major moment of modern intellectual history. He believes his approach to be a parasitical technique, a methodology which will be eventually accepted as yet another aspect of Marxism as a whole. Sartre starts with the question of dialectic, attacks on the idea of dialectic developed by Marx and Engels. He claims that the advocates of dialectic of nature imposed human idea on nature and then attempted to drive knowledge of man from the laws of nature. Sartre's alignment of existentialism with Marxism endeavours to reveal the point of insertion of individual in the particular social class. The family is considered to be the vital mediator between the class and the person, it is within this primary unit that children unknowingly don the social roles imposed upon by adults, both parents and significant others.[51] Here the individuals confronted with class values, which in the uncertain depths of childhood, are internalised as virtual absolutes.

He observes that for the majority of us, our beliefs and prejudices are virtually unsurpassable precisely because they have first have been experienced during childhood. Irrational responses and resistance to reason are artifacts of these early years, a period a class interest are interiorised as personal shackles.[52] Thus Sartre cautions that class bias should not be entirely as ascribed to the individual confrontation with the means of production as either as capitalist extraction of surplus value or proletarian victim of that process of exploitation. He claims that many attitudes and prejudices are acquired prior to leaving the family itself, i.e. each child lives the reality of the social class without the confines of the home. Sartre's expressed aim is to penetrate the Gramscian concept of "past".[53] He is intent upon locating those childhood conditionings which will enable him to discover how a individuals' actions are influenced by "not only the present determinations but also weight of his history".[54] Here Sartre proposes to classify the intersection of the history, social structure, and biography.

Unlike Marx, Sartre holds the view that the totalisation starts with individual. In the process of totalisation, individual creates different social structures such as group infusion, pledged group, structured group and sovereign group. For Sartre scarcity is the mark of our collectivism which constitutes the history.[55] Because of scarcity alienation arises between human beings. Scarcity is the setting for human in an alien mode, for the becoming counter final of the finalities orienting human praxis. "Scarcity ... the negative unity of multiplicity of men", and this unity is negative in relation to men because it is transmitted to men by matter in so far as matter is non-human.[56] Counter finality is often taken to be the expression of material resistance to the individual's own praxis. As Sartre himself expressed it, "matter alienates in itself the action which works it, not because it is itself a force nor even because it is inertia, but because its inertia allows it to absorb the labour power of others and turn it back against everyone."[57] For Sartre human practice comes to be a counter finality to the finality of free human praxis. Sartre presents a detailed description of structures created by man to overcome the obstacles of scarcity and alienation. There are three necessary conditions for counter finality according to Sartre: material disposition, becoming the inert of human praxis and seriality. Human praxis is a struggle to transform the material world. The world is also passive, or inert on which man strives in a material world to attain certain goals such as new social environment, new relations of production and new social relations. Sartre gives the example of the Chinese peasants for effectively cutting down trees for fires and other purposes and expose themselves to the disasters and floods. Inert human praxis bifurcates into contradictory condition of being both human (i.e. Active negative) and non-human (i.e. passive positivity)[58]. Thus man becomes the enemy of man (Le contra homme—man becomes anti-man) tormented by their own inventions in the world of practico-inert. Reforesting is the only way to prevent flood but it would come in the preview of serial collective. Series is a collection people who are united only by external proximity not through any ideological commitment, and it is due the scarcity of something. It is due to some exterior force of attention and has no internal structure except that of otherness. Otherness within a collective form makes the relationship between the members of the series.ie group. In this serial collective each member looses individuality and relation of identity. Because each individual is no longer their own, and each individual is doing the same thing in collective. That is, each member is committed to act as the member of the group. As Sartre puts it "passive unity— is for praxis unity as other and in the domain of other".[59] Human groups according to Sartre should be understood with reference to horizontal complexity and vertical complexity. Horizontal complexity corresponds to the social structure. It involves the specific relations of the group to the dominant social institutions. The historical dimension is accounted from the vertical complexity, which refers to the group activity surging from the past and the particular sequence by which the institutions came to be formed. The integration of these two has three phases. The first phase is one of situating a person within the social structure; this involves straightforward analysis of society. The second phase is the regressive explanation of the personal history. At this point Sartre introduces his existentialist approach in order to amplify the conventional Marxist approach. The final phase entails moving from past to the present in an attempt to grasp the current situation of the individual. Sartre claims that these threefold methods will progressively determine a biography....by examining the period by studying the biography.[60]

Sartre is presenting a concrete account of classification through the detailed analysis of specific individual. He claims that each person internalises various determinations such as the family, the relations of production, social institutions and lived experience and these interiorisations are revealed in the individual's beliefs and actions.[61] He also considers "family relationship is primary with respect to any other relationship."[62] Sartre agrees with Engels that "it is men themselves who make history, but within in a given environment which conditions them."[63] To him the individual is both a product and a producer of history.

Sartre first concerns himself with the process whereby a person moves beyond the existing situation. It is here he introduced project and praxis. He regards the project to the person's choice of one course of action from among a number of alternatives. The actions do not remain but are continuously modified in accordance with the changing circumstances. Praxis refers to the actual surpassing of the existing situation in order to realise the particular end outlined in the project itself. That leads to the formation of a new society. Therefore, the dialectical process begins with individual praxis towards totalisation, which is temporal matter. It is through the human need that the relation between man (human being) and the world occurred. It is not a social relation, but a natural one, "a quasi –human status as a passive totality"[64] (from the point of view of an organic being seeking its being in it).

Sartre fails to make a distinction between Marxist interpretation of objectification and alienation (reification) he deprived the very meaning of revolutionary theory of Marx, the overcoming of alienation, transformation of alienated human relation to genuine human relation through the transformation of mode of production and social transformation. This kind of alienation Sartre being considering here belongs to objectification as such and not identical to exploitation but it is rather the conditions of the possibility of the latter. Until and unless we confront these problems, all these conditions will threaten the finality of human praxis, our capability to obtain the end, which is the transformation of the society. Sartre's notion of project and praxis are not original, they bear a resemblance to Marxian conception of human labor. According to Marx, "A spider conducts operations which resemble those of a weaver, and a bee puts the shame many architects in the construction of her cells. But what distinguishes the worst architect from the best of bees is this: the architect raises his structure in his imagination before he erects it in reality. At the end of every labor process we get a result that already existed in the imagination of the laborer at its commencement. He not only effects a change of form in the material on which he works, but also realizes a purpose of his own".[65] In Sartre's terminology the imagined goal corresponds to the project, the actual building of the structure refers to the human praxis. What Sartre outlines is how the choice of project is also influenced by the particular history of the individual. He insists that the original childhood project will really influence his future attitudes and behaviour. It is at this point he introduces his interpretation of the Marxian concept of alienation.[66] He maintains that in the eyes of most Marxists "everything seems to happen as if men experienced their alienation and their reification first in their own work, wherein actuality each one lives first as child, in his parents work.[67] According to Sartre, people continue to live this alienation, products of their parents design; they are never fully able to overcome this early distortion of character

Nevertheless Sartre's use of alienation is problematic in this content. It is highly debatable whether his term is in fact compatible with the Marxian concept. Unfortunately Sartre himself sheds little light on this controversy. In his career he employed alienation in various ways. However since becoming Marxist has been neglected explicitly, Sartre outlines his current version of the term. Later, in the interview with Benny Levy, Sartre completely dismissed relations of production as a primary one. He observes: "I don't believe that the relations production is the primary one….. There are neighborhoods of workers who have settled in the cities….. What unites them more profoundly beyond the mode of production, is that they are human beings…. All Marx's superstructures are fine work, but it is utterly false, because the primary relationship with individual to individual is something,….family relationship is primary with respect to any other relationship".[68] As a result, we are forced to construct our own interpretation of Sartre's alienation on the basis of his earlier writings.

In Sartre's earlier writings, we have existentialism with subjectivity, individualism and absolute freedom pushed to its limits. The limit situation of existentialism is its own negation and Sartre's conception of human reality is just based on this negation. If the individual is taken in isolation from society and posed against it, if subjectivity is detached from objective being and if existence is separated from essence then what remains is either brute unconscious being or void and fantasy. Sartre realises, like all other existentialists, freedom is the absolute negation of freedom in bad faith and objectivity, and the desire to be in a fantasy (God).

For Sartre, freedom naturally tends to be in-itself and thus it is absurd freedom. It is absurd also because it is a freedom to choose, but not a freedom of not choosing. Only in the imperialist phase of capitalist society, on the other hand, even the bourgeois concept of freedom comes to end with the end of competition and action and freedom may be suspended into an absurd fundamental project of 'private appropriation of the world'. Private appropriation is, thus, projected as the essential element of the being of Sartre's for-itself and as such it not only mystifies the actual historicity of relations of production in a capitalist society but lends it an ontological meaning and justification. In fact, the fundamental problem of philosophy, the problem of primacy of mind or matter is here again of primary importance. Sartre is opposed to materialism and though he tries seriously to give a realist semblance to his being-for-itself and being-in-itself, he retains the mind-body dualism and even treats nature and body idealistically as a relation of bad-faith (alienation).

Hegel is, in this sense, in spite of being an objective idealist, the leader of all the subjective idealists (existentialists) so far as they conceive alienation as identical with otherness or objectivity. All existentialists, without exception, either deny object as untruth (Kierkegaard, Jaspers), or pose it in absolute antithesis to subject. Sartre goes one step ahead of them by devising the theory of desire to be object or to be alienated as the fundamental project of man's being.

Even though Sartre does not conceive consciousness as a substantive being, he gives all being to it, to its nothingness. Nothingness, on the other hand, posited as absolute freedom of the individual subject, is conceived as self-nullifying as, thingness, as bondage, and every social relation is seen as invariably involving alienation. Thus man's alienation or bad-faith or his state of bondage is projected as an eternal (ahistorical), untranscendable state of existence.

The idealist and false existentialist notion of reality of man comes to light in its glaring contradictions in Sartre's philosophy. He bases his idea of freedom of man on the negation of the idea of God and then makes man a fundamental project of becoming God; of becoming a contradictory idea, an idea which does not allow any freedom for man. He does not see that the very idea of God is an expression of man's self-alienation, as Feuerbach has already proved it. Another aspect of the idealist notion of freedom has been and remains with Sartre its interiority as opposed to exteriority. Freedom is internal negation of freedom. It is so conceived only because the practical activity of man, the act of labour through which he objectifies his subjective powers is not seen as an act of creation of the realm of freedom in the world, as an act of objectively changing and thus controlling nature.

Sartre, of course, has seen the limits of the existentialist philosophy and gravitated towards Marxism in his later works. But even after accepting the Marxist interpretation of history as valid, he retains existentialist premises either in pure or veiled forms. We can see how he views man and his estrangement, especially in his later major philosophical work, *The Critique of Dialectical Reason.* While discussing the alienated objectification of individual and collective praxis, Sartre writes, "Should we describe this as alienation? Obviously we should, in that he returns to himself as other. However, a distinction must be made; alienation in Marxist sense begins with exploitation. Should we go back to Hegel who sees alienation as a constant characteristic of all kinds of objectification? Yes and No. We must realise that original relation and materiality as passivity oblique man to objectify himself, in a milieu which is not his own, and to treat an inorganic totality as his own objective reality. It is this relation between interiority and exteriority which originally constituted praxis as a relation of the organism to its material environment; and there can be no doubt that as soon as man begins to designate himself not as the mere reproduction of his life, but as the ensemble of products which reproduce his life, he discovers himself as Other in the world of objectivity. Totalized matter, as inert objectification perpetuated by inertia, is in effect non-human or even anti-human...."[69] Here we are reminded of Marx's saying that man through his labour humanises nature. The contrast, which shows forth between Sartre and Marx's conception of the act and result of objectification (labour), originates from his adherence to Hegel's idealism. Marx's criticism of Hegel's concept of nature as something defective applies to Sartre also. If man is a natural being then his freedom can be realised in nature itself, in realising the necessity and not by nihiliating nature. Sartre's alienation may be theoretically sound; it may capture the lived experience of certain individuals in the capitalist society. Man evolves out of nature, and if he is alienated from nature, there should be a way of restoring the original bond of Man with it. At the same time man is social by nature and the individual is human only when he is social. Furthermore, existence is never without essence and if there is any contradiction between essence (real determinations of man's being), and his existence (his particular being), it cannot be overcome by negative essence, but by transforming the existence, by changing dehumanising conditions of Man's being. Marx rightly said, "the philosophers have interpreted the world, in various ways, the point, however is to change it." Unfortunately, even after adopting the Marxist ideology, Sartre could not change his own childhood class-bound reification of consciousness.

NOTES

1. Jean Paul Sartre, *Being and Nothingness*, Trans. Hazel E. Barnes, (New York, Philosophical Library, 1956), 3.
2. Ibid., 5.
3. Ibid., 3-5.
4. Ibid., 24-25.
5. Ibid., 126.
6. Every page of Sartre's Being and Nothingness analysis is markedly influenced by the Heideggerian Concept of Being. Ibid., 34.
7. Ibid., 39.
8. Ibid., 58.
9. Ibid., 59.
10. Ibid., 36.
11. Ibid.,84.
12. Ibid.,86.

13. Ibid.,567 also in Jean Paul Sartre, *Existentialism and Humanism,* trans, P. Mairet.(London, Methuen),34.
14. Sartre, Existentialism and, 29.
15. Jean Paul Sartre, *Iron in the Soul,* Trans. H. Barnes, (Harmondsworth, Penguin), 216.
16. Ibid.,217.
17. Ibid., 225.
18. Sartre, Being and, 429.
19. Ibid., 429-430.
20. Ibid., 430.
21. Ibid., 89.
22. Ibid., 88.
23. Ibid., 99.
24. Stephen Priest, *Jean Paul Sartre: Basic Writings,* (London, Routledge, 2001), 214.
25. Sartre, Being and, (101-22).
26. Ibid., 102.
27. Ibid., 103.
28. Ibid.
29. Ibid., 340.
30. Ibid., 302.
31. Ibid., 352.
32. George Wilhelm Frederic Hegel, *Phenomenology of the Spirit,* (Oxford, Oxford University Press), 112-119. He regards the struggle between master and slave as a struggle for recognition but that the same indicates that among these contending sides, the slave is the one who creates freedom through his labour and actually the master is free at the cost of the slave's freedom.
33. Sartre, Being and, 358.
34. Ibid., 475.
35. Ibid.
36. Ibid., 489.
37. Ibid.
38. Ibid., 532-533.
39. Ibid., 534.
40. Ibid., 536-37.
41. Ibid., 546.
42. Ibid.
43. Ibid., 547.
44. Ibid., 555.
45. Ibid.
46. Ibid., 722.

47. Ibid., 724.
48. Ibid.
49. Ibid., 784..
50. Ibid.
51. Jean Paul Sartre, *The Search for Method,* (New York, Random House, 1963 (b)), 60-62.
52. Ibid., 62.
53. Carl, Manzani. ed. The Open Marxism of Antonio Gramsci, (New York: Cameron Associates, 1957), 48. Antonio Gramsci recognised the necessity for an open Marxism, a vital and comprehensive view of social reality. Gramsci realises that if one's individuality is a totality of scientific relations; personal changes will modify the overall complex in which the individual is embedded. In Gramsci's estimation each individual is both the synthesis of contemporary relationships and the summary of the entire past."
54. Sartre, *The Search*, 60.
55. Jean Paul Sartre, *Critique of Dialectical Reason,* Trans. Sheridan Smith, (London, New Left Books, 1976), 81.
56. Ibid.,127.
57. Ibid.,151.
58. Ibid., 163.
59. Ibid.
60. Michael Weinstein A. Deens, Sartre and Humanist Traditions in Sociology, in Mary Warnock, ed.,(New York, Doubleday and co.,1971),.346.
61. Jean Paul Sartre, Itinerary of Thought, (*New Left Review*,1969), 45.
62. Jean Paul Sartre, Benny Levy, Hope Now: The 1980 Interviews, trans Adrian van den Hoven, (Chicago, Chicago University Press, 1996), 86.
63. Sartre, *Search for*, 31.
64. Sartre , *Critique of*,. 81.
65. Karl Marx, *Capital*, Vol. 1, (New York, International Publishers, 1967), 178.
66. Sartre, *Search for*, 62.
67. Ibid.
68. Sartre, *Hope Now*, 86.
69. Sartre, *Critique of*, 227.

BIBLIOGRAPHY

Aaron, R., *Sartre's Marxism, Encounter*, Vol. 24, 1964.

Aronson, Ronald, *Jean Paul Sartre: Philosophy in the World,* London:

Verso, 1980.'

Avineri, Shlomo, *The Social and Political Thought of Karl Marx*, Cambridge: Cambridge University Press, 1968.

Blackham, H.J., *Reality, Man and Existence: Essential Works of Existentialism*, New York: Bantam Books, 1965.

Bell, Daniel, *The End of Ideology*, Gencoe III: Free Press,1960.

Desan Wilfred, *The Marxism of Jean Paul Sartre*, New York: Doubleday Co.,1966.

Doland, Palumbo, *The Crisis of Faith-Father-Son Ruptures, and Alienation-from- the Self: Their Interconnection in the Works of Sartre and Camus*, Johns Hopkins University Press,Vol. 44, No. 3 (March, 1982) -12.17, https//www.jstor.org/stable/44376086

Drake, David, Sartre and May 1968: An Intellectual in Crisis, *Sartre Studies International*, Vol. 3, No. 1, 1997, 43-65, https//www.jstor.org/stable/23511087.

Fleming, Michael, Sartre on Violence: Not So Aambivalent?, *Sartre Studies Internatonal*, Vol. 17, No. 1, 2011, (20 40), https//www.jstor.org/stable/23512862.

Habermas, Jurgen, *The New Conservatism: The Cultural Criticism and the Historians Debate*, Oxford: Polity Press, 1989.

Hegel, G.W.F. *Phenomenology of the Spirit*, trans. A.V. Miller, Oxford: Clarendon Press.1979.

Heidegger, Martin, *Being and Time*, trans. Macquarrie and Robinson, Oxford: Basil Blackwell, 1962.

Heinemann, F.H., *Existentialism and the Modern Predicament*, New York: Harper and Row, 1958.

Hoffman, K., *Existential Philosophy: A Study of its Past and Present Forms*, New York: Harvard University, 1949.

Jearas, Norman, Essence and Appearance: Aspects of Fetishism in Karl Marx's Capital, *New Left Review* 66, 6983, 1971.

Kirkpatrick, Kate, Sartre: An Augustinian Atheist, *Sartre Studies International*, Vol. 21, No. 1, 2015, 1-20. https//www.jstor.org./stable/24720557.

Marx, Karl, *On Religion*, Moscow: Progress Publishers, 1976.

Marx, Karl, *The German Ideology*, Moscow: The Progress Publishers, 1974.

Marx, Karl, *The Capital* , Vol. 1, New York: International Publishers, 1967.

Marx, Karl, Engels, 1971, *Economic and Philosophic Manuscripts of 1844*, Moscow: Progress Publishers, 1971 (1974).

Sartre, Jean Paul *The Transcendence of Ego*, trans. F. Williams, New York: Noonday Press, 1962.

Sartre, Jean Paul, *Adieux: A Farewell to Sartre by Simone de Beauvoir*, trans. Patrick O'Brian, London: Penguin, 1985.

Sartre, Jean Paul, *Being and Nothingness*, trans. H. Barnes, New York: Philosophical Library, 1956.

Sartre, Jean Paul, Benny Levy, *Hope Now: The 1980 Interviews*, trans. Adrian van den Hoven, Chicago: Chicago University Press, 1996.

Sartre, Jean Paul, *Existentialism and Humanism*, trans. P. Mairet, London: Methuen, 1948.

Sartre, Jean Paul, *Imagination*, trans. F. Williams, Ann Arbor, Michigan: Michigan University Press, 1962a.

Sartre, Jean Paul, *Literary and Philosophical Essays*, trans. A. Michaelson, London: Rider, 1962b.

Sartre, Jean Paul, *Nausea*, trans. B. Alexander, New York: New Directions, 1949.

Sartre, Jean Paul, *No Exit*, trans. G, Steward and L. Abel, Harmondsworth: Penguin, 1969a.

Sartre, Jean Paul, Sartre: An interview in *New York Review of Books*. March, 26, Vol. XIV, No. 6, 1970.

Sartre, Jean Paul, *The Age of Reason and the Reprieve*, trans, E. Sutton, New York: Penguin, 1947.

Sartre, Jean Paul, *The Dirty Hands*, trans, G. Steward and L. Abel, Harmondsworth: Penguin, 1969b.

Sartre, Jean Paul, *The Emotions*: Outline of a Theory, trans. B Frechtman, New York: Philosophical Library, 1948.

Sartre, Jean Paul, *The Flies*, trans. G. Steward and L. Abel. Harmondsworth: Penguin, 1969c.

Sartre, Jean Paul, The Wall, trans. Alexander in *Existentialism: From Dostoevsky to Sartre*. New York: W. Kaufmann, 1956.

Sartre, Jean Paul, Itinerary of a Thought. *New Left Review*, 1969d, 43-66.

Sartre, Jean Paul, *The Search for a Method*, New York: Random House, 1963a.

Sartre, Jean Paul, *The Words: An Autobiography*, trans. B Frechtman, New York: Penguin, 1964.

Sartre, Jean Paul, Sartre on Genet (Question and Method, pp. 31-64) in R.D. Laing and D. Cooper (eds.) *Reason and Violence*, London: Tavistock Publications, 1963b.

Svenaeus, Frederick, The Phenomenology of Falling III: An Explication Critique, and Improvement of Sartre's Theory of Embodiment and Alienation, *Human Studies*, Vol. 1, 2009, (53-66) https//www.jstor.org/stable/40270700

Weinstein, Michael A., Deens, Sartre and Humanist Traditions in Sociology, 357-86, in Mary Warnock (ed.) *Sartre*, Garden City New York: Doubleday and Co., 1971.

7

The Untimely Marx

Marx's Critique of Political Economy and the Political Dimension of Critical Economics[1]

Riccardo Bellofiore

Introduction

My generation—I began my studies of economic theories in 1973, but somehow had been introduced to Marxian theory already in the late 1960s—has been informed by the great tradition of Maurice Dobb and Paul M. Sweezy.[2] To be sure, we came of age by committing a sort of patricide towards these figures. I don't regret my intellectual path, which is evident in my teaching. My distance from the view about Marx regarding to economic theory that was dominant in the 1950s and 60s is significant. However, as time goes by, I feel that my generation has lost something important: personally, I have always tried to stress not only the discontinuity, but also the continuity with Dobb and Sweezy. They were giants, within the larger conversation of economic theory: like Sraffa, they were respected and quoted by mainstream academics. More than that, they were able to understand the different languages of the contrasting theories, an art that seems to be lost today. With very few exceptions, the Marxists of my generation became insulated individuals, if not sects, creating an idiosyncratic world (many incommensurable worlds, actually), not knowledgeable of other theories, very often even unable to communicate among themselves.

This Chapter provides a sort of methodological introduction to *Das Kapital*. I am questioning the meaning of critique versus criticism, the distinction between fetish-character and fetishism, the role of dialectics, and the difference between reading, interpreting and reconstructing. Afterwards, I will focus especially on some key points of Volume I. At the centre of the discussion are: the multiple meanings of abstract labour and socialisation, the role of money as a commodity for the labour theory of value, the 'method of comparison' in grounding valorisation (the emergence of gross profits) as the constitution of capital from class struggle in production, the real subsumption of labour to capital, Marx's two notions of competition, and the macro-monetary class perspective in capitalist reproduction. The conclusion looks at the relevance of the Marxian legacy at the beginning of the 21st century.

The Meaning of Critique

The first issue to be dealt with is to understand the meaning of the subtitle of *Das Kapital*: 'A Critique of Political Economy'. To begin, we have to understand what *Political Economy* means for Marx, and then to understand what *Critique* means here. Marx distinguished Vulgar Political Economy, on the one side, and Classical Political Economy on the other side. Vulgar economics—a label which applies to a large part of economic theory since the 1870s until today—stops at superficial appearances: these appearances are nothing but an (illusory) *semblance*. In the Marxian vocabulary they are instances of *Schein*. Vulgar economists focus on circulation, without referring circulation back to production. Classical Political Economy is altogether a different thing. For Marx, it is made of true contributions to scientific knowledge of capital. According to Marx, political economy begins with William Petty. Afterwards, its long theoretical development, with few exceptions, takes place under the sign of the labour theory of value. The main protagonists of this version were François Quesnay and the Physiocrats, Adam Smith, but especially David Ricardo. It was science (*Wissenschaft*).

Though it was marked by a bourgeois imprinting, Classical Political Economy has provided essential elements for understanding capitalism. Ricardo especially linked value to the labour contained in commodities, and he did that in a way that was attempting to construct a coherent value theory as price theory, even though, according to Marx, this attempt ultimately failed. The point here is that Vulgar economics stops at the "semblance", the superficial world of circulation, whereas Classical Political Economy makes it possible to discern the inner reality of capital, and goes behind circulation, reaching production. It is, however, an unfinished and limited scientific project. That is why Marx thinks Political Economy needs to be developed *critically*, to fully exploit its scientific potentiality: political economy, according to Marx, must become Critical Political Economy. Critical Political Economy, however, is not on the same conceptual level as the Critique of Political Economy. But an essential moment in Marx's discourse is the consideration that the scientific discourse of Political Economy must be improved and advanced, and this continued development is delivered by Marx himself in his Critical Political Economy, so that a Critique of Political Economy could be provided: science has to be undertaken, so that that science itself is put in question. I will show, however, that it is also true that Critical Political Economy is possible only from the point of view of the Critique of Political Economy: the science of capital may be achieved only when its historical partiality and determination are considered.

Political Economy, as well as Critical Political Economy, deals with the question: "how does capital produce?" The question which is more fundamental, and which is the starting point of the Critique of Political Economy is: "how is capital produced"? This means that the exposition does not begin with capital as already constituted but as something *yet to be constituted*: the main focus of Volume I is thus exactly that *Konstitution*. Classical Political Economy, up to a point, goes beyond semblance (or *Schein*), and approaches—although never quite reaching it fully—*appearance* as *phenomenal manifestation* (or *Erscheinung*). That is: the theory goes beyond the mere superficial layer of circulation, towards the layer of the inner reality; but it is unable to link the two moments in *exposition* (or *Darstellung*).[3]

This is what is accomplished by the Critique of Political Economy. As I will show, Marx also argues that hidden within the *Darstellung* there is a movement from the inner to the outer: within the "exposition" of the totality, which *appears,* manifests itself phenomenally as *circular* (capital producing capital), we have to discover an "expression" (Marx uses the verb *aus-drücken*), which is *linear* (labour producing capital). This method is, of course, the debt that Marx owes to Hegel, however with fundamental transformations which I will discuss later.

For the moment rather, let me look at a sort of Kantian moment in the meaning of critique. In Marx, "critique" also refers to the enquiry about the *conditions of possibility* of political economy. It is not Kantian in the full sense, because in Marx's critique is not transcendental, is not something abstract and general. The conditions of possibility to which he refers have a determinate historical dimension: they are related to a specific structure, to what Marx following Hegel refers to as *determination of form*. The conditions of possibility have something to do, first of all, with the market, or better with the universalisation of exchange, *commodity exchange,* in what is *a monetary economy* from the start. This is a point on which many interpreters of Marx insist and leads directly to the characterisation of Marx's value theory as a *monetary value theory* (*of labour*).[4]

There is, however, a second point about the notion of critique that must be clarified from the beginning: I have already hinted at this. The Critique of Political Economy is not just an "advance" within political economy as a science (*Wissenschaft*), nor is it just a synonym for Critical Political Economy. Critical political economy is only part of the story in *Das Kapital*. To be sure, I am not among those who insist on such a strong separation between the Critique of Political Economy and Critical Political Economy that there is not any overlap between them. Rather, I think that these two moments of critique should be articulated together. Certainly, one loses all the innovation of Marx if s/he does not see that the Critique of Political Economy cannot be reduced to a particular version of political economy as Critical Political Economy. There is no doubt that we discover here something very strange for economists and social scientists: the fact that Marx, while deepening the scientific knowledge of capital, at the same time, is *critiquing that very scientific knowledge itself*; and through this critique of the theoretical and epistemological terrain of Political Economy, at the same time he proposes *a critique of its object*, and in the last instance a critique of the reality of capital itself.

Marx is in fact forging a new theoretical continent. From my point of view, it is important to understand that Marx does not break altogether with Classical Political Economy and with Ricardo, and the continuity is important. But the discontinuity too is important, and in a way even more important, because the discontinuity sheds light on the same scientific results. You cannot understand Marx's continuity with Classical Political Economy (culminating in Critical Political Economy) without looking at the latter by considering the discontinuity that Marx introduces.

A third important qualification: critique is not criticism, *Kritik* is not *Kritizismus*. In a nutshell: for *criticism* I mean the pointing out of errors, of category mistakes, of contradictions in an opponent's theory. Most of the Marxists, both economists and philosophers, understand the Critique of Political Economy in this way. This is wrong. *Critique*, contrary to criticism, recognises the inner truth of political economy; it does not merely criticise its shortcomings. In fact, if one reads Marx carefully, one sees that even while he was a forceful critic of Vulgar Political Economists, he also took them seriously, and was prepared to learn from them (the first names that come to my mind are Malthus and Samuel Bailey).

After these first three points, let me move on to a more substantial question: why is a Critique of Political Economy necessary, what are the fundamental limits that Political Economy cannot cross? Marx's reasoning can be put forward in this way: the Critique of Political Economy has as its pivot point the *duality of labour*, concrete labour and abstract labour, corresponding to the duality of the commodity as use value and exchange value. Moreover, Marx sees in exchange value the form of value as such. Classical Political Economy, and especially Ricardo, hinted (though confusedly) at the notion of a substance of value, and hence at the notion of the magnitude of value, but could not develop the notion of the *form of value*. Thus, Classical Political Economy and Ricardo himself did not establish a proper notion of labour, nor of money, as preliminary to the inquiry of the universal monetary capitalist exchange of commodities. Behind these two flaws there is a third basic inadequacy: Classical Political Economy never adequately grasped the distinction between labour *power* and *living* labour. This, of course, is well known—in a sense, familiar territory. What is less understood is that, for Marx, "labour" refers to three poles: labour power, living labour and—most crucially—the workers as *living bearers of labour power*. This triad is fundamental in the Critique of Political Economy as it deals with the *constitution of capital as a social relation*.

The fourth failure of Classical Political Economy is the absence of a *theory of crisis* as something unavoidable for capital. In a sense, there is, in fact, the idea that crisis is conceptually foreign to capital, which is fundamentally an "equilibrium" reality (this is the perspective of Ricardo and Jean-Baptiste Say), or alternatively there is the idea that crisis is so much the essence of capital that it is fundamentally a "disequilibrium" reality (this is the perspective of Malthus and Sismondi), such that capitalism itself is actually impossible in its pure form. Therefore, there is never crisis in capitalism, properly speaking: capital can experience minor disturbances, immediately corrected by the market, or cannot exist altogether without immediately collapsing. If this is, in fact, the Critique of Political Economy, it is clear why it is a critique of the science of capital as inherently bourgeois. Grasping the triad of "labour"—where labour power refers to workers as the living bearers of labour capacity, and the subjects who actually work actualise living labour as the use of labour power—means understanding capital as an *historically specific reality that exists under the sign of alienation, reification and exploitation*.

The Critique of Political Economy is not immediately a critique of capital itself. Marx thinks that reality can only be appropriated through theory, as "object of knowledge". At the same time, this theoretical/logical Critique of Political Economy offers the needed conceptual instruments for understanding capital, and then for practically subverting it. To be more precise: Marx is neither a traditional materialist nor an idealist thinker; his approach is that of a practical materialist (this was a key point in Alfred Schmidt).[5] The term practical takes us back to the Theses on Feuerbach, and especially the second thesis: "[t]he question whether objective truth can be attributed to human thinking is not a question of theory but is a practical question. The human being must prove the truth, i.e. the reality and power, the this-sidedness of his thinking, in practice."[6]

This means that the exposition (*Darstellung*) can be accomplished critically only from the perspective of an emancipatory radical transformation of reality. Praxis is not only the horizon of critique: it is also, in part, its *precondition*, since Marx could construct his theoretical Critique of Political Economy because *in practice* workers' struggles had begun to put in question not only the naturalness of capitalist social relations, they also put into question capitalist technology (this point was very well argued by Wal Suchting, and from a different point of view by Edward P. Thompson).[7]

I have already outlined that Marx's exposition (*Darstellung*) is *dialectical*. This dialectical method includes *Forschung*, an analytical enquiry, through which Marx arrived at the point that the whole can be exhibited (*dargestellt*) as a structural system, seemingly closed in itself. This method, as I said, goes back to Hegel.[8] In a very different but comparable conceptual setting, something similar can be found in *Lire le Capital*.[9] The Althusserians speak however of *structure* rather than *form*. In both cases we have "a process without subject[s]". The point in Althusser is epistemological, and somehow ahistorical. In the Frankfurt constellation of thinkers it is the mark of the specific capitalist totality, *the Whole as the Untrue*, and its validity is limited to that historical reality. In Marx's use of Hegel, there is a Subject behind the process without the subjects, and this Subject is Capital (homologous to Hegel's *Geist*).

A few more words are in order here since we are touching on the deepest meaning of Critique of Political Economy. According to Marx, capital is a Fetish, but an automatic Fetish, turning into a dominating Subject that 'overgrasps' all the moments of the totality (*das übergreifende Subjekt*, in Chapter 4 of Volume 1). A key ingredient to understand *Das Kapital* is to comprehend the distinction between *Fetisch-Charakter* and *Fetischismus*: fetish character and fetishism. Capital as a thing (actually, as the Thing, the automatic Fetish, the Subject), exactly like value and money, *truly* possesses social powers. Hence, the attribution of social powers to capital (to money, to value) is not illusory: it is an "appearance", meaning the *phenomenal manifestation* (or *Erscheinung*) of "things as they are", but *only in the specific capitalist historical determination*. The mystification, the illusion, the fetishism, are the *naturalisation* of these social powers, as they refer to things as things: this is a *semblance* (or *Schein*), which is of course produced by the same fetish-character nature of value, money, capital. From here, it follows that relations between people *appear* (that is, *erscheint*: manifest phenomenally) as relations between things, *as in fact they are*.

This is, however, only half the truth. The Critique of Political Economy answers not only the question "how capital?", i.e. its self-valorising feature, but also the question "why capital?", i.e. *from where this valorisation originates*. Non-human capital reality is brought back to some kind of human practice hidden behind capital as a thing: capital as a social relation, which has at its core class struggle, and more specifically class struggle in production.[10] Most of *Das Kapital,* Volume I, is devoted to this idea. Last but not least, systematic dialectics for Marx is a method which is not universal: it can be properly applied only to capital: this is what Helmut Reichelt calls the "method of withdrawal" (*Methode auf Wiederruf*).[11] There is no Diamat in Marx: no dialectical materialism of the Stalinist/Leninist variety. There is not even Hegel's logic of the positing of the presupposition as a universal ahistorical method. Dialectics pertains to those quite strange and paradoxical objects—Hans-Georg Backhaus calls these objects deranged, displaced and perverted (*the Verrückte Formen*)—that are capital, money and value.[12] In other words, the reference to dialectics is not only epistemological, it is also ontological: it is the ontology of Capital as homologous to Absolute Spirit. Dialectics disappears when capital disappears.

Reading, Interpreting and Reconstructing

To write about Marx in a proper and useful way, we must make clear the difference between *reading, interpreting* and *reconstructing*. In relation to "reading" I mean *an appraisal of the text that does not hide the ambivalences and ambiguities, and sometimes incoherencies,* of the book. A more sophisticated stage is what I call "interpretation". For "interpretation" I mean the attempt to rebuild the Marxian system staying close to what is recognised as its inner logic: *re-reading Marx according to Marx,* to quote the title of an essay by Cesare Luporini.[13] In relation to this, there is an idea that ambivalences, ambiguities, incoherencies can be solved and overcome *without any break from or revision of Marx*. I became convinced long ago that neither reading nor interpretation are able to dissolve the difficulties and contradictions of the Critique of Political Economy as we inherited it.

A third move must be undertaken: "reconstruction". Reconstruction very often means—using the relevant expression by Backhaus—*going with Marx against Marx*. Ambiguities and ambivalences, difficulties and contradictions can be overcome only in going against some of Marx's propositions, but with Marx in the sense of applying the method he proposes: exploiting in full, as Marx did not, the uniqueness of his monetary (labour) theory of value, turning it into a *macro-monetary theory of capitalist production of (surplus) value*.[14] What this actually means will become clearer toward the end of this article.

My discussion is aimed at the intersection of interpretation and reconstruction, and it presupposes a careful reading. In my understanding, going with Marx against Marx is the contemporary way to be a Marxian, and not a Marxist. This distinction was originally formulated by Maximilien Rubel,[15] who thought that all Marxists were distorting Marx's message. The exceptions were Marxians like Rosa Luxemburg, Henryk Grossmann, Paul Mattick, and Karl Korsch.[16]

In my view, as I said, being Marxian means to provide a Critique of political economy after Marx, and to deal with contemporary capitalism. Hence, Marxians cannot only confine themselves to what Marx wrote—a conceptual innovation beyond Marx is needed. Marx was the first to do something similar, constantly revising the same volume I, and not publishing the sequel because, as he said, he still had to learn and digest the lessons of the changes in 1870s capitalism.

I agree with Karl Korsch that Marx's theory must be "historicised"—must be read backwards through the questions of today. I will not go into detail here, but the attentive reader will recognise that my points of entry for my 'reconstruction' are the crisis of the 1960s and 70s (in particular, what I learned from the workers in the years of the class struggle at FIAT), i.e. the Social Crisis or the Great Stagflation, and the current structural crisis, i.e. the so-called Great Recession (or, better, Lesser Depression). This is actually a very Marxian standpoint: reading the authors of the past backwards, from their own questions distilled from assessment of the scientific debate, in order to go forward, as Marx did in *The Theories of Surplus*

Value (the same method we find in Schumpeter's *History of Economic Analysis*, in Böhm-Bawerk's *Capital and Interest*, and also in Sraffa's *Lectures on the Advanced Theory of Value*). One does not go to the 1861-63 Manuscripts to know what exactly Smith or Ricardo actually said. However, in my case, mine is not an arbitrary reading: it extracts what is already there in the texts, and this can be shown rigorously.

The paradox is this: in proceeding this way, what I am able to provide—I am once more paraphrasing Hans-Georg Backhaus—are just *fragments of a systematic reasoning*. I think that the reason for this outcome is that Marx intended to be systematic, but didn't actually succeeded. The intention is important, as is its failure. I have seen the best minds amongst Hegelian Marxists, some of them my friends, engage in attempts to "rewrite" Marx in Hegelian fashion, mainly by mimicking the *Science of Logic*. One can count, however, just as many Hegelian readings of *Das Kapital* as there are authors: indeed more, as some self-criticise their previous attempts and produce other and more refined versions of their Hegelian Marx. Here I part company with them because I feel that we are forced to remain in a fragmentary reading of Marx. The point is that this fragment of systematic reasoning is essential to understanding capital, and to fighting against it.

A Quick Journey Through *Das Kapital*, Volume I

Value and Money, Ghost and Chrisalys

At the beginning of *Das Kapital*, Marx looks at the universal exchange of commodities as the universal exchange of products of labour to be exchanged on the market. However, a problem arises: if one takes the *single* commodity, and scrutinises it carefully, one cannot detect value anywhere, one only sees the body of its use value. Value is just a *ghost*. To put it bluntly: strictly speaking, at this stage of the exposition, value does not exist; it is an ethereal entity. But Marx is a materialist: he argues that, to exist, the ghost must *take possession* of a body. We find ourselves precisely in the middle of a *gothic novel*.

In the first Chapter Marx moves from *value as content*,

which he discusses in Section one and two of Chapter 1, to *value as form* and the *form of value*, in Chapter 3. If you stop at Chapters 1 and 2, as many Marxists do, you may be justified in thinking that value is simply labour contained. Most, if not all, authors speak of "labour embodied": but Marx never used this expression, so widespread in translations all over the world, for abstract labour. Only *concrete* labour ends up being *embodied* in the use value which is its output (the German verb here is *verkörpern*). For abstract labour, Marx rather uses the expression labour *contained* (the German verb here is *enthalten*). The *concrete* labour producing *money as a commodity* (which exactly is *value embodied*) *mirrors* the abstract labour of the commodities exchanged with gold as money.

Value as a Ghost is now *exhibited* (*darstellt*) in the use value of gold as a commodity. What then is the abstract labour of commodities? It presents itself at this stage of the argument as a labour which is *not* immediately social. As an *immediately private labour*, the labour spent by individual producers selling on the market *becomes social in commodity circulation*, in the monetary exchange of commodities. It is a progressive coming into being of abstract labour and value: abstract labour as *not-yet-social* becomes abstract labour as *mediately social* labour. Looking *backwards*, abstract labour is that labour which *has become social* on the market through the metamorphosis of commodities with gold as a use value (embodying value): that is, through the equalisation in monetary exchange with the concrete labour producing gold (as the universal equivalent). This part of Marx's argument is totally *dialectical and Hegelian*. It is important to note that the concrete labour producing gold, which here is "money as a commodity", is the *only* immediately social labour. Thus we have to carefully distinguish the abstract labour hidden within the commodities as not-immediately-social-labour and the *concrete* labour producing money as a commodity as an immediately-social-labour.

Marx is referring not to some generic ahistorical exchange, but to a universal "commodity exchange" (*Waren Austausch*), which for him cannot but be *immediately monetary*. Marx is putting forward a perspective that was completely new at the time, and which stays quite unique afterwards: a *monetary analysis* distancing itself from *real analysis* (I borrow this distinction from Schumpeter's *History of Economic Analysis*), where money is introduced at the very beginning of the theory, with the universal exchange of commodities being immediately monetary, and where, most importantly, not only money is exhibiting value, but also *the very category of value is deficient without integrating money from the start in its fuller definition*. Let me add that Marx's argument may give the impression that the *social objectivity* of value and abstract labour exists *only* in the final circulation of commodities. This is certainly part of Marx's argument: what Michael Heinrich calls the ex-post socialisation, *Nachträgliche Vergesellschaftung*, of commodities' abstract labour.[17] I'll return on this later on.

We have witnessed a *miracle*: the ghost has really taken possession of a body. This embodiment is also pictured by Marx as an incarnation (*Inkarnation*) and even as a *transubstantiation*. The theological terminology, exactly like the gothic novel terminology, is essential to understand Marx as a social scientist. After Marx the gothic novelist and Marx the Christian theologian, we meet Marx the entomologist. Marx defines money as money as a *chrysalis*. The challenge for theory is to develop money *as money* into money *as capital*, the chrysalis into a *butterfly*: money as *finance*, as capital begetting more money, value valorising itself begetting surplus value, in a continuous spiral. But how is this process possible?

A Monetary Value Theory of Labour, Thanks to Money as a Commodity

Marx in the first part of the volume, and already in the first chapter, is presenting two arguments at once. The first argument is that abstract labour and value exist only in the exchange of commodities. The second argument is that abstract labour and the value that is *materialised* in final commodity circulation, expresses a movement from the inner to the outer.

Here we have an *expression* (or *Ausdruck*) in a strong meaning: the *exteriorisation of something internal*, and—most important—something that according to Marx is *already* commensurable, at least *tentatively social*, before final exchange. It is a social objectivity that somehow must *exist* as such, not just within but also *before* final exchange.

The apparent contradiction disappears when we recognise that, contrary to most interpreters, *money as a commodity* must be seen not as a dispensable assumption due to historical contingencies (because of the monetary system of his time), but as an essential moment in his value theory of labour, as a crucial notion linking value to a determinate social form of labour. When commodities are produced for universal exchange they come to the market with a price tag, a *money-name*: this money-name already (*ex-ante*) *socially homogenises commodities*. Marx adds in chapters two and three that this money-name goes together with *an already given* value of money: the given value of money is *fixed at the point of production of gold as a commodity*. When gold is sold against all the other commodities—this is Marx's position, presented without ambiguity in his book—the exchange of commodities and gold is *not yet* monetary, it is properly speaking *barter*, because at the hole that is the point of entrance of gold in the monetary circuit, money is just a commodity. We are dealing with an *unmittelbare Produktenaustausch*; yes, it is an exchange, but rigorously speaking it is an exchange *of products, not of commodities*: because to be a commodity means to be exchanged with money, and here the exchange is *not yet* mediated by money. It is a sale without a purchase, which "fixes" the exchange ratios that enables the price-tag to give a quantitative determination of value before final exchange.

The great and unique accomplishment by Marx was to present a *monetary value theory*. From my point of view, the weakness is that this monetary value theory is *grounded on original barter* (paradoxically, this is a possible point of contact with Ludwig von Mises: but don't tell Marxists, they would not understand).

From the Chrysalis to the Buttefly: The Method of Comparison and the Constitution of Capital

In the first three Chapters, and actually until Chapter 7, Marx deals with commodities that are already produced. After Chapter 7, however, he deals with the (capitalist) process of production of commodities: hence, we have to consider *a monetary theory of production of (surplus) value*, based on the determinate form of labour, which is historically specific, and this specificity is also affecting the notion of abstract labour.

Marx, especially in Chapter 4, pictures capital as *a gigantic Fetish* which is also *a gigantic Subject*, or *Subjekt*. Marx is talking about capital as a Subject in the same sense that Hegel's *Geist* is a Subjekt.[18] The reference to Hegel is *ontological*, not just epistemological. Marx uses the expression *übergreifenden Subjekt*: an "overgrasping and dominating Subject".[19] This overgrasping/dominating Subject, as I outlined, is *positing its own presupposition*. In this new reality, emerging but very different from commodity as such and money as such, the destination of the production process is not use value (like in simple circulation) anymore, it is not concrete wealth (*Reichtum*) anymore. It is value (*Wert*): or if you like, *abstract wealth*, the *opposite* of Reichtum. So value-in-process is encompassed by the word *valorisation* (or *Verwertung*).

How Butterfly, which is Capital, comes to life, how does it evolve from the Chrysalis? The answer is in Chapter 7. In the second section of that chapter the theme is the valorisation process. Here Marx provides the answer to the question that Vulgar Political Economy did not pose and that Classical Political Economy was not able to solve: where does surplus value, gross profits, spring from? Marx's is a kind of "genetic" argument about the *origin* of surplus value. In my view, there isn't a dialectical derivation, nor is Marx's argument in continuity with Hegel's method. In Chapter 7 we rather have a *constitutive* process [*Konstitution*] that breaks the closed totality and is grounded in class struggle within production:

Marx's is a *method of comparison*. He compares two

configurations. The first one seems to be hypothetical, but in fact it depicts something very important about the actual capitalist reality. The second introduces a dynamic change. In fact, both configurations are real and immanent to capitalist reality. Marx begins from an economy where the *would-be* capitalists advance money in the hope of getting more money. They buy labour power, paying the wage (variable capital), and they buy the means of production (constant capital), but extract from the workers a living labour equal to necessary labour, i.e. the labour needed to produce their subsistence. In this situation, of course, there would be no profits: it is a configuration akin to Schumpeter's *circular flow* (a simple reproduction where surplus value is absent). Here prices cannot but be proportional to values (simple or direct prices). This supposedly hypothetical situation is in fact depicting something very real: an economic system able to reproduce the workers according to the *necessary labour*, as a definite quantitative magnitude. The second step of the comparison is based not on a Smithian deduction from the wages—as actually, in different forms, Croce and even Rubin thought—but from the *actual lengthening of living labour* beyond the configuration imagined in the first step. It may come as a surprise to most interpreters, and surely to Marxists, but one of the very few authors who saw quite clearly the nature of Marx's method of comparison and its originality was Sraffa, in 1940, in a note on the *Use of the Notion of Surplus-Value*.

According to this perspective, in capitalism production is nothing but the *consumption* of workers: the new value within the period strictly depends on the *living* labour extracted from the human bearers of labour power. The only other author I know putting the same stress on this point as I do today is Massimiliano Tomba.[20] No peanut theory of surplus value is possible. This, and nothing else, is Marx's explanation of the origin of surplus value. This is the *ground* of the value theory of labour, tracing back (new) value to (living) labour. The new value must be exhibited in money, and comes only from the *objectification* of living labour. The *fluid* of living labour, when it becomes objective and fixed in the commodity, may be called *direct labour* (what is, unfortunately, mistaken for living labour in most of the literature about Marx). Direct labour, of course, is itself *dead* labour, and it is *given* after the production process: *living* labour, in Marx, as worker's activity (*Arbeit*) is inherently *variable* (this is a point raised by Rowthorn).[21]

This is the *first*, most important, meaning of *exploitation*: the quantitative and qualitative determination of the actual working time within the working day. *Quantitative*: how much (total living) labour time is extorted from workers. *Qualitative*: to allow that extortion, capital has to enter into the organisation and technological determination of the labour process. This is something which constitutes an absolute historical novelty.

Relative Surplus Value and Dynamic Competition

Chapter 12 is another of my favourite chapters, together with Chapter 7. In this chapter, Marx provides an answer to a vital question. As I outlined before, the "microeconomic" mechanism leading to the "macro" result of the extraction of absolute surplus value is easy to understand. It is in the interest of the single capitalist to *absolutely* lengthen the working day, because the more he forces on the worker a surplus labour, the more s/he obtains profits. It is not so with relative surplus value, because relative surplus value is something determined only at the *systemic* level, from the lowering of the value of labour power. If there is a rise in the *productive power of labour* which is generalised in the economy, what will follow is a reduction of the prices of wage goods: when the value of labour power goes down, the surplus value in the new value goes up *relatively*. The same can be argued about a rise in the *intensity of labour*. This macro result—this new equilibrium following a technological innovation and/or an organisational innovation—is not pursued intentionally by the single capitalist, nor it is driving their individual behaviour.

Marx originally intended to approach the logic of capital in two distinct and successive moments. The first step was the inquiry about *capital in general* (all that it is common to capitals); the second step was the inquiry about the *many capitals* (competition among capitals). The second step should have been dealt with only after he had completed the first. Marx eventually included competition already in Volume I, Chapter 12. To understand why, let us ask: what is "competition" for Marx? Competition has two meanings in Marx, and these two meanings are not well understood by interpreters, or are conflated. I think they need to be distinguished, and this distinction may become in some cases even an opposition. On the one hand, Marx took the notion of competition prevalent in Ricardo and in the Classicals: it refers to the *tendency of the rate of profit to be equalised among the different branches of production*, because of the mobility of capital. A similar though not identical notion of competition can be found in Walras, and even more in Marshall. This kind of competition gives rise to the discrepancy between simple or direct prices (the prices proportional to the labour contained in commodities) and production prices (the capitalist prices embodying an equal rate of profit). This competition is discussed in Volume III. In Volume I, we find another notion of competition altogether: the competition within industries, or *within branches of production*, where *many capitals are struggling in a fight to the death through the introduction of innovations*.

Prices—also the simple or direct prices—are established as a *social* or *market* value as the *monetary expression of the (socially necessary) labour time*, which may well be different from the individual value determined by the individual labour time contained. Those who introduce a new machine, a new organisation of labour, etc., lower their individual labour time *below* the socially necessary labour time: as a consequence, their individual value drops below the social (or market) value, and they beget an extra surplus value. The same process can be replicated for the prices of production. Innovators can wage a *war* against the other firms producing the same use value by beginning to decrease the selling price, and thereby stealing the market from other capitalists. This kind of competition is a *cut-throat* competition. It is a competition of the many capitals struggling so that they can win an extra surplus value: and they cannot avoid this competition lest they be thrown out of the market. As I am going to show, in Part 7 on reproduction, Marx highlights the *macro-social* (class and monetary) foundation of the capitalist process as the pumping out of new value from the *working class* (and thus of the extraction of surplus value) by *total capital*. Here, in Chapter 12, Marx discusses the *micro* mechanism grounding the *macro* outcome of the extraction of relative surplus value.

Competition within industries provides the rational individual behaviour leading to the prevalence of what Marx calls the *specific capitalist mode of production,* grounded in the interaction between the "relative" and the "absolute" extractions of surplus value. There were certainly antecendents of this in Classicals, but these were asides with respect to the main line of argumentation, the view of competition as the equality of the rate of profits between industries. Schumpeter borrowed this second view of competition from Marx and made it the founding principle, together with the credit theory of money, of his own system. His debt to Marx was openly recognised in the introduction to the Japanese translation of *The Theory of Economic Developm*ent, and in *Capitalism, Socialism and Democracy*.

The Real Subsumption of Labour to Capital

Chapters 13 to 15 are about *simple cooperation, division of labour in manufacturing*, and *machinofacture*. With machines we have a *real subsumption of labour to capital*. Now, the techniques and the same nature of labour—the actual capitalist labour processes—are *form-determined*. Use value is shaped by value, and the duality internal to the commodity is recomposed under the dominance of the valueform. With machinofacture, workers become the appendage of the material conditions of production. The commodity is the product of the *collective worker*: the single worker is a worker whose labour is *not* concrete anymore, because the single worker does not produce a commodity any more. The commodity can only now be the product of the *immediately socialised labour* in the immediate labour process. Abstract labour is now the living labour of the wage workers within the units of collective labour organised and planned by firms in competition, that is within the immediately private labour of capitalist producers who have to become social on the commodity market. *We have here the paradox of an ex-ante immediately socialised labour which must still become social labour ex-post.*

Under the real subsumption of labour to capital, *Reichtum*, wealth as *concrete wealth is actually produced only by capital, and capital alone*: not by labour. Capital *designs the technology, puts in action the techniques, builds an organisation of labour*: labour as concrete labour is just a cog of this mechanism.[22] But this Fetish does not produce anything, unless it becomes a *vampire*, unless it is able to *pumping living labour out from the workers*. This living labour, generating abstract wealth, value and surplus value, is already abstract labour, a labour as generic as the money and surplus money it produces. *While the use value productivity goes back entirely to capital, the value productivity goes back entirely to (abstract) living labour*: more precisely, to capital's success in winning the class struggle in production. Here I agree with Chris Arthur: capital must incorporate workers (living labour power), as an internal other. This is actually the second meaning of the *embodiment* we find in Marx: not taking possession of a body (we saw that Marx uses the German verb v*erkörpern* for this); rather, being made internal as part of capital's "body" (the German verb is here *einverleiben*).

What is this capital's labouring body, the body of the collective "immediately socialised worker"? Thanks to the buying and selling of labour power, capital inserts the workers as human living labour power bearers into an automatic "monstrous" machine, and puts them to work. Capitalists transform value, i.e. past labour, in an objectified and lifeless form: that is, properly speaking, into capital. *Capital is value performing its own valorisation process, a Subject which, once it has internalised living labour powers, begins to "work" like an animated monster, "as if it were by love possessed".*

Reproduction

In Section 7 Marx is anticipating the heretical monetary macroeconomics of the twentieth century. I am referring to Wicksell, Schumpeter, the Keynes of the *Treatise on Money*, and later to the French-Italian contemporary circuit theory of money. The difference between Marx and these authors being that, as de Brunhoff insisted, Marx was mostly writing within the tradition of the monetary theory of credit, and these "heretics" were and are (like me) committed to the alternative view of the credit theory of money.[23]

The similarity is that the reasoning about the class relation and divide is explicitly set within an initial *macro-monetary* setting. Total capital advances the money wage-bill as *finance for production* in order to buy labour power from the working class.[24] In Chapter 23, Marx writes that to have a clear understanding of what is really going on we have to abandon the perspective of the single capitalist and the single worker, and look instead at the capitalist *class* and the working *class*. The capitalist class advances money drafts to workers, order notes, that are given back by the latter to the former to get their share of what they have produced. In this transaction, the so-called money "veil" performs an essential function: capital includes in its own mechanism workers as its internal other, and the means of subsistence (as the variable capital buying labour power) are the means to get living labour power.

In fact, in the *Results of the Immediate Process of Production*, Marx even writes that it is not the workers that acquire the means of subsistence, but that the means of subsistence buy the workers. Marx has no ambiguity here in clarifying that what has to be taken as given is the *real wage of the working class as a whole*—a point which is lost in most of contemporary Marxist economics: individual workers may have freedom of choice about their individual basket of consumption goods, but that is definitely not true for workers as a class; they have to buy what the capitalist class leave them as available goods. This is the same conclusion that the monetary heretics reach, but also the same conclusion that follows from Keynes' view of the investments as the autonomous driving component in private effective demand; and, even more so, the same conclusion as Kalecki. It is, without doubt, a *macro-monetary theory of the capitalist production and distribution of new value and surplus value*.

The Ex Ante Monetary Socialisation of Labour

A quite explicit consequence of Marx's new viewpoint—a consequence which, once again, is missed in most readings—is that the "macro" logic (the *logic of the totality*)—is not only different, but *unique, prior and opposite* to the "micro" logic: what "appears" from point of view of the "micro" logic, the logic of "individuals", what more properly speaking was a phenomenal manifestation (an *Erscheinung*) in the earlier sections, is now revealed as an illusory semblance (a *Schein*). We have to look back down the path we have travelled, we must read *Capital I backwards*.

Marx began with money and the commodity, then he moved to capital and how it is produced. The single capitalist was taken to be an average representative of total capital. On the labour market, the phenomenal manifestation means that workers and capitalists are free and equal subjects. This is *not* false, at that layer of the inquiry. With reproduction and now assuming the standpoint of the totality, the inquiry is transposed into a directly social, macro, monetary, class perspective. This is a very different outlook than the one taken by the so-called "macro-monetary approaches" within Marxism today: their logic is just a logic of *aggregation*. My alternative *macro foundation* leads to opposite conclusions compared to the micro logic. This is apparent in the fact that the working class is tied to capital as a whole by a relation of *slavery*: the free and equal bargaining of the individual worker was just a necessary "objective illusion".

When reading Marx, one must be warned that the meaning of categories changes along the way in his *Darstellung*, in exposition. This does not mean that the previous meaning of a category is cancelled; it is rather a deeper understanding leading to a "sublation" (*Aufhebung*), where the prior sense is *conserved and overcome*.

Regarding to the *Neue Marx-Lektüre, the point to understand* is that the *a posteriori* socialisation of labour in capitalism *as universalised monetary exchange of commodities* is preceded by an abstraction of labour already anticipated *within immediate production*. The single worker as producer is substituted by the collective, associated worker: *socialised* labour in production as a technical necessity. This technique is *dictated by Technology*, hence by the *form-determination* of the "first world", the so-called "real" world. The meaning of *Arbeit*, labour, in Marx's *Capital* is always human *activity* expended in production. In capitalist production there are *not* two labours, but only *one*. It can, however, be regarded from two angles; as *concrete* labour producing use values, and as *abstract* labour (in becoming) producing value "in potency".

The inclusion of workers as bearers of labour power in the capitalist labour process needs to be mediated by a *monetary* process of *imprinting*, that occurs in the buying and selling of labour power *prior to* immediate production and the final circulation of commodities. This *ante-validation* through money-capital is a forward-looking, *a priori*, socialisation of labour and production.[25]

The Untimely Marx

A centenary—and of course even more so a bicentenary—is the opportunity to draw a sort of balance sheet of an author. Marx, we all know, has been at the judgement bar since the fall of the Berlin Wall and the collapse of the USSR. Talk about a "crisis of Marxism" is recurrent since the end of nineteenth century. And rightly so: the reason is straightforward, and it has to do with Marx's practical materialism.[26] Marx is an instance where the failure(s) of his project of "liberation" and "exit" from the capital relation puts in question his oeuvre. It is not Marxism to be in a crisis. It is Marx himself, and since long.

The reference to Marx is possible only as long as the Critique of Political Economy is also the *critique of the present*. If the above outline of contemporary capitalism is valid, the challenge to Marxian theory is extreme. Let me put it in this way. According to Marx, capital—better, Capital—produces an increasing *concentration* that goes in tandem with increasing *centralisation*. I argue, however, that in current capitalism we witness *centralisation without concentration*.

In Marx's views, concentration with centralisation meant that, in order to exploit the social productive power of workers that capital itself generates, it has to coalesce a collective worker that is *immediately socialised* in production. This immediate socialisation not only indicates that capital is obliged to put workers together to extract living labour, obtain new value, and gain gross profits; it also reveals that it is forced to create a possibility of collective resistance, opposition, and antagonism: a reality where the labour process becomes a contested terrain (so much so that Paolo Sylos Labini viewed workers' struggles and their effects on profits as a positive force leading to innovation and development). Only from a point of view such as this one, the pretence of naturalness and immortality of capitalism can be doubted, and the interrogation about a different social relation—let us call it "socialism"—could be advanced. Otherwise, a history beyond capitalism is just a utopian dream.

Contemporary capitalism seems to break the unity between these two moments, which are united in Marx: the productive side and the conflictual side of the "immediate socialisation" of labour within production. If one wishes to move toward a serious understanding of this reality, the newspaper to read is not a Bolshevik or Luxemburghian one: it is the *Financial Times*. On September 8, 2016 it published an article by Sarah O'Connor, titled "When your boss is an algorythm".[27] According to Jeremias Prassl, a Law Professor at Oxford University, interviewed by Sarah O'Connor, the algorithmic management techniques of Uber and Deliveroo, champions of the so-called gig economy, are "Taylorism 2.0":

algorithms provide a degree of control and oversight that even the most hardened Taylorists could never have dreamt of. Workers are dubbed as self-employed people. The connection among them is made extremely difficult, exactly as it is in the reality of *in-house-outsourcing*, depicted in movies like *The Navigators*, by Ken Loach.

In the new "neoliberal" capitalism, opportunities of rapacious exploitation, like the ones depicted in the article, are everywhere. As Sarah O'Connor reports, "[i]t's hard to spread the word when you don't even know who your colleagues are. But the couriers [of Uber] have an idea. They open their apps as customers and order food to be delivered to them. As Uber Eats couriers arrive with pizzas at the place their app has sent them, the strikers tell them about the protest and urge them to join in. Algorithmic management, meet algorithmic rebellion." In the UK the struggle went to court, and workers are nowadays again winning battles. In fact, with the new technologies, we are in a 21st century economic reality, resembling an early 19th century social configuration. This is something that is going on also in much more advanced productive realities, not only in the gig economy. That early nineteenth century was the period marking the making of the English working class. This early 21st century marks the making of the global working class. We are not witnessing the end of history, we are rather facing a challenge.

No ready-made answer can be found in the complex layered conceptual architecture of *Das Kapital*: it has always been too abstract to provide recipes, exactly the reason for it can still be useful today, as long as we still live within capital social relations. But to understand, and struggle against, this new shape of the "automatic Fetish" and of the "mechanic Monster", Marx remains, as French would say, *incontournable*. To the question if Marx is timely, the answer can therefore only be: no. Marx is very *untimely*, in the meaning attributed to this term by Friedrich Nietzsche. Untimely: that is, *acting counter to our own time, and thereby acting on our time and, let us hope, for the benefit of a time to come.*

NOTES

1. The present Chapter is part of a larger paper which was presented, under different titles, in Warsaw, October 2017, as well as in other occasions in Roccella Jonica, Rome, Milan, and Piacenza. The paper originally presented in Patna as the Maurice Dobb Memorial Lecture at the conference *Karl Marx: Life, Ideas and Influence. A Critical Examination on the Occasion of the Bicentenary*, "Is There Life on Marx? The Critique of Political Economy as a Macro-Monetary Theory of Capitalist Production", was too long to be included in its entirety in this volume, and it has been published in *PSL Quarterly Review*, Vol 71, n. 287 (2018), under the title "Forever Young? Marx's Critique of Political Economy after 200 years". The present version is a slightly amended version of the opening and closure of that paper. I wish to thank Lord Meghnad Desai for the invitation to the enlightening conference in Patna: Desai has been one of my great sources of inspirations for his writings on Marx as well as on the Austrians.
2. See especially Dobb (1937) and Sweezy ([1942] 1970).
3. In this work I very often refer to the meaning Marx gave to some German words, most of them already present in Hegel. Translations quite always lose that meaning. On this, the reader may consult Bellofiore (2014).
4. Rubin ([1928] 1973, ([1926-1928] 2018), Adorno ([1966] 1990; [1968] 2002) and the *Neue Marx-Lektüre*, Colletti ([1969a] 1972; [1969b] 1973), Napoleoni ([1973] 1975).
5. Cf. Schmidt ([1962] 1971; [1971] 1981).
6. https://www.marxists.org/archive/marx/works/1845/theses/theses.htm [last consulted, March 29, 2019.
7. See Suchting (1995) and Thompson ([1963] 1991).
8. It is what Finelli (1987) labels the method of *positing the presupposition*.
9. Althusser et al. (2016); an essay by Jacques Rancière (2016) in the first edition of this book is especially important here, and it is a sort of bridge towards Hegelian terminology. Cf. also Schmidt ([1962] 1971; [1971] 1981).
10. This is a point rightly stressed by Balibar ([1993] 1995).
11. Cf. Helmut Reichelt ([1970] 2001).
12. Cf. Hans-Georg Backhaus (1997).
13. See in particular Luporini (1974).
14. I use the expression in a very different way than Fred Moseley (2015). For a criticism, see Bellofiore (2004).

15. Cf. Rubel ([1974] 2000).
16. The most representative references are Luxemburg ([1925] 2013), Grossmann ([1941] 1977), Mattick (1969), Korsch (1938).
17. Cf. Heinrich (1999). On all this, see Bellofiore (2018a). The argument of this essay is developed in a much longer Italian book: cf. Bellofiore (2018b).
18. On this point, the interpretations by Arthur (2002), Postone (1993), and my own converge
19. *Overgrasping* is the new English term proposed for *übergreifen* by T.F. Geraets, W.A. Suchting and H.S. Harris in their translation of the Encyclopaedia Logic (Hegel, [1830] 1991). It is the Subject that "comprehends", "reaches back" and "overgrasps" the opposition within the moments of the totality.
20. Tomba, M. ([2011], 2012).
21. Cf. Rowthorn, B. (1974).
22. I am here giving my own interpretation of the important book by Frison (1993).
23. Cf. De Brunhoff ([1967] 2016).
24. My debt here is towards Graziani ([1983] 1997a and [1986] 1997b)
25. In this view, the idea that in the production of knowledge there are a subject and an object, separate and prior to science, and that science can be divorced from experimentation, is radically contested. Science, as Ian Hacking would say, is representing *and* intervening. With all their differences, such attack against the traditional epistemology trap is common to such diverse authors as Hegel, Marx, Freud, and Wittgenstein.
26. https://www.ft.com/content/88fdc58e-754f-11e6-b60a-de4532d5ea35
27. In the references, the first date refers to the original edition or the date of the manuscripts, the second date refers to the edition used.

REFERENCES

Adorno, T.W. ([1966] 1990), *Negative Dialectics*, London: Routledge.

Adorno, T.W. ([1968] 2002), *Introduction to Sociology*, Stanford: Stanford University Press.

Althusser, L., Balibar É., Establet R., Macherey P. and Rancière J. (2016), *Reading Capital: The Complete Edition*. London: Verso.

Arthur, C.J. (2002), *The New Dialectic and Marx's 'Capital'*, Leiden and Boston: Brill.

Backhaus, H.-G. (1997), *Dialektik der Wertform. Untersuchungen zur*

Marxschen Ökonomiekritik, Freiburg: ça ira.

Balibar, É. ([1993] 1995), *The Philosophy of Marx*. London: Verso.

Bellofiore, R. (2004), "Marx and the Macro-Economic Foundation of Microeconomics", in Bellofiore R. and Taylor N. (eds.), *The Constitution of Capital: Essays on Volume One of Marx's Capital* (pp. 170-210), Basingstoke: Palgrave Macmillan.

Bellofiore, R. (2014), "Lost in Translation: Once Again on the Marx–Hegel Connection", in Moseley F. and Smith T. (eds.), *Marx's Capital and Hegel's Logic. A Reexamination* (pp. 164-188), Leiden: Brill.

Bellofiore, R. (2018a), "The Adventures of Vergesellschaftung", *Consecutio Rerum*, 2 (5), available at: http://www.consecutio.org/2018/11/the-adventures-of-vergesellschaftung/.

Bellofiore, R. (2018b), *Le avventure della socializzazione. Dalla teoria monetaria del valore alla teoria macromonetaria della produzione capitalistica*, Milano: Mimesis.

Colletti, L. ([1969a] 1972), *From Rousseau to Lenin*, London: NLB.

Colletti, L. ([1969b] 1973), *Marxism and Hegel*, London: NLB.

De Brunhoff, S. ([1967] 2016), *Marx on Money*, London: Verso.

Dobb, M. (1937), *Political Economy and Capitalism: Some Essays in Economic Tradition*, London: Routledge.

Finelli, R. (1987), *Astrazione e Dialettica dal Romanticismo al Capitalismo (saggio su Marx)*, Roma: Bulzoni.

Frison, G. (1993), "Linnaeus, Beckmann, Marx and the Foundation of Technology. Between Natural and Social Sciences: a Hypothesis of an Ideal Type. Second and Third Part: Beckmann, Marx, Technology and Classical Economics", *History and Technology*, 10 (2-3), pp. 161-173.

Graziani, A. ([1983] 1997a), "Let's Rehabilitate the Theory of Value", *International Journal of Political Economy*, 27 (2), pp. 21-25.

Graziani, A. ([1986] 1997b), "The Marxist Theory of Money", *International Journal of Political Economy*, 27 (2), pp. 26-50.

Grossmann, H. ([1941] 1977), "Marx, Classical Political Economy and the Problem of Dynamics", *Capital and Class*, 1 (2), pp. 32-55 (Part I); 1 (3), pp. 67-99 (Part II).

Hegel, G.W.F. ([1830] 1991), *The Encyclopaedia Logic*: Part I of the *Encyclopaedia of Philosophical Sciences* with the "Zusätze", translated from the 3rd edition, edited by T.F. Geraets, W.A. Suchting and H.S. Harris, Indianapolis: Hackett.

Heinrich, M. (1999), *Die Wissenschaft vom Wert. Die Marxsche Kritik der politischen* Ökonomie *zwischen wissenschaftlicher Revolution und klassischer Tradition*, Münster: Westfälisches Dampfboot.

Korsch, K. (1938), *Karl Marx*, London: Chapman & Hall.

Luporini, C. (1974), *Dialettica e Materialismo*, Roma: Editori Riuniti.

Luxemburg, R. ([1925] 2013), *Introduction to Political Economy*, in *The Complete Works of Rosa Luxemburg*, Volume I: Economic Writings 1 (pp. 89-300), London: Verso.

Mattick, P. (1969), *Marx and Keynes. The Limits of the Mixed Economy*, Boston: Extending Horizons Books/Porter Sargent Publisher.

Moseley, F. (2015), *Money and Totality. A Macro-Monetary Interpretation of Marx's Logic in* Capital *and the End of the "Transformation Problem"*, Leiden: Brill.

Napoleoni, C. ([1973b] 1975), *Smith Ricardo Marx*, Oxford: Blackwell.

Postone, M. (1993), *Time, Labor and Social Domination. A Reinterpretation of Marx's Critical Theory*, Cambridge: Cambridge University Press.

Rancière, J. (2016), "The Concept of Critique and the Critique of Political Economy: From the 1844 Manuscripts to Capital", in Althusser L., Balibar É., Establet R., Macherey P. and Rancière J., *Reading Capital: The Complete Edition* (pp. 62-134), London: Verso.

Reichelt, H. ([1970] 2001), *Zur logischen Struktur des Kapitalbegriffs bei Karl Marx*, Freiburg: ça ira.

Rowthorn, B. (1974), "Neo-Classicism, Neo-Ricardianism and Marxism", *New Left Review*, 86, pp. 63-87.

Rubel, M. ([1974] 2000), *Marx Critique du Marxisme*, Paris: Payot.

Rubin, I.I. ([1928] 1973), *Essay on Marx's Theory of Value*, 3rd edition, Montreal: Black Rose.

Rubin, I.I. ([1926-1928] 2018), "Essay on Marx's Theory of Money", in Day R.B. and Gaido D. (eds.), *Responses to Marx's Capital: From Rudolf Hilferding to Isaak Illich Rubin* (pp. 619-727), Leiden: Brill.

Schmidt, A. ([1962] 1971), *The Concept of Nature in Marx*, London: New Left Books.

Schmidt, A. ([1971] 1981), *History and Structure. An Essay on Hegelian-Marxist and Structuralist Theories of History*. Cambridge (MA): MIT Press.

Suchting, W. (1995), *'Critique', 'Ideology', and 'Science' in Marx*, mimeo.

Sweezy, P.M. ([1942] 1970), *The Theory of Capitalist Development. Principles of Marxian Political Economy*, New York: Monthly Review Press.

Thompson, E.P. ([1963] 1991), *The Making of the English Working Class*, London: Penguin Books.

Tomba, M. ([2011], 2012), *Marx's Temporalities*, Leiden: Brill.

8

Guevara and Marx

Critical Remake of an Old Film

Roberto Massari

First Half: OUVERTURE: Scene 1 [**La Paz, 1996**] Scene 2 [**Dar es Salaam,** 1965]—FLASHBACK: Scene 3 [**Lima,** 1952] Scene 4 [**Rome, 1969**]

Interval: Scene 5 [**Sierra Maestra, 1956-58**]

Second Half: ORTHODOXY STORY: Scene 6 [**from Havana to Moscow, 1959-63**]—HERESY STORY: Scene 7 [**from Moscow to Havana, 1963-65**]—MARXIST STORY: Scene 8 [**Prague, 1966**]—FADE-OUT: Scene 9 [**Vallegrande, October 9, 2017**]—THE END (WORKS CITED)

First Half

OUVERTURE

Scene 1 [La Paz, 1996]

At 10:30 am on Tuesday, October 1, 1996, five visibly excited people took the lift down the 30 metres to the *Banco Central de Bolivia* basement. Three were journalists, one a photographer and the fifth a researcher of Guevara: for the first time, the Bolivian government had given them free access to the "A-73" safe-deposit box in which the original copy of Che's Bolivian diary was and is still kept.

However, the box contained other very important material, as Carlos Soria Galvarro Terán (1944)—my great friend, companion in research and leading scholar of Che in Bolivia [at the time together with Humberto Vázquez Viaña

(1937-2013)]—was to discover with great emotion In fact, they found *a*) the original copy in Spanish of Pombo's diary, which was believed to have disappeared after its translation into English; *b*) evaluation forms of all the guerrilla members; *c*) the red loose-leaf notebook with the diary pages from November 7 to December 31, 1966 (in addition to notes and drafts of press releases); and *d*) the German leatherette agenda with the diary pages from January 1 to October 7, 1967.

But it is exactly at the end of this agenda, in the five final pages, that Carlos made the most disturbing discovery for we researchers into Che and where from it starts this reflection of mine on the relationship between Guevara and Marx: these five pages contained a list of 109 book titles (15 of which marked with a red cross), divided by months (to be reduced in quantity) from November 1966 to September 1967. This was completely new documentation that showed the deep interest Che had continued to nurture for study and theoretical elaboration up to the last hours of his life, despite finding himself in desperate circumstances and knowing that he was by then destined to defeat (military).

Carlos let me have the photos of the list and I published it in colour (to highlight the red crosses) in number 2 of *Che Guevara. Quaderni della Fondazione/Cuadernos de la Fundación* [CGQF], 1999, pp. 261-3.

The titles cited covered a wide range of themes and did not seem to refer to a particular bibliographic scheme. We scholars thought that they could be divided roughly into six categories: 1) philosophy and science; 2) political and military doctrine; 3) Latin American history and society; 4) Bolivian history, society and anthropology; 5) novels and world fiction; and 6) working tools such as dictionaries, statistical repertoires and medical issues.

The first group is the one of interest here and could include—besides N. Machiavelli (*The Prince and Other Political Writings*), G.W.F. Hegel (*Phenomenology of Spirit*) and L. Morgan (*Ancient Society*)—works on Marxism or of Marxist inspiration such as the following:

C.D.H. Cole, *Political Orgnisation;*

B. Croce, [with the title used in Spanish] *La historia como hazaña de la* libertad—(*The philosophy of History and the Duty of Freedom*)];

M.A. Dinnik, *History of Philosophy I;*

F. Engels, *Ludwig Feuerbach and the End of Classical German Philosophy, Dialectics of Nature;*

M. Djilas, *The New Class;*

V. Lenin, *The Development of Capitalism in Russia, Materialism and Empirio-Criticism, Certain Features of the Historical Development of Marxism, Philosophical Notebooks;*

Liu Shaoqi, *Internationalism and Nationalism;*

G. Lukács, *The Young Hegel and the Problems of Capitalist Society;*

Mao Zedong, *On Practice;*

K. Marx, *Critique of Hegel's Philosophy of Right;*

R. Mondolfo, *Historical Materialism in F. Engels;*

L. Trotsky, *The Permanent Revolution, History of the Russian Revolution I and II;*

J. Stalin, *Marxism and the National and Colonial Question, The National Question and Leninism, Problems of Leninism;*

C. Wright Mills, *The Marxists*.

A last name on the list—the only one for the month of September 1967—was first roughly identified as "F.O. Nietzsche", bringing a sparkle to the eyes of those who were already hoping to write an essay on Che's potential "supermanliness". However, Carlos Soria later better deciphered the name and established that it was the great military expert Ferdinand Otto Miksche (1904-1992) and his work *Secret Forces* [cf. *Cgqf*. No. 8/2010, p. 273].

For many years we did not know how to interpret that list of books, so wide but also so apparently disordered as to make one suspect that instead it must have had its own order, albeit very hidden. How else could it be explained that it had been jotted down in a diary that functioned as a military diary and in a situation that was certainly not conducive to study? Moreover, the quantity of over a hundred books (some in large volumes) would have been too excessive for imagining that Che could have taken them with him during guerrilla movements. And if he had left those books in hiding places built by him in camps prepared in the early months—and thus confiscated by the army after their discovery—they would surely have re-emerged in the "clandestine" market of Guevarian objects run for years by some of the officers who had taken part in counter-guerrilla operations: the military, in fact, privately sold everything that belonged to Che, and his supposed "travelling library" would certainly have had very high starting bids.

All that remained was to think of a wish list formulated by a Marxist scholar such as Guevara, who had a wide range of interests and had already proved to be a great devourer of books throughout his life. Or, alternatively, to think that it was a precise reading plan, in which the "Marxological" sector was of particular importance.

This second hypothesis turned out to be correct, but we were only able to confirm it some time later, with the emergence of a new document which had remained unpublished for a long time despite the importance it would have had "in the heat of the moment" for a precise definition of the most authentic Guevarian theoretical dimension. The wave of nonsense written after his death in books and articles on Che's "Marxism-Lenism" and on his presumed orthodoxy could have been avoided thanks to the letter I am about to examine and which provides the explanatory key to the "Bolivian" reading scheme mentioned here.

Scene 2 [Dar es Salaam, 1965]

Holed up in the house of the Cuban ambassador in Tanzania (Pablo Rivalta, 1925-2005), recovering from the defeat of the military expedition in Congo ("la historia de un *fracaso*", as Guevara himself called it) and before moving to Prague, Che wrote an important letter to Armando Hart Dávalos (1930-2017) on December 4, 1965. Armando Hart was a historic leader of the July 26 Movement [M26-7], husband of the founder of Casa de la Américas (Haydée Santamaría Cuadrado [1920-1980]) and father of "Trotskyist-Guevarist" Celia Hart Santamaría (1963-2008), as she described herself in her last few years, before dying in a car accident. Armando Hart was the first Minister of Education in the Cuban government, from 1959 to 1965. He was then to become Minister of Culture from 1976 to 1997 and would leave a series of theoretical works, among which it is worth mentioning here the essay on *Marx, Engels and the Human Condition* (2005). We will see why.

After a premise in which Guevara informed Armando Hart of his revival of interest in studies on philosophy, the letter developed two fundamental themes: 1) desolate observation of the state into which studies on Marxism in Cuba were falling due to the lack of material except those produced in the Soviet world; 2) a well-structured study plan to be approved and implemented as soon as possible.

It should be noted that the premise contained Che's admission that he had twice tried to deepen his understanding of the philosophy of "maestro Hegel", always ending up defeated but with the conviction of having to start philosophical studies from scratch (see point 2).

Regarding the first point, Guevara said that there was no serious Marxist material in Cuba, excluding *"the Soviet bricks that have the disadvantage of not letting you think, because the party has done it for you and you have to digest"*. A method that Che defined as "anti-Marxist" and was based on the poor quality of available books (mostly of Soviet origin). Books that were published both for editorial convenience (since the USSR contributed financially, I add) and for *"seguidismo ideológico"* [ideological tailism/khvostism] towards "Soviet and French authors". By the latter, Guevara intended to refer to the official Marxists of the PCF—which at that time were the vogue, not only in France but also in various other Communist parties—gathered under the supervision of Roger Garaudy (1913-2012), at the time still a Stalinist, before embarking on the many turnabouts that were to lead him to convert to Islam in 1982.

Regarding to the second point, it is not difficult to recognise an interpretative grid applicable to an important part of the reading plan that Che was to draw up in Bolivia about a year later, which has already been mentioned. This previous study project (which was personal, but which the Ministry should have also organised for the Cuban people) appeared divided into eight sections. And for each section some authors were indicated to be published or gone into further:

1. *The History of Philosophy* to be set within the work of a possibly Marxist scholar (mention was made of Michail Aleksandrovič Dinnik [1896-1971], author of a history of philosophy in 5 volumes), without obviously neglecting Hegel.
2. *The Great Dialectics and Materialists.* To begin with, Guevara cited Democritus, Eraclitus and Leucippus, but the Bolivian notes help us understand that he was also thinking of the work of Rodolfo Mondolfo (1877-1976), a well-known Jewish Italian Marxist who emigrated to Argentina in 1939 to escape the racial laws adopted by fascism. His history of *El Pensamiento Antiguo* (Ancient Thought) had been translated from Italian and published in various editions, starting in 1942.
3. *Modern Philosophers.* No names were made in particular, but Che did not exclude the publication of "idealist authors", provided they were accompanied by a critical apparatus.
4. *Classics on Economy and Precursors.* Adam Smith, the Physiocrats, etc.
5. *Marx and Marxist Thought.* Guevara complained that some fundamental Marxist texts were non-existent in Cuba and proposed the publication of works by Marx-Engels, Kautsky, Hilferding, Luxemburg, Lenin, Stalin "and many contemporary Marxists who are not totally scholastic". This latter opinion was linked to point 7.
6. *Construction of Socialism.* With particular attention to rulers of the past and the contributions of philosophers, economists and statisticians.

7. *Heterodox and Capitalist Theorists* (unfortunately collected under the same section). In addition to Soviet revisionism (for which Guevara could not but cite the Khrushchev of the time), among the heterodox theorists he included Trotsky, accompanied by a cryptic annotation, almost as if to say that the time had come to take note that *he had also* existed and "had written" things. Among the theorists of capitalism, Marshall, Keynes and Schumpeter were cited as examples to "be analysed thoroughly".
8. *Polemics*. With the caution that Marxist thought had advanced precisely thanks to polemics, Guevara declared that one could not continue to know Proudhon's *Philosophy of Poverty* only through Marx's *Poverty of Philosophy*. It was necessary to go to the sources. Rodbertus, Dühring, revisionism (here referring to that of German social democracy), the controversies of the 1920s in the USSR. This section was indicated by Che as the most important and the aim of a polemic directed against rampant conformism in the Cuban party and in the whole of the pro-Soviet world was evident. And it is no coincidence that the theme of "seguidismo" ["tailism"] reappeared in the conclusion of the letter, with a hint of veiled complicity addressed fraternally to Armando Hart against "the current makers of ideological orientation" to whom, according to Che, it would not have been "prudent" to show that type of study project.

An invitation to "prudence" that Armando Hart took a little too literally, deciding to keep such a precious text hidden for some decades. But in addition to Che's well-founded concerns, he had a special reason for not circulating the letter (and daughter Celia told me [in October 2006] that she could not forgive him when she came to know about it): the Cuban Minister of Education had and perhaps still had some special sympathies for Trotsky and had jealously kept it secret since it had never emerged in any of his books. But Guevara—the only Cuban leader who had occasionally been interested in the Trotsky question—had somehow learned of it. For this reason, when he named the famous "heretic" in the letter, addressing Armando Hart he called him *"tu amigo Trotsky"* ["your friend Trotsky"]. In the Cuba of 1965, a month before the Tricontinental Conference (January 1966), in which the concluding speech by Fidel Castro (1926-2016) was going to mark officially and definitively the passage of Cuba into the Soviet field (which had already occurred in substance some time earlier), the suspicion of Trotskyist sympathies would have been incompatible with the government post he held. This is why the letter "disappeared" for over thirty years.

It would be published for the first time in September 1997 in *Contracorriente* (Year III, No. 9) and then by Hart himself in 2005, in the book on Marx and Engels cited earlier (pp. XLIII-XLVIII), with photostatic reproduction of the original pages.

It was in this way, only after having seen a text so precious for establishing the level of reflection on Marxism achieved by Guevara, that it became possible for those of us interested in doing so to provide a valid explanation for the reading plan sketched in the agenda of the Bolivian diary. In the words taken from *Otro Mundo es Posible* by Néstor Kohan (b. 1967), the leading scholar on Che in Argentina:

> This letter allows us to grasp the degree of maturity achieved by Che *regarding the need to seek an autonomous philosophical and ideological alternative to Marxist 'orthodoxy'*, including both the official culture of the Soviet Union and the officialism existing at the time in China (*Otro mundo es posible*, p. 155).

At the time he wrote such an important letter, Guevara was going through a period of tumultuous transition, perhaps the most unstable and certainly the most dramatic of his life: he left Cuba and he had been defeated in the *great economic debate*; he resigned from government offices and had no citizenship; he was deprived of the support of his great friend Ahmed Ben Bella (1916-2012) who was overturned in June 1965 by the coup d'état of Houari Boumédiène (1932-1978) with which the decline of the Algerian revolution began; he had gone through the Congolese disaster; he was hostile to the Soviet policy of peaceful coexistence, and a lucid and fierce critic of the model of construction of socialism in the USSR; he was aware of the involution that the Cuban revolution was experiencing, anxious to return to what he considered to be a genuine revolutionary practice (guerrilla war); and he was wary of the theoretical certainties touted as "orthodox Marxism" and "Leninism".

It was clear that the theoretical reflection he wished to resume in a systematic and almost "professional" form—and about which he had first spoken to Armando Hart (perhaps because he too had the faint smell of heresy...)—was in turn a product of more recent political delusions. There remained only the doubt about how ancient in the theoretical field were the "genetic" roots of those delusions which the new reflections should have remedied.

FLASHBACK

Scene 3 [Lima, 1952]

To answer, it is necessary to step back in time to the first encounter with Marxism that the young Ernesto had personally experienced in Lima, Peru, during a period of his life in which he had already decided to engage in the search for his own path outside Argentina. That is, outside a great country where, in the early 1950s, the ideological alternative for a young radical who wanted to fight for ideals of social emancipation risked being crushed between two main poles: *anti-communist Peronism* or *Stalinist anti-imperialism.* There were certainly no alternatives of the third or fourth type, "better" but lesser, since the homeland of Domingo Faustino Sarmiento (1811-1888) and of the continental movement of *University Reform* ("el Grito de Córdoba" of 1918) had offered the main culture broth for heretical or heterodox currents more than any other Latin American country, perhaps second only to Mexico. But for some time the young Ernesto had no sense of it or did not feel the need for it.

Of some interest in the history of his theoretical training is the fact that at the end of high school he had begun to compile a "philosophical dictionary", of which there are some excerpts and the description given by his childhood friend in Alta Gracia, José (Pepe) González Aguilar (b. 1928?).

The Guevara spouses were anti-Peronists but they were not Marxists, Catholics but not practising. The mother (Celia de la Serna y Llosa [1906-1965]) was a very independent woman, radical and endowed with considerable intellectual interests, which were non-conformist for the time and the environment in which she lived: her influence was decisive on Ernesto's training and this is recognised by many, starting with the second of the brothers (Roberto Guevara [b. 1932]) who spoke to me about it with great emphasis for the first time in November 1992.

The group of friends belonged mostly to anti-fascist and anti-Francoist families, but they were not communist. An exception was university friend Tita Infante (d. 1976), with whom Ernesto maintained a long and intense exchange of letters starting in 1947, which she corresponded with feelings that went beyond mere friendship. Tita was enrolled in the Communist Youth of the Faculty of Medicine of Buenos Aires, and Ernesto sometimes communicated to her the progress made in reading the first Marxist texts. According to the testimony of Celia Guevara de la Serna (sister of Che, b. 1929)—reported by Adys Cupull (b. 1937) and Froilán González (b. 1943) (in *Cálida Presencia,* p. 12)—it was she who introduced him to the reading of Aníbal Ponce (1898-1938), the great Argentine psychologist who died in Mexico, of whose extensive work the two read in particular the most properly Marxist works: *Education and Class Struggle, The Wind in the World* and above all (and fundamental for the future development of a Marxist ethics by Che) *Bourgeois and Proletarian Humanism.*

In the circle of friends, an exception was represented by "Petiso", the companion on the famous motorcycle trip—

Alberto Granado Jiménez (1922-2011)—the biochemist who since his university years had been linked to the Argentine Communist Party which was than headed by a notorious exponent of Stalinism, the Italian Victorio Codovilla (1894-1970).

And it was during the journey with Granado that the young Ernesto had the opportunity to frequent Dr. Hugo Pesce (1900-1969), the Italian-trained and internationally renowned leprologist who was a specialist in physiology, passionate about philosophy and an intellectual with a "formidable Marxist culture"—as Ernesto described him in a letter to his father (Don Ernesto Guevara Lynch [1900-1987]). Pesce was a member of the Peruvian Communist Party and in 1929, at the Communist Conference of Buenos Aires, he was one of the two Mariateguian delegates, that is followers of José Carlos Mariátegui (1894-1930), the main Latin American Marxist whose thinking from that moment began to have a considerable influence on the formation of the young Ernesto, above all in stimulating an early "discovery" of the *indigenous social question,* Andean in particular.

It cannot be excluded, in fact, that the theoretical interest of Ernesto for the *indios* (born initially from the passion for pre-Columbian archaeology and only later transformed into the theme of anti-imperialist struggle) and for the work of Mariátegui began right in the home of Hugo Pesce. He had the two young friends lodged in a hospital, but he often had them as guests at mealtimes. From their diaries we know what a positive influence the conversations with that direct pupil of Mariátegui—in turn, a man of Marxist science and dialectics—had on Ernesto. If Guevara's Marxism really took off from there—as the main biographers are inclined to think—it must be said that it could not have had a better start in the political and philosophical sense.

"Coming at the right moment in his own quest for a guiding social philosophy, Pesce's beliefs and personal example offered a potential structure to emulate. From then on, the idea that he should find something similar for himself began forming in Ernesto's mind. As for Marxism-Leninism, he was interested, but he still had to acquire more knowledge before committing himself to a particular ideology" (Anderson, pp. 85-6).

The respect that Guevara was to keep till the end for this complex and fascinating figure of doctor/militant/Marxist (a clear reflection of what Ernesto himself aspired to become, finding a sort of "alter-super-ego" in Pesce), is confirmed by the words he wrote to him in 1962 as a dedication in the book *La Guerra de Guerrillas* (Guerrilla Warfare):

> To Doctor Hugo Pesce who will provoke, perhaps unknowingly, a major change in my attitude towards life and society, with the usual adventurous enthusiasm, but aimed at ends which are more harmonious with the needs of America [of the American continent, ed.]. Fraternally, Che Guevara.

Scene 4 [Rome, 1969]

By pure chance, the second decisive influence on Ernesto Guevara's adherence to Marxism was also Peruvian, in the person of a young economist with unmistakable Inca traits, a militant of the left wing of Apra (*Alianza Popular Revolucionaria Americana* [American Popular Revolutionary Alliance] founded in 1924 in Mexico by Víctor Raúl Haya de la Torre [1895-1979]), a refugee in Guatemala and politically active in the world of the exiles: Hilda Gadea Acosta (1925-1974), Che's first wife and mother of Hildita (1956-1995). Her personal story as a woman first long courted, then wife and mother, as "professor" of Marxism for Che, as a companion of struggle in Guatemala in 1954 and in Mexico till almost the launching of Granma in 1956, intertwined with years that were fundamental for Ernesto's theoretical itinerary: the years in which his definitive adherence to Marxism took place, primarily for ideological reasons but also for political tasks and those related to struggle. A perfect union of theory and praxis which was difficult to find exemplified in the "Manuals" or in other famous exponents of "Marxism-Leninism".

They were "decisive years" for the birth of this figure

which has now become one of the most emblematic of 20th century revolutionary Marxism, as the title of the book rightly recalls (*Años Decisivos*, 1972): the book that Hilda decided to write to recount that human and political story. Thanks to that decision (suffered, as I can personally testify), it has left us an irreplaceable, theoretically elaborate, sincere and reliable testimony, enriched by the further merit of describing also from within, thus in psychological terms, such an important ideological transformation of Ernesto Guevara.

In addition to the task of recounting the Guatemalan-Mexican story of Che, Hilda had, however, taken on another task to be fulfilled, given that her brother Ricardo Gadea (b. 1939, leader of the *Movimiento de izquierda revolucionaria* [Mir]—Revolutionary Left Movement) was in prison in Peru, together with other famous political prisoners such as Hugo Blanco (b. 1934), Héctor Béjar (b. 1935) and Elio Portocarrero Ríos (b. 1941), who were always at risk of their lives. Given that in Italy there were some well-known personalities from the world of culture (composer Luigi Nono [1924-1990], painter Ennio Calabria [b. 1937] and others) willing to engage in a campaign of denunciation, Hilda chose Italy to give life to a Committee of Solidarity with Peruvian political prisoners, spending long periods there between 1969 and 1971. The year before in Cuba (where I had been a guest of the Government from July to December 1968) a strong understanding and beautiful friendship had been created between the two of us, so she asked me to help her set up and direct the Committee. All this was made easier by the fact that in Rome Hilda lived in the house of my sister Rossana (b. 1940), where I also stayed for a while because I did not yet have a permanent home. And it was there that she began to write the book of memories on Che and it was me who, through a fortuitous series of events, was the first or one of the first "readers" to whom Hilda recounted what could later be read in her book.

Everything that happened between Guatemala and Mexico is now a known story, recounted in the main biographies; but in the late 1960s, Hilda was the only direct and reliable source of Che's Marxist training, given that she had been his "teacher": this was able to happen because she was more prepared than Ernesto, having a degree in economics, and above all because she had an anti-orthodox Marxist training with roots in Apra (therefore more genuinely Latin American) and not Sovietic (that is, Stalinist and dogmatic).

I have already provided an account of those "Roman" conversations with Hilda in my book of 1987 *Che Guevara. Pensiero e Politica Dell'utopia* [Che Guevara. Pensamiento y Política de la Utopía], and it is not the case to repeat here. It may be interesting, however, to mention the titles or names of the authors that the two read, commented on and discussed (sometimes even animatedly as Che wrote in a letter to the family): Tolstoy, Gorky, Dostoevsky, Kropotkin (*Memoirs of a revolutionary*), Engels (*Antidühring, Origins of the Family, Socialism: Utopian and Scientific,* etc.), Lenin (*What is to be Done?, Imperialism*) and of course various works by Marx, in addition to *The Communist Manifesto* and *Capital*. About the latter, Hilda wrote:

> ...and *Capital* by Marx, with which I was more familiar for my studies of economics (p. 36)].

Wanting to summarise Hilda Gadea's point of view regarding that phase of intense theoretical sharing and fresh and enthusiastic Guevarian adherence to Marxism, I must say that in the conversations she had with me she placed the emphasis on two aspects which were then indeed crucial and which time has instead dispersed among the mists of the theoretical divergences that are now surpassed and obsolete.

In the first place, Hilda kept alive and transmitted to Ernesto the conception that the revolution in the backward, dependent or developing countries cannot rely on the national bourgeoisie, neither as such—that is collectively in historical concretions of certain dependent capitalist classes (those which when I talked to her I referred to as "sub-imperialistic")—nor on their allegedly progressive sectors. These sectors appeared inevitably marked by class interests that ultimately would have led them to clash with the processes of real social emancipation, both in the rural world and with the urban proletariat. Regarding to Hilda and to the credit of Guevara, it must be recognised that he never failed in this fundamental political intuition derived from the best theoretical tradition of 20th century revolutionary Marxism.

Secondly, she tried to win Ernesto over to a radical critique of Soviet Marxism, both for the responsibilities it had in the past for the degenerative process of the October revolution, and for its contemporary policy of convergence with imperialism in maintenance of the global status quo. It is true, however, that Hilda harboured illusions about Chinese communism, and at the time the USSR-China conflict was a burning topic. We will see that Guevara will not always listen to her on this double aspect of a single international reality born in Yalta and will go through oscillations in favour of and against Soviet Marxism, for and against so-called "Maoism", unfortunately losing life before arriving at a superior synthesis of both these refusals.

But more about that later.

On the commitment Ernesto put into the study of Marxism in the years of Guatemala and Mexico (1954-56), we also have three testimonies of his friends or future companions on the expedition to Cuba. Mario Dalmau de la Cruz, a Cuban exiled in Guatemala after having participated in the attack on the Moncada Barracks, talks about it (Ernesto "had read a whole Marxist library" in *Granma* of October 29, 1967). Darío López talks about it and tells us that it was Che who chose the Marxist works in the library of the training camp for those taking part in the Granma expedition and that the Mexican police would seize (in *Granma* of October 16, 1967).

And it is talked about by Argentine Ricardo Rojo (1923-1996), the travelling companion who wrote the first highly contested biography of Guevara and who invented the famous phrase erroneously attributed to Che (*"Hay que endurecerse, pero sin perder la ternura jamás"* ["One has to grow hard but without ever losing tenderness "]). Rojo informs us that thanks to the friendship with Arnaldo Orfila Reynal (1897-1998), the Argentine who ran the largest publishing company in Mexico (Fondo de Cultura Económica—FCE), Guevara could put himself to selling books and therefore had access to many works that otherwise he would not have been able to buy:

> The classics of Marxism, the collection of the works of Lenin, texts relating to the military strategy of the Spanish Civil War passed before Guevara's greedy eyes during the night, and in the morning they returned to the leather folder with which they visited offices and private houses (*Mi Amigo el Che*, p. 87).

The director of FCE provided Che with the three volumes of *Capital* and—whether he had read them in full or not, given the limited time available and the difficulties of study that they involved—he found himself within a few months giving lessons to Cubans of the 26th July Movement on Marxism and Marx. The latter now jokingly called by him "San Carlos", ironically referring to the "heroes" of the *Holy Family*.

Ernesto communicates his new commitment in a somewhat coded letter sent to his mother on June 17, 1955. And similarly he writes to the beloved aunt Beatriz Guevara Lynch on January 8, 1956:

> ... I often read Saint Charles and his disciples, I dream of going to study the cortisone [the countries beyond the border (*ed.*)] with one of these French girls who know everything... .

The theme of "San Carlos" appears in various other letters of the period sent to loved ones: on April 15, 1956 to his father; between August and September to his mother; towards October to Tita Infante ("assiduous reader of Carlitos and Federiquitos and others 'itos'"); again in October to his mother ("Now St Charles is primordial, is the axis, and will be in the years when the spheroid allows me in to its outermost layer".

There can be no doubt, therefore, that while adherence to Marxism was initiated in conversations with Hugo Pesce, it was actually built with the avalanche of readings carried out in Guatemala and Mexico, partly under the guidance of Hilda

Gadea, in part under the pressure of events and new political commitments including the military training given by the Spanish Civil War general Alberto Bayo y Giroud (1892-1967), his arrest and Mexican prison, and final preparation for the Granma expedition.

In between there was also "discovery" of the *class struggle*, the real, armed and mass struggle, which was workers in social composition and demands: it was the Bolivian revolution that started in 1952 and which Guevara experienced as a direct witness in the summer of 1953. And this decisive experience should also be seen as one of the elements that won Guevara over to Marxism, above all to a characteristic and more authentic conception, for which the commitment in practice should never have been separated from the theoretical elaboration. However, on the importance of the first Bolivian experience of the young Ernesto, one can only refer to other works.

The same applies to the experience of the failed revolution of Jacobo Árbenz (1913-1971) in Guatemala: an event in which Guevara saw his first true revolutionary dream frustrated and in which he actively participated in a mass struggle for the first time. Disillusioned by the conciliatory and submissive behaviour of the local communist party, the *Partido Guatemalteco del Trabajo* (Pgt) [Guatemalan Party of Labour] he drew up a negative balance of that experience in his first political article. He also blocked his adherence to the party he was about to join, having understood that it was not enough to call oneself "Marxist" to actually be so: his distrust towards the party form as such began from that moment. In the course of his intense political life as a fighter for the cause of the revolution he was not to join any party that was really such. Instead, he was a member and active member of the M26-7 and of its armed expression (the *Exército Rebelde*) as long as this movement survived. In fact, it is known that Guevara left Cuba before the constitution of the Cuban Communist Party (PCC) was formalised and the October 1965 designation of its Central Committee of which Che was never part.

INTERVAL

Scene 5 [Sierra Maestra, 1956-58]

The interval was real: an authentic "epistemological" break it could be said with Althusserian irony, since between departure for the Granma expedition and the victorious conclusion of the Las Villas campaign—which Guevara ended with the battle of Santa Clara which gave rise to his "legend»—there was an interruption in philosophical reflection on Marxism texts and reading itself of the texts. The interruption lasted a little more than two years, starting with the departure from Tuxpan (when the only person with a previous military experience was the Italian Gino Doné [1924-2008] who had taken part in the Resistance in Veneto), passing through occupation of the two main military strongholds in Havana—under the leadership of Che and Camilo Cienfuegos (1932-1959)—and ending with the establishment of the new regime headed by Fidel Castro. They were times of guerrilla warfare on the mountains and attacks in the cities, strikes, agrarian reform, expropriation and nationalisation, and the creation of a new state structure. Certainly not times of theoretical reflection, of study or of exploring the Marxian message.

Guevara's *Episodes of the Cuban Revolutionary War* and the memoires of various fighters give the perception of a profound disregard for the problems of political theory by the Castro leadership—in this very differently from what had happened in the first period of the Russian Revolution—and one gets the impression that Che was closed in a sort of theoretical self-isolation. He admitted this himself in writing to the political figure that I personally consider to have been the most representative of the Cuban revolution (commander René Ramos Latour [«Daniel", 1932-1958]), who died in combat, but only after having stood up to Che in a controversy that deserves the greatest attention and instead, out of political hypocrisy, is almost always ignored or in any case belittled.

On December 14, 1957, Che wrote him a long letter, very critical of the positions of the *llano* (the M26-7 in the cities where Daniel had been the main leader after the death of Frank País [1934-1957]), stating:

> I am, *through my ideological preparation,* one of those who believe that *the solution of the problems in the world is to be found behind the so-called Iron Curtain* and I consider this movement as one of the many provoked by the anxiety of the bourgeoisie to free itself from the economic chains of imperialism.

I have always considered *Fidel as an authentic leader of the left bourgeoisie,* even if his personality is characterised by personal qualities of extraordinary value, which place him far above his class.

With this spirit I started the struggle: honestly *without the hope of going beyond liberation of the country, willing to leave* when the conditions of the next struggle turn all the action of the Movement to the right (towards what you represent" (my italics)].

It would be too long here to explain the subject of the polemic that is however of the greatest interest for understanding the dynamics of the Cuban revolution, and in any case I have already done so in detail on other occasions. But at least two aspects must be kept in mind: *a*) Guevara had come to consider himself definitively part of the communist (Soviet) camp and, *as a Marxist,* he considered himself an isolated militant within a bourgeois democratic movement like the M26-7 and, although he was engaged in an armed struggle, he was willing to trust only up to a certain point (here Hilda Gadea's teaching was evident); *b*) as early as 1957 he believed he could not conclude his revolutionary action within the Cuban movement and, with authentic prophetic spirit, announced his intention to leave for "other lands of the world»—as was to happen less than ten years later—if his ideological training should become incompatible with the ongoing revolutionary process. It was unequivocal proof of the internationalist spirit that animated his recent adherence to communism, although for the moment it coincided with the Soviet orientation.

It was much, but it was also everything. Nothing more of interest for our reflection on the evolution of his Marxism can be obtained from the years on the Sierra Maestra and the first formation of the new Cuban regime.

Second Half

ORTHODOXY STORY

Scene 6 [from Havana to Moscow, 1959-63]

As is well known, the revolutionary government assigned commander Guevara with tasks of great importance, but all within the economic sphere as president of the Banco Nacional de Cuba, in a first phase, and then as Minister of Industry (at the time unified in a single ministry) till the day of his resignation became operational between the end of 1964 and the spring of 1965.

He was also entrusted with important missions abroad which he carried out almost as a real foreign minister—at the United Nations, the Organisation of American States (Oas), the Comecon countries, the new African nations and various national liberation movements—becoming a sort of "itinerant ambassador" of the Cuban revolution. This very important part of his government activity goes beyond our reflection. Practically all biographies of Che speak about it, but for an overview and a direct testimony, I recommend in particular *Caminos del Che* by commander "Papito" Jorge Serguera (1932-2009) who, thanks to his total identification with the secret directives of the Cuban government, found himself playing a major role in very "delicate" operations: for example, as ambassador to Algiers at the time of Ben Bella or in charge of relations with Juan Domingo Perón (1895-1974) in Spanish exile.

Che's years as Minister of Industry are years in which he takes up his studies of Marxism again, as well as of the various other subjects necessary for the management of his Ministry: a field in which he had to learn everything from scratch, but in which he demonstrated really exceptional learning skills. It is obvious that the particular nature of the position led him to deepen his study of Marx and followers, especially in the field of critique of political economy. But as we shall see in the next scene, this did not produce *economicistic*-type derivations in him. Far from it.

And even his assiduous and hyperactive frequentation of factories and other production centres did not make him a "workerist". From this point of view his anti-dogmatic and originally unorthodox Marxist training constituted an effective vaccine against deformations that would have been "natural" in a neophyte of communist statism, admirer for a whole first phase of the Soviet model and the works of its ideologues in the economic field; these began to circulate in Cuba in Spanish long before the country officially became part of the Comecon [Cmea] (1972). This part of Guevarian activity and economic formation has been largely reconstructed by his former deputy minister, Orlando Borrego (b. 1936) in the 2001 book *Che, el Camino Del Fuego* (in particular in the first five chapters).

The best anthology of Che texts devoted to economic issues was instead published on the occasion of the 20th anniversary of his death, edited by historian Juan José Soto Valdespino (*Temas Económicos*, 1988). Obviously, it could not contain the Guevarian texts dedicated to the polemics with Soviet economic conceptions, publication of which was delayed by the Cuban government until 2006, when the Ussr had no longer existed for about 15 years (I will talk about this later). For a more up-to-date study of Che's economic ideas, one can resort to *Introducción al Pensamiento Marxista* (Introduction to Marxist Thought) edited by Néstor Kohan for the Cátedra Ernesto Che Guevara of the Madres de la Plaza de Mayo.

Outside the commitment in the economic field, Che continued to read as much as possible of Marx and official Marxism, being totally identified for this phase in the policy of rapprochement with the Soviets that Fidel Castro undertook on the island starting from the first months after revolutionary victory. On this road Guevara played a leading role in proposing that the State Publishing Company should publish theoretical texts produced beyond the "Iron Curtain", but above all in the difficult task of "rehabilitating" the local Communist party (the *Partido Socialista Popular* [PSP). In addition to the original hostility towards the M26-7 and the absence as a ruling group (but not as grassroots militants) from the revolutionary process, this party had also to be forgiven for the support given in 1940-44 to the first government of Fulgencio Batista (1901-1973)—in which it had taken part with two ministers—and subsequent relationships of ambiguous collaboration with the second government (after the Batista coup of 1952), even coming to oppose attempts to overthrow him such as, for example, the attack on Moncada Barracks.

Did Guevara know about these past collaborationist episodes of the PSP? It is difficult to say to what extent and up to which point, also because after the victory of 1959 all the possible compromising documents about the PSP of Blas Roca (1908-1987) disappeared from the Havana main library, as I was able to verify in person in 1968. But after the seizure of power, Che's identification with the Soviet model was so strong as to push him to underestimate these episodes of Cuban Stalinism. He was to come to regret it bitterly later, when the hardest attacks on his management of industry were to come precisely from the former PSP while, after his disappearance, the apparatus of international Soviet propaganda would launch a campaign of slander about his alleged loss of reason, so much so as to have become Trotskyist.

But in the early 1960s, none of this seemed to be on the horizon for minister Guevara. In fact, these are the years in which his Marxism is homologous with the dogmatic and scholastic standards of the Soviet brand of "dialectical materialism»—the notorious *Diamat*—pushing him to formulations imbued with vulgar evolutionism and mechanicism that only later he would reject.

The basic and most famous text for this "scientistic" reduction of Marxism is "Notes for the Study of the Ideology of the Cuban Revolution" (in *Verde Olivo*, October 1960) in which the adherence to Marxism in the ambit of the social sciences is equated with the definition that the scientist self-attributes in the field of natural, physical or mathematical sciences. The comparisons that Guevara provides are very significant when he states that no one will ask a physicist if he is "Newtonian" or a biologist if he is "Pasteurian" because they are these by definition and by natural impulse. And even if new research and new facts lead to changing the initial positions, there will always remain a background of truth in the tools used to reach presumed scientific certainties. And this is what happens to those who consider themselves Marxist and actually are. The "scientific-naturalistic" comparison with Marxism continues citing Einstein with relativity and Planck with quantum theory which, according to Guevara, have taken nothing away from the greatness of Newton: they have *surpassed* him but only in the sense that "the English scientist represents the necessary passage" for this further development (*Escritos y Discursos*, IV, p. 203).

Guevara does not escape from a conclusion definable as deterministic and evolutionistic at the same time, when he states that there are "truths so evident, so inherent in the conscience of peoples, that it is useless to discuss them. One must be 'Marxist' with the same naturalness with which one is 'Newtonian' in physics or 'Pasteurian' in biology" (pp. 202-3). This is a not even a refined way of affirming a dogmatic conception of social science, that is to say, in the case of Marxism.

Continuing the analogy with the mathematics in which we have had "a Greek Pythagoras, an Italian Galileo, an English Newton, a German Gauss, a Russian Lobachevsky, an Einstein, etc.", Guevara states that also in the social sciences the itinerary of a great process of accumulation of knowledge could be traced from Democritus to Marx—but this, I add, in total disregard for the discontinuity that Marxism attributes to the historical dialectic marked by ruptures, leaps, rearrangements and syntheses. But by now Marx has become for Che not only the scholar who "interprets history and understands its dynamics", but also he who "foresees future events", who "prophesies" (further on he even speaks of the "predictions of Marx the scientist"), who is "architect of his own destiny" and, besides interpreting nature, now has the tools to "transform it". Hence the obvious reference to the need for revolutionary action as a logical consequence of so much scientific knowledge of nature, history and the world made possible by Marxism, now considered definetely to be a science.

This flatly materialistic vision was certainly derived from very simplistic interpretations of works by Engels (*Anti-Dühring, Dialectics of Nature, Socialism: Utopian and Scientific*) and Lenin (*Materialism and Empirio-Criticism*) which are not cited here, but which Ernesto had read in Guatemala and Mexico. The equation of Marxism with the mathematical, physical or biological sciences—which had been a common currency for Marxology in the Stalinist period—now opens into the grossest philosophical evolutionism when Guevara draws a line of continuity between "Marx, Engels, Lenin, Stalin and Mao Zedong", even going so far as to include the "new Soviet and Chinese rulers" in this pyramid scheme of presumably Marxist thinking (*Escritos y Discursos*, p. 204]): of all these, according to Che, one should have followed "the body of doctrine" and even "the example" (but on Kruschev he would change his mind shortly thereafter ...).

It would be ungenerous to continue with other quotations from this naive listing of the presumed scientific-naturalistic merits of Marxism—which strangely however is never called here "dialectical materialism" according to what instead Stalinist tradition would have prescribed—and if anything we should take it up with how many (many, too many) have indicated in this article one of the top peaks reached by Guevara in his re-elaboration of Marxism. Unfortunately, C. Wright Mills (1916-1962)—who included this unique Che text in his famous anthology *The Marxists (1962)*—is one of these.

(Guevara will reciprocate by including in his own *Apuntes* (Notes) of 1966—which we will speak of—various passages taken from *The Marxists*.)

Regarding to the "Marxism" of Marx there is not much more, because the rest of the article launches itself into a very imaginative analysis of the progress of the Cuban revolution which I leave out here without remorse. In the past, however, I devoted some attention to the hasty manner in which Che had dismissed some statements in that text from of the two founding fathers related to Mexico and Bolivar. Here I limit myself to mentioning the piece by Guevara, but for my comment I refer to the detailed analysis I made in *Che Guevara. Pensamiento y Política de la Utopía*, pp. 54-9. With a word of caution: as incredible as it may seem, the piece of criticism of Marx that I am about to mention was suppressed, in an evident attempt at censorship, by the editors of *Escritos y Discursos* in 9 volumes of *Editorial de Ciencias Sociales* (which is the collection that is normally used for the works of Che after 1957): see to believe Vol. IV, p. 203. Moreover, in the past the Guevara Foundation has identified various other examples of censure in this "official" collection and in other Cuban editions of the *Works of Che*, then making the denunciation of such a scandalous and ridiculous situation public (see *CGQF* No. 6/2006, pp. 73-84).

But since the right hand of bureaucracy often ignores what the left does, the piece can be found entirely reproduced in the collection of *Works 1957-1967*, curated not by chance by the Casa de las Américas in 1970, when it was directed by an intelligent and anti-conformist woman like Haydée Santamaría. From there I report it in full, both because it is a beautiful piece by Che (which does not seem to have softened the soul of the censors), and as a humble tribute to Marx on the occasion of his 200th birthday:

> Marx as a thinker, as a scholar of the social sciences and of the capitalist system in which he lived, can obviously be accused of some inaccuracies. We Latin Americans, for example, cannot

> agree with his judgment on Bolivar and with the analysis which, together with Engels, Marx made of Mexicans, taking for granted certain theories about race or nationality which are inadmissible today. But great men, discoverers of luminous truths, survive in spite of their small errors, which serve to make them more human: they can make mistakes without this damaging our clear awareness of the level reached by these giants of thought. And for this reason we say that the essential truths of Marxism are an integral part of the cultural and scientific community of peoples and we accept them with the naturalness that comes from something that needs no further discussion (pp. 93-4).

The criticisms that Guevara addressed to Marx-Engelsian texts on Latin America could refer to some entries compiled by Marx and Engels for the *New American Cyclopaedia* (published in New York in 16 volumes between 1858 and 1863, under the direction of Charles Anderson Dana [1819-1897], also director for some twenty years of the *New York Daily Tribune*), but above all to a letter from Marx to Engels dated December 2, 1854 (in *Complete Works*, XXXIX, p. 434).

After having reconstructed the complicated story, in my comment I openly agreed with the two great friends and disagreed with Guevara. But I added a much more serious consideration about the fact that, in the essay dedicated by Che to analysis of the ideology of the Cuban revolution, there was no mention of the great *libertadores* (liberators), no mention of any Latin American thinker or writer involved in the anti-Spanish ideological struggle, not even José Martí (1853-1895) himself. Greek philosophers, physicists and mathematicians from various eras were mentioned, as well as a lot of Marx, but no one indigenous to Cuba or Latin America. A foolishness certainly produced by the anxiety of the neophyte who wanted to show himself more Marxist than Marx, flaunting an acquired familiarity with his work, but that cannot fail to leave one taken aback. More than the vulgar materialist conception of Marxism exhibited therein, it is the absence of references to Latin American ideologies or political conceptions which constitutes the most serious deficiency of that unfortunate text, which was so popular at the time and may still continue to delight.

This was not, however, an isolated case because in other texts of the period there were similar reductive and distorted visions of the Marxist method of analysis, accompanied by a clear ignorance of the great tradition of debate that had developed during the entire 20th century starting from the original Marxian legacy.

See, for example, the most interesting interview ever with Guevara. I refer of course to my friend Maurice Zeitlin (b. 1935) who interviewed Che on September 14, 1961, and immediately published the interview in *Root and Branch* (photostatic copy in *CGQF* No. 9/2014, pp. 219-26), a magazine based at the University of Berkeley in California, which was repeated on various occasions (see for example *Cuba, an American Tragedy*). For the occasion, despite having touched on political topics of great theoretical actuality, Guevara repeated in synthesis the previous materialistic vulgate, including the comparison with biology which, as a doctor, he was evidently fond of:

> We regard Marxism as a science in development, just as, say, biology is a science. One biologist adds to what others have done, while working in his own special field. Our specialty is Cuba (p. 54).

To make the comparison with biology even clearer (and more serious), in the subsequent answer Guevara extended it also to Lenin: a "eulogy" that he would have to regret later (in 1964) when he was to clearly distance himself from fundamental aspects of the Leninist vulgate:

> The value of Lenin is enormous—in the same sense in which a major biologist's work is valuable to other biologists. He is probably the leader who has brought the most to the theory of revolution. He was able to apply Marxism in a given moment to the problems of the State, and to emerge with laws of universal validity.

This is the interview in which Guevara, pressed by Zeitlin (who in fact offered an exemplary model of behaviour for a true "interviewer" who does not want to remain passive and supine in the face of the answers of the person being interviewed), had to recognise that he was not familiar with great figures of socialism like Eugene Debs (1855-1926) or Rosa Luxemburg (1871-1919). As for the latter, he formulated only a kind of ungenerous epitaph, saying that "she was a great revolutionary and she died a revolutionary, as a consequence of her political mistakes" (p. 54). Six years later, the same words could have been applied to the Bolivian Guevara, just as ungenerously.

The use of the formula "dialectical materialism" appears widely in a speech given by Guevara during a prize-giving at the Ministry of Industry on January 31, 1962 (*Escritos y Discursos*, VI, pp. 79-90). After enthusiastically praising a book by Blas Roca, Che presents a sort of synthesis of the degree of understanding of Marxism he had achieved in that phase, totally unbalanced on the side of the last Engels, as was now unanimously accepted in Soviet Marxology.

The passage that follows (p. 81) brings together *a*) the naively materialistic (and in any case unfounded) theory of the existence of *two* sciences, the bourgeois and the proletarian; *b*) the attribution to Engels even the paternity of theory for the origin of life on earth; *c*) the applicability of the dialectical materialistic method to all aspects of reality (with Stalin we had reached linguistics and genetics); and *d*) and the de facto identification of such a method with non-capitalist science, thus with "proletarian" science, even if not further specified.

In short, Guevara shows an integral adherence to the theory of Diamat and its claims of cultural hegemony over every aspect of individual and social life.

> The concept of life that dialectical materialism offers us is different from the concept of life that capitalism offers us: the concept of the sciences of dialectical materialism is also different. Many years ago, Engels had defined life as a way of being of albuminoid material; it was a new concept, something that at the time revolutionised ideas [...]. For this reason we must look for such bases, learn to think correctly through the method

> of dialectical materialism in every field, not only in political discussions or on specific occasions, but for applying it as a method in every scientific or practical task that we have to fulfil. All interpretations of the technique, and above all interpretation of the economy, change enormously if examined in the light of dialectical materialism or under the false lights of capitalist conceptions.

Moreover, if the Che Minister of Industry displayed uncritical adherence to the conceptions of Soviet Marxism in the first years of the revolution this was due to the fact that those conceptions were naively imported and accepted in all their crude and brutal mechanicism by the entire Cuban leadership. By some passively, by others actively: among these and first of all Guevara and Raúl Castro (b. 1931), considered from the beginning the only other "communist" present in the leadership of M26-7. They were then to be joined by Osmany Cienfuegos (b. 1931), immediately after the death of his brother Camilo, coming from the PSP and future leader of the Organisation *of Solidarity with the People of Asia, Africa and Latin America* (Ospaaal).

These are also the years when ideological work (propaganda, cadre schools and publication of the main magazines) ended up in the hands of the leaders shaped in the old PSP who in the meantime had been called to be part of the new Cuban leadership. They were entrusted practically—and for a few crucial years—with the management of the properly "cultural" activity of the party in view of a true fact: namely that they were the only ones to have some sort of theoretical preparation.

But even this is a page that Che was to rewrite radically in his ideal testament of March 1965 (*Socialism and Man in Cuba,* see the edition edited by Argentine José "Pancho" Aricó [1931-1991]), denouncing the "socialist realism" and official culture that, under the pretext of being "within reach of all", was in reality "within the reach of officials" that is, of the bureaucracy. In that text he was also to make a harsh criticism of "the scholasticism that has held back the development of Marxist philosophy" and the fact that "a formally exact representation of nature" has been converted into "a mechanical representation of the social reality that was wanted to be shown".

On May 30, 1963, Guevara had written a laudatory preface, which verged on ingenuity and apologetic intent, for a book published in Cuba by the *United Party of the Cuban Socialist Revolution* (PURSC). This was the name of the intermediate party that existed practically only on paper—from March 1962 to October 1965—in the phase in which Fidel Castro imposed the unification of a single organisation of the three main political currents that had survived in Cuba: the pro-Soviet communists of the PSP, *Directorio Revolucionario 13 de Marzo* and M26-7. Those who did not share that choice (the most famous case was Carlos Franqui [1921-2010], author of *Libro de lo Doce*) was excluded or emigrated abroad.

The title was high-sounding (*El Partido Marxista-Leninista*), but in reality it was a question of some of Fidel Castro's speeches added to one of the most "celebrated" liturgical texts in the Soviet world, namely *Manual of Marxism-Leninism* by Otto Wilhelm Kuusinen (1881-1964). He had been the historic leader of Finnish Stalinism who remained unscathed through decades of purges and political wrangling, "famous" for having been placed at the head of the puppet government created by the Soviets when they had vainly attempted to occupy Finland (1939-40) according to the clauses of the Secret Protocol that had accompanied the Pact signed by Stalin (Molotov) with Hitler (von Ribbentrop).

The preface by Guevara to that pamphlet can be considered as the lowest point he reached in the exaltation of "naturalistic materialism", that is, of Soviet-type Marxism-Leninism. A date that marks the limit in the theoretical degradation of his Marxism and after which there began to re-emerge with difficulty the anti-conformist, lucid and anti-dogmatic Marxist, who had admired the Mariateguian Hugo Pesce years earlier and had listened, but not sufficiently, to the theoretical counsels of young leftist member of Apra Hilda Gadea.

Guevara's commitment to bringing Cuba closer to the USSR and identifying the ideological aims of the Cuban revolution with the Marxist vulgate spread by the Soviet propaganda apparatus was enthusiastically reconstructed (and in large part invented) in a book of "Guevarological-Marxist Paleontology", published in Russian in 1972 and in Spanish (Editorial Progreso of Moscow) in 1975. The title was simple—*Årnðsto Cð Gðvara (Ernesto Če Gevara* [*Ernesto Che Guevara*])—but the background of the author, Iosif P. Lavretskij, was less simple, being the pseudonym of a Soviet secret police agent, also hidden behind another name as we have shown in *CGQF* No. 4/2001 (see note)*. The pages in which the Kgb emissary most celebrates the pro-Sovietic commitment of Che are 183-205 of the Russian edition and 178-98 of the Spanish edition.

[* For some time it was believed that Iosif P. Lavretskij was a Soviet scholar, although there remained the suspicion that he could be identified with a Lithuanian-Russian author of works on Guevara: Iosif Romual'dovič Grigulevič (1913-1988). At one point it was clear that Grigulevič and Lavretskij were two different names and surnames of one author: the first was a physical person, an agent of the NKUD and then of the KGB (with the name of "Teodoro Castro Bonnefil"), involved in various important murders (Nin, Trotsky, etc.) and at some point commissioned to kill also the president of Yugoslavia Tito; the second was one of his pseudonyms. The library catalogues of Harvard University in the United States report that the two names identify the same author. On p. 427 of his book *La Vida en Rojo, una Biografía del Che Guevara* (1997), Jorge Castañeda Gutman (b. 1953) wrote that "Lavretskij" was the pseudonym behind which Soviet historian and KGB agent Josef Grigulevič hid. In June 2001 in a speech at the conference of the Guevara Foundation in Acquapendente, Zbigniew M. Kowalewski (b. 1943), the leading Polish scholar of Che, confirmed that "Lavretskij" was the pseudonym of Grigulevič, a former Soviet secret police officer. At the same meeting, Czech scholar Vladimír Klofáč reported that Miloslav Ransdorf (1953-2016), Vice President of the Communist Party of Bohemia and Moravia, had indicated the name Lavretskij/ Grigulevič (thus associating the two names) in the note on p. 50 of the book *Muž Svědomí* (Man of Conscience). *Ernesto Che Guevara*, Nakladatelství Futura, Prague 2000. All these hypotheses were definitively confirmed by the publication of the Archive of Vasilij Nikitič Mitrochin (1922-2004) in 1999-2000 and, posthumously, in 2005. I add a little curiosity: in the "Reading Plan in Bolivia", Che included *Pancho Villa* by the same I. Lavretskij in the books listed in November 1966.]

HERESY STORY

Scene 7 [from Moscow to Havana, 1963-65]

The starting scene for describing this intellectual revival of Guevara's Marxism is set in Moscow and he described it himself in one of the *stenographic recordings* of the bi-monthly conversations he held at the Ministry of Industry from 1962 to 1964. Here we are especially interested in some of the recordings of Che's last year in Cuba as a minister. They are informal but precious materials; even more precious because they have not been re-elaborated or reviewed thus, reflecting Che's immediate—and by no means diplomatic—thoughts. These recordings were published in 1967 (but Guevara had already been able to see the drafts in 1966) in Vol. VI of the first extremely limited edition (around two hundred copies) of his works, edited by Orlando Borrego (*El Che en la Revolución Cubana*). In Cuba they were never republished, nor ever included in collections of his works and therefore for a long time they could be read above all in editions and translations made abroad: the first were in French, edited by Michael Löwy (b. 1938) and published by Maspero (1932-2015), and in Italian by *il Manifesto* in 1969 and then in my collection of *Scritti Scelti* [Selected Writings] of Che in 1993. Until they were finally included in the volume of *Apuntes*, published in Cuba in 2006.

The scene takes place on December 5, 1964 in the Cuban embassy in Moscow where Che is listened to by some fifty Soviet students, but also challenged by some of them regarding his theory of the priority of moral incentives, based on the growth of conscience of workers more than the use of material incentives.

> At this point, when (the problems) began to be posed, the confrontation became violent. The Bible—namely the *Manual*—because unfortunately the Bible here was not the *Capital* but the *Manual*. Some points began to be challenged, while things that were dangerously capitalist were also said: it was then that the question of revisionism emerged (*Apuntes*, p. 369).

It is important to point out that the "Manual" ironically referred to here is the *Manual of Political Economy* of the Academy of Sciences of the USSR, to which Guevara was to dedicate a whole volume of devastating criticism at the beginning of 1966 and which we will return to.

For now it is important to establish that the atmosphere changed in Moscow with regard to Commander Guevara (considered "glorious" above all for his military exploits and not for his Marxism) and that the criticisms he addressed in the meantime to Soviet economic conceptions left their mark. He is no longer the ultra-Soviet apologist, slavish supporter of the almost metaphysical superiority of dialectical materialism, but an intellectual in a "revisionist" crisis, as he is accused of in Moscow, who has now understood that for the emancipation of the human being "the exact method to do so has not been found in any country and in some cases people have fallen into the extremes that today we call 'Stalinists'" (September 12, 1964, p. 548)].

And since in Moscow no doubt on fundamental questions of this nature is allowed, one can imagine what reaction could have been caused by the negative judgements on Soviet economic management that Che had formulated during the *great economic debate*. The verdict could not be anything other than the classic *Damnatio Iudicii*, Propaedeutic to *Damnatio Memoriae*: it was clearly "Trotskyism".

> But because I am identified with the budgetary financing system, I get confused with that of Trotskyism. They say that the Chinese are also fractionists and Trotskyists, and they put the San Benito

> [a penitential garment of the Inquisition (*ed.*)] even on me (p. 370).
>
> And so it was there, precisely in the Soviet Union, that greater clarity could be achieved. Does this mean that it is about revisionism up to Trotskyism, passing through the middle? [...] Rather, Trotskyism emerges from two sides: one (the one that least attracts me) comes from the side of the Trotskyists who say that there is a series of things that Trotsky had already said. I believe only one thing, and it is that one must have the capacity to destroy all the contrary ideas on a given subject or let the ideas express themselves. The opinion according to which they should be destroyed with blows is not an opinion that brings benefits (p. 369).

To understand the true Marxist maturation of Che it is essential to read carefully and go into the ideas that are scattered among the stenographic recordings, mixed with a thousand other problems (the operation of factories, problems of workers, polemics of opponents, negative but not yet drastic judgements on the economic ideas of the Soviets). It is not easy to reconstruct the thread running through Guevarian reflection and it is not even possible to summarise it here. I will limit myself to pointing out two references to Marx's works which have a great qualitative importance for our reflection.

The first concerns the "young Marx". It was the mid-1960s and in France the stir produced by the great controversy over Marxian humanism (which can be reconstructed starting from the *Writings of the Young Marx on Philosophy* and the *Manuscripts of 1844*) had not yet died down, both because of the rigidly anti-humanist positions of Althusser (1918-1990) and of the stance taken by Soviet ideologues. Guevara appears clearly fascinated by the controversy and comes out on the side of the humanism of the young Marx. He had already done so in the course of the economic debate, citing it explicitly: he returns to it in the virtually contemporary conversation of December 21, 1963.

He reconstructs the terms of the controversy, admits that the "Hegelian" language of the young Marx is not that of the "mature" Marx (author of *Capital*), but affirms that the basic Marxian thesis—according to which the development of society corresponds to the development of its economic contradictions in relation to the class struggle—was already contained in the Marx of 1844.

The reconstruction made by Guevara of this starting point acquires a particular value because it leads it back to the Marx of maximum acquired maturity, expressed in the text in which the philosopher of Trier had given his own conception of socialist society and of the transition to it: the *Critique of the Gotha Programme.* And this is the second important reference to Marx that flows through various conversations (e.g. pp. 270, 309, 311-12).

The attention given by Che to the Marx of 1844 and to the Marx of *Critique of the Gotha Programme* leads him to develop his own personal hobby-horse, namely the importance of the *subjective* element for Marxism not only during the revolutionary struggle, but also during the transition to socialism, of the construction of the new society and of the *new man*. According to Guevara, there cannot be communism that does not make Marxian "concerns" with respect to the *humanistic* nature of revolution its own. Indeed, there can be no revolution if the right role and the right importance are not attributed to the subjective commitment—in the *ethical* sense—of the worker considered as a class.

This characteristic position of Guevarian Marxism allowed Michael Löwy to speak first of the *revolutionary humanism* of Che (*La Pensée de Che Guevara*, 1970). It was then to be my turn to take up the concept and develop it extensively in my frequently cited 1987 monograph: Che's entire philosophy or vision of the world can be summed up in this phrase—*revolutionary humanism*.

Over time I have become increasingly convinced that any attempt to place Che's theoretical heritage outside of his personal and original revolutionary humanism makes it practically impossible to explain his behaviour: not only of his relationship which was experienced existentially and with extreme coherence between theory and praxis, but not even his ethics of socialism and personal commitment. From this point of view, a commitment that was very Sartre-like, and it is no coincidence that Jean-Paul Sartre (1905-1980) was able to recognise great personal and intellectual qualities in him as early as 1960 (*Visit to Cuba*).

In conversations and in other texts, Guevara also takes on the Marxian problem of *alienation* which, as we know, was a fundamental element of Marx's criticism of Hegel and, in my personal opinion, the main element of *philosophical* differentiation from Hegelian statism for an entire initial phase, and of *political* differentiation for the rest of Marx's life.

While it is not part of my reflection, it is interesting to recall that Guevara contrasts the idea of transition to Marx's socialism (starting from the relationship between given subjective consciousness and the process of self-emancipation from the mechanisms of capitalist alienation) with the uncertainties and real turning points that he rightly attributes to Lenin without, however, giving the question the importance it deserves.

During the conversations, Guevara talks about his change of judgement with respect to Lenin. The vulgate of "Marxism-Leninism" no longer belongs to his baggage of ideas, even if the process that led him to this view is in a sense historically reversed: Guevara does not like the Nep, because he does not like the idea that elements of the market, methods of capitalist functioning, are reintroduced in an economy of transition to socialism. He does not accept it for the USSR and Cuba of his days, and retrospectively does not accept it for the Russia of the 1920s. Hence a drastic review of the judgement about Lenin, which is now presented in conflict with the essence of *Critique of the Gotha Programme* (pp. 310-12, 316, 324-6), or even with his *State and Revolution*, previously admired and cited by Guevara.

Many of the ideas expressed in the conversations at the Ministry of Industry are reflected in the articles written almost simultaneously for the *great economic debate*. The discussion took place roughly between the beginning of 1963 and the end of 1964. The interventions appeared *freely* in several Cuban journals and not only the main leaders of each sector of the economy took part in the discussion—from industry to banks, with the sole exception of Fidel Castro who did not take part—but also some famous European economists such as Charles Bettelheim (1913-2006) and Ernest Mandel (1923-1995) without forgetting the importance attributed to that discussion by the *Monthly Review* of Paul Sweezy (1910-2004) and Leo Huberman (1903-1968). The best presentation of that historical discussion has been given in *O Debate Econômico em Cuba* by Luiz Bernardo Pericás (b. 1969).

An additional note should be added regarding the sources used by Che to become familiar with the personal story of Marx and Engels. He certainly read part of the correspondence between the two which had been available for some time in Spanish, but his favourite source was *The Life of Marx* by Franz Mehring (1846-1919). He cites it expressly on more than one occasion. For example, in the conversation of October 2, 1964 (p. 325) when he affirms the need to publish the famous biography (which he describes as "moving") in Cuba and emphasises in particular the importance that Mehring attributed to Marx's polemic with Ferdinand Lassalle (1825-1864). Unfortunately Che does not develop the theme and it is a real pity because we could have better understood his attitude towards the statist conception of socialism, on which I have always had doubts that Guevara was a convinced adept.

On the other hand, I have no evidence that Guevara could have read the monumental biography dedicated to *Karl Marx and Friedrich Engels* by Auguste Cornu (1888-1981), the first half of the Spanish translation of which was published by the Instituto del Libro in Havana in an enormous volume of over 700 pages only in 1967, although—I have been told—on explicit request made by Che before leaving.

But Guevara did something more than simply recommend Mehring's biography. He made it a real compendium, which can be read as "Síntesis Biográfica de Marx y Engels", either in its natural location—within the *Notes* as a chapter endowed with a propaedeutic theoretical function with respect to the subsequent polemic with the Soviets—or as a banally commercial operation (by Ocean Press), that is as a separate booklet, devoid of notes and information explaining the reasons for such an extrapolation: it is a further damage which is added to the many others done to the possibility of a scientific edition of Che's Works. In this case, the Guevarian project of actualising the heritage of Marx and Engels aimed at the focus of the controversy with the Soviets has been also hit.

MARXIST STORY

Scene 8 [Prague, 1966]

At this point we must devote attention to this polemic, trying first of all to imagine the scene: after the lengthy confinement in the Cuban ambassador's house in Dar es Salaam, there is a drastic change of continent—from Africa to the heart of old Europe; a large villa on the outskirts of Prague; the semi-clandestine coexistence (Cuban-Czechoslovak "Operation Manuel") with some of the closest companions ("Pombo" [b. 1940] and "Tuma" [1940-1967]); chess games; study and writing.

Che remained there from March till July 1966, when he returned to Cuba to prepare for Bolivia, which in the meantime was definitively decided as a political goal, having abandoned during summer the previously chosen objective—namely, Peru. (All of this has been reconstructed and documented in detail by Humberto Vázquez Viaña, *Una Guerrilla Para el Che*). And there Guevara writes the work that is used to define "The Prague Notebooks" (but published as *Apuntes Críticos a la Economía Política* [Critical Notes on Political Economy], although Che's target was really the *Manual of Political Economy* of the USSR Academy of Sciences). An enormous work of recompilation of texts (starting from the biographical compendium of Marx-Engels mentioned above), with long pieces hand-copied from works especially by Marx-Engels and Lenin, but also by Mao Zedong. It seems right, however, to add to this work of anthology recompilation also the passages that Guevara copies in a separate booklet, in the same months or in a period somewhat later which, unfortunately, we have not been able to identify better. This booklet, together with the "Green Book" with poetic passages, was to reappear among his personal items sold in Bolivia after his death: in this case bought by the Feltrinelli Publishing House, but without further specification.

The booklet was published in a very bad edition by the same Italian publishing house with errors and a ridiculous title (*Before Dying. Notes and Reading Notes*). It should however be taken seriously because it contains excerpts from *The Marxists* by C. Wright Mills, from the Works of Marx-Engels, of Lenin and Stalin, from Lukács, from the already mentioned M.A. Dinnik and from various works by Trotsky. From a quantitative point of view, Trotsky's passages prevail heavily over all the other authors mentioned and the passage taken from his *History of the Russian Revolution* is accompanied by the following comment:

> It is a fascinating book, but it is impossible to make a criticism because it is important to consider that the historian is also *protagonist* of events. However, it sheds light on a whole series of events of the great revolution that had been overshadowed by myth. At the same time, it makes isolated affirmations the validity of which is still absolute today. Ultimately, if we neglect the personality of the author and stick to the book, this should be considered a source of primary importance for study of the Russian revolution (p. 94).

The Cuban government succeeded in preventing publication of *The Prague Notebooks* until 2006 (the *Apuntes* [the Notes]), but then had to yield not only to pressure exerted by the International Guevara Foundation, but also because some salient parts critical of the USSR had already appeared in 2001 in the book by Orlando Borrego, *Che, el Camino del Fuego*. And among the passages reported and commented by the former Sugar Minister was the prologue by Che ("Necesidad de este book" [Necessity of the Book]) in which, in addition to the many Guevarian statements inspired by Marxism that dismissed the Soviet claim to march towards socialism, the following lapidary statement referring to the USSR stood out:

> La superestructura capitalista fue influenciando cada vez en forma más marcada las relaciones de producción y los conflictos provocados por la hibridación que significó la Nep se están resolviendo hoy a favor de la superestructura: ***se está regresando al capitalismo*** (*Apuntes*, p. 27; Borrego, p. 382) [emphasis by Che (*ed.*)].
>
> [The capitalist superstructure has come to influence production relations in an ever more marked form, and the conflicts caused by hybridisation that Nep meant are being resolved today in favour of the superstructure: ***there is a return to capitalism***.]

A similar prophecy formulated in the same months in which Fidel Castro decided to definitively enter the Soviet bloc may perhaps leave one indifferent nowadays, since everyone can see how it has actually come true. At the time, however, it implied a great intellectual courage by a sort of deputy head of state, legendary commander for the Soviet military world, who had matured the second phase of his youthful adherence to Marxism in prone admiration of the USSR as the homeland of socialism. Any analysis of Che's thought that does not take into account this profound transformation and instead presents a unilateral and stable vision over time of his economic conceptions does not deserve the slightest consideration. But unfortunately, for many years the books dedicated to Guevara that offer such a monochromatic and therefore deeply erroneous vision of his thought have represented almost the rule in the publishing output of Cuba or by authors related to it. I could mention Cuban, Chilean, Italian, American [Unitedstatians] etc. examples, but it would be an ungenerous way of being pitiless with the intellectual poverty of an entire generation which in the past I called "Latin-American *nomenklatura* [nomenclature]" and which is now finally beginning to die out.

The *Notes* are a very demanding work from a theoretical point of view and should be examined piece by piece, given that each paragraph refers critically to another paragraph of the notorious Soviet *Manual* . The language is very technical and demonstrates a new familiarity with the basic texts of Marxism: mostly *Capital*. The references to Lenin also abound, cited in part positively and in part to challenge certain decisons taken after the end of war communism (a topic Guevara does not speak about, even if one might presume that, generally speaking, he tended to favour it). It is evident, however, that Che totally ignored the "heretical" literature dedicated to Soviet Russia since when Lenin himself was alive. Of this great theoretical laboratory, marked by famous names of Marxism and beyond, Guevara had no hint and this was his great theoretical limit.

However, it must also be said that Che lived only 39 years, many of them travelling or fighting arms in hand for his ideals.

With regard to *Notes*, what interests us most is that there is wide recourse to *Critique of the Gotha Programme*, both as direct references, and above all as adherence to its substance. This work of the last Marx is commonly considered as the maximum concentration of his utopian vision (as I have also interpreted it in my introduction to a bilingual Italian edition of 2008) and there is no doubt that even for Che this is its most characteristic meaning. Let us not forget that a year earlier (March 1965), returning from the trip to Africa, he had delivered to the *Marcha* magazine in Montevideo his utopian text par excellence—*Socialism and Man in Cuba*—in which the inspiration from that famous text by Marx was clearly felt.

Finally, it should be mentioned that the manuscript of a study programme is also included in *The Prague Notebooks* ("Plan Tentativo" [Draft Plan]). We have already recalled two other study plans drafted in the same two-year period, and this is the second in order of time. It is also the most organic and detailed, given that it has the form of a general index for a book to be written, a sort of scheme for a great monograph on the social history of humanity: from pre-capitalist production modes to imperialism, passing through slave societies and feudalism; from the Marxian categories of interpretation of capitalist development (including a broad summary of *Capital*) to a definition of the economy of the transitional phase (the whole of the third part); to finally arrive at the problem of building socialism (fourth and last part). Death was to prevent him from carrying out this ambitious project, about which he certainly continued to think during the guerrilla war in Bolivia, as demonstrated by the readings plan mentioned at the beginning and which is now confirmed as a series of bibliographic notes drawn up month by month as part of a *wish list of readings* to be completed.

Published too late to have any influence on the theoretical training of the new generations of Cuban intellectuals, *Notes* will remain forever in the history of Marxism as proof of the highest level of understanding of Marxian theoretical heritage achieved by Guevara. But they will also be considered as the most complete testimony of his lucid capacity of analytical prediction in relation to a political world—*his* political world—which shone for dullness of mind if not real blindness with regard to the imminent fate of the Soviet bureaucratic regime.

FADE-OUT...

Scene 9 [Vallegrande, October 9, 2017]

The scene is composite, polychrome and multiple-sound. On the large clearing for what in the past was to become the Vallegrande airport in Bolivia, some thousands of people convened by the government of President Evo Morales are gathered to celebrate the 50th anniversary of Che's fall in combat. There are many multi-coloured flags, but mostly red with the silhouette of Korda's famous photo, Andean and Caribbean music, and the banners of political, trade union and cultural associations of various Latin American origins. In the days that preceded, scholars of Guevarism from various parts of the world had spoken: the author came from Italy but, incredibly, was the only one from Europe.

"Che lives" is the slogan most repeated, but the church-shaped building erected on the site where the bones of Guevara were found is there to testify to the contrary. And that tomb is mentally associated with the Cuban Mausoleum of Santa Clara, inside which the atmosphere is even more strongly mystical and religious according to a Cuban hagiographic tradition, already started in October 1967. For those wishing to deepen or extend the discourse on this evolution of the figure of Guevara—anti-materialistic (hence anti-Marxian), mystical and popular-irrational—a fascinating research has been conducted for years by a professor emeritus of art history at the University of California (Los Angeles): David Kunzle (b. 1936), *Chesucristo. The Fusion in Image and Word of Che Guevara and Jesus Christ* .

Che is dead, of that there is no doubt. But through the reflection conducted so far what is dead is above all *his relationship with Marx*. And this did not happen fifty years after La Higuera, but while the famous Commander was still alive. In fact, after the wealth of theoretical references contained in *The Prague Notebooks*, no further reflections by Che on issues related to Marxism can be found. We have the titles of the works that he would have liked to read or read again at the end of the Bolivian Diary, but the names of Marx, Lenin or other famous Marxists are totally absent from that famous diary. Trotsky is the exception but only because that day (July 31, 1967) Guevara complains of the loss of one of his books. The reader can easily verify all this because since 1996 there has also been a name index for the Bolivian Diary: I put it together for the version I edited of the *Illustrated Bolivian Diary* and it is the only one existing in the world. And I have always wondered whether this incredible shortcoming—namely that there exists no edition of the Diary (not even in Cuba) with a proper index of names—is not a symptom of the theoretical disinterest in the last ideological evolution of Che.

If in the first years after the defeat in Bolivia the lack of interest could have had political reasons—since Guevara was totally indigestible for the capitalist countries, but even more so for the countries of the alleged "real socialism" (including China and indeed in pride of place given that there news was ever even given of his death)—as time passed there were other reasons that could explain why the Guevara/Marx union lost much of its potential theoretical attraction.

First, there was the fact that Che's polemic against the USSR had lost much of its interest and its subversive potential after the collapse of the Soviet Empire in 1991 (and yet in Cuba it had long been forbidden to talk about it ever since the end of the 1960s). It should also be added that the Guevarian reflection on the theme of alienation (whether Marxian, Sartrian or humanist) was soon overwhelmed by the birth of the myth of his person and the hijacking of it by the mass society of the spectacle.

This reabsorption of the figure of Che which could not avoid sweeping away his relationship with Marxism has been magnificently described in one of the most beautiful books written on contemporary "Guevarism", that is, on how the world of culture and entertainment lives on and exploits his figure so many years after his death: see Michael Casey (b. 1967), *Che's Afterlife. The Legacy of an Image.*

If the communist and internationalist connotation of his political action, the fascination of his rebellion against any conformism, the ethical value of his renunciation of the management of state power (a unique case in the history of the twentieth century), and his original theorisation of the theory-priaxis relationship that I have defined as "revolutionary humanism" all have been lost, could his relationship with Marx have possibly survived?

Of course not.

All that remains is to close our remake of the old film with a famous aphorism by Woody Allen:

> Marx is dead, Guevara is dead ... and I'm not feeling too well myself.

THE END

(translated by Phil Harris, June 2018)

BIBLIOGRAPHY

Anderson, Jon Lee, *Che Guevara. A Revolutionary Life*, Bantam Press, London 1997.

Borrego, Orlando, *Che, el Camino del Fuego*, Imagen Contemporánea, Havana 2001.

Borrego, Orlando (edited by), *El Che en la Revolución Cubana*, 6 Vols., Minaz [Sugar Ministry], Havana 1967.

Casey, Michael, *Che's afterlife. The Legacy of an Image*, Vintage Books, New York 2009.

Cátedra Ernesto Che Guevara, *Introducción al Pensamiento Marxista*, edited by Néstor Kohan, Ediciones Madres de Plaza de Mayo / La Rosa Blindada, Buenos Aires 2003.

Che Guevara. Quaderni della Fondazione/Cuadernos de la Fundación/ Notebooks of the Foundation, (CGQF), Massari editore, Bolsena 1998-2016, Nos. 1-10.

Cupull, Adys-González, Froilán, *Cálida Presencia. Su Amistad con Tita Infante*, ed. Oriente, Santiago de Cuba 1995.

Franqui, Carlos, *El libro de los doce*, Instituto del Libro, Havana 1967 (Ediciones Huracán, Havana 1968).

Gadea Acosta, Hilda, *Che Guevara. Años Decisivos*, Aguilar, Mexico 1972 [*I miei anni con il Che*, Erre emme (Massari ed.), Rome 1995]

Guevara, Ernesto Che, *Apuntes Críticos a la Economía Politica*, Ciencias Sociales, Havana 2006.

Guevara, Ernesto Che, *Illustrated Bolivian Diary*, edited by Roberto Massari, Editora política (Havana) / Massari editore (Rome) 1996.

Guevara, Ernesto Che, *Escritos y Discursos*, 9 Vols., Ciencias Sociales, Havana 1977.

Guevara, Ernesto Che, *Marx y Engels. Una Síntesis Biográfica*, Centro de Estudios Che Guevara (Havana) / Ocean Press (Sur), 2007.

Guevara, Ernesto Che, *Obras 1957-1967*, 2 Vols., Casa de las Américas, Havana 1970.

Guevara, Ernesto Che, *Prima di Morire. Appunti e Note di Lettura*, Feltrinelli, Milan 1998.

Guevara, Ernesto Che, *Scritti Scelti*, edited by Roberto Massari, 2 vols., Erre emme (Massari ed.), Rome 1996[3].

Guevara, Ernesto Che, *El Socialismo y el Hombre Nuevo*, edited by José Aricó, Siglo XXI, Mexico (1977) 1979[2].

Guevara, Ernesto Che, *Temas Económicos*, edited by Juan José Soto Valdespino, Ciencias Sociales, Havana 1988.

Guevara, Ernesto Che and others, *El Gran Debate Sobre la Economía en Cuba (1963-1964)*, Ciencias Sociales, Havana 2004.

Hart Dávalos, Armando, *Marx, Engels y la Condición Humana. Una Visión Desde Cuba*, Ciencias Sociales, Havana 2005.

Kohan, Néstor, *Otro Mundo es Posible*, Nuestra América, Buenos Aires 2003

Kunzle, David, *Chesucristo. The Fusion in Image and Word of Che Guevara and Jesus Christ*, with a Postface by Roberto Massari, De Gruyter, Berlin/Boston 2016 [Massari ed., Bolsena 2016].

Лаврецкий, Иосиф, *Årnðsto Cð Gðvara*, Molodaja Gvardija, Moskva 1972 [Lavretski, Iosif, *Ernesto Che Guevara*, Editorial Progreso, Moscow 1975].

Löwy, Michael, *La Pensée de Che Guevara*, Maspero, Paris.

Massari, Roberto, *Che Guevara. Pensamiento y Política de la Utopía*, Txalaparta, Tafalla (Navarroa)/Buenos Aires 1992-2004[8] [*Che Guevara. Pensiero e Politica dell'Utopia*, Erre emme (Massari ed.), Roma (1987) 1994[5]].

Pericás, Luis Bernardo, *Che Guevara e o Debate Econômico em Cuba*, Xamã editora, São Paulo 2004 [*Che Guevara and the Economic Debate in Cuba*, Atropos Press, New York/Dresden 2009; *Che Guevara y el Debate Económico en Cuba*, Corregidor, Buenos Aires 2011].

Rojo, Ricardo, *Mi Amigo el Che*, (J. Álvarez, Buenos Aires 1968), Editorial Sudamericana, Buenos Aires 1998 [Mondadori, Milan 1968].

Sartre, Jean-Paul, *Sartre Visita a Cuba*, Ediciones Revolución, Havana 1961 [*Visita a Cuba*, Massari ed., Bolsena 2005].

Serguera Riverí, Jorge ("Papito"), *Caminos del Che. Datos Inéditos de su Vida*, Plaza y Valdés, Mexico 1997.

Soria Galvarro Terán, Carlos, *Andares del Che en Bolivia*, Cienflores, Ituzaingó (Buenos Aires) 2014.

Soria Galvarro T., Carlos (ed.), *Campaña del Che en Bolivia*, Huellas, La Paz 1997.

Vázquez Viaña, Humberto, *Una Guerrilla Para el Che. Antecedentes*, 2ª enlarged edition, El País, Santa Cruz de la Sierra 2008 [*La Guerriglia del Che in Bolivia. Antecedenti*, Massari ed., Bolsena 2003].

Zeitlin, Maurice-Sheer, Robert, *Cuba. Tragedy in Our Hemisphere*, Grove Press, New York 1963 [*Cuba, An American Tragedy* (enlarged edition) Harmondsworth, Penguin Books, 1964, pp. 186-95].

Many of the various scholars mentioned in the text are members of the International Guevara Foundation. To allow the reader to identify them, the composition of the Editorial Board of *Quaderni/Cuadernos Che Guevara*, theoretical body of the Foundation, is as follows:

Roberto Massari [*Dir.*], Aldo Garzia [*Man. Dir.*], Enrica Matricoti, Roberto Savio, Aldo Zanchetta (*Italy*), Néstor Kohan (*Argentina*), Michael Casey (*Australia*), Carlos Soria Galvarro Terán (*Bolivia*), Luiz Bernardo Pericás (*Brazil*), Adys Cupull, Froilán González (*Cuba*), Michael Löwy (*France*), Richard Harris (*Hawaii*), Ricardo Gadea Acosta (*Peru*), Zbigniew Marcin Kowalewski (*Poland*), David Kunzle, James Petras, Margaret Randall, Maurice Zeitlin (*USA*), Douglas Bravo (*Venezuela*), Antonella Marazzi (*Editorial Assistant*)

In memoriam: Humberto Vázquez Viaña (*Bolivia*), Celia Hart Santamaría, Fernando Martínez Heredia (*Cuba*), Sergio De Santis, Giulio Girardi (*Italy*).

SYNOPSIS

The old film refers to the many written and spoken platitudes about Guevara's relationship with Marx in the years when there was the attempt to downscale this relationship within the canons of the orthodoxy of Soviet-inspired Marxism. In reality, the history of this relationship was very complicated and subject to continuous and major changes. The essay by Massari reconstructs these changes in the form of film scenes in which the reader jumps from one place to another of the Planet (La Paz, Dar es Salaam, Lima, Rome, Moscow, Havana, Prague and finally Bolivia) to follow directly the reflection on Marx by a man of action who was also a scholar with great reading and writing skills.

From the examination of almost unknown and ignored documentary material—such as the notes on books to read in the *Bolivian Diary* written during the guerrilla war in Bolivia in 1966-67, preceded by the letter to Armando Hart of December 1965—a totally new view of Guevara's relationship with Marxism, and with the social sciences in general, is obtained.

Massari describes the early development of Che's

Marxism (anti-orthodox and culturally vivacious) before analysing the more intensely pro-Soviet period and thus the adherence to the principles of *Diamat* (dialectical materialism). He then describes the transition phase embodied in the "great economic debate" in Cuba and concludes with Guevara's harsh criticism of the Soviet model of which we can now speak openly considering that Che's main book on the subject was made public in 2006.

Massari is one of the oldest living scholars of Guevara and since 1998 has been president of the International Che Guevara Foundation. He has devoted several essays to both Marx and Che.

9

Historical Process and Gender Essentialism from a Dialectical Point of View:
A Contribution to a Marxian Feminist Theory

Edoardo Schinco

1. Introduction: The Marxian Framework

There is no room for doubt that Marxism and feminism have had a very controversial relation. On the one side, feminists have deeply criticized Marx's theory. On the other side, however, it is true that Marxist thinkers—such as Engels, with his book on *The Origin of the Family, Private Property and Family*—gave to feminists some theoretical tool to address discrimination- and submission-related issues. In general, both socialist and Marxist theories played a central role in feminist debate during the 19th and 20th century because of their criticism against classic liberalism. This fight indirectly helped feminists in defining a new understanding of family. Indeed, one of the main goals Marxist analysis of classic liberalism tried to achieve was the de-naturalisation of the capitalist mode of production. In the *Economic and Philosophic Manuscripts of 1844*, Karl Marx already attempted to point out how the eternal economic laws described by liberal thinkers were rather contingent laws, dependent on capitalism itself:

> Die Nationalökonomie geht vom Faktum des Privateigentums aus. Sie erklärt uns dasselbe nicht. Sie faßt den materiellen Prozeß des Privateigentums, den es in der Wirklichkeit durchmacht,

> in allgemeine, abstrakte Formeln, die ihr dann als Gesetze gelten. Sie begreift diese Gesetze nicht, d.h., sie zeigt nicht nach, wie sie aus dem Wesen des Privateigentums hervorgehn. Die Nationalökonomie gibt uns keinen Aufschluß über den Grund der Teilung von Arbeit und Kapital, von Kapital und Erde. Wenn sie z. B. das Verhältnis des Arbeitslohns zum Profit des Kapitals bestimmt, so gilt ihn als letzter Grund das Interesse der Kapitalisten; d.h., sie unterstellt, was sie entwickeln soll. (Marx 1968a, 510)

In all his works, he stressed the fallacious circularity characterising the typical reasoning of economists. That is, classical economics assumed historical features of the capitalist mode of production without providing any explanation about the genesis of them. In this way, those features were understood as universal and fundamental elements of any mode of production. In so doing, they were turned into unchangeable eternal economic laws. Moreover, this move implicitly produced an apology for capitalist system itself. If capitalism was just the pure expression of economic laws, there was no reason to complain about that, nor was it possible to improve capitalism at all. In his famous 1857 *Introduction*, Marx declared *apertis verbis*:

> "Die Bestimmungen, die für die Produktion überhaupt gelten, müssen grade gesondert werden, damit über der Einheit—die schon daraus hervorgeht, daß das Subjekt, die Menschheit, und das Objekt, die Natur, dieselben—die wesentliche Verschiedenheit nicht vergessen wird. In diesem Vergessen liegt z.B. die ganze Weisheit der modernen Ökonomen, die die Ewigkeit und Harmonie der bestehenden sozialen Verhältnisse beweisen. Z.B. keine Produktion möglich, ohne ein Produktionsinstrument, wäre dies Instrument auch nur die Hand. Keine möglich ohne vergangne, aufgehäufte Arbeit, wäre diese Arbeit auch nur die Fertigkeit, die in der Hand des Wilden durch wiederholte Übung angesammelt und konzentriert ist. Das Kapital ist unter andrem auch Produktionsinstrument, auch vergangne, objektivierte Arbeit. Also ist das Kapital ein allgemeines, ewiges Naturverhältnis; d.h., wenn ich grade das Spezifische weglasse, was „Produktionsinstrument", „aufgehäufte Arbeit" erst zum

> Kapital macht. Die ganze Geschichte der Produktionsverhältnisse erscheint daher z.B. bei Carey als eine durch die Regierungen böswillig veranlaßte Verfälschung." (Marx 1971, 617)

By calling dogmas of classical economics into questions, Marx rejected that theoretical naturalization of capitalist categories brought about by liberal thinkers. However, unfortunately Marx did not deeply address issues connected with women's condition within the society. The most important exceptions were some parts of *The Capital* and the 1848 *Manifesto of the Communist Party*. On the one side, *The Capital* extensively described the historical evolution of capitalism, especially in the chapter regarding the working day (Chapter 8 in the 1867 edition). There, Marx talked about the exploitation of women's and children's labour. In so doing, he partially succeeded in underlining the different impact of capitalism on different subjects, according to their own age, class, and—what is more important here—sex (Marx 1968b, 245-320). On the other side, the *Manifesto* sporadically focused its attention on women's condition. Nonetheless it was enough to outline an informal Marxian theory of family as social institution. For example, Marx drew a significant parallel between the subordination in the workplace and the subordination within the household. As the worker was submitted to capitalist's arbitrary decision, so the wife was submitted to the husband's will. In this sense, Marx tried to underscore that the family had to be understood as a social institution, a part of the society as a whole (Marx, Engels 1972). He just sketched this connection. Anyway, all the suggestions he gave in this regard are still useful to understand the consistency of Marx's position on family expressed *in nuce* there. Generally speaking, it seems that contact points between family and mode of production are substantially two.

At first, the mode of production defines the "external" form of the family. To put it differently, the mode of production plays a central role in determining what "family" means and, hence, who legitimately belongs to the family. As we know, the composition of family changed over time, and—for instance—

the contemporary nuclear family has not so much in common with Ancient Roman *familia*, of which servants were also part. Furthermore, the position of family within the social totality changed over time as well. Comparing Aristotle's *Politics* and modern contractarian theories, it is evident how family is no longer the "social cell" in modern age's perspective. On the opposite, it was individuals that became both the logic and historical *prius*; that is, they became the source of legitimation for any social institution. In addition, secondarily, the mode of production also defines the "internal" structure of the family. It shapes in a certain way the kind of relations existing among individuals within the household. The absolute power of *pater familias* in the Ancient Roman family was replaced by a different relationship in modern—bourgeois—family. Clearly, here as elsewhere, features of family institution can be separately analysed from the social context only in an abstract way. *De facto*, society and family are strictly intertwined, and they condition each other by virtue of their dialectic relation. Therefore, it is no wonder that Marx found a strong similarity between submission between worker and capitalist and submission between wife and husband.

2.a. The Marxian Contribution to Feminism...

At this point, a possible feminist use of the Marxian framework starts to loom quite clearly. Indeed, Marx's criticism against the naturalisation of classic economics' dogmas could be easily transferred in other social domains. Thus, following this path, feminists called into question the illusory eternity of "traditional" family structure and "traditional" family ties. The family as a natural institution was turned into a social construction changing over time. At this time, between the 19th and 20th century, feminists still accepted the existence of the two sexes—male and female—but they partially restricted the normative value of sex itself. They denied the possibility to univocally deduce a specific form of family—the "natural" family—by simply analysing the inner essence of the two sexes. On the contrary, they took account of a set of natural relations between men and women, but at the same time they stressed the historical evolution of family, that is, the social shell surrounding and shaping relations between the two sexes.

Moreover, according to a new understanding of equality, feminists employed Marxist and socialist theory in order to criticise the concept of formal equality. This liberal equality, indeed, was a mere equality of opportunity deriving from individuals' negative rights. Regarding to feminist issues, it only implied an equal treatment for all the people regardless of their sex or gender. Unlike this liberal position, feminists reframed the concept of equality in order to take one's sex into account. The category of "sexual difference" became central within this framework, and feminists' efforts reversed the discriminatory use of sex by employing that category to develop a broader concept of justice. First feminists harshly criticised the reasoning of conservative people, who tried to justify women's submission to men through an analysis of biological differences between the two sexes. On the one hand, conservative people's discriminatory intent was manifest. Women were naturally inferior to men, so there was no possibility for them to compete with their male counterparts. On the other hand, that intent was hypocritically hidden. Women were naturally weaker than men. They needed to be protected and overwatched by men because of their inner fragility. Therefore—conservative people argued—male paternalism was not to be understood as male oppression; on the contrary, such a system of protections and constraints was established in women's own interests. It was against this double conservative perspective that first feminists stressed formal equality between men and women. They did not deny the set of biological differences naturally distinguishing men from women. Still, they denied the relevance of these differences with regard to any legal and political discourse. They neutralised conservative people's strategies by preventing them from taking sexual differences into account. Notwithstanding that, the insufficiency of formal equality led feminists to reframe and improve their concept of equality later. As conservative people, these second-wave feminists put at the heart of their reasoning the idea of "sexual difference", but they stressed those biological differences only to show how the abstract, formal equality could not provide an appropriate protection for sexually different people situated in a different position within the society.

A brilliant example of this new understanding of justice was perfectly remarked by the US Court of Appeals, Ninth Circuit in a 1985 landmark case regarding the 1978 *Pregnancy Discrimination Act*. By enacting this act, Congress wanted to give exceptional protection to pregnant women and, generally, to prohibit discriminations on the basis of pregnancy. Previously, indeed, the existing protection offered by the *Title VII* of the *Civil Rights Act* of 1964 had showed its limits. For example, in the well-known 1974 *Geduldig v. Aiello* case the Court had established that the *Equal Protection Clause* could not provide legal protections for cases in which discrimination was based on pregnancy-related issues. After all, according to formal equality criteria, if men and women had to be treated equally, it was impossible to take pregnancy into account since men could not get pregnant. On the contrary, in *California Federal Savings and Loan Association v. Guerra* (the above-mentioned 1985 case) the Court ruled against pregnancy-neutral policies and legal blindness to pregnancy. Instead, it underlined that it was necessary to take account of pregnancy, even if only in a specific non-discriminatory way: "Congress intended to reverse Gilbert, to require employers to include pregnancy disability leave in their otherwise comprehensive benefit packages, and thus to construct a floor beneath which pregnancy disability benefits may not drop—not a ceiling above which they may not rise." (*California Federal Savings and Loan Association v. Guerra* 1985, 393)

2.b. ...and its Limits

By briefly describing the influence of Marxian thought on Western feminism, we did not want to reduce the whole feminist perspective to a mere development of some of Marx's incidental suggestions. Of course, feminist speculation has gradually embodied multiple theories or it has autonomously developed its own theory by reformulating previous points of views. Sometimes, feminism has even devised a theoretical and practical framework completely *ex novo*. Nonetheless, it is true that feminism and Marxism moved at the same pace for some decades. The radicalism of Marx's theory and its crucial idea to drastically transform the contemporary capitalist society in order to get rid of all its essential inequalities, strengthened this temporary alliance. Furthermore, the set of policies enacted by the Soviet government in the matter of equality between men and women marked an important step towards a gender-fair society. In a few years, the Soviet regime legalised abortion and divorce, gave women a broader range of work opportunities and new labour laws regarding maternity-leave and insurances. Lenin's 1920 famous speech *On International Women's Day* on March 4th summarised quite well the strong and weak points of the Marxist approach to the woman question. Lenin distinguished two diverse degrees of equality between the two sexes. The first goal was to achieve a full legal equality improving bourgeois freedoms. The second degree was to reform the labour market and create appropriate conditions in the workplace both to boost women's agency and to set them free from "domestic slavery":

> One of the most flagrant manifestations of this inconsistency [of capitalist promises] is the inferior position of woman compared with man. Not a single bourgeois state, not even the most progressive, republican democratic state, has brought about complete equality of rights. But the Soviet Republic of Russia promptly wiped out, without any exception, every trace of inequality in the legal status of women and secured her complete equality in its laws. [...] The working women's movement has for its objective the fight for the economic and social, and not merely formal, equality of woman. The main task is to draw the women into socially productive labor, extricate them from "domestic slavery", free them of their stultifying and humiliating resignation to the perpetual and exclusive atmosphere of the kitchen and nursery. (Lenin 1950)

Lenin's discourse made his well-known political foresight clear. This discourse perfectly mirrored what Marx expressed *in nuce* in relation to women's emancipation. For this reason, it was evident the direct connection that Lenin—according to Marx's view—established between full emancipation of women and improvement of material conditions *stricto sensu*. As Marxist theory suggested, to improve those conditions meant to improve women's general conditions in society as well. Surely, this assumption has been true for a very long time. Still, in the long run, this peculiar perspective openly showed its inner limits.

To better clarify this point, let us start by focusing on the controversial idea of the imminent coming of the communist phase within Soviet Russia's overall development. In his well-known 1917 pamphlet *The State and Revolution*, Lenin used Marx's and Engels's various contributions to shed light on their official position about the death of the state under communism. Unlike anarchism, Marxism did not affirm the abolition of the state *ex abrupto*. Instead, Lenin suggested that the state would have been employed by the revolutionary party in order to facilitate the passage from the capitalist mode of production to the communist one. This transitory phase would have been characterised by a "socialist economy", whose imperfect economic features—compared to the successive "communist economy"—have been partially described by Marx in his 1875 *Critique of Gotha Programme*, according to the well-known principle "from each according to one's ability, to each according to one's needs" (Lenin 1974). Lenin's intents aside, history later showed how this interpretation of Marx's and Engels's thought turned into a powerful tool of governance into Stalin's hands. Instead of being a mere transitory "moment", this "socialist stage" of Soviet Russia became eternal and served as an excuse for Stalin to increase the state power and to procrastinate more and more the eschatological final coming of a communist society. *Mutatis mutandis*, the problematic history of the relation between Marxism and feminism followed the same pattern. In general, Marxist thinkers developed a very interesting framework—consistent with Marx's assertions, as Losurdo masterfully explained (Losurdo 2013)—to address feminist issues, avoiding a shallow theoretical reductionism. They knew that any actual situation is always made up of a wide range of factors. Therefore, they found a way to address all the factors involved by systematising them in a well-ordered hierarchy. They promptly distinguished between a social main contradiction (*Hauptwiderspruch*) and secondary contradictions (*Nebenswidersprüche*). The former was always the class struggle, that is, the essential antagonism between opposite social classes, changing according to the mode of production. The class struggle's logical priority was due to the fact that this crucial contradiction shaped all the other social elements and assigned them a new role within the social totality. Hence, the latter—that is all the other social contradictions—were necessarily subordinated to the class struggle. In light of this, the achievement of new rights for female workers became the key-word of feminist politics in Western communist countries.

The history of the German Democratic Republic (DDR) is a brilliant example of this theoretical trend. There, the communist government enacted many policies in order to broaden the set of rights and protections for women. In addition, official feminist groups certainly played a proactive role and supported the government's effort to improve women's social standing. However, the government's main focus only continued to be on female workers' conditions. The government devised many training programmes for female workers. Indeed, helping women to become skilled workers was seen as a fundamental step, or even the only way, to pursue women's full emancipation. This approach was perfectly consistent with the official Marxist ideology since the woman question was understood as a part of the broader social question. Hence, women's specific interests were perceived as less important than class interests. Once again, communist guidelines on equality between men and women brought about a very significant improvement of women's condition. Still, roughly speaking, the implicit price to pay for women was the reduction of one's self-realisation to self-realisation *as worker*. At the end, the general framework did not change so much from the above-mentioned Lenin's perspective on women's emancipation. For this reason, when women's rights organisations started to highlight different aspects of the woman question and ask for the deconstruction of other kinds of gender inequality, this old-fashioned Marxist position revealed its inner weak points. Compared to many capitalist Western countries, women's condition in DDR improved fast, but mainly in only one direction. Indeed, communist strategy seemed not to address the whole spectrum of domestic slavery-related issues insofar as the household remained a mainly female domain. DDR attempts to introduce women in the national workforce did not affect widespread understanding of women's traditional role. Women were not either workers or stay-at-home mothers. Rather, they had to be both workers and mothers. The new social position of women as workers did not replace their classic role of mother at all; instead, DDR politics aimed to integrate the alternative dimensions of work and motherhood (Karl 2011, 203-216). As soon as the international feminist movement grew and got increasingly stronger, feminist reaction was not long in coming.

3. The Feminist Reaction and the Critique of Universalism

a. Sexual Difference

The 1960s and 70s marked a turning point for feminists all around the world. Feminist thinkers developed more and more an independent point of view, calling into question their alliance with socialist and Marxist groups. Investigating those previously progressive positions, the feminist movement denounced their partial failures. Even if socialism and Marxism gave a decisive boost to women's emancipation once, they ended up overshadowing the whole range of women's interests and rights. Furthermore, they fuelled a paternalistic approach since they prevented women from thinking about themselves in a completely autonomous way. Italian feminist Carla Lonzi openly explained the reasons of this radical position in some of her crucial writings about feminism, such as *The Manifesto of the Feminine Revolt* (1970) or *Let's Spit on Hegel* (1974):

> [in questi scritti] prevaleva lo sdegno per essermi accorta che la cultura maschile in ogni suo aspetto aveva teorizzato l'inferiorità della donna. Per questo la sua inferiorizzazione appare del tutto naturale. Le donne stesse accettano di considerarsi "seconde" se chi le convince sembra loro meritare la stima del genere umano: Marx, Lenin, Freud e tutti gli altri. Mi sono sentita stimolata a confutare alcuni tra i principi fondamentali del patriarcato, non solo di quello passato o presente, ma di quello prospettato dalle ideologie rivoluzionarie. [...] La chiave femminista operava come una rivelazione. Il bisogno di esprimersi è stato da noi accolto come sinonimo stesso di liberazione. *Sputiamo su Hegel* l'ho scritto perché ero rimasta molto turbata constatando che quasi la totalità delle femministe italiane dava più credito alla lotta di classe che alla loro stessa oppressione. [...] L'oppressione della donna è il risultato di millenni: il capitalismo l'ha ereditato piuttosto che prodotto. Il sorgere della proprietà privata ha espresso uno squilibrio tra i sessi come bisogno di potere di ciascun uomo su ciascuna donna, intanto che si definivano i rapporti di potere tra gli uomini. Interpretare su basi economiche il destino che ci ha accompagnate fino a oggi significa chiamare in causa un meccanismo di cui si ignora l'impulso motore. (Lonzi 2010 1-2, 15-16)

This updated version of feminism refused to subsume the woman question under the different concept of the social question. Even if those two questions could not be merely juxtaposed, they could not just overlap. The provocative claim to spit on "Hegel"—assumed as the metaphor for the entire Marxist universe—meant to suggest women to think outside the box with regard to their own oppression. By replacing old categories, such as the Hegelian master-slave dialectic, with new ones, it was possible for feminists to shed significant light on unexplored sides of women's patriarchal oppression. Marxism and socialism aside, those years also played a central role in the evolution of Western feminism since thinkers further expanded the above-mentioned critique of formal equality. Born under the sign of "sexual difference", the second wave of feminism ended up drastically criticising the concept of universalism itself. In this regard, many kinds of influences—theoretical, practical, and historical—converged in feminist thought and brought about this radical shift. Surely, the concept of "difference" implied the rejection of a certain 20th century version of philosophical universalism. The well-founded suspicion against universalism pushed feminists to look for an alliance with other minorities, once again. The risk of any universalism was its possibility to turn into a power device guaranteeing the hegemony of the ruling social group over the subaltern ones. As the failure of human rights' rhetoric had shown in the past, the "universal" subject involved in that kind of universal discourses was surreptitiously defined through the hegemonic group's typical features. For example, the 1789 French *Declaration of the Rights of the Man and of the Citizen* virtually referred to every human being. Nonetheless, when Olympe de Gouges challenged the male authority with her 1791 *Declaration of the Rights of Woman and the Female Citizen*, the revolutionary regime did not hesitate to condemn and executed her by the guillotine. Here as elsewhere, feminists pointed out the dangers lurking behind this illusory claim for universal rights. In that context, it did not take such a long time for that general and abstract "human being" to show oneself to be the portrait of the white heterosexual man. Therefore, since Simone de Beauvoir's 1949 landmark book *Le Deuxième Sexe,* feminist speculation gradually decided to re-orient its reflection on the peculiarity of being-a-woman, compared with being-a-man.

Along with this feminist perspective, the more general reflection on cultural hegemony and subaltern non-Western cultures pushed radical thinkers to call European culture's presumed superiority into question. Marxist-related scholars, such as Frantz Fanon, tried to restore the dignity of colonised and marginalised cultures. In particular, the main effort—an effort common to all the minorities—was to fight against the sense of submission and inferiority that submitted people introjected over the centuries (for example, see Fanon 1952; Fanon 1961). The progressive re-evaluation of subaltern cultures against Western hegemony underlined the philosophical necessity to give minorities the actual opportunity to develop their own alternative points of view. Postcolonial studies worked in this direction. They tried to deconstruct the biased widespread understanding of non-Western cultures as naïve or barbarian by showing their inner complex functioning. Because of these common interests, postcolonial studies and the rising third-wave of feminism mutually supported each other. Anyway, in relation to the development of feminism, French post-structuralism also played a very central role.

b. Michel Foucault and the Third Wave of Feminism

Among the other scholars, Michel Foucault exercised a great influence on Western feminism because of both his "genealogical" works regarding the concept of sexuality and his anti-universalist philosophical perspective. Traces of this double influence are clear in Judith Butler's philosophical framework and deeply affected the third wave of feminism. For example, Butler's crucial notion of gender performativity, expressed in her 1990 landmark book *Gender Trouble,* openly mirrored Foucauldian reflection on the process of subjectivation. It is worth spending a few words more about the concept of "subjectivation" since French philosophers Pierre Dardot and Christian Laval already noted the partial consistency of these considerations with Marx's classic framework (Dardot, Laval 2010). Foucault's idea is that a subject is not an entity that can be examined abstractly, separated from the actual context in which that subject comes into being. Rather, it is necessary to focus on the continuous process of social construction of subjects. Since there is no such thing as a pre-social disembodied individual, material processes of power define different kinds of subjects over time. Hence, in regard to feminism, Judith Butler broadened Foucault's analysis and applied these intuitions to sexuality, especially denouncing the social construction of gender:

> Gender ought not to be construed as a stable identity or locus of agency from which various acts follow; rather, gender is an identity tenuously constituted in time, instituted in an exterior space through a stylized repetition of acts. The effect of gender is produced through the stylization of the body and, hence, must be understood as the mundane way in which bodily gestures, movements, and styles of various kinds constitute the illusion of an abiding gendered self. This formulation moves the conception of gender off the ground of a substantial model of identity to one that requires a conception of gender as a constituted social temporality. Significantly, if gender is instituted through acts which are internally discontinuous, then the appearance of substance is precisely that, a constructed identity, a performative accomplishment which the mundane social audience, including the actors themselves, come to believe and to perform in the mode of belief. (Butler 2002, 179)

Along with other significant consequences, this Foucauldian position clearly stressed the importance of history. To put it differently, according to Foucault, it would be nonsense to think of subjects in previous historical stages without employing a different theoretical lens. In the same way, Marx thematised in his works a certain relation between the mode of production and subjects. We can give two short examples, here. On the one hand, we could refer to *On the Jewish Question*, and to the description of the kind of subject shaped by modern society. There, the separation of civil society from the state brought about the rise of an isolated human being, focused on one's self-interest, and for whom the others were merely understood as limits to one's own happiness:

> Die Freiheit ist also das Recht, alles zu tun und zu treiben,

> was keinem andern schadet. Die Grenze, in welcher sich jeder dem andern unschädlich bewegen kann, ist durch das Gesetz bestimmt, wie die Grenze zweier Felder durch den Zaunpfahl bestimmt ist. Es handelt sich um die Freiheit des Menschen als isolierter auf sich zurückgezogener Monade. [...] Das Menschenrecht des Privateigentums ist also das Recht, willkürlich (à son gré), ohne Beziehung auf andre Menschen, unabhängig von der Gesellschaft, sein Vermögen zu genießen und über dasselbe zu disponieren, das Recht des Eigennutzes. Jene individuelle Freiheit, wie diese Nutzanwendung derselben, bilden die Grundlage der bürgerlichen Gesellschaft. Sie läßt jeden Menschen im andern Menschen nicht die Verwirklichung, sondern vielmehr die Schranke seiner Freiheit finden. (Marx 1976, 364-365)

On the other hand, the young Marx dedicated a substantial part of his 1844 *Economic and Philosophic Manuscripts* to depicting the communist revolution, not only as a mere economic revolution, but also as an anthropological one:

> Wie das Privateigentum nur der sinnliche Ausdruck davon ist, daß der Mensch zugleich gegenständlich für sich wird und zugleich vielmehr sich als ein fremder und unmenschlicher Gegenstand wird, daß seine Lebensäußerung seine Lebensentäußerung ist, seine Verwirklichung seine Entwirklichung, eine fremde Wirklichkeit ist, so ist die positive Aufhebung des Privateigentums, d.h. die sinnliche Aneignung des menschlichen Wesens und Lebens, des gegenständlichen Menschen, der menschlichen Werke für und durch den Menschen, nicht nur im Sinne des unmittelbaren, einseitigen Genusses zu fassen, nicht nur im Sinne des Besitzens, im Sinne des Habens. Der Mensch eignet sich sein allseitiges Wesen auf eine allseitige Art an, also als ein totaler Mensch. Jedes seiner menschlichen Verhältnisse zur Welt, Sehn, Hören, Riechen, Schmecken, Fühlen, Denken, Anschauen, Empfinden, Wollen, Tätigsein, Lieben, kurz, alle Organe seiner Individualität, wie die Organe, welche unmittelbar in ihrer Form als gemeinschaftliche Organe sind, sind in ihrem gegenständlichen Verhalten oder in ihrem Verhalten zum Gegenstand die Aneignung desselben. (Marx 1968a, 540)

Here, it is not necessary to distinguish between a young

Marx and an old one—according to Althusser's useful advice regarding the Marxian *coupure épistémologique*—since this kind of "anthropological" considerations can be easily found in old Marx's works as well.

Before reaching the conclusion of this paper, we have to take account of a last aspect of this question in order to put Marxian theory and contemporary feminism in connection once again. This aspect is the post-structuralist rejection of both universalism and essentialism, and Marx's dialectic conception of human essence.

4. The Essence of the Human Being in Marx's Dialectic Framework

Marxist tradition furiously struggled on some crucial key points in Marx's thought. Along with economic questions regarding communist society's actual configuration, philosophical topics caused a few problems to Marxist scholars. Two factors came into play, here. On the one side, the lack of a critical edition of Marx's collected works prevented scholars from correctly addressing those issues. The so-called "transformation problem"—that is, the transformation of commodities' values into prices in Marx's economic theory—is probably the best example in this regard (Fineschi 2001). On the other side, both the limited philosophical education of many Marxist scholars and the dogmatism of a certain orthodox Marxism prevented those scholars from developing an in-depth analysis of the dialectic element in Marx's theory. In this sense, up-to-date studies, based on the latest edition of MEGA^2, persuasively showed the partial correctness of Althusser's claim. There is no room for doubt that Marx's theoretical framework underwent an evolutionary process marking a *coupure épistémologique*, an epistemological rupture between different phases of Marx's speculation. In particular, as Roberto Fineschi suggests, this gradual movement led Marx far from a naive starting essentialism (Fineschi 2006). In the wake of Feuerbach's critique of religion (1841-1845), the young Marx explicitly assumed a Feuerbachian point of view. In so doing, the essence of the human being became a central element of his theory. By broadening the Feuerbachian examination of religion, Marx employed human essence as a theoretical tool to denounce widespread alienation in the capitalist society. The cure for alienation, this peculiar "disease" of modern society, was to abolish private property, and hence the capitalist system, *in order to set the human essence free from alienation by establishing a new society in harmony with the human essence itself*. Thus, according to what has been said, in young Marx's view the human essence is a "given", an abstract thing that is defined once and for all. It has to be restored through social actions since human existence in modern society has been tainted by capitalism. Therefore, it is no wonder that young Marx's philosophical position presented all the typical weak points of an essentialist theory. As abstract and eternal, human essence was completely ahistorical, that is, its fundamental features were not affected by the historical process at all. Also, the restoration of human essence took the shape of an eschatological final moment, that is, of a theological Palingenesis aiming to cleanse the world of all its evil.

However, the continuous evolution of Marx's thought gradually brought him away from his previous essentialist position. A first criticism to *The Holy Family*'s evident essentialism was made by Gustav Julius in his significant article *Der Streit der sichtbaren mit der unsichtbaren Menschkirche oder Kritik der Kritik der kritischen Kritik*, published in the second volume of the 1845 *Wigand's Vierteljahrschrift*. Anyway, it was the reading of Max Stiner's one-of-a-kind 1844 book *The Ego and its Own* to represent a pivotal event for Marx's position. In his harsh attack against every essentialism, Stirner pointed out how the Feuerbachian "man" and its "human essence" were nothing more than a secular translation of previous religious and metaphysical entities. Even if Marx never admitted the influence of Stirner's work on his speculation, the partial correspondence between Marx and Engels and recent studies regarding the *Entstehungsgeschichte* of *The German Ideology* made clear the impact of Stirner on Marx. Derrida's well-known reflection on this point already stressed this aspect (Derrida 2006). After reading Stirner, Karl Marx drastically changed his opinion about Feuerbach's theoretical limits and openly affirmed his philosophical distance from all Left Hegelians, such as Bruno Bauer and Feuerbach, in the first part of *The German Ideology*. Incidentally, in this context Marx also provided a new definition of human essence, showing a decisive shift towards a more dialectic theory:

> Sie zeigt, daß die Geschichte nicht damit endigt, sich ins "Selbstbewußtsein" als "Geist vom Geist" aufzulösen, sondern daß in ihr auf jeder Stufe ein materielles Resultat, eine Summe von Produktionskräften, ein historisch geschaffnes Verhältnis zur Natur und der Individuen zueinander sich vorfindet, die jeder Generation von ihrer Vorgängerin überliefert wird [...]. Diese Summe von Produktionskräften, Kapitalien und sozialen Verkehrsformen, die jedes Individuum und jede Generation als etwas Gegebenes vorfindet, ist der reale Grund dessen, was sich die Philosophen als "Substanz" und "Wesen des Menschen" vorgestellt, was sie apotheosiert und bekämpft haben, ein realer Grund, der dadurch nicht im Mindesten in seinen Wirkungen und Einflüssen auf die Entwicklung der Menschen gestört wird, daß diese Philosophen als "Selbstbewußtsein" und "Einzige" dagegen rebellieren. (Marx 1969, 38)

At this point, it is evident that human essence was no longer understood as an abstract, ahistorical entity. Instead, it was defined as the sum of productive forces and capitals left by a previous generation for the next one. In this sense, the human essence became something dynamic and history-related. There was no such thing as an eternal, unchangeable human essence. On the contrary, "human essence" could be only used as a formal expression referring to ever-developing actual contents. The connection with a specific mode of production prevented the concept of "human essence" from having random contents; rather, those contents were always linked to a certain form of social and economic organisation. In this way, the human essence expressed a universality that was never given once and for all. Against every metaphysical definition of the "human essence", Marx employed dialectics to define a reflection taking account of the role of the historical development without renouncing to the crucial element of universality.

Strangely, it seems that Marx was not aware of his gradual convergence with Hegel's point of view. The interpretation of Hegelian thought he inherited from Left Hegelians conditioned his understanding of Hegel's philosophy for his whole life. Notwithstanding widespread misunderstandings, indeed, Hegel never theorised a totalitarian philosophical system in which all the particularities ended up being absorbed by an oppressive universality. From his dialectic perspective, the philosophical system—representing the full self-comprehension of an age—was in a condition of precarious balance. On the contrary, the concluded system had to be reopened every time because of the historical movement, and hence the philosophical reflection had to start conceptualising reality over and over again. Therefore, Hegel rejected metaphysical and pre-historical (hence, ahistorical) definition of any essence too. In his 1820 *Philosophy of Right*, for example, the universal idea of right was exposed in its actual development since there was no possibility to separate the essence of right from its historical evolution:

> Die Rechtswissenschaft ist ein Teil der Philosophie. Sie hat daher die Idee als welche die Vernunft eines Gegenstandes ist, aus dem Begriffe zu entwickeln, oder, was dasselbe ist, der eigenen immanenten Entwicklung der Sache selbst zuzusehen. Als Teil hat sie einen bestimmten Anfangspunkt, welcher das Resultat und die Wahrheit von dem ist, was vorhergeht, und was den sogenannten Beweis desselben ausmacht. [...] Der Boden des Rechts ist überhaupt das Geistige, und seine nähere Stelle und Ausgangspunkt der Wille, welcher frei ist, so daß die Freiheit seine Substanz und Bestimmung ausmacht, und das Rechtssystem das Reich der verwirklichten Freiheit, die Welt des Geistes aus ihm selbst hervorgebracht, als eine zweite Natur, ist. (Hegel 1911, 18, 27)

Esoteric philosophical terminology aside, Hegel also explained his dialectic conception in the well-known *Preface* to the *Phenomenology of Spirit*, in 1807:

> Es kömmt nach meiner Einsicht, welche sich durch die Darstellung des Systems selbst rechtfertigen muß, alles darauf an, das Wahre nicht als Substanz, sondern ebensosehr als Subjekt aufzufassen und auszudrücken. Zugleich ist zu bemerken, daß die Substantialität sosehr das Allgemeine oder die Unmittelbarkeit des Wissens als diejenige, welche Sein oder Unmittelbarkeit für das Wissen ist, in sich schließt. [...] Die lebendige Substanz ist ferner das Sein, welches in Wahrheit Subjekt, oder, was dasselbe heißt, welches in Wahrheit wirklich ist, nur insofern sie die Bewegung des Sich-selbst-setzens, oder die Vermittlung des Sich-anders-werdens mit sich selbst ist. [...] Nur diese sich wiederherstellende Gleichheit oder die Reflexion im Anderssein in sich selbst—nicht eine ursprüngliche Einheit als solche, oder unmittelbare als solche, ist das Wahre. Es ist das Werden seiner selbst, der Kreis, der sein Ende als seinen Zweck voraussetzt und zum Anfange hat, und nur durch die Ausführung und sein Ende wirklich ist. (Hegel 2012)

Hegel's dialectic reflection ushered in a new way of understanding essence and essentialism. Within this framework, the universal element of essence stopped being a category having unchangeable contents. Rather, the connection with history made it dynamic and adaptative. That was the conception of human essence the old Marx assumed and further developed, even if he never made it completely explicit. And it is exactly this conception that seems to show us a way to bridge the gap between contemporary post-structuralist feminism and Marxist theory.

5. Marxism and Post-Structuralist Feminism

As said before, contemporary feminism inherited a theoretical feeling of rejection for universalism from French post-structuralism. Many French *maîtres à penser* opposed dialectic thought, pointing out the risk of dissolving particularities into universality. By comparing Foucault's view with Hegel's above-mentioned assertions about freedom, it is easy to grasp the whole range of theoretical differences at play here:

> Je n'ai pas voulu dire que la quantité de liberté avait augmenté entre le début du XVIIIe siècle et, disons, le XIXe. Je ne l'ai pas dit pour deux raisons. [...] C'est qu'il ne faut pas considérer que la liberté, ce soit un universel qui présenterait, à travers le temps, un accomplissement progressif ou des variations quantitatives ou des amputations plus ou moins graves, des occultations plus ou moins importantes. Ce n'est pas un universel qui se particulariserait avec le temps et avec la géographie. La liberté, ce n'est pas une surface blanche avec, ici et là et de temps en temps, des cases noires plus ou moins nombreuses. La liberté, ce n'est jamais rien d'autre—mais c'est déjà beaucoup—qu'un rapport actuel entre gouvernants et gouvernés, un rapport où la mesure du "trop peu" de liberté qui existe est donnée par le "encore plus" de liberté qui est demandé. (Foucault 2004, 64)

Hegel attempted to bridge the gap between transcendence and immanence by assuming a universality always *in fieri*. Foucault aimed to reduce every transcendence to an absolute immanence, instead. One of the most common risks of this position is the implicit relativism. If there is no such thing as an absolute concept of freedom, so there is no possibility to show how freedom increased or decreased in different societies. To be more precise, we should say that such a question is rather a misleading one from a Foucauldian point of view. No wonder, therefore, if a similar accusation has also been made against the third-wave of feminism because of its rejection of universalism. Indeed, by using Foucault's thought, contemporary feminism deepened the critical analysis of universalism as a form of hidden cultural hegemony, that is, a sort of Trojan horse against subaltern cultures. According to this view, universal concepts mainly work as a tool to normalise and to discipline, to proclaim who belongs to a given group and who has to live as an excluded from the society. For example, it happened that feminists of sexual difference ended up harshly denigrating transgender people because of their impossibility to fit the established binary sexual criteria (to be either male or female). The abstract definition of both men's and women's essence brought about a reification of men's and women's essential features. Therefore, transgender people were stigmatised by a framework *a priori* unable to take them into account. To put it differently, they were considered to be abnormalities, errors or even direct products of patriarchy. Third wave of feminism labelled this kind of feminists as TERFs, that is, trans-exclusionary radical feminists (Butler 2014).

As Marxists, we should ask here if the "dialectic essentialism"—that is, a conception understanding the essence as a historically dynamic universality—is doomed to produce the same discriminations and to fail in taking account of the latest feminist and trans issues. Admittedly, this does not seem to be the case. The example of transgender people is particularly significant in this regard. After all, to think about transgender people necessarily implies to refer to overall social and technological development. Surely transgender people—that is, people having a gender identity that differs from the sex assigned at birth—existed before the last century. However, the actual possibility for them to modify their "natural" sex is *de facto* strictly dependent from the evolution of biomedical technologies. The possibility to undergo specific medical treatments, such as hormone replacement therapy or sex reassignment surgery, only became feasible after a certain historical moment. Since 1930—or maybe some years before—when the first sex reassignment surgery was performed in Germany, philosophical dialectic speculation had to take account of a new element with regard to existing previous ideas of what "man" and "woman" meant (Stryker 2017, 45-78). Could we not assume this episode as a turning point for the dialectical evolution of men's and women's essence? Could we not regard this pivotal event as a decisive moment—maybe, not the first in time—to finally call into question the long-lasting assumption of gender binary? According to both Marx and Foucault's position, we should not employ anachronistic elements to provide an analysis of a historical situation, or a certain configuration of power.

Therefore, without being deterministic, it would be possible to understand the contemporary rise of transgender issues as a side effect of an unavoidable dissolution of a previous understanding of what gender and sex are. In turn, this dissolution could be seen as the last moment of a chain reaction—both ideal and material at one time—triggered by a technological development taking place in a specific environment. In other words, that development could have worked as a condition of possibility to set free some existing theoretical possibilities prevented from being fully developed until that moment. So, the concept of an ever-growing human essence—and its internal distinction in male and female essence—has to be repeatedly rethought and broadened, in order to include what can be "fully" conceptualised only in the contemporary age. As Foucault suggests, there is no "neutral" knowledge since every knowledge is always a product of a certain configuration of power. Therefore, a shift towards a dialectic feminism—according to the principles we described—within a Marxian framework could give us effective theoretical tools to comprehend the meaning of contemporary feminism itself, included its crucial focus on the concept of "gender" (Repo 2016).

BIBLIOGRAPHY

Butler, J. (2002 [1999]). *Gender Trouble. Feminism and the Subversion of Identity*, New York: Routledge.

Butler, (2014). "Gender Performance: The TransAdvocate interviews Judith Butler" in The TransAdvocate, May 1, 2014. Source: http://transadvocate.com/gender-performance-the-transadvocate-interviews-judith-butler_n_13652.htm

California Federal Savings and Loan Association v. Guerra (1985). 758 F.2d

Dardot, P., Laval, C. (2010). *La nouvelle raison du monde. Essai sur la société néolibérale*, Paris : La Découverte.

Derrida, J. (2006 [1993]), *Spectres of Marx. The State of the Debt, the Work of Mourning and the New International*, trans. by P. Kamuf, London: Routledge.

Fanon, F. (1952). *Peau noire, masques blancs*, Paris : Éditions du Seuil.

Fanon, F. (2002 [1961]). *Les damnés de la terre*, Paris : La Découverte.

Fineschi, R. (2001). *Introduzione* in Marx K., *Il capitale. Critica dell'economia politica*, Napoli: La città del sole, pp. VII-XXXI.

Fineschi, R. (2006). *Marx e Hegel. Contributi a una rilettura*, Roma: Carocci.

Foucault, M. (2004). *Naissance de la biopolitique. Cours au Collège de France (1978-1979)*, Seuil : Gallimard.

Hegel, G.W.F. (1911 [1821]). *Grundlinien der Philosophie des Rechts*, Berlin: Felix Meiner Verlag.

Hegel, G.F.W. (2012 [1807]). *Phänomenologie des Geistes*, Ebook, Gutenberg Projekt-DE. Source: http://www.gutenberg.org/cache/epub/6698/pg6698-images.html

Karl, M. (2011). *Die Geschichte der Frauenbewegung*, Stuttgart: Reclam.

Lenin, V. (1950 [1920]). *On International Women's Day*, trans. by S. Ryan, London: Lawrence & Wishart. Source: https://www.marxists.org/archive/lenin/works/1920/mar/04.htm

Lenin, V. (1974 [1917]), The State and Revolution. The Marxist Theory of the State and the Tasks of the Proletariat in the Revolution in V. Lenin, *Collected Works*, trans. by S. Apresyan and J. Riordon, Moscow: Progress Publishers, Vol. 5, pp. 389-497.

Lonzi, C. (2010), *Sputiamo su Hegel*, Milano: *et al.*

Losurdo, D. (2013). *La lotta di classe. Una storia politica e filosofica*, Roma-Bari: Laterza.

Marx, K. (1968a). Ökonomisch-philosophische Manuskripte aus dem Jahre 1844 in Marx K., Engels F., *Werke*, Ergänzungsband, 1. Teil, Berlin/DDR: Dietz Verlag, S. 465-588.

Marx, K. (1968b). *Das Kapital. Band I. Kritik der politischen Ökonomie* in Marx K., Engels F., *Werke*, Band 23, Bd. I, Dritter Abschnitt, Berlin/DDR: Dietz Verlag.

Marx, K. (1971). *Einleitung [zur Kritik der politischen Ökonomie]* in Marx K., Engels F., *Werke*, Band 13, 7. Auflage 1971, Berlin/DDR: Dietz Verlag, S. 615-641.

Marx, K. (1976). *Zur Judenfrage* in Marx K., Engels F., *Werke*, Band 1, Berlin/DDR Dietz Verlag, S. 347-377.

Marx, K., Engels F. (1969). *Die deutsche Ideologie. Kritik der neuesten deutschen Philosophie in ihren Repräsentanten Feuerbach, B. Bauer und Stirner und des deutschen Sozialismus in seinen verschiedenen Propheten* in Marx K., Engels F., *Werke*, Band 3, Berlin/DDR: Dietz Verlag, S. 5-530.

Marx, K., Engels F. (1972). *Manifest der Kommunistischen Partei* in Marx K., Engels F., Werke, Band 4,6, Berlin/DDR: Dietz Verlag, S. 459-493.

Repo, J. (2016). *The Biopolitics of Gender*, Oxford: Oxford University.

Stryker, S. (2017 [2008]). *Transgender History. The Roots of Today's Revolution*, New York: Seal Press.

10

Revolution, Emancipation and Social Reproduction

Chirashree Das Gupta

I

While contested opinion(s) on socialist experiences of the twentieth century is all-pervasive, the academic literature on this has been relatively thinly spread. The quantum of views and opinions stand on a knowledge base that is narrow and the 'known' far exceeds the 'unknown' in a literature highly charged by ideological standpoints defined largely by 'ways of seeing'. The political economy focus has often been on questions around the organisation of production and productive forces—evaluations largely based on a 'productivist' paradigm. But, the reorganisation of social reproduction way beyond the tenets of *welfarism* had been the greatest promise of revolutionary emancipation from patriarchy and social oppression—i.e. from the tyranny of family, private property and the state; and the conscious political attempt of collectivism rather than individualism forming the basis of new 'individualities' (Tomba 2013).

A radical transition from the capitalist system to socialism is different from all previous social changes known in history because it marks the beginning of an entirely different social organisation—change from a class society to classless society. This kind of paradigmatic change in human civilisation could hardly have been peaceful and smooth. Similar episodes of retrogression had happened when capitalism was replacing another class-based system, feudalism. The terrain would be much more contested naturally in the case of transcending the class system altogether. Retrogression and defeat of socialism in the erstwhile USSR and East European countries have often been attributed to planning, state control, over centralisation and denial of individual choice in the realm of the economy while on the other hand, arguments or rather ideological positions would like to condemn socialism as a system that curbs democratic rights and denies political competition.

There was euphoria around the conclusion that the collapse of the USSR and the Eastern European socialist systems served as 'proof' of the inherently unviable and unsustainable nature of the socialist system. But, instead of explaining why that development occurred such readings actually dispenses with the need for any rigorous examination of the history of socialism. The ideological bias underlying such sweeping conclusions are partly demonstrated in the fact that it is premised on a historical determinism that is also simultaneously denied while questioning the 'inevitability' of the ultimate demise of capitalism. This contradiction is even more stark if a fundamental difference between the two systems is recognised—namely that while capitalism is a spontaneous system, socialism is not inherently so (Roy, Mazumdar and Das Gupta, 2015).

Efforts have hardly been made to understand in detail the contested system of 'actually existing socialism', and understand the conflicts of change. A non-determinist and non-productivist conceptualising of socialism has to be adopted as the entry point of reference. This brief paper has the modest aim of bringing to the fore some observations derived from commentaries on 'actually existing socialisms' that could be taken into account for an informed debate on the praxis of building socialism (Roy, Mazumdar and Das Gupta 2015). Based on a Marxist-Feminist framework linking theory, perspective and method, this paper is an endeavour to critically survey the methods by which the reorganisation of social production and reproduction in societies attempting a socialist transformation had been approached to extend and add to the contested terrain of the historicisation of socialist experiences of the twentieth century.

This is a relatively less explored area in the impressionistic literature around the socialist experiences that have gained credence especially since the 1990s. The scholarship on actual socialist transition(s) is thin. Access to works is also limited given both the political and cultural hegemony and limits of Anglophone scholarship in a world structured by Anglophone imperial domination. This forms the premise of the question on method. The denial of a materialist analysis and of social class as central objects of study in mainstream social science in US academia had been evident since the 1950s and 60s in the shaping of disciplinary imperatives at the height of Cold War politics. After the intellectual upheaval of the 'dependency theory' and the 'structuralist school', mainstream social science in the USA consistently rejected the idea that social classes should be objects of study. There was substantial material and intellectual investment during the Reagan period in a particular strand of culture and area studies that took the lead in formulating ideas of 'hybridity' and 'fragmented forms' and 'fluid identities' rather than 'structured social formations' like race and class as the counter to different branches of cultural relativism, essentialism and idealism that emanated as the 'new' theory from the mainstream of US academia (Gendzier 1985; Leys 1996; Roediger 2006). These intellectual models ran a serious 'risk that one's subject would be deconstructed into fragments united only by the common experience of an incommunicable identity crisis'. This risk stems from the emphasis on 'cultural collisions, confrontations and dialogues of the deaf 'and statements 'devoid of meaning' rising from the separation of the 'cultural' from the 'material' in the recasting of 'social history' and 'studies of society' in a form where the ambiguity of the 'narrator' and the 'non-specificity' of 'subject position' were premised over earlier analytical narratives based on the material construction of social relations that defined the structures of society

(Hobsbawm 1998). The dominant economic paradigm can

> *...only distinguish between private and state property—it cannot conceptualize either capitalist private property or socialized property and thus is incapable of illuminating the process of transition from the former to the latter.* (Roy et al 2015: 6)

The resolution of capitalism's contradictions involved the abolition of private property whose fundamental result was to place the social process of production within the control of society—the elimination therefore of the anarchy and spontaneity of capitalism. Engels (1880) argued:

> With the seizing of the means of production by society, production of commodities is done away with, and, simultaneously, the mastery of the product over the producer. Anarchy in social production is replaced by systematic, definite organization. The struggle for individual existence disappears. Then, for the first time, man, in a certain sense, is finally marked off from the rest of the animal kingdom, and emerges from mere animal conditions of existence into really human ones. The whole sphere of the conditions of life which environ man, and which have hitherto ruled man, now comes under the dominion and control of man, who for the first time becomes the real, conscious lord of nature, because he has now become master of his own social organization. The laws of his own social action, hitherto standing face-to-face with man as laws of Nature foreign to, and dominating him, will then be used with full understanding, and so mastered by him. Man's own social organization, hitherto confronting him as a necessity imposed by Nature and history, now becomes the result of his own free action. The extraneous objective forces that have, hitherto, governed history, pass under the control of man himself. Only from that time will man himself, more and more consciously, make his own history—only from that time will the social causes set in movement by him have, in the main and in a constantly growing measure, the results intended by him. It is the ascent of man from the kingdom of necessity to the kingdom of freedom.

However, the subsequent disciplinary divides of power-knowledge diffused *only in its manifestation* but entrenched in structural root of the patriarchal reproduction(s) of social classes and their institutional units of organization (Poulantzas 1978) has largely bypassed the so-called Marxian economics of actual socialist transition (Dobb 1969; Kornai 1979; Wilczynski 2017). However, in Marx's vision of the 'rich individuality', this aspect was central.

Rosa Luxemburg had captured this relationship between the wage system and patriarchy in 1912 succinctly when she wrote:

> As long as capitalism and the wage system rule, only that kind of work is considered productive which produces surplus value, which creates capitalist profit. From this point of view, the music-hall dancer whose legs sweep profit into her employer's pocket is a productive worker, whereas all the toil of the proletarian women and mothers in the four walls of their homes is considered unproductive. This sounds brutal and insane, but corresponds exactly to the brutality and insanity of our present capitalist economy. And seeing this brutal reality clearly and sharply is the proletarian woman's first task. (Luxemburg 2004: 241)

The attempts at 'theorising' of the socialist experiences have largely been based on abstractions informed by fragmented readings of the developments in China and the erstwhile USSR. An early attempt of critiquing such expositions led Dunayevskaya to lament in 1944 in the *American Economic Review* that 'theory' had been replaced by 'applied' economics in the USSR (Dunayevskaya 1944, 1984). Thus apart from the lack of 'newness' in scholarship, the sociological genealogy of the attempts at 'Marxist' theorising in the judgment(s) of socialist attempts at social transformation is a task at hand in terms of the implications of the level of abstraction on which the critique rests and to what extent it helps us to understand the processes of social transformation towards the creation of an emancipatory society breaking free of alienation. In doing so, the attempt is not only to break away from the class basis of production relations, but also transform the domain of state-society relationships from the aegis of the nation-state (Stalin 1913).

Multiple strands of later Marxist interpretations have

tried to locate the conflicts and contests of changing class relations in the attempts at social transformation. The abstract conceptualisation of conflict, contest and the dialectics of transformation have been limited to the sphere of production in a somewhat direct conflict with Marx's and earlier Marxist understanding of the institutional unit(s) of organisation of society. In doing so, the individual and the collective get conceived in terms of a conceptualisation of class relations that abstracts away from the role of the patriarchal family as the unit of organisation of society in a semi-feudal semi-capitalist context within a nation-state and the spatio-temporal location of that nation-state within the hierarchy of nation-states defined by imperialism. However, the transformative aspects of actually existing socialism(s) lay in not only the change in the institutional zone of production and appropriation of surplus, but the re-conceptualisation of the radical transformation needed in the sphere of social reproduction informed by a Marxist understanding of gender, patriarchy and 'human nature' in a context where the transformative potential of socialist revolution became historically limited to small pockets of the world (Marx 1959; Lenin 1916; Bebel 1910; Kollontai 1909; Trotsky 1923; Davis 1981; Bannerji et al. 2001; Brown 2013)

II

Our point of departure is rooted in two inter-connected Marxist Feminist paradigmatic premises. First, patriarchy is endogenous to the construct of the macroeconomy. The actual macroeconomic construct of patriarchy within which the social hierarchy of paid and unpaid labour operates is very much a historical process in its social and economic specificity both in terms of time and space. Thus the ahistorical abstraction of homoeconomicus based market systems is inadequate in its explanatory capacity either as point of entry or as a point of departure in understanding/analysing attempted socialist transitions.

Second, the transformative aspects of actually existing

socialism(s) did not lie in the change in the institutional zone of production and appropriation of surplus and by extension the potential and limits of 'growth of productive forces' which has been the focus of debates on socialist production. It lay in the re-conceptualisation of the radical transformation needed in the sphere of social reproduction informed by a Marxist understanding of social oppression, patriarchy and exploitation. Based on this Marxist-Feminist conceptualisation of social transformation, the rest of this paper is an endeavour to critically survey the methods by which the institutional reorganisation of reproduction in societies attempting a revolutionary transformation had been approached through a brief study of three attempted transformations—the Russian, Chinese and the Cuban revolutions. In this part of the paper, we argue that assuming the growth of productive forces as the focus of extensive transformation rather than egalitarian institutionalisation of social reproduction can largely undermine the material dialectics of revolutionary emancipation.

In the socialist transitions of the twentieth century in the USSR, China, Cuba and Tanzania, attempts to address this contradiction had been central to the process of transformation (Croll 1981). In each of these societies, right after the revolution, the securing of a new and secure material base had been severe—largely attributable to the isolations and penalties associated with the breaking away from the imperial axes of material power. In the 'conceptualisation of revolution within a revolution', collectivisation of production and abolition of private property rights played an important role in the Soviet Union, China and Cuba in raising new standards in food, health-care, housing, education and clothing and providing women visibility and better remuneration as workers. Having successfully abolished semi-feudal and semi-capitalist private property rights, the question of reorgansing social reproduction and its relationship to organisation of production became the key question in terms of not only the quest for emancipation but also the survival of the peoples in each of these contexts amidst hostile geopolitics.

In Tanzania, on the other hand, *ujama* after independence entailed the drawing in of women into the paid labour force in agriculture through the process of villagization. However the bulk of the land (70 per cent in 1980) remained under private ownership. In that sense, while it lasted, the first condition of reorganisation of property which had been possible in the USSR, China and Cuba could not be achieved in Tanzania (Croll 1981). This foreclosed the possibility of an emancipatory restructuring of social reproduction at the very beginning of Ujama.

There is of course a significant question that have been raised about socialist experiments in terms of the creation of a hierarchical technocracy that had its inherent class logic that 'assumes people on the top are the only real subjects of creating new society and the capitalist objectification of the worker continues to remain in the process of carrying out commands down the line' (Roy, Mazumdar and Das Gupta 2015). But even more fundamental to the process of social restructuring was the problem that while the old appropriators of the surplus had been done away with in the course of the revolution, the producers of the surplus were not the owners of the surplus (Roy, Mazumdar and Das Gupta 2015). This production of the surplus while geared towards the end of a better material life for all, had to fundamentally address the question of not only the wage-surplus relationship but also the sexual division of productive and reproductive labour in the determination of this relationship. The relationship between the collective enterprise system and the family has been the twin locus of determination of the wage-surplus relationship in the organisation of societies attempting social transformation in which the sexual division of both productive and reproductive labour has paid a pivotal role in a. the determination of the wage-surplus relationship itself b. making the social basis of patriarchy mutable in progressive ways but reversal of that mutability in the face of crises of production and/or reproduction.

Cuba is an example where direct attempts to break the basis of the patriarchal family were muted by the compulsions of the enterprise based production system. In Cuba, after the revolution, the emphasis was on employment, distribution and re-distribution with women and children as the locus of the system. A shift from material to moral incentives in the organisation of production was at the centre of socialist envisioning in Cuba. But by the 1970s, the material conditions of increasing problems of production given the blockade (despite Soviet assistance) led to the tying of distribution to wage and enterprises were expected to generate the surplus for re-distribution. The Cuban Federation of `Women rallied thousands of women for 'volunteer work' for both productive and reproductive labour (41 million women in five years) along with incorporation of women in the paid work-force (one hundred thousand every year). The proportion of women opting out of the paid workforce was very high (76 per cent in a single year). Women's political participation was also very low in the early 1970s. This was the context of the adoption of the Family Code in 1975 which directly addressed inequality within the home. However, this intervention, coincided with the compulsions of the reversal from moral incentives to production to the wage-surplus enterprise system (Nazzari 1983). This undid many of the egalitarian premises of the Family Code.

In 1948, the greatest problem facing Chinese families was identified as extreme poverty, very high child and adult mortality rates and health deprivation even among the more affluent sections of society. In October and November 1948, on the eve of the Chinese Revolution, 1492 children were picked up from the streets and cremated in the Municipal Crematorium (Osborne 1948). China's social transformation after the revolution was contingent on people's communes and brigades as the 'new' institutional bases of enterprise in the spheres of both production and reproduction (Dong 2014) apart from the promulgation of the new family code of 1950. China's attempts from the time of introduction of private land-use rights on one hand and despite the Cultural Revolution on the other is an illustration of the direct relationship between the relationship between family and private property in structurally foreclosing any departure of social reproduction from patriarchy. With the reorganisation of land after decollectivisation, the structural roots of the patriarchal family became strengthened with women as daughter in laws taking on an active role in farming along with fathers-in-law while the husbands migrated to non-agricultural employment to 'feed' the land (van der Pleog et al., 2014). This phenomenon became more pronounced after the institutionalisation of the wage-surplus relationship as the basis of enterprise since 1978, the changes in the family code (Marriage Law) of 1980 which formalised the property relationships in marriage and subsequent formal re-introduction of private property rights in 2007.

The attempts in the USSR in its early phase started with the decriminalisation of homosexuality in 1918 (the first constitution in the world to do so) and the conscious cultural attempt to create conditions for breaking the basis of the sexual division of labour through the Family Code of 1918 to break away from the unit of organisation of society in terms of the reproduction of the patriarchal monogamous family. The Code established legalised abortion, facilitated divorce at the request of either spouse without requiring any ground. It abolished "illegitimacy" and entitled all children to parental support. It gave legal credence to 'collective fatherhood' But the most important feature was that marriage did not create joint property between spouses: a woman retained full control of her earnings after marriage, and neither spouse had any claim on the property of the other (Goldman 1993). In the Soviet Union, this was accompanied by more and more political participation by women in public affairs at the level of the Soviets within the pyramidal structure of political power (Lapidus 1975). At the same time, there was a thinning out of women's political power at the topmost levels of the pyramid which was a significant reversal of the conditions that prevailed in the first few years after the revolution in the USSR.

Alexandra Kollontai in 1921 outlined the problematic "in the 'hypocritical way' in which 'sexual problems' were relegated to the realm of 'private matters' that are not worth the effort and attention of the collective". At the same time, she pointed to the 'spontaneous wave of new attempts of living developing from within the social fabric'. Thus Kollontai captured the contradictions of property relationships, class contradictions and individualistic morality that was the basis of alienation even as the new society under the Bolsheviks was trying to find ways of social organisation to address these contradictions (Kollontai 2017). Leon Trotsky in 1923 in Pravda formulated the contradictions emerging within the 'comunist family' due to the larger transformations in the Soviet Union in the first decade after the revolution. He argued that:

> The physical preparations for the conditions of the new life and the new family, again, cannot fundamentally be separated from the general work of socialist construction. The workers' state must become wealthier in order that it may be possible seriously to tackle the public education of children and the releasing of the family from the burden of the kitchen and the laundry. Socialisation of family housekeeping and public education of children are unthinkable without a marked improvement in our economics as a whole. We need more socialist economic forms. Only under such conditions can we free the family from the functions and cares that now oppress and disintegrate it. Washing must be done by a public laundry, catering by a public restaurant, sewing by a public workshop. Children must be educated by good public teachers who have a real vocation for the work. Then the bond between husband and wife would be freed from everything external and accidental, and the one would cease to absorb the life of the other. Genuine equality would at last be established. The bond will depend on mutual attachment. And on that account particularly, it will acquire inner stability, not the same, of course, for everyone, but compulsory for no one.
>
> Thus, the way to the new family is twofold: (a) the raising of the standard of culture and education of the working class and

> the individuals composing the class; (b) an improvement in the material conditions of the class organized by the state. The two processes are intimately connected with one another. (Trotsky 1923)

This was indeed the understanding that informed the adoption of the 1918 family code and concomitant changes to organisation of property rights. But the code became more and more difficult to operate because of the contradictions some of which were captured by Kollontai and Trotsky in their writings. Kollontai traced the adverse consequences from the time of the adoption of the New Economic Policy of 1922 and the devastating effect it had on the lives of women, some of which were captured in her works of fiction. She showed how men in pursuit of aggrandizement as part of the new technocracy took advantage of egalitarian values nurtured by the revolution in the reinforcement of patriarchy (Kollontai 1927; Kollontai 1929). By 1926, the new family code did away with 'collective paternity', recognised the need for protection of women especially after divorce and legalised adoption into the family after it was clear that ideal arrangements of 'collective paternity' was actually increasing women's oppression and strengthening patriarchy (Lapidus 1975). But it was the 1936 code which undid much of the advances and shifted the burden of social reproduction back on women within the patriarchal family (Lapidus 1975), re-criminalised homosexuality to the point where the Marriage Council of Philadelphia in the USA in 1948 ironically celebrated aspects of women's activities, standards of healthcare and education in what they perceived as 'fulfiling the vital function of strengthening of families in the Soviet Union' as opposed to the situation in the USA (Mudd 1948).

What led to this reversal? The usual explanation has been that the loss of life suffered by the Soviet Union led to this shift in women's institutional role in biological reproduction to maintain the population. Without minimising the impact of the war that led to many social problems including high levels of alcoholism and domestic abuse by men, Soviet history shows that this impetus continued beyond the logic of loss of life and the horrors of war. Our argument is that the state of continuous siege of the Soviet Union led to a the continuation of a productivist paradigm founded on an enterprise system based on a wage-surplus relationship that necessarily entailed relegating social reproduction to the realm of the 'family'. The nation-state's project of producing more and more surplus (which was perceived as necessary under the prevailing conditions), entailed a shift in the locus of social transformation from the hidden abode of reproduction to the visible abode of production. Beyond a well-functioning welfare state, the class project of transformation of the institutional basis of social organisation was abandoned to the cause of productivism in the context of the geopolitical situation that led to this shift. The wage-surplus relationship that necessarily entails sexual division of both unpaid reproductive work and unpaid labour in production constituted the fundamental reason for this regression in social transformation.

Thus, we can conclude that assuming the growth of productive forces as the focus of extensive transformation (irrespective of whether it was historical compulsion or historical choice) rather than egalitarian institutionalisation of social reproduction largely undermined the material dialectics of revolutionary emancipation in each of these transitions. Irrespective of the 'ways of seeing' and the bitter debates on these socialist transitions, what is common to each transition is the concrete question of the radical transformation of the family, private property and the nation-state in sustenance of the surplus for social reproduction. Even as each such transformative attempt challenged the global hegemony of imperialism, it also threw open the questions of the material limits of socialist emancipation within a system of nation-states. This paper does not propose definitive answers as there can be none, but in conclusion makes a plea for a Marxist Feminist conception of state-society relations which would help to unravel the institutional linkages between enterprise and family in the material historical dialectic of production-reproduction in the specific context of the attempted revolutionary transformations to socialism in and since the twentieth century.

REFERENCES

Bannerji, H., S. Mojab and J. Whitehead. 2001 (eds), *Of Property and Propriety: The Role of Gender and Class in Imperialism and Nationalism*, University of Toronto Press.

Bebel, A. 1910. *Woman and Socialism* https://www.marxists.org/archive/bebel/1879/woman-socialism/index.htm Last accessed on March 30, 2019.

Brown, H. 2013. *Marx on Gender and the Family*, Haymarket.

Croll, E.J. 1981. Women in Rural Production and Reproduction in the Soviet Union, China, Cuba and Tanzania: Socialist Development Experiences, *Signs* 7(1).

Davis, A.Y. 1981. *Women, Race and Class*, Random House, New York.

Dobb, M. 1969. *Welfare Economics and the Economics of Socialism:Towards a Commonsense Critique*, Cambridge University Press.

Dong, Z. 2014. Mao Zedong and the Independent and Comprehensive Industrial System and the Modernization of New China, *World Review of Political Economy* 5(4).

Dunayevskaya, R. 1944. A New Revision of Marxian Economics, 1944, *American Economic Review* 34(3).

Engels, F. 1880. *Socialism: Utopian and Scientific* https://www.marxists.org/archive/marx/works/1880/soc-utop/index.htm Last accessed on March 30, 2019.

Gendzier, I.L. 1985. *Managing Political Change: Social Scientists and the Third World*, Westview Press 1985.

Goldman, W. 1993. *Women, The State and Revolution: Soviet Family Policy, 1917-1936*, Cambridge University Press.

Hobsbawm, E. 1998. *On History*, Abacus 1998: 261.

Kollontai, A. 1909. The Social Basis of the Women's Question, https://www.marxists.org/archive/kollonta/1909/social-basis.htm Last accessed on March 30, 2019.

Kollontai, A. 2017. 'Sexual Relations and the Class Struggle', in *The Soviet Women: Selected Essays*, LeftWord.

Kollontai, A. 1929. *Red Love*, Seven Arts Publishing Co., New York.

Kollontai, A. 1929. *A Great Love*, The Vanguard Press, New York.

Kornai , J. 1979. 'Resource Constrained versus Demand Constrained Systems', *Ecoometrica*, 47(4), pp. 801-819.

Lapidus, G.W. 1975. Political Leadership, Participation and Leadership: Women in the Soviets, *Comparative Politics* 8(1).

Lenin, V.I. 1916. *Imperialism: The Highest Stage of Capitalism* https://www.marxists.org/archive/lenin/works/1916/imp-hsc/ Last accessed on March 30, 2019.

Leys, C. 1996. *The Rise and Fall of Development Theory*, James Currey.

Luxemburg, R. 1912. *Women's Suffrage and Class Struggle*. https://www.marxists.org/archive/luxemburg/1912/05/12.htm Last accessed on March 30, 2019.

Luxemburg, R. 2004, *The Rosa Luxemburg Reader*, (eds.), P. Hudis and K.B. Anderson, Monthly Review Press, New York.

Marx, K. 1959. *Economic and Philosophic Manuscripts of 1844*, Progress Publishers; Indian edition, Aakar Books, Delhi, 2016.

Mudd, E.H. 1948. The Family in the Soviet Union, *Marriage and Family Living* 10(1).

Nazzari, M. 1983. The 'Woman Question' in Cuba: An Analysis of Material Constraints in its Solution, *Signs* 9(2).

Osborne, E.G. 1948. Problems of the Chinese Family, *Marriage and Family Living* 10(1).

Poulantzas, N. 1978. *State, Power, Socialism*, NLB 1978.

Roediger, D. 2006. The Retreat from Race and Class, *Monthly Review*, 58 (3). July-August .

Roy, S., S. Mazumdar and C. Das Gupta. 2015. *Socialist Experiences and Methods in Social Science*, Mimeo p. 2.

Stalin, J.V. 1913. *Marxism and the National Question* https://www.marxists.org/reference/archive/stalin/works/1913/03.htm Last Accessed on March 30, 2019.

Tomba, M. 2013. *Marx's Temporalities*.

Trotsky, L. 1923. *From the Old Family to the New* https://www.marxists.org/archive/trotsky/women/life/23_07_13.htm Last accessed on March 30, 2017.

van der Ploeg, J.D., J. Ye and I. Pan. 2014. Peasants, Time and the Land: The Social Organization of Farming in China, *Journal of Rural Studies* 36:172-181.

Wilczynski, J. 2017. *The Economics of Socialism After World War II: 1945-1990*, Routledge.

11

Manufacturing Profits: Modes of Surplus Extraction at the Lower End of the Global Value Chain

Archana Aggarwal

Global Value Chains (GVCs) are the face of globalised production now. The last few decades have seen the emergence of the international division of labour in the form of GVCs. Firms located in different parts of the world undertake different aspects of production and distribution of a commodity. Countries like India are situated at low value adding segments of the GVC and maintain their competitiveness by providing cheap labour. India has become a hub for the automobile supply chain as well as the 'manufacturer' of readymade garments and also consumer electronic goods for global 'buyers'. Most recently, it has become an attractive destination for assembly of mobile phones. The National Capital Region (NCR) of Delhi and surrounding areas has evolved as an important centre for various kinds of manufacturing activities, especially in the last three or four decades. There are more than 50 industrial clusters in NCR besides a number of micro enterprises concentrations in the National Capital Territory[1] (NCT) Delhi. Industrialisation in NCR is concentrated in the sub-regions of Uttar Pradesh (general manufacturing), Haryana (automobile, electronics, and textiles) and Rajasthan (marble, leather, and textiles). The textile industry has the largest number of units and is also the largest employer of workforce (Economic Profile of NCR 2015).

This paper examines the methods and mechanisms employed by firms located in the automobile, apparel and consumer electronics GVCs in the NCR, in order to extract surplus and profits. The observations are primarily based on interviews with workers employed in some of these firms. The analysis uses Marxian theory to understand the modes of surplus extraction employed by capital in these industries. Section I discusses the concept of GVC and the distinction between producer-driven and buyer-driven value chains. It also gives an overview of the situation in five plants in the NCR region which provides the basis for analysis in Section II of the paper. The case studies used for analysis in this paper are based on the interviews with the workers of the following factories and industries: 1. Maruti Suzuki India Limited located in Manesar, Haryana; 2. A vendor company for automobile OEM (Original Equipment Manufacturer) including Maruti; 3. Garment workers working in the garment firms in Udyog Vihar, Haryana; 4. A subsidiary of a global producer of consumer electronics, Greater Noida; and 5. A mobile manufacturer in Greater Noida and a phone assembling company at Noida.[2]

Section I: Global Value Chains

A value chain refers to all the value adding activities in the production and distribution of a commodity undertaken by different firms but linked together. Value chains can exist within and across countries. In the latter case, they are referred to as Global Value Chains. Various firms in the chain may be linked together through 'sub-contracting' relations or as 'buyers and sellers' of a part or whole of the commodity. Different firms are located at different levels in the value chain in correspondence to the level of 'value addition' done by them.

Gereffi (2003) shows how two types of international economic networks exist; 'producer-driven' value chains and 'buyer-driven' value chains. Both these networks are led by large, usually, transnational corporations. In the case of 'producer-driven' value chains, transnational manufacturers coordinate the production networks and such chains are common in capital and technology intensive industries such as automobiles. Buyer-driven GVCs, on the other hand, are characterised by large retailers and branded manufacturers, subcontracting to, or buying from, decentralised production networks spread across the world, especially in the low wage developing countries. These are visible in labour intensive industries such as apparel and consumer electronics. Amongst these firms, the transnational corporations located in the developed world are the 'lead firms' and act as the global buyers. They are able to capture the major share of profits by their effective control on high value adding segments of the value chain such as R&D intensive operations and also through their monopoly on markets and finances. Take the example of Apple where the value added in China from assembly, testing, and packaging is just about three per cent or less of the output price (Bose and Pratap, 2016).

(A) *Producer Driven Chains: Automobiles*

The emerging economies saw a rapid spread of the automobile industry in the 1990s. This was the period where the industry stagnated in the traditional home for automobiles, i.e. Triad economies and flourished in the rest of the world. The value chain in the automobile industry is usually described by reference to a number of tiers. The supply chain is such that 'Tier 1 suppliers' are those selling directly to the car makers or assemblers and 'Tier 2' suppliers are those selling directly to the 'Tier 1' firms, and so on. In India, it was only with the arrival of Suzuki in partnership with Maruti and the forming of the Suzuki-Maruti company, that the face of the automobile industry changed in the early 1990s. In 1992, the Indian government reduced its share in the publicly owned Maruti Company and allowed the Suzuki Motor Corporation of Japan to become the largest shareholder. Maruti went on to capture 70 per cent of passenger car sales of India. By the end of the 1990s, the overwhelming majority of all passenger cars in India was produced by eight firms of which six were multinational ventures. The supply chain underwent a transformation with multinational companies working closely with local suppliers. Thus the component supply chain developed rapidly and the value of component trading doubled between 1997 and 2001. At present, India's automobile industry has global scale participation mainly in component manufacturing and assembly.

Maruti Suzuki India Limited, Manesar (Haryana)

As mentioned above, Maruti-Suzuki India Limited is practically the synonym for the Indian automobile industry. The company has a long and eventful history. When the first Maruti plant was set up in the early 1980s, it was a profitable public sector enterprise. The enterprise was privatised over time starting as a joint venture with Suzuki Motor Corporation of Japan in 1992. By 2002, Suzuki had a controlling stake in the company. From three plants in Gurgaon, Maruti Suzuki expanded to set up a plant in Manesar in 2006. Manesar in Haryana developed as an industrial cluster largely due to Maruti Suzuki. The company attracted an entire supply chain of component producers. Some of these were joint ventures, in which Suzuki-Maruti held a substantial stake, while others were independent domestic firms (Sutton). In the last few decades, Maruti has also become a synonym for workers' struggles and repression on the workers.[3]

Automobile Vendor Company, Manesar (Haryana)

Manufacturer of Exhaust Maniflod, Case Differential & Steering Knuckle, this company caters to the needs of passenger cars and commercial vehicles for a number of companies including Maruti. This is an example of a Tier 1 company in the supply chain for automobiles. Located in the automobile cluster of Manesar, the company has a Foundry and a Machine Shop. The former employs unskilled workers, whereas the workers in the Machine Shop are often graduates from ITIs. The Foundry has nearly 350 workers, of which only a handful is in the category of regular workers, the rest are employed on a contractual basis through labour contractors. The Machine Shop, on the other hand, has 180 regular workers and some contractual workers. Apart from these, there are 10-15 workers employed for packaging, loading, unloading, cleaning and other miscellaneous tasks.

The conditions of employment are different at the Foundry and the Machine Plant. The Foundry works on two shifts of 12 hours each, with shifts changing at 7 am and at 7 pm. The workers employed here are forced to work all seven days a week. Although they receive overtime (OT) wages for the work on Sunday, but the overtime rate is the same as non-overtime, in violation of the law that requires a double rate for overtime. Even on national holidays like 15th August, the work continues discreetly in the night shift. The timing of the salary payment to these workers is delayed and irregular, with the Foundry workers getting paid later than others. The Machine Shop has more than 350 workers employed in three shifts starting at 7 am, 3 pm and 11 pm. Around 50-60 regular workers and 5-10 contractual workers work in each shift. They have a half hour break for lunch and are supposed to have a holiday on Sunday. However, there are times when they have to report for OT (at single rate even here) on Sundays and failing to do this, they are not allowed to enter the factory for the next few days and accordingly, the wages are deducted. The basic wage for a helper grade worker is Rs. 8,279 per month (2017) which is the same for a new entrant as well as experienced workers. However, based on the worker's experience and management's discretion, the experienced workers get some annual increments. Apart from the basic wage, the only other component of wage is an Attendance Bonus of 15 per cent in a situation of full 26-day attendance. There is no dearness allowance. PF is deducted at 12 per cent and ESI at 1.75 per cent. A machine operator draws a salary of Rs. 13,500 after 5 years of experience including the overtime. According to the workers, the accounting of OT hours of the workers is often fudged by the management and as a rule,

10-15 hours of overtime remains unpaid. Not only this, but in case a worker needs to stay back on account of excessive production targets, it is not treated as OT but is simply part of that day's regular work. Apart from this, verbal and even physical abuse by the management is quite commonplace.

(*B*) *Buyer-Driven Chains: Apparel and Consumer Electronics*

i) *Garments*

Buyer-driven value chains are characterised by the lead firms being "retailers, marketers and branded manufacturers" (Gereffi 2003). Apparel and consumer electronics are good examples of these. In the case of garments, for instance, the lead firms in the developed countries either subcontract production to the firms in the developing countries or simply act as buyers of readymade garments which are produced by the firms in the developing countries. These lead firms often act as 'manufacturers without factories". The garment industry has gone through multiple phases of geographical relocation. Mezzadri and Srivastava (2015) show how the East Asian economies used the exports of garments to further their national development. A crucial basis was use of wage differentials. However with a partial erosion of these differentials, by the late 1970s, there was a "second, wider process of industrial relocation." This included countries of Latin America, South East Asia, South Asia, especially China. India's entry in the above global garment market took place towards the 1980s. "In Asia, by 2013, the top 5 garment exporters were, respectively, China, Hong Kong, Bangladesh, Vietnam, and India" (Mezzadri and Srivastava). India exports primarily to the US and European Union. Apart from the ability to provide 'diversified' garments, India's advantage also lies in low labour costs. According to the World Bank data of the world's 25 leading apparel exporters in 1980, 1990 and 2000, quoted by Gereffi (2003); labour costs (wages and fringe benefits) in India was merely .39 US$/hour in 1998 compared to 10.12 US$/hour in the United States. Only four countries had labour costs below India, i.e. Indonesia, Vietnam, Bangladesh and Pakistan.

ii) New Connections: Mobile Phones

'Make in India' initiative by the Indian government, attracted a host of smart phone manufacturers. This initiative slashed the tax on locally manufactured handsets to 2 per cent, compared to 12.5 per cent duty on imported, completely-built handsets. Given this, and given a huge potential market in India, manufacturing handsets in India became logical. A number of Chinese phone manufacturers have relocated or subcontracted production to India. Chinese smart phone company set up a manufacturing plant in Greater Noida in December 2015. In another case, two other phone manufacturers began to get the handsets made by a company which set up base in Noida in August, 2016. Both these companies (Greater Noida and Noida) have used the services of labour contractors to supply workers as and when they needed them.

Garment Workers in Udyog Vihar (Haryana)[4]

The Haryana Industrial belt known as Udyog Vihar developed as a cluster for garment exports in the 1990s when manufacturing units relocated from parts of Delhi to Udyog Vihar. This happened both due to mandatory moving of industrial units from Delhi and in response to heavy tax concessions provided by the Haryana government. The garment production in Udyog Vihar takes place in registered manufacturing units and in fabricator units. Some of the larger manufacturing units could even employ 1,000 workers but there are smaller units too, employing 400-500 workers. These units are registered under the Factories Act and they take orders directly from the global brands or indirectly via the buying houses. Fabricator units take orders from the registered manufacturing units operating within this region, i.e. the registered units sub-contract a part of their work to the fabricator units. Fabricator units often work illegally and vary in size from those employing 10 workers to those with 500 workers. Some part of the work is outsourced to and done by home-based women workers. A vast majority of the workers are migrants from Uttar Pradesh and Bihar and many are Muslims belonging to the 'julaha' community. Despite living in the Delhi-NCR area for as long as 20 years at times, most of the workers do not have a voter card. Almost all the workers (95 per cent to 99 per cent) are employed through labour contractors and not directly by the company. Unlike garment workers in other parts of the country, the NCR is dominated by male workers in this sector.

The workers are employed in various departments of the garment units such as sampling, quality control production or sewing, finishing, etc. The production takes place under a 'chain system' or an assembly line. Here, many workers sit in a row and the garment passes from one worker to the other where each of them is responsible for a small part of the work such as stitching the collar or stitching one arm of the shirt. The rows or columns of workers are supervised by 'supervisors' who are responsible for meeting the production targets and hence keep urging the workers to work faster and faster. The monthly wages differ from one kind of worker to another and are based on an eight-hour working day (9 am to 5:30 pm) with a half an hour break for lunch. This is in accordance with the minimum wages stipulated by the Haryana government but is grossly inadequate to lead a dignified life in Delhi-NCR. Even these wages have been falling in real terms.

The horribly depressed wages force the workers to work overtime in order to increase their monthly earnings. With overtime of at least 3-4 hours every day (and Sundays), the workers manage to make monthly earnings of around Rs.10,000. Legally, the wages for overtime work is supposed to be double the usual wage, however overtime at single rate is the norm in Udyog Vihar. There is also a continuous pressure to increase the intensity and pace of work. The workers claim that they are regularly harassed, not paid adequately and also verbally and physically abused by the company management and the bouncer-turned guards. Also, the industry is known for frequent accidents and injuries.

After putting in long hours of back breaking work, virtually the entire workforce comes back to dank and cramped rooms in many villages on the Haryana-Delhi border such as Kapashera and Dharuhera. The rooms shared by workers are tiny, overpriced and come with a long list of conditions imposed by the landlords. The threat of eviction is also always present. Most of the workers cannot afford to live with their families who stay back in the native villages.

Subsidiary of an Electronics Major, Greater Noida (Uttar Pradesh)

India is also emerging as a production hub for the electronics industry with many global electronics brands, Original Equipment Manufacturers and Original Design Manufacturers (OEMs and ODMs) including Foxconn getting production done in India and Indonesia. A well-known global name in the field of consumer electronics set up a production plant in Greater Noida in 1998. This company is a wholly owned subsidiary of the parent company and undertakes assembling of consumer electronic goods. The technology intensive components are imported. The Greater Noida plant is a multi-product plant with a total of 12 assembly lines including two lines for refrigerators, one for microwave, two for washing machines and three for air conditioners. On the shop floor, there are roughly 2,000 workers of whom 850 are permanent. Of these, about 100-150 are women and only a small number; i.e. around 50-60 are local. Apart from the permanent workers, around 1,200 contractual workers also do the same work. The contract workers are not paid directly by the Company but by the labour contractors, who incidentally deduct their own share from the wages of the workers. In 2016, the oldest and the most senior permanent workers who were employed since the setting up of the plant in 1998 roughly earned a wage of Rs. 30,000 per month of which Rs. 18,000 was the basic pay. Annually, the workers got an increment of Rs. 1,500-2,000 (this used to be Rs. 1,000 a few years ago). Workers have a 9-hour working day from 9 am to 6 pm with a half an hour break for lunch and two tea breaks of 15 minutes each. In case of overtime, it is supposed to begin after another ten minutes of tea break once the regular day gets over at 6 pm. As will be seen later, these breaks have been systematically reduced in some or the other way. There has also been a continuous increase in productivity through automation and a rising intensification of work.

Mobile Phone Manufacturer, Greater Noida (Uttar Pradesh)[5]

All the workers in this plant are ITI graduates and 100 per cent of the workers are contractual. The workers work in different shifts; the regular shift is for 9 hours while two other shifts are 8 hours each. The workers are required to work for all 30 days without any leave for which they are paid Rs. 9,300 per month. After deducting PF and ESI, each worker gets only about Rs. 7,100 for 30 days of work. The company has a policy of deducting Rs. 2,000 from the salary for the absence of a single day of work and if perfect attendance is met, a reward of an extra Rs. 2,000 is added to the salary. The award has not really been given till now but absence for even a day leads to more than 20 per cent deduction in salary. During the entire day's work, the workers get half an hour of lunch break and 10 minutes of tea break. Besides these breaks, if a worker leaves the assembly line even for going to the washroom, he is penalised. Workers also complain of regular harassment and verbal abuse by the supervisors. They work with a target of assembling 160 phones per hour. Not meeting the target has resulted in termination of the services of the entire line of workers. The PF amount can be claimed by a worker only after 6 months of service but the Company follows a practice of not retaining a worker for more than 5 months. In the recent months workers have not been receiving even the stipulated Rs. 7,100. In July 2017, some workers received less than Rs. 4,000 as salary. Terminations and dismissals without notice is quite the norm here. The workers may enter the factory for their shift only to be told that they are part of "Left" category and they could leave. The word

Left symbolises termination from the job. No explanation is provided. The land on which the Company stands belongs to Jaganpur village but the Company has hardly employed even 10 young people from the village. They have a policy of getting workers from distant areas in a bid to prevent unionisation.

Assembler of Mobile Phones, Noida

Three different labour contractors supply workers to this company. Like most of the manufacturing units that have come to India since the 2015 drive, the nature of hiring is purely contractual with a clause that the workers can be terminated at any point of their tenure without any prior notice. The management began laying off workers after Diwali in November 2018. Over 50 workers were laid off in the first three weeks of November. On November 29, 2018, the company resorted to mass termination resulting in protests by the workers and police action against them. The Company only hires ITI and polytechnic graduates and recruitment is usually on the wage scale of Rs. 12,000 per month with a PF deduction of 8 per cent per month. However, they are paid only Rs. 9,200 per month. Although some workers are given ID cards, these have the names of contracting companies and not of the company where they were employed. The cards have an expiry date of 11 months from the day of hiring though, sometimes, the workers are ousted much earlier, as was the case in November layoff. The working hours are nine per day with compulsory overtime (OT) of 3 hours for which they are paid Rs. 100 per hour. An hour of 'leisure time' is given for lunch and tea, which is subtracted from the total number of working hours which means that for 12 hours a day that a worker spends in the company, he is paid only for 11 hours. Since November 2018 with reduction in production, OT had been scrapped, making it very difficult for workers to sustain themselves. Most of the workers lived in rented accommodation nearby which cost them at least Rs. 4,000 per month.

Section II: Dynamic of Capital Accumulation

This section discusses the dynamic of capital accumulation in the industries in NCR. As pointed out by Marx, accumulation of capital or expansion of value is the motivation for production under capitalism. The capitalist is concerned about profits and the hidden basis of the profits is surplus value. Surplus value is created through appropriation of the worker's labour. During the course of production, workers add more value (labour put in) than what they are compensated for (value of labour power). This gives rise to surplus value which is then realised by the capitalist by selling the product of labour.[6]

Let us first focus on the generation of surplus in the course of production. The working day can be divided into two parts, necessary labour and surplus labour. The product of necessary labour time accrues to the worker in the form of wages, whereas the product of surplus labour time is appropriated by the capitalist in the form of surplus value. The basis for valorisation of capital or expansion of the value of capital is the rate of surplus value which is defined as ratio of surplus value (*s*) to variable capital (value of labour power, *v*) or s/v. Marx talks about two basic possibilities for increasing the rate of surplus value and thus the valorisation of capital; i) production of *absolute surplus value* and ii) production of *relative surplus value.* The former or the *absolute surplus value* is increased, when, given the value of labour power *v*, surplus value or *s* is increased (*higher s with same v raises the ratio* s/v). This can be done by increasing the surplus labour time, which in turn can be done by various measures. An important measure is to make the workers work for longer hours or increasing the length of the working day. With a legally mandated working day, this can also be achieved by using the working hours better through reducing the break times or "by no longer counting certain job preparations as part of the working time" (Heinrich, 2013, p. 104). Accelerating up or increasing the intensity of work has a similar effect since it leads to more surplus labour in the same working hours. It is not surprising, therefore, that the conflict between capital and labour is quite often centred on the use of labour time. Lack of unionisation or repression on existing unions enables the capitalist to increase the portion of surplus labour time through one or more of the mechanisms described here.

The rate of surplus value can also be increased by increasing relative surplus value, when, given the length of the working day, necessary labour time, v, is reduced (*lower v with same s raises the ratio* s/v). This can be done by decrease in the value of means of subsistence necessary for reproduction of labourer. For this, there needs to be an increase in productivity in the sectors producing the means of subsistence. However, *v* can also be reduced by reducing the extent of the amount of means of subsistence necessary for reproduction of labourer. Just like labour time, the value of labour power or *v* is also impacted by the struggle between capital and labour (apart from other historical and cultural factors). Once again, weak labour unions can lead to a fall in the *extent* of means of subsistence considered necessary for the reproduction of labour power.

Another method to increase profits is to increase the productivity so that the same amount of products can be made with fewer units of labour. This often happens through introduction of machinery.[7] If a shortening of the working day does not accompany the increase in productivity, it means that, the innovating capitalist can obtain extra surplus value and extra profits (even if temporarily so). What is seen in practice is that a rise in productivity through the introduction of machines results in longer work hours, multiple shifts and night shifts in order to avoid 'idle machine time'. In the industries under discussion, increase in productivity is rarely accompanied by a proportionate rise in the workers' standard of living or a shortened work day, implying that workers create a larger sum of value than what they receive as wages. Thus increase in productivity also leads to an increase in surplus value and the rate of surplus value.

How the globally integrated industries located in the NCR employ many of the mechanisms described above, in order to increase the surplus value and profits.

1. *Increasing the Length of Working Day*

Whether it is the automobile sector, or electronics or garments, all of them have long working hours for the worker. The working day in most industries is usually 9 hours with half an hour lunch break and one or two tea breaks of 10 minutes each. There are units where the scheduled work day is 12 hours, for example, the Foundry unit of auto vendor in Manesar, which produces components for automobiles. Further, working beyond the scheduled hours or overtime work is a norm in most cases. As per law, wages for overtime work should be double of normal wages, but practically, this was non-existent in all the industries which were surveyed. On one hand, low wages lead workers to seek overtime work on a regular basis but on the other hand, overtime is also forced by the employer and failing to show up for overtime often leads to dismissal or threat of dismissal. According to the workers, in Maruti's Manesar plant, between 2006 and 2011, workers would be kept back indiscriminately for long hours but no overtime was given for staying back. In the vendor company, the workers in the machine shop are supposed to have a weekly day off on Sunday. However, there are times when they have to show up for OT (at single rate) on Sundays and failing to do this, they are not allowed to enter the factory for the next few days and accordingly the wages are deducted.

In the units producing readymade garments in Udyog Vihar, Gurgaon, the norm is overtime of 100 hours per month (although legal cap on overtime is 50 hours per quarter or three months) per worker. During the peak months, it is not uncommon for the workers to be working till after midnight. Interestingly, although, workers themselves need overtime work, there are situations where a worker may be asked to quit if he/she cannot put in the overtime hours when the employer demands it. The garment producers have devised a novel mechanism to increase the working day. Many of them employ a piece rate worker and a time rate worker in the same 'chain' or assembly line. The workers who are paid wages according to the number of pieces produced are interested in increasing the pieces produced even if it means working more hours per day. This means that even time rate workers are forced to work for long hours on account of pressure exerted by the piece rate workers.

2. *Reduction of Breaks*

As discussed earlier, reduction of breaks during the course of the working day result in extracting more labour during the course of the day. Producer of consumer electronics, subsidiary of global electronics major, located in Noida, has perfected the art of extracting extra labour for 35 minutes every day from each worker. Although the work day is supposed to start at 9 am, the workers are expected to report at 8.30 am, do some exercises, take instructions and clean up the work station. Almost as a routine, the production line is started 15 minutes before the scheduled time and carries on till 10 minutes after 6 pm. Also in order to accommodate 10 minutes of the tea break before the overtime shift, the scheduled tea breaks have been reduced to 10 minutes each. In other words, if a worker (usually women workers) does not stay on for overtime, she gets only 50 minutes of break during the day instead of an hour. This means that each worker puts in 25-40 minutes of extra work almost on a daily basis (15 minutes before 9 am, 10 minutes after 6 pm and 10 minutes of reduced breaks). It should be noted that workers are not paid for this extra work. According to the workers, 5-6 refrigerators get assembled in 1 minute which means that 75 lakh extra fridges are assembled simply in the unpaid extra time extracted in this 'extra' 25-40 minutes per worker every day. It generates enough revenues so as to pay the entire wage bill of the production workers.

In a similar manner, the workers alleged that in Maruti's Manesar plant, the already short tea breaks were further reduced by a minute per break (before 2011). According to the workers of auto vendor company, Manesar, they are not provided with any relievers so that in case some worker needs to use the toilet, he has to request another worker to take over his task as well. The workers of mobile phone company in Greater Noida, reported a similar situation—they are penalised for taking toilet breaks. The attempts to reduce breaks by a few minutes or the attempts to increase the working day by a few minutes, show how crucial this labour time is for generating surplus and profits. In the Noida phone assembling company, the break hour is deducted before calculating the hours for which wages are paid.

3. Ensuring Maximal Attendance Through Attendance Bonus

In many industries, attendance is incentivised (or absence is penalised) through a farcical attendance bonus. This ensures that workers do not take (or are not allowed to) take any day off. Let us look at some illustrations: Phone manufacturing company in Greater Noida expects workers to work for 30 days per month without any day off, in order to be eligible for attendance bonus. Even this attendance bonus (even though namesake) was scrapped after August 4, 2017. Similarly, auto vendor company of Manesar claims to give an attendance bonus to those workers who are present for 26 days per month (entire month excluding one off day per week). It is a different matter that till date, no worker has received this bonus.

4. Acceleration and Intensification of Work

Intensification of work has been a common feature across industries. The pace of work has increased continuously leading to intensification of work per unit of time. This means that more labour is put in per unit of time and is tantamount to increasing the absolute surplus.

At the Gurgaon plant of Maruti, the index of hours required to produce cars reduced continuously from 100 in 2001 to 76.15 in 2002, 59.36 in 2003 and 37.95 in 2006 (PUDR 2007). According to some workers of Maruti's plant at Manesar, from 2006-11, the work pressure was immense as work at two stations was combined into one, in effect, doubling the amount of work for each person. Despite carrying water bottles, workers did not get enough time to even drink water. The intensity of work had risen to such high levels that the time needed to assemble one car had been contracted to 45-46 seconds which forced the workers to work at brutally high speeds.

The auto vendor company has seen so much intensification of work that accidents have become fairly common in this factory. The workers attribute regular accidents to excessive workload. The workers complain of being fatigued and overworked and despite this, the production targets have been going up continuously. For instance, a terminated worker from VMC (Vertical Machine Control) said that within a span of 5 years, the production target in a single shift almost doubled from 60 pieces to 110 pieces. And this was done without changing the machines physically, simply by increasing the speed of the machines.

In the garment industry, nearly 20 years ago, there was a transition from a system of 'full piece tailor' wherein each worker was responsible for making the garment in its entirety, to 'chain system' or the assembly line where each assembly line has many workers, each responsible for cutting or stitching a small part of the garment. Supervisors are deployed to ensure that workers meet rising production targets. More recently, in order to supervise and increase the work intensity in the garment industry, devices such as stop watches and magnetic cards were adopted. According to the workers, production targets had increased three fold within a span of 5 years. Production targets have become so punishing that when one worker collapsed on his seat in a factory of Orient Craft Limited in 2014, other workers realised this only after some time had elapsed as they did not have the time to raise their heads from their sewing machines. The pace of work is also enhanced by keeping a piece rate worker in the same assembly line as a time rate worker. This ensures that the piece rate worker, himself puts pressure on other workers to work faster.

5. Increase in the Productivity

We have already seen how automation and an increase in productivity enables the capitalist to extract greater surplus and more profits. In practice, it is often difficult to distinguish between the effects of increase in productivity, i.e. increase in output per unit of labour and increase in intensification, i.e. increase in labour per unit of time. Both show up as increase in output per labourer. There has been a continuous increase in the number of cars per unit of 'direct worker' in the case of Maruti or Maruti Suzuki. The cars per direct worker (per year) increased from 77 in 1995-96 to 107 in 1999-2000 (PUDR 2001). As stated earlier, the index of hours required to produce cars reduced continuously. To take another example, in the electronics manufacturing company at Greater Noida, nearly 300 workers at the Greater Noida factory produced 1,000 units of electronic products per day in 2003 whereas ten to twelve years later, the production rose by 250 per cent to 2,500 units, whereas the number of workers undertaking this production fell by 40 per cent, to 180. Firstly, the company has been undertaking continuous automation to increase productivity. This has resulted in workers having to work faster. For example, a fridge compressor used to be assembled in 5 seconds a few years ago but over time, this has been continuously reduced and today the 'Takt Time' is only 3 seconds. (This has created a situation where the worker cannot even scratch himself/herself or remove a fly from his/her body during work).

6. Depressed Wages

The workers in most cases are not fully compensated for the value of their labour power. The wages are supposed to cover the 'cost of reproduction of labour power' and this must include the means necessary to maintain the worker in his normal state as a working individual. In other words, wages should cover the cost of sustenance of the worker's family and include the means necessary for the worker's replacements, i.e. the livelihood of his/her children. This is not a fixed sum but depends on historical, cultural factors and, more importantly, on the balance of power between capital and labour.

In Indian industry in general and the sectors and industries under discussion specifically, the following observations can be made:

i) Wages are lower than what is needed for a 'decent living'.
ii) Wages are falling in real terms.
iii) Cost of reproduction of industrial worker is partly being borne by the agricultural sector.
iv) The productivity increases are not resulting in increase in wages. In other words, the increase in output per worker is not going to the worker.

Although, the legally stipulated minimum wages are provided in most cases, but this minimum has become the *maximum* possible wage. The workers hardly, if ever, get a wage higher than the *minimum wage*. Virtually none of the industries pay a Dearness Allowance to the workers.

In fact, the basic pay of the 'sampling tailor' (tailors who makes samples and are most privileged amongst all tailors in the garment industry) fell continuously in real terms between 2007 and 2014. In 2015, the basic pay of these tailors was a meagre Rs. 6,500 per month. Adding various allowances (house rent allowance, travel allowance and dearness allowance), the monthly wage became Rs. 8,800. The production tailors received a monthly wage of Rs. 6,500 in April 2015 but there were no further allowances. In a similar manner, the wages paid by mobile phone manufacturers in 2017 was merely Rs. 9,300 per month (and after deduction of PF and ESI merely Rs. 7,100). None of the workers of this company have ever managed to get the PF since they were removed before the completion of the necessary period for withdrawal of PF, i.e. 6 months. The monthly wage in auto vendor company was Rs. 8,279 in 2017 which is the legal minimum wage set by the Haryana government. *These low wages make overtime work essential for the workers in order to make ends meet, thus increasing the length of the working day.* Even with overtime, the workers in the garment industry were able to earn merely Rs. 10,000 per month. The workers also face arbitrary deduction in wages in many industries. In the units of garment manufacturers in Gurgaon, a 10-minute delay can lead to deduction of one hour's wages.

The wages are much lower than the figure of Rs. 18,000 calculated by India's 7th Central Pay Commission as a need-based minimum wage (NBMW) for the *lowest* ranked staff in government (RUPE 2018).[8] In fact, if we look at the garment sector in particular, even with both husband and wife working, the family wage turns out to be less than this figure. These low wages have also been falling in real terms. This can be exemplified by looking at the basic pay of sampling tailors in the garment industry. The following chart is based on payslips of the workers and Labour Bureau Statistics.

Basic Pay of a Sampling Tailor Over the Years			
Years	**Basic Pay (Monthly)** *(Rupees) (Nominal terms)*	**Price Index** *(CPIIW)*	**Salary Adjusted for Price Change** *(Basic salary in real terms)*
2007	3,900	131	2,977.09
2008	3,976	141.6	2,819.85
2009	4,304	157	2,741.4
2010	4,739	175.9	2,708.0
2011	5,031	191.5	2,634.0
2012	5,400 (approx.)	209.3	2,583.7
2013	5,600 (approx.)	232.16	2,413.7
2014	6,030	246.9	2,451.2
2015	6,200		

Source: Compiled by the Author based on payslips of the workers and Labour Bureau Statistics.

The result becomes even starker if we look at the auto industry for the entire country. This is an industry which saw considerable growth in the decade of 2000-01 to 2009-

10. Despite being one of the better paying industries, real wages in the auto sector—i.e. after discounting for inflation—actually fell continuously in the period 2000-01 to 2009-10. However in nominal terms, annual wages in this industry rose from Rs. 79,446 in 2000-01 to Rs. 88,671 in 2004-05 to Rs. 109,575 in 2009-10 (Aspects of Indian Economy, No. 52).

Chart 1: Real Wages of Auto Industry Workers (in 2000–01 Rs.)

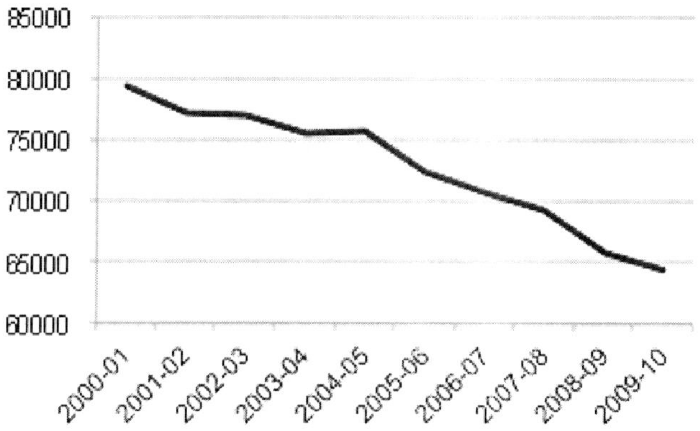

Source: *Aspects of Indian Economy, No. 52*

The fact that workers are not even paid the value of labour power is evident from the fact that they need to supplement their incomes through multiple sources. In the garment sector, most of the workers are unable to get their families to live with them. Also a large majority of the workers get rations from their native villages. These can be regarded as 'reverse remittances' from the agricultural sector. The workers of phone manufacturer of Greater Noida choose to commute from their native villages, which may be as far as 80 kilometres, in order to save on the living costs by renting a place near the factory. Thus for the worker households, who have migrated from the villages, rural connections are retained as a 'second base of material provision in the city' (*Aspects of Indian Economy, Nos. 71&72*). A portion of consumption of the worker household is met from the agrarian sector, whether it is in the form of sustenance of a part of the family in the village or procuring rations from the village.

Further, the workers have not benefited from productivity increases in various industries. Productivity increases have not provided them either shorter working hours or a rise in real wages. In fact, in some cases, the number of shifts has increased so that the machine is not left idle. The workers employed in the Foundry of auto vendor at Manesar reported that there are two shifts of 12 hours each and the production is carried out discreetly even during public holidays such as 15th August (Day of Indian Independence). In the automobile sector as a whole, wages as a share of value added have fallen from 27.4 per cent in 2000-01 to 15.4 per cent in 2009-10. This is due to a rise in value added per worker accompanied by a fall in real wage per worker (*Aspects of Indian Economy, No. 52*).

Chart 3: Wages as % of Net Value Added in Auto Industry

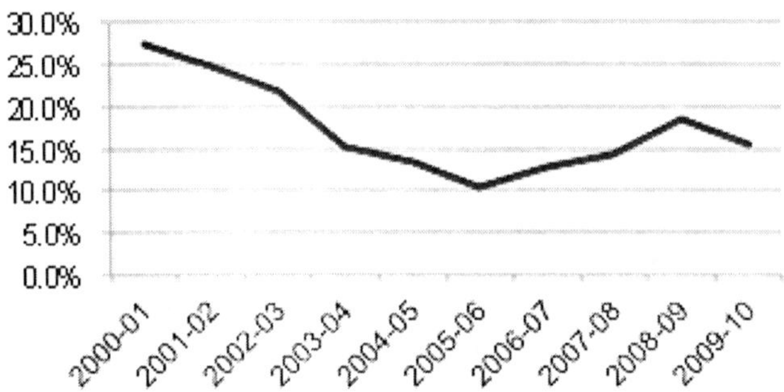

Source: Behind the Present Wave of Unrest in the Auto Sector
http://www.rupe-india.org/52/auto.html#note1

7. Weakening of Labour and Repression on Workers' Unions

The degree to which, capital, can employ the various methods of surplus extraction depends on the relative strength of capital and labour. For instance, the capitalist tries to lengthen the work day, whereas labour tries to shorten it. Eventually the struggle between capital and labour (class of capitalists and the working class) establishes a work-day which becomes the norm or to quote Marx, 'between equal rights, force decides' (Heinrich 2012). Hence, it stands to reason that capital would try to weaken the collective strength of labour through multiple ways. The globally integrated industries in the NCR are no exception. As it is, the competitive advantage for these industries is based on low labour costs. Pervasive use of contractual labour, migrant labour and a universal unleashing of repression on trade unions are simply means to weaken labour and increase surplus extraction.

Contractualisation

About 95 to 99 per cent of the *garment* workers are hired through the labour contractors and are contractual workers. At phone manufacturer in Greater Noida, the workforce is entirely contractual. In electronics company, only 850 out of 2,000 are permanent workers. The contractual workers do not get any increments. At auto vendor at Manesar, all workers in Foundry are contractual workers and 10 per cent of machine shop workers are contractual. In Maruti Company's Gurgaon plant, permanent workers were increasingly replaced by contractual workers with the company being taken over by Suzuki. Nearly half of the permanent workers had been removed by 2007. The Manesar plant started with less than 40 per cent workers employed as permanent workers. In this plant, an incident of violence occurred on July 18, 2012, in which a few management officials and workers were injured and an HR manager was tragically killed. The company changed the worker composition drastically after the flashpoint of 2012. The proportion of contract workers has been increased and these workers are now called Temporary workers (TW–Type I and Type II). TW-I are hired for 7 months. After seven months, a few selected amongst TW-I are hired as TW-II workers but again for only 7 months. It has become almost impossible for a contract worker to become permanent. In the case of manufacturing mobile phones, even the pretence of hiring the workers is given up since it is only their 'services' which are bought from the vendors (labour contractors) for a short period of time. They are not 'hired' and hence cannot be 'fired' by the parent company.

Attempts to Stop the Unionisation of Workers

In the conflict between capital and labour, the balance is sought to be tilted in favour of capital by scuttling varied attempts by the workers to come together and organise themselves. In this, capital is backed firmly by the Indian state. The foremost example is of Maruti Suzuki Udyog Ltd. Prior to 2000, Maruti Udyog Employees' Union (MUEU) was one of the largest unions in the organised sector in India. This union was systematically crushed and several workers were dismissed or coerced into accepting Voluntary Retirement Scheme (VRS). The Manesar plant did not have an elected union till mid-2011 and the workers were represented by the management controlled union of the Gurgaon plant. In 2011-12, after persistent efforts of the workers to overcome hurdles created by the management, which even saw termination and transfer of some of them, the workers' union at the Maruti factory was formed. As a consequence of the struggle by the union, there has been some improvement in the work conditions. However, the incident of July 2012 became a flashpoint and what followed was a spate of dismissals and arrests of workers. After a trial of around five years the Sessions Court pronounced its judgment in March 2017, convicting 31 accused workers in the case and acquitting 117 others. Thirteen workers have been awarded life sentences. Today, the workers have organised themselves as Provisional Committee of Maruti Suzuki Workers' Union (MSWU) and are working in association with MSWU inside the plant. Even now, the Maruti management is busy devising several strategies to prevent the workers from joining the union. Some of these are: carefully hiring workers from a lower economic background who are sole supporters of their families, not hiring workers from neighbouring areas, hiring workers on short-term contracts, purposely keeping a large gap in the salaries of permanent and contract workers (about three times) to prevent their unity, etc. Transfers to other plants are also used to prevent workers from coming together. The attitude of the Maruti management can be seen even in relation to vendor companies. Earlier, Maruti would penalise the vendor companies if they could not deliver on time, on account of a strike, but now, the Maruti management extends help to the vendor company for breaking the strike.

The story is not very different in the case of auto vendor company at Manesar. The workers took the initiative to come together and form a union in 2016. The ten workers, who had led the initiative, were all terminated on some pretext or the other. Terminations, transfers, verbal and physical abuse became routine since then. Open and direct threats were given to some workers in a 'meeting' with the owner, whereas others were forced to sign papers stating that they were not involved in the formation of the union. Besides muscle power, monetary incentives have been used for buying out workers and for forcing them to leave the factory premises. The workers went ahead with applying for registration of the union and submitted a demand notice to the Assistant Labour Commissioner's (ALC) office in Gurgaon. The persistence on part of the workers and intimidation and harassment on the part of the management continued till the writing of this paper. Ever since the workers tried to organise themselves, the management has been attempting segregation of the workers on the basis of training—ITI, Polytechnic and BE degree—and has begun fixing differentiated wages for them.

The story is not very different in the case of electronics company of Noida. Here too, attempts for formation of unions were initiated in 2016. Since then, the management has resorted to assaults, harassment, and intimidation of the workers. In complicity with the company management, the Delhi Labour Commissioner also rejected the application for union formation in July 2016. However, the workers managed to obtain a certificate of registration for their union in August 2017. Immediately, the management wrote an application to the Registrar, who cancelled the registration certificate in January 2018. This is despite the fact that according to the Trade Unions Act, the Registrar does not have the powers to cancel registration on an application by a third party.

Conclusion

Use of the Marxian method provides a useful insight into the methods employed by capital to extract more and more surplus from labour. This surplus extraction, allows the Indian capital to compete internationally and also forms the basis of huge profits for the transnational corporations. An overwhelming use of non-regular workers, long hours of work, overtime, reduced breaks, wages lower than the value of labour power, increasing the productivity of labour without accompanying wage increases in the same proportion and intensification of work are common across all sectors and industries in the area under study. Another universal feature is repression of organisation and unionisation of workers which tilts the balance heavily in favour of capital, facilitating the surplus extraction and capital accumulation. Eventually, the extent of surplus extraction depends on the relative strength of capital vs. labour. Hence it is not surprising that both global capital and the industries in the emerging economies adopt strategies to weaken labour. It is clearly the 'low road to flexibility' which helps to generate profits at the higher ends of GVCs.

NOTES

1. A cluster is defined as an area with a radius of 60 kms with more than 100 units in related and complementary business (UNIDO).
2. The names of most of the companies are being withheld on purpose. The interviews with the workers have been conducted by the author along with voluntary groups such as 'Perspectives' and 'People's Union for Democratic Rights' over a period of last five years. Some of the case studies have been published as booklets.
3. The details of the situation in this plant is given in Section II along with the analysis.
4. Based on Simmering Rage (Aggarwal, A. 2015) and Tailor–Made

Lives (Perspectives and PUDR 2015).

5. Based on a fact-finding conducted into an incident of large-scale dismissal of workers in 2017.
6. In Marxian terms, value of any commodity comprises of three components; constant capital *c*, i.e. the value of machines and materials, variable capital; *v*, i.e. value of labour power and surplus value *s* which is appropriated by the capitalist.
7. The capitalist is interested in the rate of profit which is the surplus as a ratio of total capital outlay on constant and variable capital (s/v). Although introduction of machinery increases c but v is reduced due to reduction in labour time. When the costs, for the individual capitalist, fall below the social average, this capitalist obtains extra profits.
8. NBMW of Rs. 16,000 does not include any component for skills.

BIBLIOGRAPHY

Aggarwal, A. (2015). 'Piece by Piece', *Himal Sothasian, Labour and its Discontents*, March 2015.

Apex Cluster Development Services Pvt. Ltd. (2015), 'Final Report Economic Profile of NCR', Submitted to National Capital Region Planning Board.

Bose, A.J.C. and Pratap, S. (2016). 'Value Chains and Worker Illfare: Some Comments', *Business Analyst*.

Gereffi, G. and Memedovic, O. (2003). 'The Global Apparel Value Chain: What Prospects for Upgrading by Developing Countries?' United Nations Industrial Development Organisation.

Gupta, A. and Choudhury, S. (2016). 'Global Value Chains: Indian Automobile Industry', *CCS Mid-term Report.*

Heinrich, M. (2012). *An Introduction to the Three Volumes of Karl Marx's Capital*, Monthly Review Press 2012; Indian edition, Aakar Books, 2013.

Humphrey, J. and Memedovic, O. (2003). 'The Global Automotive Industry Value Chain', UNIDO, Strategic Research and Economics Branch.

Mezzadri, A. and Srivastava, R. (2015). 'Labour Regimes in the Indian Garment Sector: Capital-Labour Relations, Social Reproduction and Labour Standards in the National Capital Region', Centre for Development Policy and Research.

People's Union for Democratic Rights: Various reports on Maruti (2001, 2007, 2013 and 2018).

Perspectives, People's Union for Democratic Rights (May 2015): 'Tailor-Made Lives'.

Research Unit for Political Economy (2012). 'Behind the Present Wave of Unrest in the Auto Sector', *Aspects of India's Economy, No. 52* http://www.rupe-india.org/52/auto.html#note1.

Research Unit for Political Economy (2018), 'India's Working Class and Its Prospects Part I', *Aspects of India's Economy, Nos. 71 & 72.*

Smith, J. (2015). ' Imperialism in the Twenty-First Century', *Monthly Review,* Vol. 67, Issue 03 (July-August, 2015).

Sutton, J. 'The Globalization Process: Auto-Component Supply Chains in China and India,' *Project Report* (London School of Economics).

12

From Hegemony to Full Control

Which Kind of Elite, If Any, is Necessary for the Masters of the Universe?

Reading Antonio Gramsci About the Role of the Intelligentsia, Yesterday and Tomorrow

Giulietto Chiesa

It is no longer the time for revolutions. At least not in the West, where the only revolution underway and under development is the technological one, controlled by the ruling classes. Many of the original features of capitalism have been swept away and replaced by a 'money map' that is, the map of abstract corporate finance, designed by the 'Banking System'. This bound the 'State' to obedience and surrender, after having been taken over, corrupted and bought.

The Bank System also cancelled the Market and rewrote the laws of the State. The new laws made the robbery—which is already the standard procedure for the Banking System—completely legal. Simultaneously, it set up the army of its exegetes (the economists), its soldiers (mainstream media) and its policemen (the secret services).

The process based on transformation and accumulation, named "commodity-money-commodity", has been mainly substituted by that of "production of money by means of money", in turn replaced and integrated by the process of "producing money from nothing". An increasingly narrow elite of "Masters of the Universe" has seized, without fighting

—rather through legal procedures—the technological and legal means to carry out these new processes. As a result, society as a whole—including the institutions of liberal democracy—has lost control over the dynamics of money. This is how our society lost democracy. Whereas the abstract corporate finance, in an obscure and unpredictable way, erodes the structure of our collective life.

I will not address here the topic of the fate of this "revolution from above" against the people. I will only say that the upheavals underway are, in my opinion, a prelude to a third world war, something that will challenge the very existence of life on this planet.

My aim is to find the explanation—or, better, multiple explanations—of the defeat of the popular forces by such Masters of Universe's general offensive. I will try to do so by introducing a theorem. I will not be able to demonstrate it here, as it is still awaiting to be fully proved, but I believe that it should be the starting point for a new, indispensable theoretical phase.

I think that the Marxian "method" is still a useful tool for the construction of a new theory. It is my opinion, however, that we need to start from an observation: the current complexity is considerably more complex than that of capitalism at its early stage. Regarding political philosophy, in fact, we still seem to be living in the days of Marx. His "critique of political economy" was a fundamental turning point that changed the face of the world. The ideas and concepts he formulated have largely affected the thought of all the economists of the present time, even those who fought it with all their strength. And yet, his ideas remained, for instance, essentially "outside" the ecosystem. That is, he did not even attempt (nor could he have, given the knowledge and the complexity of his time) to face two issues which are crucial today: the earth's limited resources and the 'singularities' that the monstrous and inhuman technological acceleration have produced within the very nature of capitalism. An acceleration that later became financial and global. He could not foresee the effects that capitalist production, by revolutionising itself, could have produced both on the evolution of the species and on the relationship between the organic and inorganic world.

It could be said that Marx's interpretation was the most effective description of what the Italian eco-physicist Luigi Sertorio defined as the "transition phase of the heat engine in the evolutionary history of the human species."

The empirical data suggests that this "transitional phase" will not make it to the middle of the 21st century. Only some of the concepts formulated by Marx will be useful in the "post-fossil fuel" era. As a result, I believe that the truly revolutionary task is to set aside the 'money map' altogether, as it imprisons the whole of mankind and forces mankind and nature into a deadly zero-sum game. We need a conscious movement of people, of human masses, able to understand the collective necessity of a struggle for survival. The political and scientific task of the present moment is to create such a theory, since "without revolutionary theory there can not be any revolution". Again, this theorem is still at the stage of definition.

Nevertheless, it is a task that requires questioning many cornerstones of Marxist revolutionary theory. One of those has been an axiom for over a century: the centrality of the working class and its nature, which is revolutionary by definition. It is not like that any more, at least in the West. The crisis of liberal democracy is visible to the naked eye in Europe today. In the US the crisis is definitive and characterised by the total disappearance of "the working-class consciousness". All of this takes place in a context in which not only has the working class been shattered and deprived of self-awareness, but also all the other social classes have disappeared. Individuals have not disappeared, but their classification in social classes—which we have all studied—has been erased.

The figure of the worker as we know it from Taylorism has long since disappeared, and the very idea of the worker has almost disappeared even from the minds of those who are still actual workers, but do not consider themselves as such.

Among the many fragmented and fragmentating jobs, most of the individual workers have no idea of how to consider themselves and of which place they take in society. Their thoughts and goals are led towards patterns of behaviour, that are at the same time based on ultra-individualism and ultra-mass culture, reinforced by moral indifference, pathological, psychic and physical degenerations nourished by morbid forms of mysticism and sensuality.

Which part of civil society, for example, is the consciousness of a young Italian man or woman expressing today? The same question is valid for their peers living near the dam of Aswan, or in a village in Uttar Pradesh. When they look at the screen of their cell phone, they are watching things that they cannot avoid desiring, even though they don't fully understand their meaning. The same happens to contemporary Italian or American youth.

In any case, these situations—along with the objects and the dynamics involved in them—have nothing to do with the village in which they live or with the history of their fathers and ancestors: they all "learn" what is offered to them, although not by reading (they are quickly unlearning how to read). An image—and furthermore the moving images of the videos—is much more easily absorbed than something written. It is pleasant to see. It is a synthesis of its own. It is authoritative and definitive. By taking the place of reality itself, the image affects the mind and transforms it.

There is no logic in the sequence of frames. A story at the centre of the screen can be told along with other stories, that are not perceived because they are hidden at the edges. They might be hidden in the furniture of a house, perhaps against the background of the main action and apparently disconnected from it, or embedded in the space between the music and the landscape, between reason and desire, between fantasy and nightmare. All the stories though—the main and the secondary ones—will be perceived simultaneously and accepted by the unconscious, beyond any rational control.

So, they "watch", as we all "watch". But none of the

"watchers" is familiar with the syntax and the grammar of this language. So you can make them think and believe what you want, according to the behaviour you wish for them to develop.

Not even the traditional intellectuals know and speak this language of motion pictures. Even the "organic intellectuals", as Gramsci used to call them, would not be able to organise the battle. It is astonishing to observe how most of them are sure to have mastered this language, while in reality they are controlled by it. It is even worse: the vast majority of them accept—more or less voluntarily—taking orders from those who use it against them. They too were, and still are, illiterate in this new language. Obviously, Gramsci could not have foreseen that in 25 years television would arrive ("God save the ugly", wrote Gore Vidal). Then computers arrived, followed by the Internet. Eventually mobile phones appeared and they alone give access to all the TV channels in the world. He could not foresee that we would have access to the virtual world, where every image can now be artificially modified, along with the voices of the speakers and their facial expressions.

Therefore, he could not foresee that the only world language now created—the language of motion pictures—potentially would have become entirely false. Neither Gramsci nor Marx could ever imagine that one day someone could accumulate vast amounts of data (metadata), and that such data would allow him or her to predict—statistically, through digital algorithms—reactions and preferences of millions or billions of individuals; or to anticipate their desires, fears, and elementary urges. "Prepare yourself to desire something, or somebody" the motto could go.

Neither of them could have predicted that currently there are sophisticated ways to skip the rational control over what we see, and what we see is seen through what we might call the "visual prosthesises". These sophisticated methods have been already studied and experimented with for decades and down to the last detail. In this way, it is possible to get into each individual's brain by stimulating his or her sexual desires, anxieties about food and primordial fears.

Obviously, we cannot blame Antonio Gramsci for failing in his forecasts. Meanwhile, we can deplore the total stupidity of those who today—while the enslavement of the masses is underway—declare that "television is dead" and at the same time fetishise the Internet, presenting it as an alternative to manipulation or even as an alternative to democracy. This can even be done without mentioning that television is still the centre of power management, no matter whether we are in a cinema, or the TV is in the traditional position in the home, or hanging on a wall, or shifted to the Web.

There are so many things it was not possible to foresee. "Let's see" (or, better, "let's watch"). This is exactly the goal pursued by those who create images. On top of that, by sitting in front of a PC, the learning processes are increasingly affected by multitasking and speed, which exclude even the slightest possibility of "mind concentration" and "discipline". The ability of overviewing what has being examined and of connecting it with its history and with the rest of our knowledge is ruled out. A project of general lowering of the intellectual level of billions of individuals is being implemented, to prevent, in fact, that some critical control function is applied over the action of the "Universal Masters". The word "project" may be misleading and should be used cautiously. It does not mean that there is a "command centre" or a control room providing guidelines about its order execution. In reality, centres like that are numerous. But this is not the point. The point is that such a "project" is the automatic effect of a radical technological mutation of human relations. It automatically depresses individual skills, leverages primordial, asocial instincts, simplifies and trivialises reality, reduces the range of languages, eliminates nuances and chiaroscuro, reduces diversity and modifies human time.

Many are not able to perceive the changes in their depth. They think it has "always been this way" and bosses have always been deceiving and manipulating their subjects. This is nonsense—the truth is exactly the opposite. It has never been the way that we are experiencing now. Never have the mighty been able to have such a pervasiveness, such hidden means to impose their power of manipulation. A power which can and does exclude any possibility of "democratic" control. A power which enables them to reach and hit the mark—in a fraction of a second—over an endless crowd of eyes and ears.

I am talking about what is happening in the West, that is, in the "highest" peak of current human development, where the traditional parties are disappearing, together with the whole conceptual system of liberal democracy. This, in turn, has succumbed to the technological change that has been imposed by the Universal Masters and which is called "American globalisation". But, if it is true that Facebook now has over two billion users, then it is clear that the expansion of the Anglo-Saxon way of life is invading a sizeable chunk of the rest of the world.

In this context, a special thought on the role that intellectuals have taken becomes particularly important. It could be, I believe, one of the "building blocks" of the new theoretical construction that is needed. In any case: the re-reading, in our time, of Gramsci's pages on intellectuals and the organisation of culture causes a sense of estrangement. There is almost nothing left of what he witnessed.

The admirable Gramscian intellectual education was entirely developed within the context of the "homo legens"—that is, the man who reads—of the rational man, of the conscious subject, who can control his own knowledge. The meticulous attention with which Gramsci outlined a reform of the school is there to show the importance that he gave to the educational process for the formation of a free individual "as a person capable of thinking, of studying, of ruling—or controlling those who rule". The "educational principle" that he describes is based on rational concepts that implied the formation of an individual capable of "adapting to the laws of nature (...) to master them in turn" and who considers "civil and state laws as (...) established by men and (which) can to be altered by men in the interests of their collective development".

Bearing in mind also that the consciousness of the individuals who need to be educated "is the result of the civil society in which (the individual) participates, and the social relations which are formed within his family, his neighbourhood, his village". It almost sounds like a quotation from Marx, where he defined the individual as "the point of intersection of his social relations". It was an apt definition, to be considered as a flash of genius, and yet largely incomplete. The human being—as underlined by the whole reasoning that we are developing here—is something immensely more complex.

There are more real things beneath the heavens than those which can be shown. Not only in the sense that the human being (as fully and completely connected with the whole ecosystem of which he is a part) is not "solely" the point of intersection of all his social relations. And therefore the topic addressed here—as part of the complexity—is not purely social and it is not purely rational. It must be addressed on multiple dimensions, on different depths, which have nothing to do with rationality. Human education cannot disregard these dimensions. Historical materialism has played a foul trick not so much on its creator, as on its imitators. Having grasped the end of the skein, they ended up thinking that there was only one tangle in the skein, while, instead, they were countless.

"One of the most important characteristics of any group that is developing towards dominance", Gramsci wrote, "is its struggle to assimilate and to conquer "ideologically" the traditional intellectuals, but this assimilation and conquest is made quicker and more efficacious the more the group in question succeeds in simultaneously elaborating its own organic intellectuals."

Here Gramsci talks about intellectuals as "clerks" working for the dominant group, i.e. those exercising the subordinate functions of "social hegemony and political government". As to say, as tools for "hegemony".

But it is a positive, creative hegemony. The exact opposite of the "single thought". And it is exactly here that a clear fracture was created between today's reality and the reality described and analysed by Gramsci.

In the context offered here, the very idea of forming an intellectual elite performing the function of social control has changed its meaning. Today there is a huge army of propagandists which depict the "present time reality" as the best of all possible worlds, a system working automatically and reproducing itself automatically, in the absence of any critical alternative. According to the inhuman spirit characterising the contemporary age, there is no longer an urgent need for addressing these problems specifically, as millions of people—or billions—eat from the same menu that is handed to them.

There is no alternative option. So, all that's left is trying to create a strategy that breaks the monopoly that the Masters of the Universe have on communication. They now have to face only one problem: how to continue to hide, from the masses, the incontrovertible facts that make us foresee the end of their project. Their "money map" is like the drawing of a big video game: it has a border, and this border cannot be crossed. As our civilisation is condemned to stay on this planet for the length of time that remains before its crisis is completed, the videogame players are forced to stay in the city where the inhuman rules of the dog-eat-dog warfare are in force.

The left, in the West, was unable to see the global cultural revolution, which completely changed even basic vocabulary. A revolution that changed the way of thinking, of consuming, of living and one which overturned the concept of time and affected the way human beings use it, by subjecting it to that of artificial prostheses, at this point indispensable. It changed human consciousness and created a virtual reality stronger than "actual" reality. An anthropological modification took place. It opened the doors to a completely new universe, one in which we now find ourselves, whose rules we are incapable of understanding. In the same way, we are unable to assess its overwhelming implications, to measure the multiple speeds of mutation, to interfere in its rules of acceleration, as it does not accept—indeed, on the contrary, it rejects—all our intervention, both as individuals and as groups. From that universe—which has already become a prison—we do not know how to escape. We do not (yet) have a theory to fight against it. We do not have the file to saw through the bars. There is no modern Gramsci who is able to analyse the current reality. Anyway, this cannot be a task for a single person. It is urgent to talk about a new figure of "collective intellectual". However, in order to create it, we need a theory, which does not yet exist. These reflections are a humble attempt to lay the groundwork for an unprecedented and—I recognise—desperate attempt, to tackle the problem.

The subordination of the "superstructure" to the "structure", assumed in a dogmatic and uncritical way, prevented us from understanding, for example, that the human being is something more than a "point of intersection". It was Sigmund Freud who opened the path of the unconscious. And, not surprisingly, the understanding of these problems has been far superior among non-Marxists and non-materialists. The publication, in the United States, of *Propaganda* by Edward Bernays, Freud's nephew, dates back to 1928. Since that day, over ninety years, this science has evolved and achieved extraordinary results. It remained unknown to most but has turned into a powerful tool for controlling and addressing the masses. Individuals became "solitary" and deprived of political representation, orphans of parties and transformed into an "audience", spectators. That's why, in the whole of the West, over only a couple of decades, the populations have lost all reactivity and passively suffer the threats imposed by the power.

As I have already noticed, some personalities understood and warned about the effects that this type of "reverse civilisation" would have produced, but they were all standing—not by chance—outside or on the sidelines of both historical and dialectical materialism. I will only mention some names and titles, of different relevance and depth. I refer to, for example, Giovanni Sartori, Pier Paolo Pasolini, Gregory Bateson, Karl Popper, Neil Postman, Guy Debord, and almost all of Noam Chomsky's work.

You may feel a certain amount of bewilderment in reading the Gramscian reflections. They belong to a world that no longer exists. And to reconsider it, it is not enough to turn off your computer. The superstructure—someone might say—has overwhelmed the structure. It prevents people from understanding how the new structure is made; it prevents us from seeing that its main production is immaterial, but extremely powerful: it is called "deception". This is why the Masters of the Universe need to reduce our "rate of understanding". And the issue concerns not only the large masses who must remain ignorant. The Masters of the Universe must be surrounded by blinkered scientists (so intensely specialised to the point of not being able to look beyond the square centimetre of their knowledge, i.e. not being able to see the complexity of the crisis) and by ignorant and dogmatic professors (who learn and teach the rules of the "Money Map" and stop in horror by the outline of the drawing). They do not need high level intellectuals.

The "Trilateral Commission" had given the crucial signal to all the "Masters of the Universe". A signal that the subordinate classes could neither read nor understand, because they were "elsewhere", fighting a class struggle that no longer existed. The message from the Trilateral Commission was the following: it is no longer time to look for 'consent' and to wear velvet gloves. The era of blandishments, consumption, liberating culture, democracy is about to end.

This is why it is necessary, for them, to disarm the masses before they become dangerous, having perceived the deception and the destiny planned for them. The technological tools already exist for exercising the new "control". The intellectual class mediator in charge of this control consists of the managers of the prefabricated messages. It is a stupid, uncreative, repetitious class. But this is exactly what has to be done, otherwise an intellectual class can become, again, dangerous. Their universities, increasingly restricted to the top of the social pyramid, will "educate" their children and their "clerks", teach their ideology, reproduce their false conscience, propagate the virtual reality. Further down they should not go, because there is nowhere to go. Their single thought is equivalent to the *"hic sunt leones"* ("here are the lions") that the emperors of the declining Roman Empire marked on their military maps. There is no future in the "Money Map". So we have no other task than looking for the way to get out of it.

13

Karl Marx and the Opium War

Eugenio Lo Sardo

Marx was familiar with the history and culture of India. Who knows if he read the famous travel book written by Ludovico de Varthema in the 16th century. But he was, like many other German students of his time, certainly familiar with Sacred text like the *Upanishads*, already quoted by the famous philosopher, Arthur Schopenhauer, in his 1818 preface to the first edition of *Die Welt als Wille und Vorstellung*. It was not just India's history and culture that he knew of, but also its economic situation. His studies were focused on the development of the British imperial system in Europe and Asia.

In an article published in the *New York Herald Tribune* (on June 25, 1853), three years before the beginning of the second opium war, he describes the country as: "An Italy of Asiatic dimensions. The same rich variety in the products of the soil, and the same dismemberment in the political configuration".

A country "which the British, dissolved into as many independent and conflicting states as it numbered towns, or even villages".

"A world", he adds, "dominated by the religion of the lingam and juggernaut; the religion of the monk, and of the bayadere".

"The misery inflicted by the British on Hindustan" was for him very different and intensive, because England had broken down the entire framework of Indian society.

The British in the East had neglected the public works provoking "the deterioration of an agriculture which is not capable of being conducted on the British principle of free competition, of laissez-faire and laissez-aller".

"From immemorial times", Marx states, "Europe received the admirable textures of Indian labour", sending in return, "precious metals, and furnishing thereby material to the goldsmith, that important member of Indian society", whose skills were so great "that even the lowest class", people going "about nearly naked, have commonly a pair of golden ear-rings and a gold ornament of some kind hung round their necks". And he adds, showing his knowledge of Hindus' habits "Rings on the fingers and toes have also been common".

It was the British intruder, according to him, who broke up the Indian handloom and destroyed the spinning-wheel. They destroyed also the so-called village system, "which gave to each of these small unions their independent organisation and distinct life".

A few lines later he clarifies his idea: "These small stereotype forms of social organism have been to the greater part dissolved, and are disappearing, not so much through the brutal interference of the British tax-gatherer and the British soldier, as to the working of English steam and English free trade". Because those family-communities were based on domestic industry, "in that peculiar combination of hand-weaving, hand-spinning and hand-tilling agriculture which gave them self-supporting power".

In conclusion the cause of the economic decline of India was the international division of work, the English had placed the spinner in Lancashire and the weaver in Bengal.

"Sweeping away both Hindu spinner and weaver, dissolved these small semi-barbarian, semi-civilised communities, by blowing up their economic basis, and thus produced the greatest, and to speak the truth, the only social revolution ever heard of in Asia".

"But, on the other side", Marx says, "we must not forget that these little communities were contaminated by distinctions of caste and by slavery, that they subjugated man to external circumstances instead of elevating man as the sovereign of circumstances, that they transformed a self-developing social state into never changing natural destiny".

So, according to Marx, the British were not in India to improve the wealth of people, like a famous historian, Macaulay, stated in 1923. But they were answering to a general law: the general law of profit. Also the opium-war was answering to the same general law: to make a profit.

Amitav Gosh in a recent interview to an Italian newspaper shared Marx's 'opinion: "Free trade was allowed only to the Westerners", he says. "China and India had commercial links for a very long time, the first had 24 per cent of the world trade and the second 2 per cent. The British were able to destroy the local industry. It was an imperialism of pure exploitation, which introduced drugs. Nothing to do with progress. The proof? After Independence India recovered" (*La Republica* October 21, 2015).

Fernand Braudel too, the well known French historian, thinks the decline of India had "an external not an internal explanation, in a word, Britain."

India was for the British an instrument thanks to which they gained access to an even larger area, coming to dominate the Asiatic super-world economy". India, he added was "deindustrialised, reduced to a role of a major producer of raw material". (*The Perspective of the World,* 522)

A few years later the quoted article, in the winter between 1857 and 1858, Marx was writing the *Grundrisse* (*Foundation of the Critique of Political Economy*, published only in 1953). They are for us very important from a theoretical point of view and extremely interesting for the links suggested between opium trade and the production of contemporary goods.

In the second chapter, dedicated to the general relation of production to distribution, exchange and consumption, Marx writes: "Production creates, produces consumption", and a few lines after he adds, "production creates the consumer", "not only supplies a material for the need, but it also supplies a need for the material". Therefore production is consumption and consumption is production. For example, an object of art creates a public which is sensitive to art and enjoys beauty.

Finally production produces consumption by creating the material for it; by determining the manner of consumption; by creating the products initially posited as an object of consumption, the manner of consumption and the motive of consumption.

Opium too, a dangerous drug, was a perfect product creating its consumers and consequentially, creating a great mass of addicted people. For the Sikhs in India the telegraph cables were the rope to hang subjected people, but it was anyway a useful tool, opium unless for medical purposes was useless and created diseases, slavery and death.

When in 1856 the Second Opium War began, Marx's workshop was ready to furnish all the necessary tools for a sharp analyses of the war. He wrote several articles in the same American newspaper to show the economic roots of the conflict and the moral issues.[1]

The English, for him, were at war without any moral justification. In England itself people like William Gladstone, the politician, and James Legge, the famous translator of Confucius, were, against the decision of the government.[2]

But why was that war necessary? According to Marx, the reason was simple, as he explains in *Das Kapital*: England "sends silver to India, and buys opium … all of which goes to China to lay down funds to purchase the silk". Not only silk but also tea. China was not interested in English merchandise, it was a market closed to it. The Chinese had always produced all they wanted. They were in credit, a huge credit towards the more industrialised countries.

In the first line of Marx's article published at the beginning of September 1858, he posed the following question: "Is it quite certain that an increase of the Chinese trade must follow upon the multiplication of its emporiums?" No, he answered, it was not true. Instead of increasing American and English exports to China, the war precipitated the commercial crisis of 1847 by "raising dreams of an inexhaustible market and by fostering false speculations".

"The Chinese, therefore, cannot take", according to Marx, "both goods and drugs; under actual circumstances, extension of the Chinese trade resolves into extension of the opium trade".

In the same month, he published another article (on September 25, 1858). "We cannot leave", he writes this time, "this part of the subject without singling out one flagrant self-contradiction of the Christianity-canting and civilisation-mongering British Government. In its imperial capacity it affects to be a thorough stranger to the contraband opium trade, and even to enter into treaties proscribing it". "Yet", he adds, "in its Indian capacity, it forces the opium cultivation upon Bengal, to the great damage of the productive resources of that country". The British Government compels also "one part of the Indian *ryots* to engage in the poppy culture; entices another part into the same by dint of money advances". The government runs everything. "It keeps the wholesale manufacture of the deleterious drug a close monopoly in its hands; watches by a whole army of official spies its growth, its delivery at appointed places, its inspissation and preparation for the taste of the Chinese consumers, its formation into packages especially adapted to the convenience of smuggling, and finally its conveyance to Calcutta". There it is "put up at auction at the government sales, and made over by the state officers to the speculators thence to pass into the hands" of the smugglers who land it in China". Every chest costed about Rs. 250 and was sold at the Calcutta auction at a price ranging from Rs. 1,210 to Rs. 1,600. "Not yet satisfied" with this complicity, the same government, "enters into express profit and loss accounts with the merchants and shippers, who embark in the hazardous operation of poisoning an empire".

Marx offers a perfect description of the opium trade, which tied the Indians and Chinese in a mortal knot.

"The Indian finances of the British Government", were then depending "not only on the opium trade with China, but on the contraband character of that trade". If the Chinese

Government had legalised the opium trade, tolerating the cultivation of the poppy in China, the Anglo-Indian exchequer would have experienced a serious catastrophe".

The British Government "openly preaching free trade ... secretly defends the monopoly of its manufacture. Whenever we look closely into the nature of British free trade, monopoly is pretty generally found to lie at the bottom of its "freedom."

Conclusions

In the articles we quoted, Marx offers a very clear picture of the economic roots of the opium war, studying it like a case in the expansion of European capitalism. The British had used the sea power to conquer the world. They were establishing, as the Portuguese before, outposts at the mouths of the most important rivers, in order to intercept the trade of a specific country, in this case India and China (The Greeks did the same while founding Alexandria in Egypt). But the merchandise we are speaking of was a peculiar one, since opium addicted consumers, created by itself its own market. The drug transformed a subject of an ancient empire into a subject of drug sellers, opening a wider gap between the government and people.

The *Grundrisse* explains to us the typical behaviour of modern capitalism: it acts in order to create the consumers, to create the necessity of consumption. These actions are not in the field of necessity; they are in the field of drive that will be coercion.

The Indo-Chinese war is an interesting example: the Indian economic system was destroyed, the internal political and economic balance of China too. Two big economies were reduced to peripheral suppliers of raw materials and their people to endemic poverty.

The Chinese opium dreamers woke up abruptly many years later. Finally they understood that the problems of their country derivated also by its economic position in the international economic system. The Indians and the Chinese, after a long fight, were able to become independent. Now

India and China are again a gigantic economy in the theatre of the world.

But people everywhere must obey, still now, the financial system's dictat and the mermaid of profit. Now more then before, Marx can help us to answer the challenges of modern times.

NOTES

1. And also in *Das Kapital* he observes that England "sends silver to India, and buys opium ... all of which goes to China to lay down funds to purchase the silk".
2. Dona Toor in 1951 (London) collected a selection of Marx's articles written in the *New York Daily Tribune* on the war in a book entitled *Marx on China, 1853-1860*.

14

Marx or Utopia and Ideology Against Wisdom

Jean-Joseph Boillot

Introduction

Marxism, a criticism of nascent capitalism, has long established itself as the hegemonic alternative system of thought in revolutionary movements. It has clearly forced capitalism to adapt and it has channelled a large number of national liberation struggles into the world, including China and Africa, where it has long represented the only real alternative to the domination of the Western world.

But certain theoretical weaknesses of the Marxist system, its quick evolution into ideology, even into religion for the Orthodox Marxist movement, transformed the utopian project of Marxist communism into a true 20th century dystopia and marginalised Karl Marx's thought as rational thought and political project.

Understanding Marx's thought trajectory, his theoretical and practical weaknesses as well as his strengths are far from being useless scientific work. Time has done its work and the dispassionate critique of Marxist thought and its utopia can usefully contribute to increasing the wisdom of the world in the search for more humane economies, more just societies and better harmony among humans and with nature.

1. The Historical Genesis of Marx's Thought

1.2. Marx's Marxism in Three Parts and the Five Great Thesis of the Original Marxism

The Marxism of Marx himself can be broken down into three parts: the philosophical Marx, the political Marx and finally the economist Marx, and it is important to understand how they form a global analytical and practical system.

1.2.1. The **philosophical** Marx first, whose essence, to keep it short, is an opposition to metaphysics and idealism with the central concept of "historical and dialectical materialism" which interprets the entire history of societies and of the world to that of the forms of production from which social classes and class struggles derive as the driving force of History. This largely explains the central place given by Marx to the economy in explaining the evolution of societies.

Without denying the importance of production relations and material life in the determination of social relations or individuals, the mechanistic vision of the determination of superstructure by material infrastructure seems not only simplistic but strongly reductionist to the point that Marx himself was often obliged to broaden his theoretical framework to analyse concrete situations as in "Les Luttes de classes en France" or for the treatment of the caste system in India. In his correspondence with Engels, he also made numerous references to the concept of the "Asiatic mode of production or despotism" in an attempt to understand the Eastern countries.

The result on a theoretical level is the absence of a fine analysis of societies in the Marxist corpus, of their real social differentiation beyond the social classes, of concepts as essential as morality, human nature, violence, nation, etc., in short, of everything that makes the human being, in favour of a central place brought to the economy and in this case the mythical "capitalist system" which was becoming dominant in the West. In his numerous texts as a journalist or columnist of political and social events all over the world, Marx himself, however, testified to a finesse of practical analysis that goes far beyond the dialectical materialist philosophy of history.

1.2.2. **Marx as an economist and political scientist** is better known. In these two economic and political fields, Marx's essential ideas can be summarised with five thesis as suggested by Erik Olin Wright (2010) in his seminal book *Envisioning Real Utopias*".

Thesis 1: The long-term unsustainability of capitalism under the effect of its own internal contradictions and in particular the law of falling rate of profit. Yet the obsession with his "labour theory of value", actually originating from the English Classical School theorists such as Adam Smith or David Ricardo, has led economic Marxism into a deadlock: not seeing capitalist competition as the very spur of innovation, of permanent revolution in production methods as well as in modes of consumption and commercial exchange, including in the financial sphere, to the point that profit rates have never been as high as they are today, for example. Moreover, Karl Marx himself demonstrates in certain texts that with machinism and technology, the creation of wealth depends less on work than on the mechanical power associated with the general scientific and technological level, what is called the "general intellect" hypothesis which would invalidate the whole theory of labour value at the heart of Marxism for decades and thus the theory of exploitation which is associated with the historical role of the proletariat.

That crises, then, are intimately linked to capitalism is not false in itself, but all forms of production have also experienced economic crises, including in Antiquity. And the French Marxist *School of Regulation* has shown precisely how capitalism has learned to regulate itself and to adapt to the specific conditions of each country more or less willingly or forcefully. The paradox of Marxism is that it may have allowed capitalism, under the pressure of its critics, to constantly adapt, whether defensively or offensively.

Thesis 2: Intensification of the anti-capitalist class struggle by increasing proletarianisation of the entire world population and polarisation into two blocks of a wealthy elite and others. The least that can be said is that this thesis also appears erroneous in the light of history. By economicism no doubt, but above all by refusing to consider the complexification of societies into classes, sub-classes, sub-sub-classes, etc. on a vertical level, but also horizontally between ethnic, national, religious and other barriers, so many divisions which have their own autonomy with regard to economics. Not to mention that pure capitalism has never enveloped the totality of production relations. Families as economic units, small and medium-sized enterprises, often non-capitalist, and finally states, which have themselves become increasingly important in modern economic life, play a major role in any modern economy.

But here again, let us recognise in the Marxist critique the paradox of having undoubtedly facilitated the end of the proletariat by integrating it in a differentiated way into the sharing of wealth and even power. This differentiation is partly due to the social struggles against capitalism, but it has largely been possible because of the successive adaptations of capitalism, particularly at the international level, as for example during the colonial phase, then more recently with the great globalisation at the end of the 20th century. These internal and external transformations allowed the emergence of mass consumption in the countries at the heart of capitalism, including the United States and Western Europe, then its extension to the emerging world such as China, India or Brazil and recently to Africa.

This reality, finally developed by Lenin for the imperialist phase of the early 20th century, justified the idea that communist revolutions could therefore finally take place in the "peripheral" countries. It seems to have worked in the case of Russia and China, but not really in connection with their economic exploitation. The most exploited colony, India, on the other hand, did not experience a communist revolution, like many other colonies, such as Brazil, where a very specific form of corporatist national capitalism appeared with Gétulio Varga in 1930.

Above all, the example of the globalisation that followed the intensive and Keynesian capitalism of the "thirty glorious" post-war years shows the paradox of an extension of world capitalism thanks to China which, as well argued by the Marxist Giovanni Arrighi (Adam Smith in Beijing, 2007), pushed Adam Smith's capitalist logic to a level never equalled in the economic history of the world. However, China is not the place of the intensification of the anti-capitalist class struggle with a proletarianisation of the whole Chinese society. Here again, despite a formidable rise in inequality, social (and regional) differentiation is at the heart of the complexification of modern production with new Chinese middle classes and the emergence of a mass consumer society since the refocusing on the domestic market in the early 2000s.

Thesis 3: The ineluctable revolutionary transformation following the Thesis 1 and 2 where capitalism will not collapse alone but will be overthrown by the oppressed classes including the proletariat and its communist vanguard party. Yet it is precisely where capitalism was dominant that it has adapted best, certainly under the action of social struggles, but largely within the framework of the parliamentary system in general and with a determining role for reformist parties and trade unions. It is indeed in the most capitalist countries that people are most attached to the democratic political framework.

Thesis 4: The transition to socialism, i.e. a production system based on collective ownership and control by democratic and egalitarian institutions. In reality, this aspect of the socialist transition was not described much by Marx, whose main text remains the Manifesto of the Communist Party of 1847 with two ideas that were repeated till the end of his days in numerous writings, articles or letters: the crucial roles of the state and of collective planning during the transition period. On a practical level, it was the really existing countries of socialism that had the task of inventing the transition, the purest of which was Soviet Russia, whose outcome or performance has been undoubtedly less catastrophic than some propagandists had wanted to make people believe, but which collapsed on its own in 1989 with the fall of the Berlin Wall and the discovery of a totalitarian, bureaucratic and economically inefficient system very well described by the Hungarian economist Janos Kornaï in particular.

As for the thesis 5 of the advent of communism under the double dynamic of the reinforcement of community solidarity and the erosion of inequalities, it foresaw the natural decline of the state and social classes with the utopian affirmation (in the literal sense of imagined future) of a normative ideal of radical egalitarianism and material abundance for all. Let us recognise the Chinese leader Mao Zedong for having broken with the first thesis with the critical foundation of his "Great Proletarian Cultural Revolution" launched in 1966: the need for a permanent revolution but also a cultural revolution to avoid the traps that he had well anticipated in the transition to socialism, namely the seizure of power by a new conservative bourgeoisie. His only problem is that he himself failed in his project in favour of the pragmatic reformer Deng Xiaoping, known in China by the formula: "Turn the indicator to the left and turn to the right".

2. Marx: Science and Ideology, Utopia and Dystopia

Despite these harsh observations on Marx's five great theses, no one can deny that he was one of the greatest thinkers of the 19th century. His critical work on the capitalist mode of production at a key moment when it would assert itself as the dominant economic system in Western countries and beyond extending to the entire planet has provided essential keys to understanding the economic, social and political mechanisms that explained both the performance and the pathologies of a system lived with immense pain by the exploited and oppressed of the "Great Transformation" well described by Karl Polanyi. Orthodox transition theorists such as Adam

Smith, Stuart Mill or David Ricardo merely described its positive effects in terms of economic progress, or like Malthus, accused overpopulation of being at the origin of the pathologies observed when poverty was exploding in all the major urban centres of the industrial revolution.

But it is here that the essential distinction made by a great philosopher, Paul Ricoeur, between science, ideology and utopia must be made.

2.1. Marx Between Science and Ideology

Marx's approach was actually aiming at criticising the liberal ideology behind the work of those who claimed to follow a purely empirical and descriptive scientific method without questioning the implicit assumptions of their science. But in so doing Marx himself fell into the Mannheim paradox, i.e. produce an ideology to criticise another ideology, in this case liberal.

Ideology intervenes because no system of domination governs by force alone. Each system of domination requires not only physical submission but also consent and cooperation, or in other terms, a form of legitimacy whose ideology provides codes of interpretation that ensure the integration of individuals by justifying the present system of authority. The same is true for the alternative forces who wish to replace the old power system.

This approach is essential to understand how Marx moved from a critique that he wished to be as rational as possible, i.e. based on reason, on a scientific approach of causal links and experimental tests, to an ideology that aimed to produce a legitimisation of his alternative vision to capitalism, of which the Manifesto of the Communist Party is probably the key book. However, this work was published when Marx was not yet thirty years old and it has obviously influenced all his subsequent work, which ultimately aimed more at supporting his political approach than being part of a purely scientific approach.

The second aspect, did Marx's ideology impose itself

by its scientific or rational relevance? No. This alternative ideology was actually competing with a whole range of other ideologies offering alternatives to liberal capitalism like other socialist movements or anarchism. But History will remember that it is the Marxist communist parties that will gradually impose themselves as the dominant force in the anti-capitalist elite. They undoubtedly succeeded thanks to the intellectual power of Marx's work, but undoubtedly more so thanks to the organisational strength of the Marxist communist movement resulting from Marx's theory of revolution led by an avant-garde party organised in an almost military manner. Lenin with his Bolshevik party, but also Mao with his political and military writings—alas not well known—would develop this theory of the revolution of a so-called proletarian avant-garde party with the practical success we know. In this sense, Marx's ideology will became hegemonic for a long period within the alternative movements to capitalism less because of its scientific basis than because of its praxis on the ground of the seizure of political power.

From this probably comes the importance of the communist utopia both during Marx's life, but even more among those who would win revolutions in the name of Marxist ideology, especially in Russia, China and Africa. Indeed, for the same philosopher Paul Ricoeur, ideology and utopia have the same link with reality: a social imaginary function capable of mobilising human energies and passions. But where ideology has the function of legitimising authority, of justifying it, "Utopia has the function of stimulating the imagination on the field of possibilities beyond the existing by making it possible to envisage radically different ways of living without worrying about their feasibility".

In this sense, Marx's communist utopia played an essential role in bringing together masses of people or intellectuals who did not share Marxist theories or his communist ideology in particular because of its violent or elitist practice of power, but who accepted it for its practical effectiveness in overthrowing capitalist regimes and because of their dream of another society.

2.2. Marx and the Long History of Utopia

Utopia, or in fact Utopias, can be characterised as imaginary creations, morally inspired conceptions aiming at a world of peace and harmony, satisfaction of basic needs or material prosperity, and not constrained by realistic considerations that touch on human psychology and the question of economic, social and political feasibility. In this sense, Utopia defines a genre, not a thematic unity. On the major subjects of society, including economic organisation, there are as many projects as there are utopias, such as for the family that some would like to see disappear or, on the contrary, reinforce for the former, or for consumption with frugal ascetism for some or, on the contrary, abundance for others. In this sense it is necessary to specify what is called Marx's communist utopia.

The utopian tradition can be traced back to Antiquity with Homer's Odyssey in the 8th century BC, and on the political field to the 5th century with the Republic of Diogenes and then with Plato and Aristotle who imagined the ideal city. Probably the most finished work remains at this time Iambule's "The Sun Island" which became the main source for Thomas More and Campinella in the 15th century when the epic and utopian style reappeared. It is actually to Thomas More that we owe the word Utopia, title of his book of 1516 which describes a perfect country, without private property, without war, without social antagonism, egalitarian, democratic, frugal certainly but guaranteeing the satisfaction of all basic needs, social protection, a retirement and an optimal balance between leisure and social or political activities. The utopian genre made a fortune since then with several hundred books that described ideal societies and marked the philosophers of the Enlightenment in Europe and many social reformers at the time of the Industrial Revolution.

However, if Marx quoted Thomas More, Mably, Morelly, Cabet, Villegardelle or Weitling, it was to take up their criticism of feudal society but not really for the meticulous description of their "communist" project, the actual word often used to describe in detail the ideal city of More and most social reformers. In fact, it would have been to his advantage to focus and analyse in detail the political, social and economic organisation proposed since they actually almost always bore totalitarian visions in terms of freedom, were frugal to the extreme and without proper History. He would have seen then that they were not only unrealistic but leading to "dystopia", i.e. the transformation of an ideal into a dark world, even a human nightmare.

On the contrary, Marx's critic of utopias focused on the socialist visions of Saint-Simon, Fourier, Lasalle, Owen, and others, including his own son-in-law Joseph Proudhon, all of whom were treated rather harshly, notably in a famous book signed by Engels, as "utopian socialists" as opposed to the "scientific socialism" attributed to Marx. These great social reformers of the 19th century were accused by Marx and Engels of proposing "immature theoretical forms compared to the degree of development of the proletariat and the productive forces". They were also accused of pursuing "chimeras" such as the projects of "Phalansteres" or worker cooperatives, while "scientific socialism" was predicting the collapse of capitalism and therefore the priority to organise the proletariat with a view to its overthrow by revolution. For the rest, in fact, Marx was content with a vague goal that was communism without property, without class and without state.

In doing so, Marx fell into the same traps as idealistic utopia with its two principles: "Want is power", implying, everything is possible; and "Necessity is the mother of invention", implying, solutions will always be found.

2.3. From Utopia to Dystopia

The paradox of economists is that we owe the description of the mechanisms of this dystopic metamorphosis to two great writers: George Orwell and Aldous Huxley.

2.3.1 The "Animal Farm" Model

On the revolutionary rupture envisaged by Marx, George

Orwell's "Animal Farm" model perfectly describes the political and economic mechanisms that not only made most Marxist revolutions fail, but above all transformed them into a rejection of any revolutionary perspective of this kind.

Written in 1945, three years before his world-famous novel *1984*, Orwell's *Animal Farm* offers an explanatory model based in fact on the historical experiences of the French and Russian revolutions. Its essential mechanism is the cynical use of popular aspirations to free themselves from an oppressive system of exploitation and the dream of a New Man to set up an economy of war and dictatorial mobilisation of the labour force that legitimises the seizure of power by a dictator and a new aristocratic class to the detriment of a proletariat more exploited than ever but now deprived of any means of resistance or opposition. The system obtained ultimately proved to be much less effective than that which was fought. The new bourgeoisie in power then negotiated a compromise with the adversary in exchange for which it retained power thanks to a totalitarian system which played on the fibre of nationalism to maintain any semblance of legitimacy.

It is difficult to deny the relevance of the model whose historical examples have multiplied since the French Revolution. George Orwell also had direct experience of it during the Spanish Civil War in 1936 where he experienced the cynicism with which the Spanish libertarian anarchists of the CNT were massacred and abandoned by the Communists of the Spanish Communist Party supported by Moscow.

The case of Leninism-Stalinism in the USSR and China is well known, but Cuba can also be mentioned in Latin America, or in Africa, the experience of Kwame Nkrumah in Ghana, whose two key works reproduce Orwell's novel almost word for word. It is *The Class Struggle in Africa* published in 1970 and even more *Africa Must Unite* published in 1963. In the middle of the turmoil of his socialist experience of Ghana, Nkrumah tried to justify the end of political freedoms, the establishment of a single party and the experience of socialist planning directly inspired by Marx's work but which failed dramatically.

Less commented upon, the case of India is also instructive. The Indian experience is a kind of attempt by Jawaharlal Nehru of a synthesis inspired by English reformist fabianism between a democratic political system avoiding totalitarian drift and a Marxist-style economic model, notably on the pattern of planification and socialist accumulation. The development strategy set out in the early 1950s by the Planning Commission led by the USSR inspired Marxist economist, P.C. Mahalabonis, turns out in reality to be a significant failure since the growth rate would not exceed 4 per cent during the First Plan of 1951-1956 and hardly more than 4 per cent during the Second Plan between 1956 and 1961. After the 1962 war against China, India entered an infernal spiral of agricultural and balance of payment crises so that its average post-independence growth rate—nicknamed the 'Hindu rate of growth'—was barely higher than population growth till the early 1980s. India owes its democratic political model to the exiting impasses of the Marxist economic model without too many difficulties, even if the transition lasted almost twenty years, which include the meanderings of Indira Gandhi during her State of Emergency from 1975 to 1977, recalling the prognostics of George Orwell on the totalitarian drifts in this kind of situation where the ideal deviates too much from the realities and the intensive use of scapegoats to explain the failure of its own policy.

2.3.2 *China and the "Brave New World"*

One could say however: what about Post-Mao China? His resounding success since the pragmatic turn of 1978 could well constitute a tangible proof of the relevance of Marx's theories concerning the Revolution and the transition phase from socialism to communism, this time well conducted after several unfortunate but ultimately acceptable experiments under any experience curve.

(a) On the one hand, the Chinese revolution was a success in the sense of the overthrow of the ancient feudal-capitalist order by a communist party inspired by Marx's thought. But inspired intelligently in the sense of a specific adaptation to China by Mao Zedong whose philosophical and practical writings are explicitly in the continuity of those of Marx. Even today, the most recent reference to the sources of the Chinese regime—Xi Jinping's book *The Governance of China*—is unambiguous: "The theoretical system of Chinese socialism is the fruit of the sinisation of Marxism. This theoretical system is the continuation, development, legacy and innovation of Marxism-Leninism and Mao Zedong's thinking. We absolutely cannot abandon Marxism-Leninism or Mao Zedong's thought, otherwise we will lose our foundations... To pursue the theoretical system of Chinese socialism in China today is to rightly pursue Marxism."

The current doctrine simply speaks of the "historical contribution to Chinese socialism made by the central leadership team of three generations, including Mao for the first, Ding Xiaoping for the second, and finally the third led by Jiang Zemin who set the case for 21st century China. Finally, Marx's communist ideal is simply put in brackets in the name of the argument that China is in "the primary phase of socialism marked by a still low level of development" justifying the continuation of the socialist transition as described by Marx. That is to say "under the leadership (read "dictatorship") of the Communist Party which must exercise all power to rebuild the country, develop productive forces, focus priorities on economic construction and on this basis only, promote in a coordinated manner the political, cultural, social and ecological construction of the country." (All these references appear in the same book by Xi Jinping)

Nevertheless, Marx's communist ideals are already present in a rhetoric typical of the "Manifesto of the Communist Party" of 1857: "The aspiration of the people to live a better life must always be the focus of our efforts (...) All happiness on earth is created by work (...) It is necessary to promote in harmony, equity and social justice, and to ensure a happy and peaceful life for a people."

(b) On the other hand, most economic and social

indicators, but also technological and what are more broadly called "human development indexes" as measured by the United Nations, all show China's rather fascinating progress. It has become the world's leading economy in terms of GDP calculated in purchasing power parity; it has one of the longest life expectancies in the world (76 years); finally, its Human Development Index rose from 0.50 to 0.74 between 1990 and 2017, even if its 90th place in the world still shows a significant gap with its competitors in the capitalist countries. But for now, the catch-up trajectory remains striking with growth continuing to exceed 6-7 per cent per year, and a growing mastery of technological innovations that brings China closer to the technical frontier of the most advanced countries. On the negative side, wealth and power inequalities, corruption and environmental degradation place China at the bottom of the list of developed countries. But these are now priorities of the transition led by the team of President Xi who took the reins of power in 2012 and the 19th Congress at the end of 2017 has decided to extend his mandate for an infinite duration and to give his thought the same status as those of Mao Zedong and Deng Xiaoping.

(c) *The Chinese Way of the "Brave New World"?*

Although the Mass is not said (over), one can propose the reading of the Chinese model through the second model of utopia-dystopia existing on the market: that of the famous novel *Brave New World* written in 1932 by Aldous Huxley, long enough to judge the maturity of a work. Unlike Orwell's models of the *Animal Farm* and 1984, Huxley describes a modern totalitarianism in which leaders became aware that the use of terror, artificial famines, imprisonment of the masses and deportation of opponents are not only inhuman but ineffective : "In an era of advanced technology, a truly efficient totalitarian state would be one in which an almighty executive committee of political leaders and their army of directors have control over a population of slaves but whom it would be useless to coerce because they would have the choice of love of their bondage."

In particular, mass manipulation methods are increasingly scientific, mixing sophisticated police control with the use of media and manipulation techniques, including chemical drugs. In return, a highly efficient economic system offers all the ingredients for mass prosperity and consumerism, including leisure, supported by massive investments in technical progress and productivity gains. The political system is that of an omnipresent state-party that promises happiness, social stability and the protection of individuals in exchange for renouncing political freedom and thinking.

All the information available on China today, its increasingly sophisticated surveillance system, and the description of the "Chinese way to happiness" is actually very similar to Huxley's model and the analyses of opponents of the regime, such as the economist Zhang (reference?) who left the country after the Tian'anmen massacre, converge towards this totalitarian society of mass prosperity.

2.3.3 *The "End and the Means" Model*

Undoubtedly, Marx cannot be blamed for having sinned for insufficient analysis of the political conditions of the transition, nor for having envisaged these pathological excesses of real socialism. But many thinkers of his century had clearly conjecturised the potential drifts of the Orwell type, and in particular the libertarians and all those which one groups today under the term of the thinkers of "Degrowth", among which John Ruskin, David Thoreau and Léon Tolstoï who greatly influenced Gandhi. All shared also a utopian path of political and economic rupture with capitalism in the name ultimately of the same ideals of Marx in terms of the end of man's exploitation by man and class oppression. Simply, the means of rupture are directly posed in relation to the ends sought.

In fact, the probable trajectory of the current Chinese model is due to the fundamental error of Marx's theory of dialectical materialism, which completely subordinates superstructure—

broadly speaking, politics, social and culture that do not exist in their own right—to the material infrastructure, that is, to his theory of modes of production. The paradox, well highlighted by Huxley, is that to sustainably establish its power, the Communist Party that wants to escape the economy of scarcity and therefore totalitarian physical repression is obliged to engage in a race for growth, for scientific and technical progress to legitimise its domination, and to follow a de facto capitalist path.

In so doing, the inversion of the end and the means leads to the disappearance of Marx's very human goal, namely freedom and equality, i.e. the human development well defined by Amartya Sen not by the accumulation of wealth but as the fulfilment and expansion of the capabilities of each individual.

3. Conclusion: The Economy of Wisdom

In conclusion, I would like to offer some positive perspectives from this theoretical journey on the evolution of Marx's works, which I recall to what extent they are rich and constituted one of the main criticisms and alternatives to capitalism throughout the 20th century before the collapse of the Marxist communist dream almost everywhere in the world.

This perspective has a name: *Wisdom*, as a rational, balanced approach but also capable of transforming proposals. It includes philosophical wisdom, political wisdom and economic wisdom. Despite the two words are rarely used together and may even appear antinomic, some great economists like Jean-Baptiste Say have precisely defined economics as the very science of wisdom.

Let us content ourselves with a simple definition of Wisdom as: "Behaviour in conformity with an ethic which combines the conscience of oneself and others, which cultivates temperance, prudence, sincerity, discernment and justice by relying on one or more reasoned knowledge."

From this point of view, Karl Marx has not been a "Wise One" in all the qualifiers quoted, with the exception of sincerity.

Beyond the use of reasoned knowledge in a completely partial way, Marx lacked at least two other essential qualifiers: ethics and caution in judgement.

Indeed, ethics is Marx's poor relation, to the point of having even had to develop the notion of a "proletarian morality" to justify his key thesis of the dictatorship of the proletariat as a method of transforming societies. The questions of violence or some basic universal principles indispensable in any life in society are especially poorly represented in Marx's writings. Secondly, prudence in analysis is a second great absence in Marx's intellectual approach who never doubts his analyses, quite the contrary. However, the evolution of capitalism has, for example, proved the resilience of the system thanks to more or less sudden but also voluntary adaptations, as shown by a very large part of the so-called orthodox economic research, i.e. that is favourable to capitalism.

We can suggest here three ways to overcome these weaknesses and offer a critical or even alternative perspective to capitalism for those who think that its pathologies outweigh the undeniable progress it generates.

3.1. The Realities of Human Nature

First, that of a judgment on man, on human nature, which goes far beyond the very restrictive framework granted by Marx on this subject: his over-determination by the economic system. In reality, as both the evolution of capitalism and of real socialism show, any economic system obeys certain laws of human nature which are neither good nor bad, but which possess intrinsic, even genetic, characteristics capable of perverting even the best economic system. I am referring in particular to the infinite quest for "power" over others, the greed to amass, to be richer than the other, anger, violence, jealousy, etc. As the philosophers Hannah Arendt and Paul Ricoeur say, the problem of power is the "most fascinating structure of existence" but it remains a sort of blind spot in our existence. The same is true in economics, where the notion has become indispensable in the analysis of markets and competition (see Joseph Stiglitz, Georges Akerlof or Paul Krugman) without, however, leading to institutional reforms capable of guaranteeing satisfactory market balances or regulation.

From this point of view, the famous Indian Panchatantra fables attributed to Vishnu Sharma and written in antiquity have long offered a fairly exhaustive vision of this human nature, in its best and worst, with behavioural models worthy of inclusion in the best economics textbooks. In fact, contemporary economic science sometimes merely repeats these fables with increasingly sophisticated behavioural or structural models of markets and institutions, whether we think of the Game or the Information theories, or behavioural analysis recently awarded to two Nobel prizes: David Kahneman and Richard H. Thaler.

I retain this essential lesson that Wisdom consists in postulating that Homo Economicus does not exist, any more than Homo Sapiens, and that it is vain to pursue utopia (even if one can and even must know how to dream about it), or to believe that one could transform all the individuals of the planet into Homo sapiens, prudent, reasoned, altruistic, etc.... One only has to work on Game theory or Daniel Kahneman's famous "Thinking Fast and Slow" model, for example, to realise that we cannot transform every human into an Einstein or Vishnu Sharma, if only because of the economic cost of each enlightened decision and the reality of information or market asymmetries.

3.2. Institutions are Always Imperfect

Which leads me to a second perspective. Any necessary progress of human wisdom, thanks in particular to education, presupposes a progress of collective institutions towards more wisdom, if only to deal here again with the mechanisms brought to light by the Game theory or that of asymmetries, including those developed by Nassim Nicholas Taleb in his theory of the unpredictable or hidden asymmetries ("Skin in the Game: Hidden Asymmetries in Daily Life"). From this point of view, Albert O. Hirschman's social science approach seems to me to provide a powerful framework for analysis.

Let us not expect perfect, ideal institutions. Let us try at least to better integrate into our scientific approach the famous "tricks of History" where when we have barely concluded the rationality of our explanatory model and its conclusions, they in reality are already exceeded (Trespassing) by a whole set of mechanisms related to the dynamics of open systems: perverse effects, linkage effects, permanent shift from the fields of economics towards the social one, then towards politics and vice versa.

This is quite simply because of the permeability between the different fields of social sciences that we tend to close, to compartmentalise for relatively legitimate reasons of rigorous analysis but at the cost of a poorly accepted loss of explanatory capacity. Marx and Marxism are a very good example of Albert Hirschman's legendary caution never to conclude definitively, especially in the social sciences, where one never has the ideal laboratory conditions to test his theory. On the other hand, Hirschman's approach to Marxism deserves to be better known with his concept of "micromarxism", i.e. the transposition of the Marxian scheme to small-scale economic and political development processes ("A Biais for Hope, Essays on Development and Latin America", 1971). Conversely, Hirschman never adhered to the claim of the vast encompassing frescoes of Marxist analysis and preferred the notions of "possibilityism" and "unintended consequences of human action" to that of probability of abstract theoretical models.

3.3. Economic Models and Limited Rationality

Hence my third line of inquiry, recently opened by the economist Dani Rodrik (Economics Rules, 2015), which cannot be accused of basic anti-Marxism: the modesty necessary in Economics, on the model of the Fables, which he himself says have generally produced better results than all economic models with scientific pretensions. Marx in particular has developed an all-encompassing, general theory of history, taking everything back to the concept of Materialism. However, such models are in reality unverifiable. Hence the rapid drift towards ideology and utopia according to his own relationship to the seizure of power. In reality, we must abandon the claim to make economics a normative science of "happiness" (welfare) and limit ourselves to a set of partial models based on realistic assumptions and thus corresponding to an imperfect world. The difference with the Fables is that partial economic models can indeed claim greater scientific rigour thanks to a set of transparent hypotheses, causal reasoning based on abstractions and the use of mathematical tools, and finally to verification tests.

In doing so, the models are multiple, specific to each subject and diverse as is the reality of the social world, and economists must abandon the very idea of a model with a universal or general vocation.

We can regret this disappearance of an all-encompassing vision of history which is quite convenient in the end, because very economical apparently in mental and time resources. Marxism, like all "isms," however, has shown that their costs were probably greater than their benefits. Human progress therefore depends on abandonment and evolution towards greater methodological and ethical wisdom.

***

Finally, Marx will have been very useful, not only for his very serious leads on a set of subjects related to the sources and effects of capitalism, but just as much for the lessons we can learn from them on what not to do if we wish to improve our understanding of our economic and social systems and guide us in an effective way on how to improve them.

15
Exploitation and Oppression Under Bourgeoisdom

C. Saratchand

1. Introduction

Traditional statements of historical materialism such as (Lange, 1963) are couched in terms of Marxist concepts of productive forces, production relations, mode of production, exploitation (private appropriation of surplus labour), etc. However it has long been recognised that historical materialism has to deal with phenomena such as gender, race, caste, communalism, etc., in other words with social oppression (Callinicos, 2002). The relation between exploitation and oppression is the subject of this paper.

It is proposed that social oppression is associated with heterogeneity within social classes[1] besides struggle between classes. Marxist writing often recognised the heterogeneity amongst the bourgeoisie. For instance (Patnaik, Chandrasekhar, and Sen, 1996; Patnaik, Chandrasekhar, and Ghosh, 2004), argued that there were two processes at play here namely, monopolisation and proliferation of the bourgeoisie. Monopolisation involves centralisation and concentration of capital. Proliferation involves the process through which new entrants make it into the ranks of the bourgeoisie.[2] The role of caste, gender, race, communalism, etc. in these processes has been significant since they were associated, for instance, with contradictions between different sections of the bourgeoisie.

However in (Marx, 2010 [1858], 2010 [1867], 2010 [1884], 2010 [1894]) it was assumed that the rate of surplus value was equal in each branch of production. This is generally equivalent to the assumption that the rate of exploitation of all workers is equal. Some of Marx's writings may be construed to imply that there is a tendency towards the creation of a homogeneous proletariat.[3] (Marx, 2010 [1867]) had pointed out that "...reproduction on a progressive scale, i.e. accumulation, reproduces the capital relation on a progressive scale, more capitalists or larger capitalists at this pole, more wage workers at that." Earlier it was argued according to (Marx and Engels, 2010 [1848]) that "Of all the classes that stand face to face with the bourgeoisie today, the proletariat alone is a really revolutionary class. The other classes decay and finally disappear in the face of Modern Industry; the proletariat is its special and essential product." However it does not follow from either of these propositions that the proletariat is homogeneous or will become so.

However this assumption that the rate of exploitation of different types of workers is unequal is neither necessary logically nor is it necessarily tenable historically.[4] Once it is admitted that the rate of exploitation of different types of workers is unequal, the factors that give rise to this inequality need to be examined. It is proposed that social oppression is associated with this phenomenon.

In order to examine the other phenomenon associated with social oppression it may be apposite to consider (Stalin, 1953 [1926])'s discussion on the heterogeneity amongst the proletariat: "....The proletariat, as a class, can be divided into three strata...One stratum is the main mass of the proletariat, its core, its permanent part, the mass of 'pure-blooded' proletarians, who have long broken off connection with the capitalist class. This stratum of the proletariat is the most reliable bulwark of Marxism...The second stratum consists of newcomers from non-proletarian classes—from the peasantry, the petty bourgeoisie or the intelligentsia. These are former members of other classes who have only recently merged with the proletariat and have brought with them into the working class their customs, their habits, their waverings and their vacillations. This stratum constitutes the most favourable soil for all sorts of anarchist, semi-anarchist and 'ultra-Left' groups...The third stratum, lastly, consists of the labour aristocracy, the upper stratum of the working class, the most well-to-do portion of the proletariat, with its propensity for compromise with the bourgeoisie, its predominant inclination to adapt itself to the powers that be, and its anxiety to "get on in life." This stratum constitutes the most favourable soil for outright reformists and opportunists."

Postponing commentary about the first and third stratum (as well as on this formulation as such) to the later sections of this paper, it may be pointed out that the existence of the second stratum of the proletariat presupposes the existence of other modes of production. But it cannot be ruled out that the persistence of other modes of production is only a matter of time if the capitalist mode of production has a tendency to eliminate other modes of production. But (Patnaik, 2009) points out that the historical experience has demonstrated that: "While retaining the concept of the mode of production, however, we must recognise that the capitalist mode of production is always located within a cluster, surrounded by pre-capitalist modes of production that are hegemonised but are nonetheless very clearly extant and by no means obliterated." The implications of this argument are examined later but it is proposed that social oppression is also associated with the existence of different modes of production.

The rest of this paper is organised as follows: Section 2 examines the implications of unequal rates of exploitation for historical materialism, Section 3 examines the relations between the mode of production and the social formation with special reference to the phenomenon of social oppression. Section 4 seeks to tie together the arguments of Sections 2 and 3 while Section 5 concludes the paper.

2. Unequal Rates of Exploitation of Workers and Social Oppression

It was assumed in (Marx, 2010 [1884], 2010 [1894]) that the rate of surplus value was the same in each branch (sector, industry) of production. If the types of concrete labour differ from the number of commodities then the sectoral rates of surplus value may be derived from the rates of exploitation of different types of workers. However besides simplicity there seems to be no reason to stick to this assumption.[5]

There is no tendency in the capitalist mode of production to overcome unequal rates of exploitation of different workers. (Marx, 2010 [1867]) did say that: "The distinction between skilled and unskilled labour rests in part on pure illusion, or, to say the least, on distinctions that have long since ceased to be real, and that survive only by virtue of a traditional convention; in part on the helpless condition of some groups of the working class, a condition that prevents them from exacting equally with the rest the value of their labour power. Accidental circumstances here play so great a part, that these two forms of labour sometimes change places. Where, for instance, the physique of the working class has deteriorated, and is, relatively speaking exhausted, which is the case in all countries with a well developed capitalist production, the lower forms of labour, which demand great expenditure of muscle, are in general considered as skilled, compared with much more delicate forms of labour; the latter sink down to the level of unskilled labour. Take as an example the labour of a brick-layer, which in England occupies a much higher level than that of a damask-weaver". In this quotation there is a reference to skilled and unskilled labour. The conversion of a given magnitude of concrete labour to abstract labour would depend on reduction ratios (Krause, 1982). The reduction ratios involve both skill and other aspects of the bargaining power among different types of workers and the balance of bargaining power between workers and capitalists. In other words, reduction ratios involve both skill differences and unequal rates of exploitation.

For the same type of concrete labour, it may be possible to an extent to speak of a more or less skilled worker such as a more skilled weaver as opposed to a less skilled weaver. But beyond a point even for the same type of concrete labour and certainly across different types of concrete labour the degree of skill cannot be determined independently of the ensemble of social relations within which the production process is carried out.

Therefore it would be the case that unequal rates of exploitation may be influenced by factors such as race, caste, gender, etc. For such a state of affairs to persist a whole host of social practices that reproduce the social differences between the two or more types of workers must prevail. This is one way of formalising the insight of (Wolpe, 1986) about the interiorisation of race (or any other type of social oppression) in the class struggle.[6]

Intersectionality is another framework that seeks to examine the relation between class, gender, race, etc (Hancock, 2016). Marxist critiques of intersectionality have included the following:

1. Intersectionality has abandoned the primacy of class but there is a need to examine how capitalist development interacts with gender, race, etc. (Eisenstein, 2018).
2. (Gimenez, 2018), in a critique of intersectionality, argues that: "When examining class at the level of analysis of the capitalist mode of production, it would make no sense to take into account gender, race or other forms of oppression. Class is identity blind. Far from being an error, or a problem in need of correction, this "blindness" indicates that the logic of class relations, exploitation and capital accumulation is indifferent to the actual individual characteristics of capitalists and workers. At this level of analysis, what matters for capitalists is that surplus labor can be extracted from workers whatever their imputed or acknowledged identities may be; capitalists themselves, these identities notwithstanding,

> ought to behave as capitalists, rationally making decisions about the use of technology, automation, location of investments, outsourcing, locking workers out, and so on, in order to maintain the profitability of their enterprises."

Since this paper is not concerned with intersectionality or its critique in detail, the above mentioned observations were selected with a view to evaluate Marxist views that were sought to be established in the light of the formulation on unequal rates of exploitation are set out here. Let us consider them seriatim.

Once it is acknowledged that race, gender, caste etc. are capable of influencing the rates of exploitation, the understanding of the relation between class and social oppression becomes more concrete once additional considerations about how class may impact social oppression are taken into account. A specific response to the issue of primacy of class (Eisenstein, 2018) will be advanced later.

For workers as a whole the rate of surplus value and the rate of exploitation are identically equal but when the rate of exploitation of different workers are unequal it is no longer necessary to argue along the lines of (Gimenez, 2018) that an analysis of the capitalist mode of production must ignore social oppression.

Two issues remain that need to be addressed. It has long been recognised that the commodity labour power is not produced by capitalists. The social reproduction theory (Bhattacharya, 2017) represents one attempt to explore the relation between the reproduction of labour power and the accumulation of capital. In terms of the formulation set out in this paper, labour expended on reproducing labour power contributes to the determination of the number of workers (new entrants) as well as part of the cost of reproducing all workers.[7]

The second issue in this context is that some have argued that the accumulation of capital requires the existence of at least some workers whose share in output may be compressed (Patnaik, 1997). If money is not based on a commodity then the existence of such workers restrains acceleration of inflation while if money is based on a commodity then the existence of such workers reduces price volatility.[8] In terms of the formulation of this section of the paper this implies that there are at least some workers who are unable to defend (almost) any level of real wages (or share of wages if the productivity of their labour is rising over time). This is the case, it has been argued because they live amidst a larger reserve army of labour as compared to other workers who are able to defend at least partially their real wages. The existence of such workers it may be argued is on account of their being socially separated from other workers. This would be associated with unequal rates of exploitation or the existence of more than one mode of production. While the former was partly examined in this section, the latter is examined in the next section.[9]

3. Capitalist Mode of Production and Social Formation

Before proceeding to a discussion of the relation between the existence of multiple modes of production in social formations and social oppression it may not be inappropriate to briefly survey the relevant literature on modes of production in social formations (Küttler, 2011). A non-exhaustive list of works which discuss these concepts include (Lange, 1963; Althusser, 2014 [1969]; Hirst and Hindess, 1975; Wolpe, 1980; Banerjee, 1985; Richards, 2013 [1986]; Patnaik, 1990; Patnaik, 2009; Jessop, 1990; Habib, 2010; Farooqui, 2010; Banaji, 2012; Graca and Zingarelli, 2015).

(Lange, 1963) defines a mode of production as follows: "The social productive forces and the production relations connected with them and based on a given type of the ownership of the means of production are jointly termed the mode of production." According to (Lange, 1963), a social formation is defined in the following passage: "We call the superstructure of a given mode of production that part of social relations (outside production relations) and of social consciousness which is indispensable for the existence of that particular mode of production. The mode of production, together with its superstructure is called the social formation or social system, and the production relations proper to a given social formation are called its economic base." Apart from many formulations which are eminently debatable, it may be noted that the possibility of a social formation encompassing several modes of production is absent in this formulation of (Lange, 1963).

However (Althusser, 2014 [1969]) provides a clear statement of this possibility: "Every concrete social formation is based on a dominant mode of production. The immediate implication is that, in every social formation, there exists more than one mode of production: at least two and often many more." This formulation was critically evaluated by many including (Hirst and Hindess, 1975).

(Wolpe, 1980) provides an extended discussion of the articulation of modes of production production in social formations.[10] In doing so, (Wolpe, 1980) distinguishes conceptually between the features of a mode of production and factors which bring about its reproduction which may involve other modes of production in a social formation. (Wolpe, 1980) distinguishes between the restricted and extended concepts of the mode of production wherein the former involves only the specification of the relations of production and the productive forces while the latter involves the relations of production, the productive forces and the factors that bring about its reproduction. On this basis, (Wolpe, 1980) argues that there are three possibilities:

1. A social formation involves two or more modes of production defined restrictively while the factors that reproduce them are external to each restrictively defined mode of production.
2. A social formation involves two or more extended modes of production while the relation between them is not necessary for the reproduction of any of them.

3. A social formation involves one dominant extended mode of production and one or more subordinate restricted modes of production. Here dominance of an extended mode of production is its ability to self-reproduce and that other modes of production are dependent on it for their reproduction.

Once a sharp conceptual distinction between the restricted and extended definition of modes of production is overcome[11] it is possible to consider the argument of (Patnaik, 2009) who points out that a capitalist mode of production is not self-contained. This proposition is based on the following argument: if both capitalists and workers are organised then steady growth and steady inflation are not possible for high rates of activity, i.e. the rate of employment and the degree of capacity utilisation. The solution to this problem lies in the fact that in the capitalist periphery there exist a set of workers whose share in output can be squeezed since they live amidst a reserve army of labour that is larger than that in the capitalist metropolis. These workers could be primary commodity producers and workers employed by metropolitan capital in the periphery. A third possibility is of workers of the periphery (or emigrants or their descendants) working in the metropolis has been implicitly considered in the previous section. Thus the capitalist mode of production does not/cannot eliminate some of the other modes of production. In other words, the capitalist mode of production is not self-reproducing. Further, colonialism was historically necessary in the making of this system (i.e. imperialism according to Patnaik, 1997; Patnaik, 2009; Patnaik and Patnaik 2016)[12] but is not necessary for its persistence.

This also implies that a key difference between the capitalist metropolis and periphery, namely the large ratio of the reserve army to the active army of the labour in the latter never attains that which prevails in the former. In different historical periods other factors that have contributed to this dichotomy between the capitalist metropolis and the periphery include the relative immobility of labour between the two, the relative immobility of productive capital between the two, the limited role of exports of the capitalist periphery to the metropolis and the price inelastic preference of the elite in the periphery for the commodities produced by metropolitan capital (Patnaik, 1997).

Though some of these factors no longer hold good at present or have become less relevant and even if the rate of growth of output is large in some parts of the capitalist periphery in the last few decades, the rate of growth of the productivity of labour is often higher resulting in the phenomenon of jobless growth, i.e. the share of workers employed in the organised sector of the capitalist periphery is declining (Patnaik, 2007b, 2007a).

The argument of (Patnaik, 2009) that pertains to this paper may be summarised in the following passage: "The capitalist mode, it follows, is both revolutionary and yet not quite revolutionary enough. It does break down the insulation of existing pre-capitalist societies; it does ruthlessly draw them into the vortex of its own accumulation process, but not necessarily by creating within them, in a dominant form, the structures of the bourgeois mode of production itself. They are transformed and hegemonised by metropolitan capitalism, but they themselves are never transformed into predominantly bourgeois societies. They may replicate within them the dichotomy characterising the system as a whole, by having an enclave of capitalism, but this is very different from their transformation into bourgeois societies." This formulation is possible since a sharp distinction between the restricted and extended definition of modes of production has been overcome.

It follows that the existence of other (including pre-capitalist) modes of production in the capitalist periphery[13] is a perennial feature of the social formation where the capitalist mode of production is dominant. Here dominance[14] of a mode of production may be defined (differently from that proposed in (Wolpe, 1980)) as following from its greater share in the surplus product.[15] Undoubtedly, this formulation could be made more concrete through historical investigation.

The persistence of some types of social oppression such as caste in India is connected to the coexistence of some pre-capitalist modes of production in a social formation where the capitalist mode of production is dominant. (Patnaik, 2017) argues that: "The experience of post-independent India, however, shows that constitutional measures meant to end caste oppression cannot do so, as long as the caste-system, i.e. the division of people into different caste-groups within a hierarchical order, remains. It is this hierarchical order itself that is oppressive. Even if through such measures, for argument's sake, *the caste distribution of persons employed within each occupation becomes the same as that of the population as a whole, which is a necessary condition for ending caste oppression*, given the enormously long history of the system and the ideology sustaining it, to which both its perpetrators and victims have subscribed in the past, such oppression will still continue in society." (emphasis added). What would be necessary for overcoming caste is not only that the caste composition of occupation be the same as the caste composition of the population but also that the caste composition of all classes (capitalists, workers, etc.) must be the same as that of the caste composition of the population. If caste (and other types of social oppression) is part of the ensemble of social relations that contingently reproduce the capitalist mode of production then it follows that the overthrow of caste cannot be merely an economic process.[16]

Discussions of caste which do not take into account its material dimension whereby many members of deprived castes are situated in non-capitalist or pre-capitalist modes of production will necessarily be incomplete (Patnaik, 2000). Likewise many members of the Muslim community in India who undergo social oppression through communalism are also situated in non-capitalist or pre-capitalist modes of production.[17] Further many women in India either expend family labour or are situated in non-capitalist or pre-capitalist modes of production.[18]

Within such a social formation, members of socially oppressed strata even when they are incorporated within the capitalist mode of production are often subject to greater exploitation which is associated with a host of socially oppressive practices which are facilitated by the bourgeoisie. The discussion about unequal rates of exploitation in the previous section now may be linked to that of the current section. Workers of oppressed strata are subject to greater exploitation and the bourgeoisie have a material interest in furthering social oppression in ways which are explored in the next section.

Some of the arguments of this paper have drawn on the following observations set out in (Marx, 2010 [1870]):

> Ireland is the bulwark of the English landed aristocracy. The exploitation of that country is not only one of the main sources of their material wealth; it is their greatest moral strength. They, in fact, represent the domination over Ireland. Ireland is therefore the cardinal means by which the English aristocracy maintain their domination in England itself...If, on the other hand, the English army and police were to be withdrawn from Ireland tomorrow, you would at once have an agrarian revolution in Ireland. But the downfall of the English aristocracy in Ireland implies and has as a necessary consequence its downfall in England. And this would provide the preliminary condition for the proletarian revolution in England. The destruction of the English landed aristocracy in Ireland is an infinitely easier operation than in England herself, because in Ireland the land question has been up to now the exclusive form of the social question because it is a question of existence, of life and death, for the immense majority of the Irish people, and because it is at the same time inseparable from the national question. Quite apart from the fact that the Irish character is more passionate and revolutionary than that of the English...As for the English bourgeoisie, it has in the first place a common interest with the English aristocracy in turning Ireland into mere pasture land which provides the English market with meat and wool at the cheapest possible prices. It is likewise interested in reducing the Irish population by eviction and forcible emigration, to such

> a small number that English capital (capital invested in land leased for farming) can function there with "security". It has the same interest in clearing the estates of Ireland as it had in the clearing of the agricultural districts of England and Scotland. The £6,000-10,000 absentee-landlord and other Irish revenues which at present flow annually to London have also to be taken into account...But the English bourgeoisie has also much more important interests in the present economy of Ireland. Owing to the constantly increasing concentration of leaseholds, Ireland constantly sends her own surplus to the English labour market, and thus forces down wages and lowers the material and moral position of the English working class...And most important of all! Every industrial and commercial centre in England now possesses a working class divided into two hostile camps, English proletarians and Irish proletarians. The ordinary English worker hates the Irish worker as a competitor who lowers his standard of life. In relation to the Irish worker he regards himself as a member of the ruling nation and consequently he becomes a tool of the English aristocrats and capitalists against Ireland, thus strengthening their domination over himself. He cherishes religious, social, and national prejudices against the Irish worker. His attitude towards him is much the same as that of the "poor whites" to the Negroes in the former slave states of the USA. The Irishman pays him back with interest in his own money. He sees in the English worker both the accomplice and the stupid tool of the English rulers in Ireland...This antagonism is artificially kept alive and intensified by the press, the pulpit, the comic papers, in short, by all the means at the disposal of the ruling classes. This antagonism is the secret of the impotence of the English working class, despite its organisation. It is the secret by which the capitalist class maintains its power. And the latter is quite aware of this.

In other words, the hegemony of the English bourgeoisie even over the English workers was tied up with English colonialism in Ireland. English colonialism in Ireland was a necessary condition for the differences between Irish immigrant workers in England and English workers and this was promoted by the English bourgeoisie and involved social oppression of the Irish in both Ireland and England.

4. Bourgeoisdom, Exploitation and Oppression

It is proposed that the social formation where the capitalist mode of production is dominant may be termed as bourgeoisdom.[19] Bourgeoisdom rather than capitalism has been proposed as a moniker for this process since it allows one to engage with propositions such as the following:

> The capitalist system is much more than the capitalist mode of production analyzed by Marx." (Patnaik, 2009).

Likewise (Marx, 2010 [1867]) had said, "As capitalist, he is only capital personified." But the bourgeoisie is the product of a historical process and is not *merely* capital personified.

How a concrete instance of bourgeoisdom is reproduced (both locally and globally) (i.e. to what extent is it an organic system[20]) can only be uncovered by historical investigation. However some theoretical reflections on this theme are set out in this section.

Bourgeoisdom involves among other things two processes: oppression is necessary for the reproduction of exploitation. To begin with, a homogeneous proletariat would also have more bargaining power than a differentiated proletariat resulting in a decline in the economy wide rate of surplus value. The bourgeoisie, after all has a material interest in greater extraction of surplus value (due to unequal rates of exploitation and differential exploitation in different modes of production) as long as it can be realised in the form of money. Further if there was a tendency towards homogenisation of the proletariat then the likelihood of their struggles involving economic resistance developing into a political struggle to overcome bourgeoisdom would have been higher.[21]

(Patnaik, 2009) had pointed out that:

> Exploitation within this totality is of diverse forms: there is above all the exploitation of workers directly employed by capital through the appropriation of surplus value; there is the exploitation of the metropolitan reserve army, which is kept in depressed living conditions and has the role of keeping down the bargaining strength of the trade unions in the metropolis;

then there are the unorganised workers in the periphery, who are exploited through unequal exchange and made to act as price takers so as to sustain the stability of the value of money; finally, there is the vast pauperised mass amidst whom these unorganised workers are placed which is also exploited, through even more depressed living conditions than the metropolitan reserve army, and upon whom the system rests ultimately for its stability. In addition to these, there are of course the different forms of exploitation by the pre-capitalist hegemonic classes."

This diversity of exploitation would not have been possible if the workers involved were not socially separated through oppression involving race, gender, caste, communalism, etc. The hegemony of the bourgeoisie is strengthened by social oppression. (Marx, 2010 [1861-63]) had asserted that:

> Bourgeois society reproduces in its own form everything against which it had fought in feudal or absolutist form."[22]

Likewise and as mentioned before the differential exploitation of the proletariat and articulation of different modes of production is a necessary condition for the reproduction of social oppression. For the purposes of this paper oppression may be defined as the ensemble of differentiated unfreedom[23] and is necessarily linked to exploitation. This formulation on oppression suggests that different types of oppression are necessarily linked and that oppression does not impinge on all oppressed in an identical manner. In other words, an individual worker may be subject to exploitation and multiple types of oppression. Further members of oppressed strata may be confronted with the hurdles created by social oppression when they seek to take advantage of the process of proliferation of the bourgeoisie. In other words, social oppression may also be to the advantage of bourgeois incumbents against their upstart rivals from oppressed strata.[24] In other words, for instance, there is no necessary tendency for the bourgeoisie or other exploiting classes in India to have the same caste composition as the caste composition of Indian society.

More generally, we assume a social formation is

composed of two non-class social groups. It is asserted that there is no tendency for the two non-class social groups to be proportionally represented among the exploiters (bourgeoisie, etc.) and the exploited (proletariat, etc.). The more oppressed non-class social group is likely to be over represented amongst the exploited. For example, the Dalits are over represented amongst the proletariat in India.[25] Neither is there any spontaneous tendency in bourgeoisdom to overcome this asymmetry (Harriss-White, 2003; Harriss-White, 2015; Harriss-White and Heyer 2014) nor is the bourgeoisie going to willingly accede to any such effort.[26] In other words, there is an objective material basis for the bourgeoisie and other exploiting classes under bourgeoisdom to facilitate social oppression.

Thus while one may endorse the proposition advanced by (Wolpe, 1990) that Apartheid is not necessary for the persistence of capitalism (bourgeoisdom) in South Africa, it is asserted that social oppression along racial lines or along other social grounds is necessary for the reproduction of bourgeoisdom both in South Africa and elsewhere. Therefore attempts at a consistent social process of inclusion are unrealisable under bourgeoisdom.

The spontaneous tendency under bourgeoisdom is for the reproduction of the proletariat as an exploited but partly fragmented class along with other exploited social classes and socially oppressed strata. In (Marx and Engels, 2010 [1848]) it is pointed out that:

> "The essential condition for the existence, and for the sway of the bourgeois class, is the formation and augmentation of capital; the condition for capital is wage-labour. Wage-labour rests exclusively on competition between the labourers. The advance of industry, whose involuntary promoter is the bourgeoisie, replaces the isolation of the labourers, due to competition, by their revolutionary combination, due to association. The development of Modern Industry, therefore, cuts from under its feet the very foundation on which the bourgeoisie produces and appropriates products. What the bourgeoisie, therefore, produces, above all, is

> its own grave-diggers. Its fall and the victory of the proletariat are equally inevitable."

However the revolutionary combination due to association of the proletariat, i.e. the formation of the revolutionary proletariat is not spontaneously accomplished by bourgeoisdom.

When (Stalin, 1953 [1926]) discussed the three strata amongst the working class, the first he said "is the main mass of the proletariat, its core, its permanent part, the mass of 'pure-blooded' proletarians, who have long broken off connection with the capitalist class. This stratum of the proletariat is the most reliable bulwark of Marxism." This section of the proletariat, i.e. the revolutionary proletariat, as mentioned before, is not produced by bourgeoisdom. The revolutionary proletariat constitutes itself through an authentic democratic social process of struggle that can combat exploitation and oppression under bourgeoisdom.

Without combating oppression and exploitation in its struggles the revolutionary proletariat cannot come into existence. Since exploitation and oppression are linked under bourgeoisdom it is not possible to combat one while disregarding the other.[27] Likewise an inability to sustain the combined struggle against oppression and exploitation will result in an unravelling of the revolutionary proletariat. A successful transcending of bourgeoisdom may be more complex than previously conceived (due to factors such as those discussed in this paper), but the struggle for it remains historically relevant and significant.

5. Conclusion

This paper has been concerned with setting out in outline a framework to examine the relation between oppression and exploitation under bourgeoisdom. Two factors have been identified in this regard, namely unequal rates of exploitation of different types of workers and the coexistence of different modes of production with one dominant mode of production in a social formation. Under bourgeoisdom, which is the social formation where the capitalist mode of production is dominant, there is no tendency for social oppression to be overcome since exploitation are oppression are organically interrelated.

A certain analogy may be drawn between the link between surplus value and profit, interest and rent and the link between class and caste, gender, race etc. A strand of writing that sought to advance the work set out in (Marx, 2010 [1867], 2010 [1884], 2010 [1894]) argued that values (or value magnitudes) and surplus value are determined independently of prices of production and profit. However, subsequent work has increasingly come over to the position that both processes are jointly determined. Likewise class, caste, gender and race are organically interrelated. This does not involve a de-prioritisation of class but a more concrete understanding of the role of class within the framework of historical materialism.

No specific formulation on the concrete link between class, race, gender, caste, etc. in any concrete social formation has been advanced in this paper. That process can only follow from historical enquiry into concrete social formations such as Indian bourgeoisdom (Currie, 1992). Some questions that may be motivated by this paper include:

Concrete investigations of the relation between oppression and exploitation in different social formations and how they may have changed over time may be undertaken (Bannerji, 2005; Velaskar, 2016).

What were the modes of production in the social formation that existed in pre-colonial India and how was the relation between exploitation and oppression structured therein (Habib, 2010; Farooqui, 2010)?

Development of formal models of interaction of gender, caste, race, etc. within the framework of the critique of political economy undertaken in (Marx, 2010 [1867], 2010 [1884], 2010 [1894]) and as developed by many others subsequently (Bhattacharya, 2017).

NOTES

1. (Lenin, 1974 [1919]) had asserted that: "Classes are large groups of people differing from each other by the place they occupy in a historically determined system of social production, by their relation (in most cases fixed and formulated in law) to the means of production, by their role in the social organisation of labour, and, consequently, by the dimensions of the share of social wealth of which they dispose and the mode of acquiring it. Classes are groups of people one of which can appropriate the labour of another owing to the different places they occupy in a definite system of social economy."
2. (Damodaran, 2008) examines this process in the Indian context. (Patnaik, Chandrasekhar, and Ghosh, 2004) seeks to explain the role of the Indian bourgeoisie in the transition from a dirigiste regime to a neoliberal set up wherein changes in the monopolisation and proliferation of the bourgeoisie play a key role.
3. An equal rate of exploitation of all workers is one aspect of a homogeneous proletariat.
4. Further it may be noted that Marx has discussed the case of unequal rates of surplus value in one of his manuscripts which is contained in (Marx, 2012 [1863-68]).
5. A mathematical statement of the implications of unequal rates of exploitation will be examined in subsequent work.
6. However (Wolpe, 1986) goes on to add that "...it also does not follow that because race, under certain conditions, may be interiorised in the class struggle, all conflicts which centre on race are, therefore, to be conceived of as class struggles. On the contrary, it will be argued that struggles focusing on race may take on a form in which class is not interiorised within them." Thus the interaction between exploitation and oppression in each case must be concretely examined.
7. (Kotz, 1994) advances a mathematical model of the relation between wage labour and family labour.
8. Excessive price volatility may hamper the ability of the state to sustain a system of commodity money.
9. There remains one other related issue that needs to be addressed. It has been argued that values (or value magnitudes) are irrelevant to the process of determination of the general rate of profit and prices of production (Steedman, 1977). However if there exists at least one section of workers whose real wage can

be squeezed then the two equalities of (Marx, 2010 [1894]): "...the sum of the profits in all spheres of production must equal the sum of the surplus values, and the sum of the prices of production of the total social product equal the sum of its value" will be relevant for the determination of the general rate of profit and the prices of production. If money is not based on a commodity then the condition that "the sum of the prices of production of the total social product equal the sum of its value" may act as a price numeraire while the condition that "the sum of the profits in all spheres of production must equal the sum of the surplus values" will contribute to the determination of the general rate of profit and the prices of production. If money is based on a commodity then there will be a hoard of money (Patnaik, 2009). As a result, both the equalities of (Marx, 2010 [1894]) mentioned above will be required to ensure the just determination of the system of equations that determine the general rate of profit and prices of production. The mathematical details of this process are not set out in this paper. This approach to the transformation problem of (Marx, 2010 [1894]) is related to the diversity among workers (and primary commodity producers) either in the capitalist metropolis or between the capitalist metropolis and the periphery. In either case more than one mode of production is involved.

10. Both (Wolpe, 1980; Jessop, 1990) point out that modes of production involve the production of commodities and ideas but as (Wolpe, 1990) points out this does not involve a lapse into subjectivism.
11. This may be the case because on the one hand, the conditions that bring about the reproduction of a mode of production may influence the character of the productive forces and the relations of production and on the other hand, the character of the productive forces and the relations of production may contribute to the process of reproduction of the mode of production.
12. In a theory of imperialism, the capitalist mode of production in both the capitalist metropolis and periphery are unequally interdependent, apart from the interdependence between capitalist and non-capitalist modes of production.
13. The petty mode of production may exist also in the capitalist metropolis as long as production units in it are not subject to the tendential process of profit rate equalisation vis-à-vis production units in the capitalist mode of production.
14. (Marx, 2010 [1894]) had argued that: "The specific economic

form, in which unpaid surplus labour is pumped out of direct producers, determines the relationship of rulers and ruled, as it grows directly out of production itself and, in turn, reacts upon it as a determining element. Upon this, however, is founded the entire formation of the economic community which grows up out of the production relations themselves, thereby simultaneously its specific political form. It is always the direct relationship of the owners of the conditions of production to the direct producers—a relation always naturally corresponding to a definite stage in the development of the methods of labour and thereby its social productivity—which reveals the innermost secret, the hidden basis of the entire social structure, and with it the political form of the relation of sovereignty and dependence, in short, the corresponding specific form of the state." Thus it may be argued that the dominant mode of production in a social formation is one whose share in the surplus product is the greatest and therefore the appropriators of the surplus product of the dominant mode of production constitute the ruling class.

15. (Croix, 1989) had argued that though the share of peasants in the population in ancient Greece and related areas was larger than that of slaves, the share of the surplus product extracted from the latter in the total surplus product was greater than that extracted from the former.
16. The question whether social oppression can be eliminated without transcending exploitation is dealt with in the following.
17. (Khalidi, 2006) examines the economic conditions of Muslims in the Indian economy.
18. Thus from the perspective of this paper (Vogel, 2018)'s critique of intersectionality where she says that: "...let me offer some thoughts about the utility of such concepts as race/class/gender and intersectionality. I view them as primarily descriptive. That is, they provide a conceptual framework for describing and investigating 'diversity', but by themselves they do not explain anything. Strictly speaking, then, they are imprecise and some would argue against using them." will hold good. Likewise when (Foley 2018) points out that "To assert the priority of a class analysis is not to claim that a worker is more important than a homemaker, or even that the worker primarily thinks of herself as a worker; indeed, based on her personal experience with spousal abuse or police brutality, she may well think of herself more as a woman, or a black person. It is to propose, however, that the ways in which productive human activity

is organised—and, in class-based society, compels the mass of the population to be divided up into various categories in order to insure that the many will labor for the benefit of the few–this class-based organisation constitutes the principal issue requiring investigation if we wish to understand the roots of social inequality," there is substantial agreement except where the category of priority is employed. The arguments of (Vogel, 2018; Foley, 2018) may be examined in the light of the arguments set out in both this section regarding the social formation as well as the previous one regarding unequal rates of exploitation of different workers.

19. The term bourgeoisdom was introduced in (Marx, 2010 [1867]).
20. "If in the fully developed bourgeois system each economic relationship presupposes the other in a bourgeois-economic form, and everything posited is thus also a premiss, that is the case with every organic system. This organic system itself has its premises as a totality, and its development into a totality consists precisely in subordinating all elements of society to itself, or in creating out of it the organs it still lacks." (Marx, 2010 [1858]). Thus an organic system reproduces its premises.
21. Revolutionary breakthroughs have often involved a meaningful incorporation of issues concerning social oppression into the class struggle thereby rendering the latter more concrete.
22. In (Marx, 2010 [1861-64]) it was argued that "But capital is in and for itself indifferent towards the specificity of every sphere of production, and where it is invested, how it is invested, and to what extent it passes from one sphere of production into another, or its distribution between the various spheres of production alters, is determined solely by the greater or lesser difficulty experienced in selling the commodities produced by one or the other sphere of production. In reality, this fluidity of capital is slowed down by frictions, which we do not need to consider here any further. But on the one hand, as we shall see later, it creates means of overcoming these frictions, in so far as they arise solely from the nature of the relation of production itself, and on the other hand, the development of the mode of production peculiar to capital removes all legal and extra-economic obstacles to its free movement in the various spheres of production. Above all it overturns all the legal or traditional barriers preventing it from buying whatever kind of labour capacity it thinks fit, or appropriating any kind of labour at all at its good pleasure. Furthermore, although labour

capacity possesses a particular shape in every particular sphere of production, as the capacity for spinning, shoemaking, blacksmithing, etc., although, in short, every particular sphere of production requires a labour capacity which has developed in a particular direction, a specialised labour capacity, that fluidity of capital, its indifference towards the particular character of the labour process it is appropriating, presupposes the same fluidity or versatility in labour, hence in the ability of the worker to employ his labour capacity. We shall see that the capitalist mode of production itself creates these economic obstacles to its own tendency, but it removes all legal and extra-economic obstacles to the versatility we are discussing." (emphasis added). In subsequent work, Marx replaced the term labour capacity with labour power.

23. Therefore oppression unlike exploitation is ab initio heterogeneous (caste, gender, race, etc.) but linked and therefore must be concretely investigated as an ensemble.
24. (Messer 2011) discusses the attack on the black bourgeoisie in Tulsa, Greenwood district of Oklahoma, USA by white mobs that was aided and abetted by the government.
25. (Heyer, 2010) discusses the conditions of Dalits in neoliberal India.
26. In this light, it is instructive to compare the formulation on caste in the 1964 programme of the Communist Party of India (Marxist) (CPI(M), 1964) and its updated version that was adopted in 2000 (CPI(M), 2000). In (CPI(M), 1964), it is stated that "Capitalist development in India, however, is not of the type which took place in Western Europe and other advanced capitalist countries. Even though developing in the capitalist way Indian society still contains within itself strong elements of pre-capitalist society. Unlike in the advanced capitalist countries where capitalism grew on the ashes of pre-capitalist society, destroyed by the rising bourgeoisie, capitalism in India was superimposed on pre-capitalist society. *Neither the British colonialists whose rule continued for over a century, nor the Indian bourgeoisie into whose hands power passed in 1947, delivered those smashing blows against pre-capitalist society* which are necessary for the free development of capitalist society and its replacement by socialist society. The present Indian society, therefore, is a peculiar combination of monopoly capitalist domination with the caste, communal and tribal institutions." (emphasis added). In other words, it is presumed in (CPI(M), 1964) that the abolition

of social institutions such as caste will allow a freer development of capitalist society. However in (CPI(M), 2000) it is stated that "The problem of caste oppression and discrimination has a long history and is deeply rooted in the pre-capitalist social system. *The society under capitalist development has compromised with the existing caste system. The Indian bourgeoisie itself fosters caste prejudices*. Working class unity presupposes unity against the caste system and the oppression of Dalits, since the vast majority of the Dalit population are part of the labouring classes. *To fight for the abolition of the caste system and all forms of social oppression through a social reform movement is an important part of the democratic revolution. The fight against caste oppression is interlinked with the struggle against class exploitation."* (emphasis added). It is possible to interpret this formulation in (CPI(M), 2000) as follows: institutions such as caste are a necessary part of bourgeoisdom.

27. In other words, under bourgeoisdom it is not possible to overcome any type of oppression tout court. (Patnaik, 2000) had argued that "...any significant advance in the context of any of the multifarious struggles occurring in society necessarily requires a change in the nature of ownership of assets, a proposition which I think can be demonstrated. It must unleash therefore a fierce social struggle around the question of ownership, which is nothing else but class-struggle, since classes are defined precisely in relation to the ownership over the means of production. Putting it differently, successful class-struggle constitutes an enabling condition for success in all other terrains of struggle."

REFERENCES

Althusser, Louis (2014 [1969]). *On the Reproduction of Capitalism: Ideology and Ideological State Apparatuses*. Originally written in 1969 and revised thereafter. First published in 1995 in French. Verso Books.

Banaji, Jairus (2012). "Mode of Production". In: *The Elgar Companion to Marxist Economics*. Ed. by Ben Fine, Alfredo Saad-Filho, and Marco Boffo. Edward Elgar Publishing, pp. 227–232.

Banerjee, Diptendra, ed. (1985). *Marxian Theory and the Third World*. Sage Publications Pvt. Ltd.

Bannerji, Himani (2005). "Building from Marx: Reflections on Class and Race". In: *Social Justice* 32.4, 102, pp. 144–160.

Bhattacharya, Tithi, ed. (2017). *Social Reproduction Theory: Remapping Class, Recentering Oppression*. Pluto Press.

Callinicos, Alex (2002). "History, Exploitation and Oppression". In: *Historical Materialism and Social Evolution*. Ed. by Paul Blackledge and Graeme Kirkpatrick. Palgrave Macmillan UK, pp. 129–162.

CPI(M) (1964). *CPI(M) Party Programme*: Adopted at the Seventh Congress of the Communist Party of India, at Calcutta, October 31 to November 7, 1964. Communist Party of India (Marxist).

——(2000). *CPI(M) Party Programme*: Updated at the Special Conference of the CPI(M) at Thiruvananthapuram, October 2000. Communist Party of India (Marxist).

Croix, Geoffrey Ernest Maurice De Ste (1989). *The Class Struggle in the Ancient Greek World: From the Archaic Age to the Arab Conquests*. Cornell University Press.

Currie, Kate (1992). "The Indian Stratification Debate: A Discursive Exposition of Problems and Issues in the Analysis of Class, Caste and Gender". In: *Dialectical Anthropology* 17.2, pp. 115–139.

Damodaran, H. (2008). *India's New Capitalists: Caste, Business, and Industry in a Modern Nation*. Palgrave Macmillan.

Eisenstein, Hester (2018). "Querying Intersectionality". In: *Science & Society* 82.2, pp. 248–261.

Farooqui, Amar (2010). "History of Social Formations in India". In: *The Marxist* XXVI.4, October–December, pp. 49–60.

Foley, Barbara (2018). "Intersectionality: A Marxist Critique". In: *Science & Society* 82.2, pp. 269–275.

Gimenez, Martha E. (2018). "Intersectionality: Marxist Critical Observations". In: *Science & Society* 82.2, pp. 261–269.

Graca, Laura da and Andrea Zingarelli, eds. (2015). *Studies on Pre-Capitalist Modes of Production*. Brill.

Habib, Irfan (2010). "Note Towards a Marxist Perception of Indian History". In: *The Marxist* XXVI.4, October–December, pp. 37–48.

Hancock, Ange-Marie (2016). *Intersectionality: An Intellectual History*. Oxford University Press.

Harriss-White, Barbara (2003). *India Working: Essays on Society and Economy*. Cambridge University Press.

——ed. (2015). *Middle India and Urban-Rural Development: Four Decades of Change*. Springer India.

Harriss-White, Barbara and J. Heyer, eds. (2014). *Indian Capitalism in Development*. Routledge.

Heyer, Judith (2010). "The Marginalisation of Dalits in a Modernising Economy". In: *The Comparative Political Economy of Development: Africa and South Asia*. Ed. by Barbara Harriss-White and Judith Heyer. Routledge, pp. 225–247.

Hirst, Paul Quentin and Barry Hindess (1975). *Pre-Capitalist Modes of*

Production. Routledge and Kegan Paul.

Jessop, Robert (1990). "Mode of Production". In: *Marxian Economics*. Ed. by John Eatwell, Murray Milgate, and Peter Newman. Springer, pp. 289–296.

Khalidi, Omar (2006). *Muslims in Indian Economy*. Three Essays Collective.

Kotz, David M. (1994). "Household Labor, Wage Labor, and the Transformation of the Family". In: *Review of Radical Political Economics* 26.2, pp. 24–56.

Krause, U. (1982). *Money and Abstract Labour: On the Analytical Foundations of Political Economy*. Translated by Rothschild, J. New Left Books.

Küttler, Wolfgang (2011). "Social Formation". In: *Historical Materialism* 19.4, pp. 229–237.

Lange, Oskar (1963). *Political Economy. Volume I*: General Problems. Pergamon Press.

Lenin, V.I. (1974 [1919]). "A Great Beginning: Heroism of the Workers in the Rear. Communist Subbotniks". In: *Collected Works of V.I. Lenin*. Vol. 29. March–August 1919. Originally published in 1919. Progress Publishers, pp. 409–434.

Marx, Karl (2012 [1863-68]). *Ökonomische Manuskripte 68–1863, MEGA2, Zweite Abteilung, Band 4, Teil III*. Akademie Verlag.

Marx, Karl (2010 [1858]). "Economic Manuscripts of 1857-58". In: *Collected Works of Karl Marx and Fredrick Engels*. Vol. 28. Marx 1857-61. Originally written in 1857-58 and published in 1943 as Grundrisse. Lawrence and Wishart.

—— (2010 [1859]). "A Contribution to the Critique of Political Economy: Part One". In: *Collected Works of Karl Marx and Fredrick Engels*. Vol. 29. Marx –1857-61. Originally published in 1859. Lawrence and Wishart, pp. 267–417.

—— (2010 [1861-63]). "Theories of Surplus Value. Adam Smith". In: *Collected Works of Karl Marx and Fredrick Engels*. Vol. 31. Karl Marx 1861-63. Lawrence and Wishart.

—— (2010 [1861-64]). "Results of the Direct Production Process". In: *Collected Works of Karl Marx and Fredrick Engels*. Vol. 34. Karl Marx 1861-64. Lawrence and Wishart.

—— (2010 [1867]). "Capital: A Critique of Political Economy Volume 1". In: *Collected Works of Karl Marx and Fredrick Engels*. Ed. by Fredrick Engels. Vol. 35. Karl Marx—*Capital* Volume I. Originally published in 1867. Lawrence and Wishart.

—— (2010 [1870]). "Marx to Sigfrid Meyer and August Vogt In New York". In: *Collected Works of Karl Marx and Fredrick Engels*. Vol.

43. *Letters 1868-70*. Originally written in 1870. Lawrence and Wishart.

—— (2010 [1884]). "Capital: A Critique of Political Economy Volume 2". In: *Collected Works of Karl Marx and Fredrick Engels*. Ed. by Fredrick Engels. Vol. 36. Karl Marx—*Capital* Volume II. Originally published in 1884. Lawrence and Wishart.

—— (2010 [1894]). "Capital: A Critique Of Political Economy Volume 3". In: *Collected Works Of Karl Marx and Fredrick Engels*. Ed. by Fredrick Engels. Vol. 37. Karl Marx—*Capital* Volume III. Originally published in 1894. Lawrence and Wishart.

Marx, Karl and Fredrick Engels (2010 [1848]). "Manifesto of the Communist Party". In: *Collected Works of Karl Marx and Fredrick Engels*. Vol. 6. Marx and Engels 1845-48. Originally published in German in 1848. Lawrence and Wishart, pp. 477–519.

Messer, Chris M. (2011). "The Tulsa Race Riot of 1921: Toward an Integrative Theory of Collective Violence". In: *Journal of Social History* 44.4, pp. 1217–1232.

Patnaik, Prabhat (1997). *Accumulation and Stability Under Capitalism*. Oxford: Clarendon Press.

—— (2000). "Notes on the Concept of Class". In: *Social Scientist* 28.9-10, pp. 3–11.

Patnaik, Prabhat (2007a). "A Model of Growth of the Contemporary Indian Economy". In: *Economic and Political Weekly*, pp. 2077–2081.

—— (2007b). "Contemporary Imperialism and the World's Labour Reserves". In: *Social Scientist* 35.5-6, pp. 3–18.

—— (2009). *The Value of Money*. Columbia University Press.

—— (2017). "Caste, Community and Belonging: The Indian Case". In: *Social Scientist* 45.1-2, pp. 73–79.

Patnaik, Prabhat, C. P. Chandrasekhar, and Jayati Ghosh (2004). "The Political Economy of the Economic Reform Strategy: The Role of the Indian Capitalist Class". In: *Class, Caste, Gender*. Ed. by Manoranjan Mohanty. Sage Publications India, pp. 89–105.

Patnaik, Prabhat, C. P. Chandrasekhar, and Abhijit Sen (1996). "The Proliferation of the Bourgeoisie and Economic Policy". In: *Class Formation and Political Transformation in Post-Colonial India*. Ed. by T. V. Sathyamurthy. Oxford University Press, pp. 55–79.

Patnaik, U., ed. (1990). *Agrarian Relations and Accumulation: The "Mode of Production" Debate in India*. Oxford University Press.

Patnaik, Utsa and Prabhat Patnaik (2016). *A Theory of Imperialism*. Columbia University Press.

Richards, Alan (2013 [1986]). *Development and Modes of Production in*

Marxian Economics: A Critical Evaluation. Routledge.
Stalin, J. V. (1953 [1926]). "The Seventh Enlarged Plenum of the E.C.C.I, November 22-December 16, 1926". In: *J.V. Stalin Works*. Vol. 9: December–July 1927. David J. Romagnolo of www.marx2mao.com created the digital version of this volume. Originally published in 1926. Foreign Languages Publishing House, pp. 1–155.
Steedman, I. (1977). *Marx After Sraffa*. New Left Books.
Velaskar, Padma (2016). "Theorising the Interaction of Caste, Class and Gender: A Feminist Sociological Approach". In: *Contributions to Indian Sociology* 50.3, pp. 389–414.
Vogel, Lise (2018). "Beyond Intersectionality". In: *Science & Society* 82.2, pp. 275–287.
Wolpe, Harold (1980). "Introduction". In: *The Articulation of Modes of Production: Essays from Economy and Society*. Ed. by Harold Wolpe. Routledge, pp. 1–43.
—— (1986). "Class Concepts, Class Struggle and Racism". In: *Theories of Race and Ethnic Relations*. Ed. by John Rex and David Mason. Cambridge University Press, 110–130.
—— (1990). *Race, Class & the Apartheid State*. Africa World Press.

Contributors

Archana Aggarwal teaches Economics at Hindu College, University of Delhi, India. Her areas of interest are Macroeconomics and Marxian Political Economy. She founded a group called *Perspectives* in 2007. As part of that group, she has undertaken field visits, both inside and outside Delhi, in order to understand issues such as agrarian distress and condition of industrial workers. Many of the findings have been published as booklets.

C. Saratchand is an Assistant Professor of Economics at Satyawati College, University of Delhi, India. His areas of specialisation are Macroeconomics and Political Economy. He has co-edited the book *Analytical Perspectives on the Indian Economy* (Aakar Books, 2019). His articles have appeared in journals such as *Social Scientist, Economic and Political Weekly, Metroeconomica, Journal of Post Keynesian Economics, International Review of Applied Economics, International Critical Thought*, etc.

Chirashree Das Gupta is an Associate Professor at the Centre for the Study of Law and Governance at Jawaharlal Nehru University, New Delhi, India. Her research and teaching have been focused on different dimensions of the political economy of institutions with a focus on patriarchy, race, caste and class and the role of law in the political economy of accumulation in trade, finance and industrialization and public policy. She has worked on the relationship between personal laws, tax and corporate governance in India. Her recent work focuses on gender, labour and social reproduction.Her major journal publications have been in the *Cambridge Journal of Economics, Rivista di Politica Economica, South Asia Multidisciplinary*

Academic Journal, and *Economic and Political Weekly*. Her book titled *State and Capital in Independent India: Institutions and Accumulation* has been published by Cambridge University Press in 2016.

Craig Brandist is a Professor of Cultural Theory and Intellectual History, and the Director of the Bakhtin Centre at the University of Sheffield, UK. He has published extensively on the work of the Bakhtin Circle, Antonio Gramsci's relationship to Russian Marxist thought and the development of sociological linguistics in the USSR. Among his major publications are: *The Bakhtin Circle: Philosophy, Culture and Politics* (Pluto Press, 2002), *Politics and the Theory of Language in the USSR 1917-1938* (Anthem Press, 2010) and *The Dimensions of Hegemony: Language, Culture and Politics in Revolutionary Russia* (Brill, 2015). He is currently working with Peter Thomas on a collection of archival documents and commentary on Gramsci's time in the USSR in the early 1920s.

Damien Ehrhardt is a tenured Associate Professor at the University of Paris-Saclay in Evry, where he is responsible for the research axe "Intercultural Mixes", part of the SLAM laboratory. Collaborator of the Schumann New Edition of Complete Works, his research concerns musicology and arts, especially 19th century German aesthetics, and intercultural communication, including works on area and transfer studies as well as transnational cultural fields. Three stays in Mithila allowed him to discover the paintings in situ and to analyze them with Helene Fleury in light of new theories on transnational cultural fields.

Edoardo Schinco has edited a new translation of Feuerbach's *Principles of the Philosophy of the Future* (2016) and published a detailed philosophical introduction to Marx's thought (Clinamen, 2019). Over the last years, he has also focused his attention on the connection between feminism and Marxism, and has delivered lectures on this subject at international conferences (2017, 2018). Currently, he is editing a new translation of Marx's and Engels's *The Holy Family* and Simone Weil's *The Need for Roots*.

Eugenio Lo Sardo directed the Italian National Archives in

Rome. He co-founded a magazine entitled *Marxiana* with Enzo Modugno in 1976, published by Dedaloeditore, with translated articles written by Jean-Paul Sartre, Max Horkeimer, Herbert Marcuse and others. He studied the economic relationships between England and the Kingdom of the Two Sicilies, which was published by Iovine, Naples in 1993. He has published many books on the history of civilization, with particular focus on the relationships between the European countries and China and India between 1500 and 1800.

Giulietto Chiesa was in the Scientific (Physics) formation at the University of Genoa. He was a Correspondent in Moscow for 20 years for two big Italian newspapers: *l'Unità*, then an organ of the Italian Communist Party (1980-1990), and *La Stampa* (2000-1991). In 2017 in Moscow, he received the Bunin Prize for his outstanding work in journalism and literature.

Hélène Fleury is a Lecturer in Visual and Heritage Studies at the University of Evry and a PhD candidate at the University of Paris-Saclay in cooperation with the Center for South Asian Studies (EHESS). Her research concerns mostly the reception and globalization of Mithila paintings (worldwide exhibitions, transcultural mediators and the construction of a transnational cultural field), and more widely interculturality and transfer studies. She made four fieldworks in Mithila in 2002 and 2017-19. She has published extensively and spoken on her subject at several international conferences.

Jean-Joseph Boillot is a Professor in Economics and Social Sciences. He is an Associate Researcher at the French Institute of International Relations IRIS where he follows the Indian economy as well as the emerging world, in particular the China-India-Africa triangle, seen as a structuring pole of the new global economy in the making. He is a Co-founder of the Euro-India Group (EIEBG), and a Member of the Cyclope Expert Group and the ISEG Scientific Council. He writes monthly columns for *Alternatives Economiques* and *Market Express*. He is the author of more than 20 books, including *L'Indeancienne au chevet de nos politiques* (Félin Publishing House, Paris 2017), *L'Economie de l'Inde* (La Découverte 3e éd. 2016, translated in English with Gyan Books), *L'Afrique pour les nuls* (First 2015), *L'Inde pour les nuls* (First 2014), *L'Innovation Jugaad* (translation et adaptation, Diateino 2013) and *Chindiafrique* (Odile Jacob 2013).

Julio Boltvinik is a Professor at El Colegio de México in México City. He has published, in English, as co-editor (with Susan A. Mann), *Peasant Poverty and Persistence in the 21st Century* (Zed Books, London, 2016) and as co-author (with Meghnad Desai and Amartya Sen), *Social Progress Index: A Proposal* (1992, UNDP). In Spanish, his books, articles and book chapters are more than 200 in number. His two more recent books in Spanish are (in translated titles): 1. (in co-authorship with Araceli Damián), *Measurement of the Poverty of México. Critical Comparative Analysis of the Methods Applied. Recommendations of Good Practices for Poverty Measurement in Mexico and Latin America*, ECLAC, United Nations, Mexico, *Serie Estudios y Perspectivas*, No. 183, 2020; and, 2. *Poverty and Human Flourishing. A Radical Perspective*, University of Zacatecas and ÍtacaEditores, Mexico City, 2020. He writes, since 1995, a weekly column called Moral Economy in the national newspaper *La Jornada*.

Kipton E. Jensen is an Associate Professor of Philosophy and the Director of the Leadership Studies Program at the Andrew Young Centre for Global Leadership at Morehouse College, Atlanta, USA. His most recent publications include a collection of Howard Thurman's *Sermons on the Parables* (Orbis Books, 2018) and *Howard Thurman: Philosophy, Civil Rights, and the Search for Common Ground* (University of South Carolina Press, 2019). His research in Botswana on the role of traditional healers and faith communities in public health was published as *Parallel Discourses: Religious Identity and HIV Prevention in Botswana* (2012). He also published *Hegel: Hovering over the Corpse of Faith and Reason* (2011). Jensen's scholarly essays deal with the philosophy of religion, social philosophy, pragmatism, nonviolence, and the philosophy of education.

Kumari Sunitha V. teaches philosophy at the Madras Christian College, Chennai, India. She is a recipient of the Nehru Fellowship from the Nehru Memorial Fund, Teen Murti House, New Delhi. She also received the General Fellowship from the Indian Council of Philosophical Research (ICPR) for the project entitled "Time and History in Heidegger's

Philosophy: A Critique". She was a Co-investigator of the research project (2014-2016) "Ethical, Legal and Medical Implications of Surrogacy in Tamil Nadu" funded by the United Board of Christian Higher Education in South Asia (UBCHEA). Her research interests include Phenomenology, Hermeneutics, Critical Theory, Philosophy of Science, and Philosophy of Gender Studies. She is the author of *Anatomy of Alienation: A Critical Study of Heidegger and Sartre* (2014), *Heidegger's Hermeneutics: A Metaplay of Polysemous Language* (2017), *Gender and Globalization: Making of a Universal Woman* (2013), and *Heidegger and Degeneration of Art* (2011).

Riccardo Bellofiore is a Full Professor of Political Economy at the University of Bergamo, Italy. He has published or edited many books, among which, in English: *The Great Recession and the Contradictions of Contemporary Capitalism* (Elgar 2014, with Giovanna Vertova), *Towards a New Understanding of Sraffa: Insights from Archival Research* (Palgrave 2014, with Scott Carter), *Rosa Luxemburg and the Critique to Political Econo*my (Routledge, 2009). His last book is in Italian: *Smith Ricardo Marx Sraffa* (Rosenberg & Sellier, 2020).

Roberto Massari has worked in the field of Industrial Sociology in France and Italy. In 1989 he founded a publishing house, which has around 350 titles in its catalogue. He is the author of essays in various fields (sociology, politics, theology, etruscology, history of music, etc.), of three novels and a documentary movie on Che Guevara. President of the Guevara International Foundation since 1998, he is moderator of the International Red Utopia Blog.

Shannon Brincat is a Senior Lecturer in Politics and International Relations at the University of the Sunshine Coast, Australia. His most recent project, *The Spiral World*, traces dialectical thinking in the Axial Age. He has been the editor of a number of collections, most recently *From International Relations to World Civilizations: The Contributions of Robert W. Cox* and *Dialectics and World Politics*. He is also a co-editor of *Global Discourse*. He has articles published in the *European Journal of International Relations, Constellations,* and the *Review of International Studies,* amongst others.